rat race blues

noal cohen & michael fitzgerald

rat race blues

the musical life of Gigi Gryce

foreword by benny golson

berkeley hills books
berkeley california

Published by:
Berkeley Hills Books, PO Box 9877, Berkeley CA 94709

Copyright:
© 2002 Noal Cohen and Michael Fitzgerald

Library of Congress Cataloging-in-Publication Data

Cohen, Noal, 1937–
   Rat race blues : the musical life of Gigi Gryce / Noal Cohen and
Michael Fitzgerald.
         p. cm.
Includes bibliographical references (p.   ), discography (p.   ), and index.
   ISBN 1-893163-25-3 (alk. paper)
   1. Gryce, Gigi. 2. Jazz musicians—United States—Biography. I.
Fitzgerald, Michael, 1970– II. Title.
   ML419.G79 C64 2002
   788.7'3165'092—dc21

                              2001008086

Distributed by:
Publishers Group West

contents

foreword vii

preface xi

acknowledgments xv

interview codes xix

introduction 1

one pensacola blues 9

two education: hartford and boston 37

three manhattan blues 79

four paris the beautiful 109

five laying the foundation 147

six on the cutting edge 185

seven in the laboratory 211

eight the out chorus 247

nine metamorphosis 307

epilogue 335

appendix a: gryce's compositions 343

appendix b: gryce's publishing holdings 365

discography 375

bibliography 419

index 427

foreword

by benny golson

I REMEMBER IT QUITE WELL. New York City had claimed another hot day as its own in the summer of 1951. I was there visiting my aunt and at the same time preparing to become yet another resident of "Mecca." Yes, a resident in what was a city of hope, where one could proleptically realize his dreams, especially if that person happened to be a young, aspiring jazz musician. Its streets were crowded with cars that identified themselves, one from the other, with loud and different-sounding horns, and whose sounds were underscored with random, intimidating epithets from its drivers. People were busily engaged in myriad, unintelligible conversations the sound of which filled the air like so many invisible, hungry locusts. And massively tall buildings stood silently forming a forest of redoubtable sentinels protecting nothing in particular. It seemed like everything that could happen *was* happening. All eventualitics seemed to be squeezed into that one day. Was this the reality or had my perception of things been exaggerated because of years of anticipation for this moment? It didn't matter. I was in New York—New York City! I was going to live there, finally. For a certainty, this was a special day. It was also the day on which I met Gigi Gryce.

Gigi was a particularly nervous person with one conspicuous quirk: constantly clearing his throat for no apparent reason. It seems he had experienced a nervous breakdown a few months prior to our meeting, and he appeared to be somewhat fragile at this point. But for all the strange little things I saw in him, I eventually saw his genius too. Yes, a quiet kind of genius that could be easily overlooked since he was hardly a braggart. In fact, his shyness took him in the other direction. He was extremely vocal about other people's talents and abilities, verbally pushing *them* to the fore. Though his life was rife with accomplishments, in order to know what they were, one had to probe, inquire, cajole, at times rummage through his past. Sometimes it seemed somewhat painful for him to reveal such things, like the symphonies he'd written that never saw a performance.

In the few short years Gigi lived in New York, it seemed just about every important jazz musician knew him. This was inevitable because of his ability as an alto saxophonist and an extremely creative writer. Many times, as the new boy in town, I was completely thrilled when visiting his apartment and Coleman Hawkins or Art Blakey or Max Roach or Howard McGhee or Hank Jones or others would call. I wanted to be in on the conversation so badly that the only thing I could think of to say was, "Tell him I said hello!" Of course, only a few actually knew who I was at the time. Gigi, knowing this, indulged me nevertheless.

He came to New York with bundles of music under his arms and even more in his mind. He was an organizer of the highest magnitude and quickly gained a reputation for it. When people—musicians, club owners, entrepreneurs—wanted quality jazz underscored with quality business, they often included Gigi in their calls. Although a graduate of the Boston Conservatory, he chose not to teach school in those early days because of devoting full time to writing and playing and becoming a well-informed business man in the marketplace. In fact, he and I later became partners in two publishing companies. Though he did not formally teach in any university then, he was always teaching. He was didactic by nature and could not envision life without intuitively teaching at every opportunity. I do not infer, however, that he was aggressive or arrogant in this. In a quite natural way, he lovingly and mercifully shared all the information he had stored in his capacious mind.

He was a great source of encouragement to all, through his music and through social encounters as well. He was always—may I emphasize always—upbuilding. I often saw him as a strong support for many who had problems of one kind or another. By 1955, we had become inseparable as friends and business partners. When I was married in 1958, he went to Washington, D.C. with me for the marriage ceremony as my best man, and I was there when his first child was born.

During the summer of 1953, we were both members of Tadd Dameron's band in Atlantic City, New Jersey. The money was short and the hours long, but we had fun. In that same band was a young Clifford Brown, Johnny Coles, initially Cecil Payne, Philly Joe Jones, and Jymie Merritt. At the end of that summer season, Gigi, Clifford, and I were recruited into the Lionel Hampton band. There we met Art Farmer, Quincy Jones, Monk Montgomery, Jimmy Cleveland, Alan Dawson, and others.

Although Gigi wrote many memorable compositions, the two most unusual that touched my heart are "Hymn to the Orient" and "Minority." Gigi played on my very first album and I recorded "Hymn to the Orient" on another. I feel "Minority" is fast becoming a jazz standard and rightly so. The melody is completely intriguing, as is the accompanying chordal structure. "Social Call" is a light, delightful melody that haunts your memory and tends to make one forget the cares of the day and kick back with love in mind rather than war. "Smoke Signal," based on the standard "Lover," is a fiery up-tempo tune that keeps the thinking processes operational—a thinking man's tune to be sure.

Gigi went on to become internationally known for his ability as a consummate musician and writer of the highest caliber. For this to happen, one must axiomatically have the talent to support the accolades. Of course, there will always be a few who slip by because of things other than talent, but in the main, talent must be extant. The other necessary element in the equation for success is often overlooked—it's opportunity. Gigi had the opportunity as a jazz musician but had none at all for his symphonic abilities. I lament over this. Would that he had had this opportunity, the opportunity I know he hoped for, the opportunity that remains elusive even in death. Many things that don't happen in life sometimes happen afterwards. Will time be kind to him after the fact, to his memory?

After perusing the contents of *Rat Race Blues: The Musical Life of Gigi Gryce*, the reader will never ever find Gigi Gryce relegated to the two-dimensional medium of vinyl discs and CDs only, but he will become as real as anyone we've ever known in life. Let's be glad that there was a musician like Gigi Gryce, and let's be glad that there were people like Noal Cohen and Michael Fitzgerald who had enough conviction and vision to recall Gigi's plethoric life with the aid of their minds, hearts, and pens. Noal, Michael— I salute you.

Benny Golson
Friedrichshafen, Germany

preface

*T*HIS BOOK IS THE RESULT of nearly a decade of serious research and half a century of casual interest. It slowly came together as we became aware of Gigi Gryce's efforts, efforts scattered across many classic albums. Although his career was brief, lasting only a decade, he seemed to be associated with the greatest, most creative artists in jazz and his writing and playing were unique and readily identifiable.

Never before has there been a thorough and exhaustive look at the entire oeuvre of Gigi Gryce, which numbered over a hundred recording sessions, most of them issued commercially. During his lifetime he was the subject of a chapter in two books (Raymond Horricks's *These Jazzmen of Our Time* and Robert Reisner's *The Jazz Titans*), and since his death he has only figured as an auxiliary to the career of Clifford Brown and as one-of-many in the school of lyrical hard bop composers. Almost no writing existed that evaluated his career, his many compositions, and his place in the history of jazz. What did exist perhaps covered one aspect but ignored several others. Only when examined in full could the range of his musical development be seen and properly assessed.

Even before beginning work on this project it was apparent that there were contradictions and errors in the biographical details and in credits and titles of compositions. We worked to verify or disprove these definitively by using multiple sources. In digging deeper, we learned that Gryce's birth and death dates have regularly been misreported and that no published account of his life was without some kind of misinformation.

"So, whatever happened to Gigi Gryce?" was a question we frequently heard, not only from fans but also some of the musicians who were close to him in the 1950s. Rumors were rampant and, if truth be told, Gryce himself contributed to the confusion. While this book cannot clear up the entire mystery, it will certainly present the clearest and most accurate account of his post-jazz life available at this time. It should be noted, however, that these years are not the focus of the book, which is concerned with the composer and performer.

Any biography of a musician must necessarily deal with that artist's recorded legacy and a complete discography was begun. This is the only comprehensive discography of Gigi Gryce ever attempted, although general discographers (Raben, Bruyninckx, Lord) included the vast majority of sessions to one extent or another. Items were added and corrections made up until weeks before submitting the manuscript for publication. Items that had been issued but never documented were included and, in most cases, new information was added to amend the earlier work. An international community of record collectors supplied rare recordings and information relating to foreign issues.

One of the first thoughts regarding research strategy was to inter-

view the musicians who knew and worked with Gryce. This logi-
cal idea led to compiling a list of survivors based on the most
accurate discography. Added to this list were family members and
then friends, co-workers, and acquaintances. The period with which
we were primarily concerned was the years 1953–1963 and in the
intervening decades a number of the participants have passed away.
Even as we were conducting our research and writing the text, we
learned of the deaths of several important colleagues: Art Taylor
(1995), Johnny Coles (1996), Gerry Mulligan (1996), Walter Bishop,
Jr. (1998), Betty Carter (1998), Jaki Byard (1999), Melba Liston
(1999), Ernie Wilkins (1999), Art Farmer (1999), Tommy Flanagan
(2001), Milt Jackson (1999), Al Grey (2000), Alan Hovhaness
(2000), Jerome Richardson (2000), Stanley Turrentine (2000), Milt
Hinton (2000), J.J. Johnson (2001), John Lewis (2001), and Makanda
Ken McIntyre (2001). Three of Gryce's sisters also passed away
during this time: Kessel Grice Jamieson (1997), Elvis Grice
Blanchard (1999), and Harriet Grice Combs (1999). Regrettably,
we were unable to communicate with some of them and, of course,
these missed opportunities can never be regained. Some other
subjects declined to be interviewed and some were impossible to
contact (though we certainly did try). In the end, we were fortunate to record over seventy-five conversations specifically on the
topic of Gigi Gryce and his music.

Each of these presented new information and interesting anec-
dotes. (The code for each quoted interview is listed in a table.) We
have tried in many cases to preserve in the text the actual words
of the interviews. In the tradition of earlier books like *Hear Me
Talkin' to Ya*, this has elements of an oral history, but here the
stories of the participants share the page with retrospection, critique, and our follow-up research, which attempts to support and
clarify the quotes. While neither of us ever met Gryce, we hope

that through the words of those who knew him, something of him may be conveyed to future readers.

Another avenue of research involved going through the periodicals and literature with a fine-tooth comb. Sometimes even the smallest mention would eventually lead to a major discovery, particularly when several items were used in conjunction with each other, and with the interviews and photographic contributions. The bibliography included here does not detail all of these, but covers the publications that contain significant coverage related to Gryce's work and the world in which he operated.

Although this book is not targeted for musicians only, a great deal of examination was conducted on Gryce's music, involving transcriptions and study of copyright deposits at the Library of Congress. It is hoped that any musical discussion here will be accessible to all readers. We anticipate that the printed compositions of Gigi Gryce will finally be made available in the near future and this will certainly generate more interest among the musical community.

We are eager to share our knowledge and enthusiasm and encourage future researchers to contact us with questions or new information. This has been a labor of love and although publication here brings some sense of finality, there will continue to be discoveries that will complete the picture of Gigi Gryce as man, musician, and teacher.

Noal Cohen & Michael Fitzgerald
June 2001

acknowledgments

RESEARCH IS ALWAYS A PROCESS that involves many connections and interactions. Via letter, telephone, email, or in person, the various pieces of this puzzle were brought together. We are extremely grateful to those individuals who provided invaluable information, insights, and materials. Without their contributions none of this could have been possible.

THANKS TO...

The players who supplied musical details as well as personal reflections: David Amram, Margie Anderson, Danny Bank, Eddie Bert, Ran Blake, Walter Bolden, Russell Boone, Bob Brookmeyer, Don Butterfield, Teddy Charles, Allan Chase, Jimmy Cleveland, Bob Cranshaw, Bill Crow, Dr. Art Davis, Bob Dorough, Al Dreares, Bunky Emerson, Julian Euell, Art Farmer, William B. Fielder, Kent Glenn, Benny Golson, Lorenzo Greenwich, Dick Griffin, Clifford Gunn, Jon Hendricks, Hank Jones, Nat Jones, Dick Katz, Wolf Knittel, Dr. Makanda Ken McIntyre, Norman Macklin, Anthony Minstein, Bob Mover, Anthony Ortega, Miles Osland, Harold

Ousley, Cecil Payne, Walter Perkins, Bob Porcelli, Benny Powell, Henri Renaud, Jerome Richardson, Sam Rivers, Bobby Rogovin, Mickey Roker, Dr. Donald Shirley, Horace Silver, Emery Smith, Clifford Solomon, Idrees Sulieman, Kellice Swaggerty, Edwin Swanston, Clark Terry, Ben Tucker, Bobby Watson, Chris White, Reggie Workman, Phil Wright, Richard Wyands.

...Family, friends, and fans of Gigi Gryce who gave accounts of their interactions with him and furnished archival materials: Chris Albertson, Harold B. Andrews, Fred Baker, Victor Christensen, Valerie Grice Claiborne, Evelyn DuBose, Esmond Edwards, Mort Fega, Ira Gitler, Rev. Jerome and Aurelia Greene, Eleanor Gryce, Tommy Gryce, Vinnie Haynes, Nat Hentoff, Raymond Horricks, Dr. Thomas James, Orrin Keepnews, Jack Lazare, Aaron Long, Louis-Victor Mialy, Daniel Pinkham, Ollie Qusim, Beatrice Rivers, Don Schlitten, Bob Weinstock, Judge Bruce Wright.

...Fellow researchers, collectors, fans, family, and friends who furnished archival materials and gave encouragement, advice, and help in contacting and locating individuals and information: Steve Albin, Ron Arfin, Abby Bass, Bill Bauer, Paul Berliner, Armin Büttner, Robert Campbell, Mark Cantor, Ann Cohen, Bruce Colgate, Bill Damm, John Delaney, David Diamond, Chris Drukker, Jim Eigo, Ken Field, Rudolf A. Flinterman, Samuel A. Floyd, Otto Flückiger, Peter Friedman, Will Friedwald, Ron Fritts, Daniel Fuller, Antonio J. García, Matt Gorney, Angelynn Grant, Sid Gribetz, David Griffith, Walter Gross, Stjepko Gut, Andrew Homzy, Peter Katz, Peter Keepnews, Brooks Kerr, Bill Kirchner, Karl Emil Knudsen, Jonathan Kutler, Andy Laverne, Howard Mandel, John Meagher, Owen McNally, Piotr Michalowski, Craig Nixon, Ted Panken, Louis Pine, Jacques Ponzio, Bob Porter, Lewis Porter, Brian Priestley, Jim Progris, Peter Pullman, Doug Ramsey,

acknowledgments

Pär Rittsel, Sherri Roberts, Norbert Ruecker, Paul Salomone, Lewis Saul, Phil Schaap, Claude Schlouch, Loren Schoenberg, Steve Schwartz, Dan Serro, Chris Sheridan, Zena Shervin, Dan Skea, Yves François Smierciak, Matthew Snyder, Evan Spring, Dave Stalker, Jeff Sultanof, David Suskin, Hiroshi Tanno, Jeroen de Valk, Stuart Vandermark, Steve Voce, Ilse Weinmann, Richard Weize, Lars Westin, Dennis Whitling, Jack Woker, Steve Wolff, Bill Wood, Edward Woods, Ben Young, François Ziegler, Art Zimmerman.

The Morroe Berger–Benny Carter Research Fund at the Institute of Jazz Studies was generous in providing financial assistance; and Benny Carter was also helpful with materials from his archives.

Unique photographs were supplied by the following: Valerie Grice Claiborne, Bob Crimi, Grayson and Jerry Dantzic, Jazz-Institut Darmstadt (collection of Joachim Ernst Berendt), Kati Meister (collection of Carole Reiff), Mosaic Images, Inc. (collection of Francis Wolff), Dale Parent (collection of Bob Parent), Ray Ross, Don Schlitten, Chuck Stewart, Ernest Zwonicek.

We also wish to thank the following organizations and institutions for assisting and facilitating our research efforts: ASCAP, BMI, Board of Education of the City of New York (Frederick J. Thomsen, Joseph Del Greco, Carmen Hillman, David Vas Nunes), Boston Conservatory (Harriet Lundberg, Shannon Hartzler), *Coda Magazine* (John Norris, Bill Smith), Escambia County Florida School District (Ann Cooper), Fantasy, Inc. (Terri Hinte), Florida Office of Vital Statistics (Priscilla Smith), Fordham University Registrar's Office, Institute of International Education (Walter Jackson), Jacogg Publications, Inc. (Ken Combs), Jazz-Institut Darmstadt (Wolfram Knauer), Juilliard School, Library of Congress (Larry Appelbaum, Rosemary C. Hanes, James Wolf), Mosaic Records, Inc. (Michael Cuscuna, Charlie Lourie, Scott Wenzel), National Archives, Pensacola Jazz Society (Dr. F. Norman Vickers), PolyGram Holding, Inc. (Marie Donoghue), Rutgers Institute of Jazz Studies (Dan Morgenstern, Ed Berger, Vincent Pelote, John Clement, Don Luck, Tad Hershorn, Annie Kuebler, Esther Smith), Second Floor Music, Inc. (Don Sickler, Maureen Sickler, Marc Ostrow), Sony Music (Kevin Gore, Scott Pascucci, Michael Roberson), Teachers College of Columbia University/Milbank Memorial Library (David Ment), University of Arkansas/Fulbright Archive (Betty Austin), University of Hartford/Hartt College of Music, U.S. Copyright Office/Reference and Bibliography Section, U.S. Information Agency/Programs Office (Effie Wingate).

Excerpts from interviews published in *Cadence Magazine* are used by permission © 2001 Cadence Magazine: *www.cadencebuilding.com.*

interview codes

All interviews conducted by Noal Cohen except as noted.

AF: Art Farmer, February 24, 1997
AG: Aurelia Green, January 10, 2001
AL: Aaron Long, August 28, 2000
AO: Anthony Ortega, December 9, 1997
BC: Bob Cranshaw, September 28, 1998
BG: Benny Golson, November 27, 2000
BK: Bill Kirchner, May 7, 2001
BM: Bob Mover, May 7, 2001
BP: Bob Porcelli, October 24, 2000
BW: Bruce Wright, November 13, 1996
CG: Clifford Gunn, June 10, 1997
CS: Clifford Solomon, May 27, 1998
CT: Clark Terry, October 8, 2000
CW: Chris White, June 18, 1998
DA: David Amram, April 13, 1999
DB: Don Butterfield, November 16, 1998
DK: Dick Katz, February 25, 1997
DS: Donald Shirley, September 15, 1998
DSch: Don Schlitten, July 11, 2000
ED: Evelyn DuBose, August 21, 2000
EG1: Eleanor Gryce, March 3, 1997
EG2: Eleanor Gryce, Feb. 24, 1998
EG5: Eleanor Gryce, December 6, 2000
EG7: Eleanor Gryce, April 17, 2001
ES: Emery Smith, September 16, 1998
ESw: Edwin Swanston, December 13, 2000
FB: Fred Baker, March 5, 1998
HJ: Hank Jones, July 5, 2000

HO: Harold Ousley, April 10, 1998
HS: Horace Silver, June 29, 1997
IG: Ira Gitler, March 17, 1997
IS: Idrees Sulieman, January 5, 1998
JC: Jimmy Cleveland, May 28, 1998
JE: Julian Euell, November 22, 1998
JG: Reverend Jerome Greene, December 13, 2000
JH: Jon Hendricks, November 18, 1997
KG: Kent Glenn, May 7, 2001
KS: Kellice Swaggerty, April 29, 1998
LG: Lorenzo Greenwich, September 21, 2000
LM: Louis-Victor Mialy, February 17, 1998
MA: Margie Anderson, October 25, 2000
MF: Mort Fega, May 18, 1998
MKM: Dr. Makanda Ken McIntyre, August 8, 2000
MO: Miles Osland, email exchange with Noal Cohen, May 7,
    2001
MR: Mickey Roker, March 3, 1997
NM: Norman Macklin, June 3, 1997
PW: Phil Wright, September 18, 2000
RW: Bob Weinstock, May 26, 1998
RWo: Reggie Workman, February 3, 1998
RWy: Richard Wyands, November 28, 1997
SR: Sam Rivers, July 11, 2000
TC1: Teddy Charles, June 10, 1998
TC2: Teddy Charles, April 25, 1999
TG1: Tommy Gryce, interviewed by Noal Cohen and David
    Griffith, August 14, 1996
TG2: Tommy Gryce, September 22, 1997
TG3: Tommy Gryce, April 2, 2001
TJ: Dr. Thomas James, August 30, 2000
VC1: Valerie Grice Claiborne, April 9, 1997
VC2: Valerie Grice Claiborne, March 10, 1999
WB: Walter Bolden, August 16, 2000
WP: Walter Perkins, October 7, 1997

introduction

W**HAT'S WRONG WITH THIS PICTURE?"**
Eleanor Gryce, Gigi Gryce's widow, poses this question as she describes how her husband, while not unique, still stood apart from many of the jazz musicians of his time. He didn't smoke. He didn't drink. He wasn't involved with drugs. His only weakness was ice cream, which he loved almost as much as the music he lived and breathed. He was serious, quiet, secretive, and very much concerned with the business aspects of music and the inability of musicians and composers to reap the proper rewards from their creations. At the height of his career as an active musician, he was almost universally respected as an alto saxophonist, composer, arranger, bandleader and mentor, and was certainly in the thick of things regarding the dynamic New York jazz scene. Yet his reserved, studious demeanor, uncompromising standards, and strong educational background rendered him something of an anomaly. He just didn't quite fit the mold. So it is perhaps not terribly surprising that Gryce's tenure in the limelight was short-

lived. Within a decade of his first commercial recordings, he had slipped into obscurity, reemerging with a new identity and a new career in education that would last twice as long as his jazz activities.

Gryce came to prominence during the 1950s, an immensely rich period in the relatively short history of jazz, a period filled not only with artistic innovations but technological advances as well. The advent of the long-playing record had allowed musicians the freedom to stretch out beyond the two- to three-minute limitation imposed by 78s. In addition, breakthroughs in recording technology, pioneered by engineers like Rudy Van Gelder, brought an unprecedented clarity and realism to the LPs being issued now in large numbers by labels both large and small. And this was the era of the working bands, groups that stayed together not just for an occasional tour, but for months and even years with a constancy of style and approach even in the face of shifting personnel: The Modern Jazz Quartet, Art Blakey's Jazz Messengers, The Horace Silver Quintet, The Byrd–Gryce Jazz Lab, The Clifford Brown–Max Roach Quintet, The Adderley Brothers. In performance and on record, these groups documented their musical evolution against the background of the changing jazz landscape. It was truly a golden age filled with enormous talents, colorful personalities, and creative brilliance.

But things were far from perfect. Racism and economic exploitation were rampant. Royalties were routinely stolen from jazz musicians by many record company executives and publishers. Unhealthy lifestyles involving drug abuse and alcoholism were commonplace and led in many unfortunate cases to shortened careers and unfulfilled potential. Gryce witnessed and was deeply affected by these problems. When his younger brother Tommy sought to follow in his footsteps and pursue a life as a jazz musician in New York, that career path was strongly discouraged by his older sibling.

Regarding Gryce's musical legacy, scrutiny of his recorded work reveals that he was a thoughtful and lyrical player who, at his peak, had developed a recognizable style and sound.

He was a player, a very good player. He was a good technician. He always had a problem with his sound. He was always trying to develop his tone because he wasn't a physically strong person. He was very nervous and kind of withdrawn type of person so his sound wasn't that wholesome, and he was always working on that. He wasn't the kind of a person who would, you know, fill up a room with his sound and make everybody stand up in awe, but he *was* a person who had his own voice. He had his own voice and that was one thing that *had to be* during the days that we all came up. You had to have your own voice, and you could hear him in any circumstance and you knew that that's Gigi in the section. You could hear him in the section or you could hear him soloing. You know that's Gigi Gryce, not only because of his tone, which wasn't the greatest tone but it was *his* tone, but also because of the way he approached the music— where he was in the whole scheme of things and how he approached the music—that was Gigi and you recognized his conversation and you recognized his rap and his sound. So, that was one thing that he accomplished in the short time that he was on the scene. (RWo)

His solos were constructed compositionally, emphasizing form at the expense of virtuosity—perhaps another reason why his work has been overlooked. But most importantly, Gryce was a complete package, a musician's musician, one who through his contributions had the ability to raise the level of any project with which he was associated. Gryce was a member of an impressive group of artists of his time who, in addition to being fine soloists, were also outstanding writers. The included John Coltrane, Kenny

Dorham, Benny Golson, Elmo Hope, Thad Jones, Duke Jordan, Booker Little, Charles Mingus, Hank Mobley, Thelonious Monk, Herbie Nichols, Horace Silver, Lucky Thompson, Bobby Timmons, Mal Waldron, and Randy Weston. Many of these were musicians with whom Gryce would have substantial and productive interactions. All of these individuals advanced the art of jazz composition, and several produced tunes that would become standards, frequently performed in a wide variety of contexts.

In this regard, Gryce is perhaps best known as the composer of "Minority," a challenging sixteen-bar line made famous by its inclusion on the 1958 Riverside LP *Everybody Digs Bill Evans* and which, since then, has been recorded numerous times by a diverse group of musicians. Another well-known Gryce composition is "Social Call," with lyrics by Jon Hendricks, which has been performed by many singers and instrumentalists since it was introduced in 1955. But these are only the tip of the iceberg. One can find documentation of over 150 Gryce compositions of which around 60 have been recorded.

Gryce was well-grounded in music and his body of work reflects his conservatory training. In many ways, his style and approach, both as a writer and instrumentalist, exemplify certain characteristics lacking in the music of today. He was all about strong melodies, form, structure, dynamics, and choice notes. This is what makes his work memorable and worthy of reinvestigation.

But Gryce's interests and activities extended beyond those usually associated with jazz musicians of his era. He was also passionately dedicated to educating his colleagues with regards to the importance of protecting their own compositions through copyright so that they, and not just the record companies, would be the beneficiaries of their creative efforts. His efforts as a music publisher were bold and groundbreaking but, sadly, contributed to his downfall and premature withdrawal from a very productive career.

Gryce was also a mentor. Slightly older than many of his colleagues, he was educated and experienced when he began working in New York. He was known and respected as a professional to whom aspiring young musicians could turn for advice and instruction, which he offered generously. He figures prominently in the early careers of many artists who would go on to eclipse him in longevity and fame. His later profession as a teacher is certainly connected to this affinity for encouraging others and for sharing his knowledge and passion for music.

In many ways, the story of Gigi Gryce is an uplifting one. He overcame institutionalized racism, poverty, the ravages of the Great Depression, and the untimely loss of his father. He was able to secure a college education, which provided him with tools that he would exploit effectively in ascending to prominence on the New York jazz scene. But while leaving a substantial legacy of recordings and compositions, his goals and aspirations were never truly fulfilled. Certainly his musical career ended prematurely in the early 1960s when his dreams were shattered in the wake of personal and professional turmoil. There was so much more he could have achieved if circumstances had been different. Yet even with these disappointments he was able to reinvent himself as a superb public-school teacher who commanded the respect and admiration of students, teachers, and parents alike.

Gryce may not have cut the widest swath among the many musicians of his era, but his is a story worth telling. It presents an individual who existed in a strange environment that stood in contradiction to many of his fundamental beliefs. Despite this, he was able to work with the absolute cream of the crop in the exceedingly competitive jazz world. He recorded for major labels as well as small independents, and those records as well as the compositions on them continue to hold interest a half-century later.

Although he was not an extrovert and was rarely interviewed, on several occasions Gryce spoke of his artistic goals. In each case, he was clear and focused about what he was trying to achieve. Over the course of his career, he ascended from sideman, to partner, to leader, and, at each step, was refining his musical conception. By the time he was co-leading the Jazz Lab group with Donald Byrd, he expressed his perspective on history and public recognition as follows:

We want to reflect all of the language of jazz and get into everybody's heart. And we're trying to develop another quality within ourselves. Too many musicians today are more concerned with winning polls or getting a lot of gigs than with making the most honest music possible, regardless of the profit you can make from it. And many of the younger players are surprisingly unaware of where they came from, of where their roots are, and that their indebtedness goes back beyond Tatum and Lester Young and to Pete Brown, Cootie Williams, Willie "The Lion" Smith, and the blues players. I've been listening to a lot of old records, and really trying to get into the history of jazz. I don't want to be just a flash on the surface of the language; I want to be really part of it.[1]

About his last group, the six-piece ensemble known as the Gigi Gryce Orch-tette, he said:

All of the arrangements are new and in a definite style for this group. We want the band to provide a full-course meal and not just the same one or two dishes over and over—with discipline and subtlety, and also the jazz feeling. We also try to get a range and variety within each piece.

The Orch-tette has also become a kind of seminar for us; there is always lots of discussion of music, about the best way to do things and the best way to reach different kinds of people with them. Of course, we always want to reach them with what we believe in and what we can do as jazz musicians, without being commercial about it.[2]

Along the way, Gryce contributed significantly to furthering form and harmony in jazz composition and was respected for his writing and arranging. Even as early as 1954, his friend Quincy Jones was noticing this.

It takes more planning to create a simple tune with pretty changes with real structure. Tunes like Johnny Mandel, Gigi Gryce, George Wallington, Tadd Dameron and, of course, Duke, write. Compositions like theirs that are carefully planned have a good chance to create new standard tunes for jazz. Maybe three out of thirty will last, but they'll certainly help. We've surely exhausted "Indiana," "Get Happy," and "Cherokee" and all the others.[3]

Gryce used his bands to document these advances, both in live performance and on numerous recordings. His academic studies in composition as well as his love of Duke Ellington's music allowed him to create music that eschewed the hackneyed head–solos–head format that had become ubiquitous during the period. Always composing, Gryce seemed never at a loss for original works, though he was not self-centered and encouraged his bandmates and musical friends to contribute to his projects. He also had no disdain for the repertoire of the Great American Songbook and for older jazz material, wrapping these in fresh new arrangements to give them his personal stamp.

The story of Gigi Gryce is intertwined with that of well-known musicians and also those who have been overlooked. The early 1950s Boston scene, the legendary 1953 Lionel Hampton tour, and the exploratory work by Teddy Charles are but three under-documented chapters in the history of jazz in which Gryce played an active role. In learning of his work, areas are illuminated which, hopefully, will merit further exploration.

Notes

1. Gigi Gryce, quoted by Nat Hentoff in liner notes to Jubilee 1059.
2. Gigi Gryce, quoted by Martin Williams in "New Ears for Jazz: A Talk with Gigi Gryce," *Metronome*, June 1961, pp. 12–13.
3. Quincy Jones, quoted by Nat Hentoff in "Counterpoint," *Down Beat*, May 5, 1954, p. 12.

pensacola blues

PENSACOLA, FLORIDA, THE BIRTHPLACE OF GIGI GRYCE, is located in the state's panhandle region near the Gulf of Mexico. It has a long and colorful history, going back to the early 1500s when Spanish traders interacted with the local natives. A hurricane in 1561 destroyed the chance of Pensacola being the oldest permanent European settlement in the United States. It existed under changing government for many years, and today there are five flags flown above the city—those of Spain, France, Britain, the Confederacy, and the United States. It remains the site of an important naval station (home to the famous "Blue Angels" flying squadron), and now also has centers of education, industry, and healthcare.

Historically, its culture has been described as very similar to that of New Orleans, the birthplace of jazz, located only 200 miles to the west. Pensacola had black, white, and Creole populations and the residents of this port city were constantly encountering new people and ideas from around the world. The 1934 City Directory gives the population within five miles of the center of the city as 42,440, and states that, at the time, the U.S. Government alone was spending over $10,000 a day there. The current population of the Pensacola metropolitan area is over 400,000, a result of the widespread migration to the Sunbelt in recent years.

Pensacola has had an active music scene and, over the years, produced some important musicians besides Gryce, including piano virtuoso Donald Shirley, guitarist/vocalist Slim Gaillard, and tenor saxophonist Herman "Junior" Cook. Around 1927 there were several local music organizations in the city: the Pensacola Symphony Orchestra and at least seven other groups including the Anderson Douglass Orchestra, a black ensemble. There was exposure to jazz through both local bands and visiting tours. Cliff Smalls of the Earl Hines orchestra remembered:

Different bands operated in different areas. Around Pensacola, for instance, you'd find Harley Toots's band, or Smiling Billy Stewart's, or the Sunset Royals. There was another band led by Ray Shep, and out in Texas there were Don Albert's, and Boots and his Buddies.[1]

The "Ray Shep" mentioned is actually Raymond Sheppard (1905–1981), later the clarinet teacher and band director of young George "Gigi" Grice. Another great modern jazz alto saxophonist, Julian "Cannonball" Adderley was born in Tampa, Florida and recalled that many of the greatest big bands played in the area. "Henderson, Kirk, Lunceford, and others used to come through on tour and there were some pretty good Florida bands: the Sunset Royal Entertainers—Dad played with them—Smiling Billy Stewart and C. S. Belton's Syncopators."[2]

Originally from Brewton, Alabama, George General Grice, Sr. (1877–1933) was one of seven surviving children of thirteen born to Harriet Grice. He ran a clothes cleaning and pressing service at

22 South Tarragona Street that specialized in cleaning Panama hats. His business was near the waterfront and he would meet the ships arriving in Pensacola to collect their laundry. Sometime between 1910 and 1912 he married Utica, Mississippi-born Rebecca Rials[3] (1890–1969) whose family had moved from Alabama to Mississippi and back to Mobile, Alabama before coming to Pensacola. Rebecca was a seamstress and assisted her husband in running the business.

George General Grice, Jr. was born in Pensacola on November 28, 1925.[4] It is only recently that the correct birth year of 1925 has become known.[5] Many sources incorrectly give the year as 1927 and it appears that Gigi (so named for his initials: G.G.) was himself responsible for the perpetuation of this inaccuracy. He had four older sisters: Harriet (1913–1999); Kessel (1916–1997); Elvis (1918–1999); Valerie (1921–); and one younger brother, Thomas (1929–). Two additional children did not survive infancy.

Music was important to the Grice family and, as was typical in those days, they always had a piano. Thomas S. Grice (born 1851), a great uncle of Gigi, had two sons, one of whom (Thomas Jr.) was known as "Baby Grice" and was mentioned by Jelly Roll Morton in his interviews with Alan Lomax:

Of course we had, ah, King Porter around there, that is I mean Porter King—the man that "King Porter Stomp" was named after. He was considered a very good piano player. And of course we had, ah…King…I disremember his name/I think his name Charlie King, another piano player around there. Baby Grice was another one that was supposed to be good. Ah, that was all in Mobile. Baby Grice was from Pensacola, Florida.[6]

Despite this intriguing association, Baby Grice was not close to his Pensacola relatives and is remembered more as a vagabond than as a professional pianist. There is no evidence that he was influential in bringing jazz to the attention of any of the Pensacola relatives.

The Grices were members of the African Methodist Episcopal Church and it was mostly church music that was heard and played in the house. Popular music and jazz were frowned upon as negative influences. When Gigi was just six years old he gave a vocal recital, singing "His Eye Is on the Sparrow," attired in a satin dress suit made by his mother, who had printed tickets for the occasion.

The piano virtuoso Donald Shirley was born in Jamaica in 1927 but grew up in Pensacola alongside Gigi and his brother Tommy. He recalled that the Grice family were known for their musical abilities:

George came from a very talented family. Two of his sisters, as I recall, played the piano. And I believe his mother played. She played as a housewife or a community person would play, nobody's Horowitz or anything like that. (DS)

The two sisters that Shirley remembered were Harriet and Kessel. They had studied with Carrie Holland Hicks (1899–1984), a local legend in the Pensacola community, at her home on West Belmont Street. The third sister, Elvis, was an accomplished singer, and, according to her sister Valerie, "She won first prize every year in the high-school musical vocal contest. She won. She was a great soloist." (VC2) Shirley recalled the contexts in which the Grice children's talents would be showcased:

I know George used to sing. It was a family-type thing. You had to try to imagine what was taking place. There were Sunday-school programs and there may have been school programs and local Tom Thumb weddings and things like that. George and his brother used to sing duets as I recall. And one of the sisters accompanied them. This was all a community effort of what was taking place in the community. And it also gave—as an adult I can look back on it and say, well, this was one of the ways that a family was able to display the moral fortitude of how they had raised their children, and how well they were doing. And it was a good forum to see that this one had not gone to reform school and this one had not gotten… so it was like any other community in that sense. It was a community effort. (DS)

The family performances continued on a regular basis (though tickets were not printed). Tommy, the youngest of the family, remembered:

We used to have talent shows every Saturday night because we were not permitted to go out to parties and things. My mother, being a very religious person, and expecting us to rise up early in the morning for Sunday church, from Sunday school all the way to the afternoon—so on Saturdays, we had our baths, we had to perform our little talent show. And at first, we performed without any instruments. My sisters, two older sisters, played piano. And Gigi and I used to play the tunes through the *Look* magazine. It was a magazine we used to roll up and hum all the marches and some of the pop tunes. We never heard of anything called bebop or swing so we'd just hum those things.[7]

Valerie, the youngest sister, was more mathematician than musician and recited multiplication tables as her contribution to the evening.

Some opportunities existed for more organized musical activity and at least Gigi and Tommy—possibly the sisters as well—participated in Reverend Edwin Shirley's choral group (Donald's father), a non-denominational community chorus. There was a weekly broadcast of this group on radio station WCOA, 1340 AM in Pensacola.

These happy times stood in stark contrast to the darker events of the day. The Great Depression hit hard, and by 1931 many were out of work. In fact, over half of the businesses in the area around the Grice cleaning shop were closed.

After the early death of her husband from a heart condition in 1933, Rebecca Grice was forced to raise the children as a single mother, although she did have the assistance of the older girls (the oldest, Harriet, was nearly 20 at the time) and their paternal grandmother. Kessel fell a semester behind in school because she was needed to help maintain the family pressing and cleaning business. By this time the country was in the depths of the Great Depression and life could not have been easy. Eventually they were forced to sell the business.

Located in an almost exclusively white area (in 1931 the Grices were one of only two black families in a nine-block stretch), 1312 West Jackson Street was "a lovely house," according to Donald Shirley. It must have pained the family greatly when they were forced to rent it out for badly needed income to make mortgage payments. For about two years around 1934, Rebecca Grice and her family were residing at 1012 North F Street, a low-rental property provided by friends. When the Works Progress Administration began finding jobs for the unemployed in 1935, Rebecca worked in a mattress factory. The older girls would do odd jobs as they could find them. By this time Kessel was teaching in Madison County, Florida.

Thomas James, a childhood friend of Gigi, remembers how difficult things were economically for the Grices:

No, they had hardly anything. The girls helped the mama. When Gigi came along he went into the service and he had the G.I. Bill and he came back and that's how he started on his education, because there wasn't nobody to give George anything. During that time, most all of the mothers in our generation stayed home. They ran the family. (TJ)

But Evelyn DuBose, another close school friend of Gigi's, spoke about the determination that was instilled in the Pensacola children of that era:

I think, I really believe that, sometimes when it's so easy, people just don't appreciate what they have. But I think because it was segregated and because survival meant you had to go to the core of your soul and figure, OK, come hell or high water I'm going to get over and beyond this. There was some kind of internal power that came by virtue of the deprivation… Sometimes having a hard time can be a motivating force. (ED)

Donald Shirley has vivid memories of the people and times. He reflected on the Grice family and what enabled them to overcome many of the obstacles they faced:

Just determination and good parenting. Other than the determination and having some concept of family unity. And that was instilled in all the brothers and sisters by the mother because I didn't know the father.

George's mother was a very stern disciplinarian as I recall. She was a very fine lady and a very churchgoing lady and was determined she was going to raise her children in the finest tradition that could be thought of at the time. And so she did, all of them. (DS)

Shirley's appraisal of Mrs. Grice is exactly in line with the comments of Valerie Grice Claiborne: "She was a widow. She wanted to bring us up strict, very strict." (VC2) Her brother Tommy qualifies this by calling her "very strict, in a loving sense." (TG1) Accordingly, church attendance was consistent and mandatory in the Grice household:

I used to see George every Sunday morning. You have to understand, I had to, against my will; I had to play the organ in my father's church. I'd been playing, I guess, just before as well as after I went to Russia to study piano. But the window that was open by the organ was right off to the street. And George's family belonged to—like keep in mind my father's was the Episcopal church—George, I believe his was a Methodist church... The name of the church was Allen Chapel.

And as they would pass, it was kind of cute really now that I look back on it. It looked like a—[Laughs] Well, have you ever seen ducks with their [ducklings] following? Well, that's what this looked like. All of them were in line... Not outwardly militarily so... And they would pass and every Sunday morning and the mother, of course, was in the back. The older girls were in the back. I don't know whether the mother was in front. I don't recall who was in front, but the older girls and then, well, the middle ones. (DS)

Many of the members of the Allen Chapel A.M.E. church were educated professionals, according to Thomas James:

Pensacola also had the largest number of black professionals—I'm talking about physicians and dentists—than any other town in Florida. And all the professionals belonged to Allen Chapel church. That church was bordered on the downtown area. Still is. And the downtown area was right there where you'd go shopping and I guess belonging to that church kind of gave you a little relationship with the other people, being that close to downtown. But people lived all over Pensacola and they lived in areas we called the tan yard and they lived in areas we called West Pensacola and all of them came on Sundays to Allen Chapel. All your physicians, all your dentists. You had Dr. Moon. You had Dr. Sunday. You had Dr. Aarons. You had Dr. Pickens, I think you had about five MDs in this little town. For dentistry you had Dr. Long. You had Dr. Boyd. You had Dr. Goose. A little area like this had eight professional doctors. That was something and they all belonged to Allen Chapel AME. (TJ)

On September 18, 1939, just as World War II was getting underway in Europe, Gigi Gryce entered Booker T. Washington high school. Also located on West Jackson Street, several blocks east of the old Grice house, this was in an overwhelmingly black neighborhood (North D Street seems to have been a demarcation line) and was an all-black school. The town's white high school was Pensacola High and by the accounts of Tommy Gryce and Evelyn DuBose, the black schools were often lacking in supplies or given tattered hand-me-down books from the white schools. Even so, there was a powerful spirit among the school community that inspired the students to overcome these obstacles.

I do know that frequently there were classes we were supposed to be having and there were no books. It was segregated, so all the things you read about and we were exposed to, somehow they projected to us, along with our families. I think that has a lot to do with it, I mean, school can't do it all, but between what the school said and our families said to us, they said, "Listen, you have no limitations, you have the power to go on and beyond," and I think most of us did. (ED)

Indeed, many of Gigi's Pensacola schoolmates went on to very successful careers in professional fields. Several of the Shirley children were doctors, Thomas James was a dentist, and Evelyn DuBose was a teacher, as were all of the Grice children.

This level of accomplishment was promoted by strong interactions between the school and the parents which helped keep the children focused and out of trouble, as Thomas James recalled:

School, family and church in this area, in this community, were all entwined. Parents were in control and anybody else's parents were in control as far as you were member of either one of these entities. Like if Mrs. Grice saw me do something wrong, she could reprimand me and I'd better listen to what Mrs. Grice said, and before I got home because she would call and tell on me, that kind of thing. See, they didn't have counselors in our high school. We just had a principal. The principal did everything, he was the disciplinarian and whatever. In these type neighborhoods it was kind of like a village whether it was the east side or west side, you were under parental control of anybody who was in that area. (TJ)

While the strong family, church, and community underpinnings undoubtedly facilitated the achievements of the black children of Pensacola, certain government programs also opened many doors to educational and economic advancement. Gigi and Tommy Gryce were beneficiaries of the training made possible through the Works Progress Administration authorized in 1935 by Congress during the Roosevelt administration, as part of the New Deal. And later, Gigi would attend college with funding provided by the GI Bill of Rights.

One of the divisions of the Federal One program instituted as part of the WPA was the Federal Music Project. At a time when nearly two-thirds of all professional musicians were out of work, the FMP, which had both educational and performing components, was a very welcome boost. At its peak in 1936, the program employed approximately 15,000 musicians.[8] These programs were especially attractive to black students who had few alternatives, and adults as well as children would participate.

When exactly Gigi began clarinet studies is unclear. By some accounts, it could have been as early as the age of nine or ten, but more likely his first lessons started three or four years later, when he was already in high school. One of the problems in this regard was the availability of an instrument, which for a long time was precluded by financial constraints.

The first director of the FMP music program in Pensacola was a trumpet player named Joseph Jessie who had arrived in Pensacola sometime shortly before 1931.

My father helped Joseph Jessie get that particular job because Joseph Jessie was unlettered. But Joseph Jessie had played jazz in several, at the time, well-known groups. I don't know, something like King Oliver, and people of that ilk. He was the first person who got the job on the WPA as a band instructor. And that was the only time that, to my knowledge, anything resembling the word "music" had been introduced to the kids of the South at that time, at least, specifically in Pensacola. (DS)

Jessie's tenure lasted only a little over a year because on May 26, 1936, he was murdered. At the age of only 10, Gigi was witness to the horrifying event:

They used to have rehearsals. My brother played baritone horn, not saxophone. My oldest brother played trumpet. That's Dr. Calvin Shirley. And Dr. Edwin Shirley played baritone horn. They would have rehearsals at a school on what we called the East Side. Now I lived on the West Side and so did George. George lived further west than I did. And they had rehearsal at a school called Spencer Bibbs. You have to understand the breakdown of what the education system was at that time. Needless to say, you know it was a segregated situation, and the facilities were not anyplace near standard or good... So Mr. Jessie did the very best he could. So wherever he could have rehearsals, he would have it. They were having rehearsal on the grounds of Spencer Bibbs, outdoors.

Now, there was some, what we would call poverty, well, economically starved families around that neighborhood. One of the boys came over with a group of his—baby brother and a couple other kids in the neighborhood. When I speak of kids, I'm speaking now between the ages of ten and eighteen or nineteen. We would call them thugs. Anyway, they began to throw pebbles in my brother's—in the bell of his baritone horn. So Mr. Jessie decided he was going to have to do what most adults would have to do and go across the street under the guise of maybe trying to find the boys' parents or let them know that they were disturbing the band rehearsal and so forth. Anyway, [one of the boys] got a gun and shot him dead. (DS)

Whether Gigi was playing in the band when this happened or was just a spectator is unclear although it seems doubtful that he had access to a clarinet at this point. What is certain is the traumatic effect this event had on the black community of Pensacola, unaccustomed as it was to its children committing acts of such senseless violence.

The successor to Joseph Jessie and first clarinet teacher of both Gigi and Tommy Gryce was Raymond Sheppard. Tommy relates how both he and his brother gained access to their first formal musical training:

And it's odd how we got into music—through a program called the WPA. It was very similar to today's welfare program. And we saw a sign on the door, at the school, on the bulletin board saying, "Musicians: We're forming a band." And this band was being formed by an outstanding saxophone player—he used to play with Noble Sissle's band, as well as Jimmie Lunceford—called Ray Shep. He was our first band instructor.[9]

But the Grice family's lack of financial resources made it hard to get hold of instruments:

So Gigi and I signed up for band, for music lessons. And all the kids laughed because they knew the condition of the family. We were not able to buy an instrument. But however, we did sign up and fortunately there was a fellow by the name of Aaron Long [who] had an instrument and he had an extra mouthpiece. And our schedule— Aaron took the first half an hour of private lessons, that was followed by Gigi and myself. And Ray Shep would give these lessons and he thought we had a clarinet. And on the way out, as Aaron finished his lesson, he would give that instrument to Gigi and Gigi would put that mouthpiece on and he'd take his lesson and on the way out Gigi would give it to me and I would use the same mouthpiece that Gigi used. OK, so we finally made the band. [Laughs] Now how we gonna do this? So I had to drop out because my mother bought a cavalry clarinet, one of those old metal clarinets. I think it was about fourteen dollars. And during that time, fourteen dollars, that was like, you're talking about eight hundred and fifty dollars or something like that. And it took her a long time to pay it off. So Gigi took the lessons and I dropped out and got into other interests. And from that he became quite a skillful clarinet player. In fact, Gigi won the state band competition for clarinet solo on *William Tell—William Tell* Overture, took the clarinet solo. And I went off into the Boy Scouts.[10]

While some members of the Pensacola community, like Donald Shirley, had a deep involvement with classical music (Shirley never played in jazz ensembles with Gigi Gryce), this "culture" was a bit new to many at Washington High.

Well, I know the band played [Laughs]—everybody played the *William Tell* Overture. That was that and *The Poet and the Peasant* Overture, those were the things that Joseph Jessie had introduced to an otherwise totally musically illiterate community. The *William Tell* Overture—and, of course, kids associated that because we could go to the movies, let's say on Saturdays or what have you, and they always associated that with the Lone Ranger. That was the kind of thing that spurred their interest in wanting to play it. (DS)

Gigi was also fortunate to have been able to study music with another professional jazz musician in the person of Harold Andrews, now known as "The Professor." At the time, Andrews was fresh out of the band of Jay McShann, with whom he sang for three months after receiving a science degree from Tuskegee Institute in Alabama. He had been tapped to replace Raymond Sheppard who was required to temporarily relinquish his post as band director until he had obtained the appropriate educational credentials. Andrews had attended music schools in New York City and had played bass for two years with Lucky Millinder. He was also proficient on guitar, banjo, piano, and alto saxophone, and was a respected vocalist. Andrews led a nine-piece band in which Gigi, its youngest member, played lead alto saxophone (probably using a borrowed horn). Andrews reflected on his experiences with Gigi:

Gigi was a proud, well-mannered young man. I knew him as he went through grade school and then to high school, where he came in contact with me as one of his teachers in the ninth grade. I taught him General Science at Booker T. Washington High School in Pensacola, Florida. During this time the federal government installed a music program in our school. This move gave many of our students a chance to select musical training as one of their training choices. Gigi excelled as a student on the clarinet and saxophone. Inasmuch as I had been previously trained as a performing professional music teacher, I had the chance, along with Raymond Sheppard and Joseph Jessie, to teach this young man. He was bright, very witty and easy to work with. Soon he was appearing on programs in the school and community. I organized a school band that gave many of the students a chance to play and get experience here in the city.[11]

Donald Shirley remembered Mr. Andrews well.

He was a member of my father's church. And he also succeeded Joe Jessie. In fact, my father got him in college. He went to Tuskegee and his mother, Mrs. Andrews, was a very close friend of my mother. But yes, George—and Harold Andrews had a—maybe that's who it was because Joe Jessie did not start, I don't believe, the jazz band. I know that Harold Andrews did and there were several kids that played in it and among them was George.

They had two bands going, two orchestras going. Harold Andrews had one. I remember Mr. Andrews wrote something called "Kokomo." And this was when we were introduced to the word copyright—of somebody writing something and owning it and that kind of thing. But anyway, he wrote something... Of course, you have to understand that this is a small community. And nothing like what you would think of as any great recording contract—and then we used to hear a lot of the good musicians who would come to Pensacola, passing through and would play for a dance. That included Lucky Millinder, Andy Kirk, people of that ilk. And Raymond Sheppard, I can tell you, Raymond Sheppard's band played equally as well. (DS)

Mr. Jessie and Mr. Andrews were significant figures in Gigi's musical development, but there was a special connection with Raymond Sheppard.

First of all, Joseph Jessie, but more importantly, there was a man by the name of Raymond Sheppard. His father was a member of my father's church. But his mother was not. [Laughs] Raymond Sheppard had the best, I would say jazz orchestra, in and around Pensacola and that included the whole state, frankly. He played alto saxophone. Well, he had tried at one time I think he also had that position of being a head of the music faction of the WPA. But it didn't last long. And I don't know quite why or what. I think that maybe he may have succeeded Joseph Jessie and then Harold Andrews came in because Harold may have been in college at the time. (DS)

Sheppard had a high regard for the talents of the young Gigi Gryce:

Gigi had what you call the wherewithal and the whatevers! Everybody was just proud to have Gigi play. Gigi looked like from out of nowhere, he just mastered that clarinet. And Raymond Sheppard was just so... He used to say "My, my. My, my." He was just phenomenal with that horn. Like he was born with it. (TJ)

Donald Shirley's recollection of Gryce was as an unusually intelligent, but musically unremarkable student.

George was a very bright youngster. So was his brother. George had a very, very keen mind, a very good one. As a matter of fact, it would not be too far to say that I would regard George as an intellectual, frankly, compared to a lot of the other people who came out of [Pensacola]. George was a very sociable person. But he had more serious verbal communicational skills than most of the people that I knew around Pensacola, of that age category. So it was not at all surprising that he would succeed at anything, really.

He was such a hell of a nice guy, so as I remember him, as a kid, and I certainly never thought that he would—he didn't manifest anything of any unusual greatness, not at that age. Now maybe to his family it may have appeared so, maybe so. The most promising trumpet player who was also in high school was a guy by the name of Herman McMillan. Now as an example, Gigi did not manifest the kind of immediate flair and talent as did Herman McMillan, to my recollection. (DS)

Shirley was already attending college when Gryce was finishing high school, so it could well be that Gigi made great strides in his final years. Valerie Grice Claiborne mentions McMillan (1923–1986), who was two years older than Gigi, as well as Shirley, as being influential to the whole family. She especially remembers when the prodigious Shirley would "get on the piano and Mother said 'Stop playing all that music in this house!' [Laughs]" (VC2)

Tommy Gryce recalled that Sheppard taught a good deal of music theory in band class and he and Donald Shirley remembered that Gigi was working with Raymond Sheppard's band even while he was in high school. Aaron Long remembered him playing in that band also after his naval service.

While Gigi was in high school, his mind was invariably on music. His brother reported that their mother would allow him to practice and Tommy would have to pick up the slack with the household chores. He often preferred to spend time alone.

He wasn't that shy, he was just quiet. He loved to dress. He didn't have that many clothes, but he always had a shirt and tie on. I never saw him in a pair of shorts or anything. In fact, in high school he was the same way—very, very studious. (TG1)

Quiet. He was very quiet and kind of self-centered. But he was friendly. George, we used to tease him about his name. George General—"General George." Used to tease him about his name. But he was as friendly as he could be. (TJ)

I don't think he was an extroverted person. I think that quite frequently when he was talking with people, he was also composing or thinking, visualizing tunes that he might be able to create. I could see that. (ED)

His school friends remember him as not particularly interested in sports; unlike the case with most of his peers, musical interests occupied much of Gigi's time.

He always practiced a lot whereas I liked to be out in the street, he wouldn't, and he'd stay home and read and do music. He'd practice on the piano when he wasn't practicing on the horn. (AL)

Music. Music was his world. Basically, that's what he committed himself at that point in his life to, music, and I think it might have been an eternal commitment. I don't know. I visited his home there in New York after he had been married and started his family because we had a very healthy relationship. Even then, it was still music. I think music was always it.

I felt that Gigi had a very exceptional genius for the music that was in his soul. It was in there and you could just feel the genius and feel his need to express it, and even though I didn't know how it would manifest itself, that I knew it would, and I'm not quite sure how it did because there are a lot of details I don't know about, but I think whatever happened was an expression of him and how he wanted it to be and that's the way it is. (ED)

Gigi devoted much time to perfecting his instrumental technique and when not practicing by himself, would study with Aaron Long sharing a Carl Fischer clarinet method book. Long also recalled that Gigi had a great interest in the piano and would spend considerable time at the keyboard learning chords and harmonies.

The Washington High School marching band, of which Gigi was a member, performed at quite a high level as Aaron Long remembered:

Only time that we traveled in high school was when we went to the music festival, which, at that time, the first music festival we went to was down to Tallahassee. And Gigi went to that one, you understand. Our school won the music festival. We had bands from Jacksonville, from other high schools in the state of Florida. They was competing, you understand. We were very fortunate. We had good musicians and we won the state festival. (AL)

The band competition to which Long refers took place right around the time of the bombing of Pearl Harbor, in late 1941.

Although Gigi was deeply involved in music, he appeared to have little interest in schoolwork. Despite being viewed as bright and articulate, his high-school grades were mediocre at best.

Booker T. Washington High School transcript, 1943

Gigi never engaged in extended discussions about his aspiration to be a professional musician.

Not really. Other than the fact that he was doing it. It wasn't a matter of talk. He was playing and he played well enough to play in both of the local jazz orchestras. He played with Raymond Sheppard for a while and I know he played for a length of time with Harold Andrews. (DS)

But Thomas James remembered Gigi as being quite single-minded regarding his career plans:

Gigi was a determined-type youngster. Gigi, once he got involved in something, he just never let go. He was very determined. Lots of ability. Lots of ability. Just really determined and he was determined to be some type of big man in the music world. (TJ)

It is likely that his early experiences with Sheppard and Andrews in terms of composition, copyright, and arranging planted seeds that would grow as Gigi became more and more committed to the field.

In his senior year of high school, Gigi formed a close bond with Evelyn DuBose who was four years his junior. More than a half century later, she recalled their relationship:

It's so hard to explain it, but mentally at that time, we were really close, but now that I know about adult relationships, I guess... I wouldn't say "friends," because we called ourselves a couple, but in reality there was not the kind of interaction that you would have if you were really... It was very sterile, but it was very real in our lives at that particular time.

Because even though it was three or four years, it still was a big gap. I just remember walking down the corridor and he started glancing. Maybe it was one of the first relationships I ever had in my whole emerging process where the guy was looking at me and I was looking at him and all we were doing was looking. That's about where it was. Perhaps because at that time if you're in the eighth or ninth grade and somebody's already in the twelfth grade, that's still, down here anyway, and during the times, a long, a great distance. Maybe he was inhibited and propelled by his values that he had been taught in his home. As I said before, it was very sterile but it was very real, in our hearts. But it wasn't really a relationship as we would know it now as adults.

The whole experience, even though I wasn't grown up enough to have a relationship that I could share with you and say we had this syrupy thing, it wasn't like that. It was good, it was fun, it was clean, it was young, it was real. (ED)

As the youngest of eleven children, DuBose was known as "Baby." Her mother died when Evelyn was only three months old and she was raised primarily by her grandmother. Her family was very protective of her and her older brothers would pick her up straight from school in a car. There was not much opportunity for social interaction with George or anyone else.

It's so funny. We would meet in the movie because before he came back from the service I wasn't supposed to be seeing the guy. But we'd be afraid to be seen in public. It was funny. It was a relationship and we claimed each other, but as adults I now know we didn't get to be with each other a lot and to know each other, but in our hearts, at that particular time, I have to reaffirm, at that particular time, that's what we felt. That's what it was in our world then. I wasn't allowed to so therefore he couldn't see me very much. (ED)

The two corresponded during the years that Gigi was in the Navy, and when he returned on leave DuBose's strict family did permit Gigi to call upon Evelyn at their home, providing he departed by 9 PM.

He would write about his devotion to me, and he had expectations about being with me always and forever. And then sometimes he would share things about whatever he was doing or whatever he was writing or whatever he was creating or whatever he projected as part of his goals for the future. That was the basic content. (ED)

Although the relationship never fully blossomed, the two kept in contact, and Gigi composed a piece entitled "Baby" dedicated to Evelyn DuBose, and recorded it while in Europe with Lionel Hampton in 1953.

Gigi was graduated from high school in June of 1943, and spent the next few months working in the local shipyard and playing in

Raymond Sheppard's band until he was drafted by the U.S. Navy. He may have attended a semester of college (probably Fall 1943) as this is indicated on his Naval record. By this point, his competency on both clarinet and alto saxophone was such that he could hold his own in professional ensembles like that of Sheppard. Furthermore, he was becoming aware of the many name bands that would perform in Pensacola. Aaron Long recalled:

Well, all of the big bands that ever played, from Louis Armstrong all the way to Cab Calloway and Duke Ellington, came to Pensacola to perform during the forties. Every big band that was played here. We'd all use to go to the band and stand around the bandstand and listen to them play, and dance and come back and listen to them play certain numbers. (AL)

On March 4, 1944, Gigi was inducted into the United States Navy and saw a great deal of the U.S. during his two-year term, traveling first to Great Lakes, Illinois (approximately 30 miles north of Chicago's Loop), then to Chapel Hill, North Carolina; Seattle, Washington; and Kodiak, Alaska; before finishing at Jacksonville, Florida. He was trained in welding but found his way into the Navy band, eventually being discharged with the rating of Musician, Second Class.[12] Those who served at the same time say that, since Gigi entered the Navy as a draftee, his transfer into the band would have required encouragement and intervention from other Great Lakes band members with whom he had become acquainted, and could not have occurred simply because he had prior musical training and experience.

The Band at Great Lakes Naval Training Center was founded by John Philip Sousa in 1917 and remains a vital part of the armed forces in the Midwest to this day. In 1942, African-Americans were accepted for limited service in the Navy in an effort to utilize this personnel pool, which was substantial but largely untapped due to discriminatory policies. Leonard Bowden, a professional musician with ROTC training at Tuskegee Institute, was appointed bandmaster at Camp Robert Smalls, a new camp organized at Great Lakes to handle the large influx of black recruits that the changed policy was expected to produce. Later, two additional camps were formed, Lawrence and Moffett. During the 1940s, over 5000 band members would pass through the Great Lakes programs, including many who had already established, or would go on to, important careers in jazz. This impressive group included trumpeters Clark Terry, Jimmy Nottingham, and Ernie Royal, arrangers Luther Henderson, Gerald Wilson, and Ernie Wilkins, bassists Major Holley and Arvell Shaw, drummer Osie Johnson, trombonists Booty Wood and Al Grey, saxophonists Lou Donaldson, Marshall Royal, John Coltrane, Jerome Richardson, Sam Rivers, and Willie Smith. Smith, the star soloist with the 1930–41 Jimmie Lunceford orchestra, directed the swing band stationed at Great Lakes.

The Great Lakes bands performed important entertainment and fundraising functions in Chicago as well as many other locations during the war years. Perhaps more importantly, the training station provided a large number of black musicians with unprecedented opportunities for professional growth, as Samuel Floyd, Jr. noted:

In sum, the Great Lakes Experience contributed to the quality of life for the individual musicians and their families, and for that of others, through its cultural enrichment efforts. It helped to prepare many for their professions. It increased knowledge, directly for those involved in the experience, and indirectly for others it affected. It made possible the further development of the intelligence of each participating individual and it certainly increased the participants' capacity for sound judgement. In other words, the Great Lakes Experience was, as far as I can determine, the greatest single educational and musical experience for blacks ever to occur in America.[13]

The proximity of Great Lakes to Chicago and its legendary jazz scene was also a singular advantage for young Navy musicians, as Clark Terry recalled:

When we had liberty on the weekends at Great Lakes, you had to either go to Chicago or Milwaukee. And it was stupid to go to Milwaukee because there was nothing there. So everybody went to Chicago. Chicago welcomed the musicians with open arms because prior to this, every time you saw a black man with a United States Navy uniform on, he had a "c" on his sleeve which was chief cook and bottle washer, you know. But when we came into Chicago on our first leave with a lyre on our sleeves—emblem for musicians, it was a totally different thing, brand new. So the whole town just took to us. And almost invariably every weekend, all the musicians would be in a situation where people would offer their homes to you. "Come and stay with me." And on top of that, on 39th and Wabash there was big place that used to be Baker's Casino which was where Joe Louis used to train, they made that into a USO. So that was the USO where all of the black sailors would go to stay. They had lots of beds and showers and food, you know, a place you could use as a headquarters. I'm sure that Gigi must have spent a little time in there unless he knew somebody right away that would have circumvented his having to go there. (CT)

Gigi's period in the Navy must have been a very exciting time for him musically, and he most certainly benefited from the programs and associations Great Lakes provided. While stationed there, he also studied briefly at the Chicago Conservatory of Music. It was probably during this time that he was able to purchase his own alto saxophone, and he had already started writing during this period, as Aaron Long recalled:

During that time when he come back from the Navy he had written quite a bit of music. He had quite a repertoire of music that he had wrote because he was in the Navy band and I imagine with him being in the Navy band they sent him to music school, you understand. I don't know what all he'd done in the Navy, but I do know he played in the Navy band. When he came back to Pensacola we got together and talked and everything and he had quite a bit of music. He played with Sheppard until he left for him to go to the Boston Conservatory. (AL)

Tommy Gryce recalled two names of important figures that his brother would have encountered in Chicago: "Goon" Gardner and Harry Curtis.

Gigi later went on to—got out of the service and he was telling me about these great alto players. And he didn't mention Bird. He mentioned a fellow by the name of Andrew Gardner, Goon Gardner. He said Goon was the alto player not Bird, said he would wipe Bird out! I think Goon played with Earl Hines's band. There was another fellow by the name of Curtis, Harry Curtis. Harry was with Cab Calloway's band. They were tremendous alto players. And then I thought, well wow, these guys, they was better than Bird, I wanna know, you know—then that sort of steered me away from really listening to Bird.[14]

Andrew "Goon" Gardner was a legendary figure who was considered one of the best alto players in Chicago in the late 1930s. He is sometimes mentioned in connection with his early association with Charlie Parker. Gardner helped Bird get work in Chicago around 1939 and later played alto in the legendary 1943 Earl Hines big band, where Parker played tenor. Tragically, there are no recordings of this landmark unit (which also included Dizzy Gillespie, Bennie Green, and Shadow Wilson) due to a recording ban. The few recordings that Gardner appears on show him to be moving in the direction of the bebop style although frequently in a jump blues environment. Gardner was listed as a member of the Navy band at Great Lakes in the March 15, 1944 issue of *Down Beat*.

Harry Curtis worked with trombonist Trummy Young for a time

and recorded with him in Chicago early in 1944, just before Gigi's arrival at Great Lakes. Leo Parker, John Malachi, and Tommy Potter were all members of the Eckstine band that recorded for National on May 2, 1945.

Next, I got a little band of my own. I picked them up in Washington and took them off to Chicago—John Malachi on piano, Tommy Potter on bass, Eddie Byrd on drums, and Leo Parker and Harry Curtis on saxes. They'd never been out of Washington before and we worked about four months. Ray Nance used to come by every night when he was in Chicago with Duke. He dug the little band. We played real soft to fit the club—tenor, alto, trombone and three rhythm.[15]

Clearly, the musicians that Gigi Gryce encountered were in on the ground floor of the bebop revolution even if they were not the best-known practitioners. In 1944, when Gigi entered the service, the music of the day was big band swing, and it was while in the Navy that Gigi first encountered the sounds of the bebop revolution. His brother Tommy recalled being introduced to the exciting new music.

When Gigi finished high school, he went into the Navy. And then he bought, on one of his leaves, he came back with some old records of Charlie Parker—"Hot House" and "Salt Peanuts" and Dizzy, and I'd never heard this music before because the first solo or the first person in jazz that I was attached to was a tenor player by the name of Flip Phillips. And I imitated Flip Phillips and Georgie Auld and then I got into Ben Webster. So, when Gigi went back to the Navy, I got the old clarinet that he had.[16]

Many of the musicians in the Navy band went directly into professional big bands after being discharged, but reports that Gryce was a short-time member of the Tiny Bradshaw band around March of 1946 remain unconfirmed. Gigi used the opportunity offered by the GI Bill to further his musical education. He returned to Pensacola for a short time before heading north with the intention of studying music.

Notes

1. Cliff Smalls quoted by Stanley Dance in *The World of Earl Hines*, p. 262.
2. Cannonball Adderley quoted by Charles Edward Smith in liner notes to *Cannonball's Sharpshooters*, EmArcy MG-36135.
3. It should be noted that Rebecca's surname has also been spelled Riels, Rails, and Ryles on various official documents.
4. George Grice, Jr. changed the spelling of the family name to Gryce as an adult. Professionally, he was known as Gigi Gryce. To avoid confusion, in this book, the surnames Grice and Gryce can be considered interchangeable and refer to the same family.
5. Photocopy of Notice of Separation from U.S. Naval Service of George General Grice, Jr. supplied by Valerie Claiborne; photograph of gravestone supplied by Valerie Claiborne, photocopy of high school transcript; Death Certificate of Basheer Qusim (George G. Grice, Jr.) provided by the Florida Office of Vital Statistics.
6. Transcript of 1938 interview with Jelly Roll Morton by Alan Lomax, provided by Peter Pullman, Library of Congress acetate no. AFS 1638 B; See also Alan Lomax, *Mister Jelly Roll: The Fortunes of Jelly Roll Morton, New Orleans Creole and "Inventor of Jazz,"* Duell, Sloan and Pierce, New York, 1950, p. 121.
7. Tommy Gryce, interviewed by Phil Schaap on WKCR-FM, New York, July 2, 1997.
8. http://www.curtainup.org/lii10204.htm
9. Tommy Gryce, interviewed by Phil Schaap on WKCR-FM, New York, July 2, 1997.
10. Tommy Gryce, interviewed by Phil Schaap on WKCR-FM, New York, July 2, 1997.
11. Harold B. Andrews, letter provided by Valerie Grice Claiborne.
12. Photocopy of Notice of Separation from U.S. Naval Service of George General Grice, Jr. supplied by Valerie Claiborne.
13. "The Great Lakes Experience: 1942–45," Samuel A. Floyd, Jr. in *The*

Black Perspective in Music 3, no. 1 (spring 1975), p. 23.

14. Tommy Gryce, interviewed by Phil Schaap on WKCR-FM, New York, July 2, 1997.

15. Trummy Young quoted by Stanley Dance in *The World of Earl Hines*, p. 224.

16. Tommy Gryce, interviewed by Phil Schaap on WKCR-FM, New York, July 2, 1997.

education: hartford & boston

*H*ARRIET, THE OLDEST, was also the first of the Grice siblings to leave Pensacola for the north. She had married a man named Charles Combs from Tallahassee, and the couple settled first in Philadelphia, where Charles worked in the shipyards, and then Hartford, Connecticut where he secured employment as clerk and supervisor of a department store warehouse.

After completing his service in the U.S. Navy, in 1946 Gryce traveled to Hartford, where he lived for about a year with Charles and Harriet. By this time, the couple had achieved a reasonable level of financial security and their home represented the most viable family situation for the advancement of Gryce's educational and professional goals. Rebecca Grice had instilled in her children the importance of education and the need for the siblings to aid each other in this regard. Thus it was quite reasonable that Harriet's home would be available for her younger brother to use not only while he applied to and attended college, but also as a jumping-off point for establishing important contacts in Boston and New York. The Grices were something of a rarity among African-American families at that time as all the children attended, and all but one completed, college. It was largely through their mutual cooperation, encouragement, and assistance that this could be realized. Tommy Gryce spoke about the family:

Her [their mother's] values and morals were so outstanding. She never really wanted him [Gigi] to become a musician or anything like that. That's how religious she was. She was a fanatic. She believed that a family was a family and that was it! You would do anything for your family. In fact, that's how we got through school. My oldest sister helped my other sister—actually paid—and it was like a chain reaction. (TG2)

Several published accounts[1] claim that Gryce attended the Julius Hartt School of Music, but the records of the Hartt School (since 1957 part of the University of Hartford) show no evidence of his enrolling.[2] Local musicians who knew him at the time also have no recollection of Gryce attending school in Hartford. Education was most certainly on his mind, however. His high-school transcripts were sent to Boston Conservatory in May of 1946, though he did not start his studies there until September of 1947. It could well be that in the interim he was working to save money so he could enroll, although the bulk of his college expenses were paid for by his veterans benefits under the Servicemen's Readjustment Act of 1944 (GI Bill of Rights), which subsidized tuition, fees, subsistence, books and supplies, equipment, and counseling services.

Gryce continued to spend time in Hartford during the period when he was at the conservatory and had strong ties to the Hartford musical scene, especially to trumpeter Clyde Board, pianists Emery Smith and Norman Macklin, and bassist Clifford Gunn. Smith recalled the time when Gryce was in Hartford:

OK well, that had to be, let me see, in the middle, late forties when he was going to Boston Conservatory. And he had a sister and her family was living here on, let's see, what was the name of that street, West Clay Street, a little small street in Hartford. And he befriended a guy by the name of Clyde Board. He had a band, "Thirteen Students of Swing." He was a trumpet player. And he had a brother who also played in that band, named Henry Board. Henry was a year older than Clyde. Clyde taught me everything about music. (ES)

According to Macklin and Smith, Board was very involved in music education in an informal manner. Gryce's interest in teaching and developing young people would eventually result in a long career in the New York City public school system. The first seeds of his inclinations in this area may have been sown in Hartford through his relationship with Board:

We were young at that time. There was a gentleman named Clyde Board, a trumpet player and he and Gigi were very good friends. And Clyde had a 13-piece band, you know, of all the kids in the neighborhood. It was very, very successful and they played the proms. Gigi used to arrange the music and he played with those groups. But he was far advanced! (NM)

We're dealing with kids, we was 14, 15, 16 years old, and we had no formal musical training, and he had the patience to teach the kids and help them along. And this band was good—the Clyde Board band—and we used to play proms and stuff like that. And he [Board] was very influential in helping a lot of children start playing music. (NM)

Gryce and Board were above the level of most of the other musicians in Hartford at that time, as Emery Smith relates:

Way ahead of everybody! [Laughs] I mean they could walk down the street and a car blows a horn and they would know what note it was. (ES)

Emery Smith spent much time in Hartford with Gryce and Clyde

39

Board and witnessed how his two mentors approached studying music and practicing their instruments:

Gigi came here and he met Clyde and Clyde was a guy that had perfect pitch, a great trumpet player, could read the impurities in the music manuscript paper. So they got together and they used to practice together at 294 Bellevue Street. That's where Clyde Board lived, up on the third floor. And I was always there. What Gigi used to do—he had written something. I remember when he wrote that tune, "Social Call." And he would write out the changes and he and Clyde taught me how to play them changes. And they would work out a tune. And he wrote some other things too.

But they used to practice together. Now here's what they would do: Gigi was playing alto and Clyde was playing trumpet. I mean they would practice like four, five, six, seven hours, you know, and here's what they would do: Clyde would practice, he had a book called *Herbert L. Clarke Trumpet Studies* and they would practice duets out of that book. And Gigi would, on the spot, he would transpose, right on the spot!

And after about two hours of going through that, then Gigi would put out his book. I think it was [Paul de Ville's 1908 book] *Universal [Method] for the Saxophone*. And Clyde would transpose out of Gigi's saxophone book. And that would go on and on and then they would sit down and write out things like "Dizzy Atmosphere." What was that other thing they used to do? [Sings] "Shaw Nuff." And they would play that stuff. I mean they would *play* it. Yeah, without a rhythm section. And then they had a little quintet that they had together that they used to play little dances we had at the YWCA in Hartford, Connecticut. They were playing all those tunes like "Now's the Time," "Anthropology," and then Gigi's tunes, things he wrote and then some of the things that Clyde had written. And that's how I got to know Gigi because he would sit down and he would say, "Play such-and-such a chord or play this chart," and then he would say, "Try these voicings." And he would sit down at the piano and show me these voicings that he wanted to hear. And then we used to do tunes like if I said, "Hey man, there's a tune that I want to learn

called 'Tenderly.'" A cat named Walter Gross wrote it and Sarah
Vaughan sang it. That's how far back that goes, so that had to be
1946 or 1947. And he said, "Well, I know the tune." Then he would
play it with his horn and I would sit at the piano and scuffle with
them chords. Then he'd say, "Well, come on, wait a minute." Then he
would sit down, show me the chords, write them out, then show me
the voicings.

That's the kind of guy Gigi—then he had a band here that played
little dances. Clyde was in that band. He played first trumpet in that
band. Gigi was the leader. And he had a tremendous band. And he
helped a lot of guys because guys had problems, you know, reading
and he would explain about the middle of the bar, you know. If
you're in 4/4 time, you don't write over the middle of the bar, so
making the reading a lot easier, you know. (ES)

Gryce was involved in the theoretical side of music and had a
firm grasp of the literature and how it applied to jazz. He was
generous in sharing his knowledge, and Emery Smith was a ben-
eficiary of this information.

I can remember a lot of times we were walking down Main Street,
usually in the summer, late spring, early summer, just walking—me,
Clyde and Gigi. And I'm listening to them cats talking about intervals
and talking about scales and talking about that kind of thing. In fact,
it was Gigi that told me, he said, "Hey man, you want to get a book
about—there's two cats that you should look at." I said who? He
said, "One guy is a guy named Nicolas Slonimsky." He wrote a book
called *A Thesaurus of Scales and Melodic Progressions*, something like that.
Back in 1947 he wrote this book and it still costs twenty-five dollars. I
know Trane used the book. The other book was in two volumes by
Joseph Schillinger. And in that was a book where he dealt with pitch
scales—pitch scales. So I went to the library and copped that. I had
to buy that Slonimsky book because it wasn't in the library. But I got
a hold of that Schillinger. (ES)

The *Thesaurus of Scales and Melodic Patterns* was published in 1947, and while it was not intended for jazz musicians, a number of notable figures have drawn inspiration from it. The association with John Coltrane is legendary (there are clear connections between the book and Coltrane's "Giant Steps") and it seems that Gryce was studying the book before Coltrane, who is reported to have come in contact with it in the mid-1950s.[3]

As jazz theory became more and more codified, Gryce kept abreast of subsequent developments. Emery Smith later encountered Gryce in New York and was referred to two books that would have been of great interest to jazz musicians, both published by Charles Colin: *Kaleidophone* (first published in 1940) was written by the Russian composer and theoretician Joseph Schillinger (1895–1943) and dealt extensively with pitch scales. The other book Gryce alerted Smith to was entitled *Chord Dictionary*, by Don Schaeffer. Gryce's interest in the works of Schillinger is worth noting. Joseph Schillinger developed a system of composition based on mathematical permutations. The two-volume work *The Schillinger System of Musical Composition* is a legendary text and was originally published in 1941 by Carl Fischer. Schillinger's composition students included George Gershwin, Benny Goodman, and Glenn Miller. Other jazz musicians who have studied the "Schillinger System" include pianist Muhal Richard Abrams and trumpeter Hobart Dotson, but his system was most widely used in the Hollywood film studios. There is a Boston jazz connection in that the original name of the Berklee College of Music was the Schillinger House. Its founder, Lawrence Berk, was another student of Schillinger's.

Smith recalls still other books to which he was referred by Gryce:

So Gigi was always up on things and he always pointed me in the direction—and there was another book he told me about, a guy named Bugs Bower, Bugs Bower in New York. He was writing a book. Yeah, shit, this is before 1950. He was writing a book called *Chords and Progressions*, in two volumes. And so I went to Charles Colin's studio and Charles Colin gave me the damn book. He knew I didn't have a pot to piss in so he said, "Take this book." And then he gave me book two and it was an eye-opener because that book two really showed you about the most popular progressions. And what Bugs Bower did, he turned me on to this guy Rameau who wrote a treatise on music a couple of hundred years ago where what he did at that time, you know this is in Europe, European music a couple hundred years ago, where he went through several compositions, many compositions and found out what the chord progressions were. And found out about taking the chord progressions and about resolving chord progressions. And he found out that most problems like V to I and then IV–V–I, that kind of thing. And that's what Gigi was telling me. You know, when you talk about it now, when I talk about it, he was talking about playing what Bach and Palestrina did. They would write something supposed to be in minor but when they ended the tune, it was always in major. And I got that from Gigi.

He loved them lines. But he understood that even with the lines, there's a chord progression. Doesn't have to be like a chord, like a four-tone chord, but there was a progression going on. And he was a very studious guy. He turned me on to Pythagoras. He called it the Pythagorean scale. And he was the one who told me, he said, "The major scale is not enough. The major scale is incomplete." I said, "What the hell do you mean?" He said, "When you play it, you play C, D, E, F, F-sharp, G, A, B, then your C."

He told me about the dominant seventh scale. He said, "You flat the seven. But you've got to add another note." So he said like C, D, E, F, G, A, B-flat, B-natural and then C. He said, "Now you see how symmetrical that is?" He said, "It's not a seven-tone scale. It's an eight-tone scale. You got half and half." You know, that kind of stuff. I learned an awful lot from little spurts from him. It wouldn't be five, ten minutes, because he said, "Now what I'm giving you, you got to play this in all keys." That's what he did. That's what him and Clyde did. (ES)

This theory of "additive" scales has also been investigated by Barry Harris and David Baker, but Gryce again seems to have been involved at an early stage.

And what he did was he would take a scale and he would flat the three—C, D, E-flat, E, F, F-sharp, G, A, B-flat, B-natural, C. And he called that a blues scale. Not that thing they got going today. I don't know what the hell that is. You know, that five-tone, six-tone thing. What he called a blues scale he said you take that and you use that, but you got to practice that in all keys, with all different kinds of progressions.

He was a bright guy... I learned an awful lot from that guy. He and Clyde, when they practiced, they would call a tune—they would say let's do that tune that Tadd Dameron used to play all the time, "Out of Nowhere"... "Casbah." [Sings] And they would go through several keys with that... They used to play fours and each time they would go to a different key. So those guys—I had the best education in the world, man, from those two guys. (ES)

Perhaps inspired by Dameron, Gryce wrote his own composition based on "Out of Nowhere" entitled "Sans Souci" (French for "without a care")—the name of a Florida city on the Gulf of Mexico.

For all his talent and ability, Clyde Board remained a strictly local legend, never traveling outside Hartford.

He was supposed to go with Buddy Johnson. Here's the story on that. Arthur Prysock was living here in Hartford, he and his brother Wilbur. We called him Red but his name was Wilbur. And Arthur was singing with—Clyde had a little small band, a quintet. He had a tenor player named Paul Cloud on tenor. He's dead. He played in Gigi's band but he just died a couple of years ago. Anyway, so Buddy Johnson came to town and he heard Prysock. Somebody brought him up to the Elks Club. He heard Prysock and he took Prysock on the road. And he was looking for a trumpet player to play lead trumpet and Prysock suggested Clyde. At that time, Clyde was going to the Hartt School of Music. Walter Bolden was there at the time also at the Hartt School of Music. You know this was after the Army. But Clyde had developed a strange disease called sphingomyelia, which is a deterioration of muscles and bones, and he had to switch from his left hand to his right hand and he wanted to finish school. So when Buddy Johnson talked to him, he turned Buddy Johnson down because he wanted to continue school. But then of course, that disease got progressively worse. He didn't leave. Then Dizzy wanted him. Dizzy was here. This was in 1957... But anyway, he came here and Clyde knew him and they used to go to Clyde's house. And Dizzy was amazed at Clyde because he could read as fast as Dizzy. And he would read, not with the horn, this is solfeggio, man. You know what I'm saying? And Dizzy wanted him in the band. He said, "No, I don't want to go." That was in 1957 because the disease had gotten to a point where he didn't trust himself being away from home, you know. That was that with Clyde. (ES)

In contrast to Board, even while living in Hartford and Boston, Gryce was also spending time in New York City (sometimes traveling with Quincy Jones) where he was able to associate with many of the legends in jazz. This was where trombonist Jimmy Cleveland first encountered Gryce.

I knew Gigi just on the scene in New York, you know from different places. Like at Nola's—everyone used to rehearse at Nola's in those days, prior to Lionel Hampton. What happened was, I came up there with the Tennessee State Collegians, a college orchestra of course, and I met a lot of people while I was there. It wasn't too long but I did a lot of running around, young and wild, you know. This was in...it was like forties, late forties though, yeah, early fifties.

At that time, the old Theresa Hotel uptown in Harlem, we were staying there and then we'd go downtown... But the circle of musicians that I came in contact with during that time, Gigi Gryce was one of them. And then Monk, I met Monk, and of course Dizzy. He [Gigi] came up to the Theresa to hear this band and I met him there. But it wasn't really—you know it's just like you go to the bar downstairs and get a beer—but he wasn't a drinker. He'd get coffee, orange juice, soda, and that was his whole life. That's the way he was—my total acquaintance with him, nothing stronger than fruit juices, sodas, etc. (JC)

Born in Tennessee in 1926, Cleveland apprenticed with the Lionel Hampton band between 1949 and 1953. By the mid-1950s he had become established as one of the most sought-after trombonists in New York demonstrating amazing facility on his instrument. While only seldom assuming the role of leader, he and Gryce would often interact at studio sessions, club dates, and concerts and the two established a close and long-lasting personal relationship. Cleveland remembered Gryce as a very serious musician who had already befriended the great pianist and composer Thelonious Monk (1917–1982).

That's right. He and Monk were together. He was all about jazz! He was just really devout! Now, I don't know what he and Monk were discussing although I knew it was musical. Gigi Gryce had a piece of music paper in his hand, a regular manuscript. And he was putting down—Monk was playing with something and Gigi said well, we could go with it this way. We could go with it that way. And they were discussing this.

He wrote a date for Monk. I don't know where it took place. He wrote some tunes for Monk, arranged some tunes for him. You know Monk was one of those geniuses that was like Gigi. This was—when did I come to New York with that band, the college band? It was between that time and when I decided to go with Lionel Hampton.

It was around that period of time that I ran into Gigi Gryce. I mean I hadn't heard too much of his work and all that sort of stuff but we were all students, so to speak. I'm sure he was doing a lot more than I was way down in Tennessee. Of course, he would have been, being on the scene, like the New York scene and the eastern scene, you see. So he was coming in contact with the same kind of people that I met down at the college when Dizzy brought his band down. Now I would say that the second time I saw them was at Beefsteak Charlie's and they were still talking music. And of course, I'd say hello because I used to go in there quite often.

Then I didn't see him then until I decided to come and stay. Now when traveling with Hamp's band, of course, we were in New York quite often and sometimes we'd be there like months, you know, working in and around the east and stuff, going back and forth, commuting kind of stuff. So that way, I got to meet everyone, Sahib Shihab and all those people that were in the band. And, of course, that was just a really, really great time for me. I thought it was just really lovely. (JC)

There was a decent amount of activity in Hartford that involved musicians such as Horace Silver (on tenor saxophone as well as piano), pianist John "Count" Steadwell, bassists Joe Calloway, Willie Ruff, and Clifford Gunn, and drummer Walter Bolden. Bolden also recalled working with Gryce in nearby New Haven, at a club called Lillian's Paradise. (WB) While at Boston Conservatory, Gryce would maintain his connections in Hartford, as Gunn explains:

He used to come down and play with me on certain nights, and stay at his sister's, and then return. I had a steady engagement at a club, and various other engagements, in which I would include Gigi on: the Sundown, the Elks Club—and there were several clubs in the area. (CG)

Emery Smith elaborates further:

There were two Elks Clubs. There was the Elks Club on Canton Street and then there was an Elks Club on Bellevue Street because they had split. So that we referred to the Elks Club on Bellevue Street as the "old folks' home" because they were older Elks. And Gigi played there. Then there was a place called the Turf Club, Turf Club up on Main Street. And then there was a place called the Golden Pheasant, a little small place. On Sunday afternoons—in those days, clubs and bars had to close on Sundays at nine o'clock. So you'd be in there on a Sunday and we'd be there with a piano player and a bass and a drummer, something like that you know. So that was one place. And then—wow, I have to think a minute here—down on Winton Street was the Club Sundown. That's where Horace [Silver], Joe [Calloway] and Walt Bolden were playing when Getz discovered them. They were playing with a guy named Harold Holt, a saxophone player, he had the gig down there. And on Monday or Tuesday, they used to bring in, because it was slow nights, the Club Sundown would bring in cats from New York like Lucky Thompson, and he brought Jug in, Gene Ammons. We called him Jug. You know why don't you? Big head! His head was bigger than mine. And Wardell Gray and he brought Charlie Parker. (ES)

Gryce spent time in these locations meeting these great players.

Oh yeah. He'd hang out there when he was in town, you know. So the Club Sundown was a great place. And then he would play dances—like at, you know, they had little social clubs—I used to have to sneak in because I didn't have no seventy-five cents for no dances—at the Northeast/Bracket School. The Bracket portion was elementary school, K–6, and the Northeast was a junior high school, seven, eight, and nine. They used the same auditorium. So he used to play dances there, used to have basketball. We had a little semi-pro basketball team and after the basketball game at the Northeast/Bracket gym, then they would have a little dance in the auditorium with his band.

Here's what they were playing. They were playing mostly rhythm-and-blues tunes and tunes like some standards, tunes like "Trust in Me," tunes like ["These Foolish Things"], those kind of tunes, you know, "Don't Blame Me." But then they would throw in—Gigi was a great writer. He had an arrangement on "The Hucklebuck" that was out of this world, man—Paul Williams's "Hucklebuck." And they would dance to that. So he knew how to program music because you're playing a dance. You can't play "Anthropology" all night long. He played tunes like Dizzy's tune, "Ow!" It's nice for dancing, what they used to call off-time dancing. [Sings] They would dance to that. But they didn't throw too many fast numbers out there because we were right at the tail end of like the Lindy Hop time. There was still some people that wanted to fling, you know, dancing the Applejack and all that kind of stuff. So that's the kind of stuff they played. And then Clyde was great at writing tunes with blues changes that were danceable and Gigi did the same thing. And then they would take standard tunes and they would write another line. You know what I'm saying? Like on "Fools Rush In," Clyde wrote a beautiful line based on "Fools Rush In." [Sings] You know, that kind of stuff. And people dancing and the mood was cool, man. I was there, man. (ES)

Emery Smith remembers that Gryce also studied saxophone and flute privately in Hartford when he would visit on weekends and during the summer. His teacher was very impressed with Gryce's ability and potential, and often provided instruction and tutelage without charge.

It has been written that Gryce led a band with a young Horace Silver while living in Hartford,[4] but this was not the case. Gryce and Silver did not meet until an encounter in Boston.

Well, Horace didn't live in Hartford. See, Horace came to Hartford— when Gigi was still going to Boston Conservatory, Horace used to come up and play on the weekends with Walter Bolden on drums and Joe Calloway on bass. Joe Calloway is since deceased. So no, he [Gigi] wouldn't have met—he probably met him when he was playing with Getz, yeah that was 1950. (ES)

Silver (1928–) was, in fact, a product of Norwalk, Connecticut and after his discovery by Getz would become a major figure in the development of hard bop, both as a pianist and composer. The ensembles he would lead, at first with drummer Art Blakey, and later on his own, became shining examples of the genre as well as incubators for a host of young and upcoming talents. Silver shared with Gryce a dedication to the concept that composers should control the rights to their works and not allow them to be given up for short-term gains, as was usually the case. Both were pioneers in the establishment of musician-controlled publishing companies.

Clifford Gunn recalls that Hartford was home to many fine musicians including trombonist Wayne Andre and others with whom Gryce had the opportunity to interact during this period:

These were fellows that played with my group. [Vibraphonist] Emil Richards and [drummer] "Skinny" Porcaro—Joe Porcaro—who moved to the West Coast in Sinatra's band. They were primarily local. Except for those who, you might say, escaped and had gone out to deeper waters—like gone on to New York. With Horace Silver's group there was Gene Nelson, a piano player. (CG)

Yeah, Gene Nelson, a piano player. That cat could play. In fact, I lived up the street from Gene's oldest brother, Percy. His father, Percy Nelson, the old man, taught me a lot about playing gigs and things. His father was a reed player, played alto. He played all the reeds—alto and clarinet. He played till he died. He was, I guess, ninety years old, playing, the old man, yeah. (ES)

Gene Nelson must have had an impact on Gryce because when Nelson died, Gryce wrote a piece entitled "In Memory of Gene." This composition has never been recorded, but Emery Smith recalled Gryce giving him and Clyde Board copies of the sheet music.

According to Clifford Gunn, Gryce had a reputation for being straight-laced, and not at all involved with drugs or alcohol.

You know, the fellows happened to have a smoke or a drink between sets and he would go out and get an ice-cream cone and sit writing arrangements on the breaks. And there were boys who indulged in the other items. He did not. (CG)

Right, he didn't smoke or drink. There was a soft drink called Tru-ade. It was an orange drink. So he would come up to Clyde with six bottles of, you know, the twelve-ounce bottles of Tru-ade. [Laughs]

And Clyde was a drinker. He wanted some steam, you know. He would say, "Goddamn, what did you bring this shit up here for?" [Laughs] (ES)

In fact, even by this time Gryce was interested in Islam, the religion he would later adopt.

He had a great sense of religious history, dealing with Asia Minor, you know, the Middle East and the Mesopotamian area, the Euphrates and all that. He talked about that all the time. So he had that great sense, a kind of a spiritual sense. (ES)

This interest was not at all uncommon among blacks during this period. Beginning in the 1940s, certain jazz musicians had converted to Islam, searching for a religion that was without ties to whites and the history of slavery. The faith they chose was traditional Islam, not the Black Muslim or Nation of Islam offshoot associated with Elijah Muhammad. While Gryce was aware of these trends, his own conversion did not occur until later.

In the 1940s, Boston Conservatory had an excellent reputation as a music school and it was not unusual for blacks to attend. Jazz trumpeter Idrees Sulieman, who would work with Gryce in the mid-1950s, was a student at the conservatory in the mid-1940s and saxophonist Sam Rivers attended at the same time as Gryce.

The well-known composer Alan Hovhaness (1911–2000) taught at the conservatory from 1948 to 1951 and Gryce studied classical composition with him. Hovhaness was a musical eclectic who drew much inspiration from folk music of many lands, ancient history, nature, and religion.

I've used all techniques, including the 12-tone technique. But I believe melody is the spring of music. The human voice was the first instrument, and I believe that all the different instruments are voices as well. So I want to give them melodies to sing. I think melodically, and without melody I don't have much interest in music.[5]

Gryce called Hovhaness "my most inspiring instructor" and it is easy to appreciate the connection that was made. Melodicism is certainly one of the predominant aspects of Gryce's music and it is his lyrical sense that sets him apart from many other jazz composers.

He gave me the desire to write; and broadened my musical outlook. Since then I've written two symphonies. Now I'm on a third. One of them—"Gashiya"—is being considered by the New York Philharmonic. And I wrote a ballet—"The Dance of the Green Witches"— which is due for a performance by the New York City Ballet.[6]

In the early 1950s, trumpeter Clark Terry would often work in Boston as a member of Count Basie's small ensemble of that period. It was there that he first met Gryce and heard "Dance of the Green Witches":

He [Gigi] was always a marvelous musician and a great player. And I remember the one thing. I used to call him "Green Witches" because he wrote a suite once called "Dance of the Green Witches" and I liked it very much because I used to always call him "Green Witches." (CT)

The nature of "Gashiya" (or "Al Gashiya") is unclear. In early 1953 Gryce copyrighted a score with this title for orchestra, narrator, and six-member chorus; however, a later copyright deposition with the same title is a single-page lead sheet looking very much like a jazz composition. In fact, "Gashiya" was performed by the Teddy Charles Tentet at a concert at Cooper Union in 1956. Teo Macero, who reviewed the concert in *Metronome* magazine, found the Gryce work to be one of the highlights of the concert and commented that it and one of Charles's compositions "contained all the necessary ingredients that go into good jazz. It was healthy, earthy and funky."[7] This description makes it seem unlikely that the New York Philharmonic would be interested in such a work. Regarding the title: "Gashiya" (The Overwhelming Event) is a Surah or chapter of the Quran—another indication of Gryce's interest in and familiarity with Islam. Several other Gryce compositions also have titles inspired by his faith.

There were other reports of Gryce's ability as a composer outside of the jazz arena such as the following taken from an article in 1955 by Nat Hentoff:

He has written piano duets for Hovhaness, and Boston violinist Grace Derran has featured several of Gryce's works for violin and some of his chamber pieces. In addition to chamber music, Gigi has written a symphony and two symphonic tone poems.[8]

Unfortunately, the whereabouts of these classical compositions is unknown. His teacher Alan Hovhaness is known to have destroyed dozens of works in "cathartic episodes"[9] and it is possible that Gryce may have done the same. One person who remembers at least seeing, if not hearing, some of Gryce's classical works was bassist Julian Euell.

The guy—he wrote concertos and sonatas and shit. Yeah, I saw them in this trunk and I wondered—I talked to Donald Byrd when I was in New York, asking him about that. We were talking about Gigi and he told me his brother had the music. He showed me all the stuff, you know, a couple of times, that he had written that were classical. (JE)

Tommy Gryce has no information on the subject and indicates that family members did not inherit any musical scores, but Sam Rivers feels these works could well have been the student compositions that Gryce was required to complete during his enrollment at Boston Conservatory.

No, I never heard any of these pieces, anything like that. But, of course, you know, that's part of graduating with a composition degree. You have to write a composition for the symphony orchestra.

So that's part of composition. It's necessary to get a degree. It's something you have to submit, you know, if you're majoring in composition. All the majors in composition have to write. (SR)

Regardless of the nature and quality of Gryce's non-jazz compositions, the publicity surrounding them would add significantly to his reputation as a talented and thoroughly trained musician, and would set him apart from most of his colleagues in the jazz world of the 1950s. There is no doubt, however, that his conservatory experience had broadened his horizons and exposed him to lasting influences. Although Gryce was perhaps not active in the classical realm after his time at the conservatory, his studies there gave him a special perspective that was respected by the New York musicians, and he established a rapport with like-minded individuals such as composer David Amram, whom he encountered a few years later in New York. Gryce's love for classical music was still there.

He was tremendously learned as a musician and an arranger, obviously. And since I was composing and he knew that I wanted to be writing, and was trying to write symphonic music—this was way back then—and chamber music that reflected the experience in jazz—was kind of into what they called both musics, although some of us were already thinking of it as one music. We used to have a lot of talks about music and harmonies. He used to talk to me—he loved Stravinsky, of course, and Bartok and he loved Duke Ellington's music and Charlie Parker, Dizzy, Monk, and very often we would listen to almost anything. He would always make a comment at a beautiful moment just to say how gorgeous that particular moment was. I think he was really in love with music and appreciated all of the fine things.

I told him one time about a beautiful piece that I had turned Paul Desmond onto which was Darius Milhaud's *The King's Chimney*, a woodwind quintet. And I had an old scratchy copy of that and I lent that to Gigi and he said, "I see what you mean, man. Those voicings are gorgeous." It was one of Milhaud's most beautiful pieces, based on the sounds of the provinces of France. And I think that Gigi, when he was in France, like all of us, was very touched by the French spirit and the flavor and also a lot of the French music, and appreciated Debussy and Ravel, especially for their harmonic sense a lot. And these were composers that we all loved, also Shostakovich and, of course, Prokofiev. These were all favorites of so many of the real musicians of our era. Of course their music was so gorgeous.

...And players like Gigi showed that you could take melody, harmony and counterpoint and, using a lot of their genius of jazz, go right back to those fundamentals and write some fantastic music, not only in the jazz idiom but in any idiom. But by using what Gigi and all of us called choice notes—that was the expression, that was the motto, choice notes, play choice notes, write choice notes, listen for the choice notes. In the vernacular, choice means the most beautiful possible notes all the time. So Gigi was always looking for perfection and for beauty and truthfulness. (DA)

Gryce's idol Charlie Parker expressed the same sentiment: "It's just music. It's playing clean and looking for the pretty notes."[10]

As in high school, Gryce was not a stellar student at Boston Conservatory, receiving only a C and C- in flute and a C- and D in history of music. Composition and counterpoint were his strongest subjects.

I mainly studied with Miss Minna Holl for theory and piano; Mr. Daniel Pinkham for music history and some phases of composition; and Mr. Lee for piano, instrumentation and counterpoint. Incidentally, Mr. Lee is the founder of a very fine music school in Shanghai, China. I think it's called the Shanghai Conservatory.[11]

In addition to these teachers from Boston Conservatory, Gryce took special lessons in composition from Madame Margaret Chaloff, the mother of the great baritone saxophonist Serge Chaloff.

BOSTON CONSERVATORY OF MUSIC
BOSTON, MASSACHUSETTS

Basheer Qusim

Record of.......GRICE.......... ....George.......... .... Home address...26 Mahl Avenue.......... Street
LAST NAME   FIRST NAME   INITIAL   Hartford, Conn.......... City

Candidate for .... Degree.......... .... Major Composition..........
Entered...Sept. 15, 1947.......... .... Graduated.......... June 6, 1952 –degree bachelor of music

PREPARATORY SCHOOL B.T. Wash. Pensacola, Fla.

		History or Civics	3
English	5	ElectivesSociology	1
For. Language German	2	Physiology	1
Mathematics	2		
Science	5		

CREDITS ACCEPTED IN ADVANCED STANDING

School	Subject	Credit

CONSERVATORY RECORD

Year	Subject	1st Sem. Grade	1st Sem. Credit	2nd Sem. Grade	2nd Sem. Credit
1947–48	Piano	B✓	2	B	2
	Clarinet	B	2	–	–
	Recital Class	#	¼		
	Basic Music I	B	3	C–	3
	Harmony I	A	2	B✓	2
	English I	D	3	D	3
	German	B–	2	C–	2
	Band	A	1	A–	¼
	Phys. Ed.	A	¼	A	¼
	Flute	–	–	C✓	2
.948–49	Piano	B–	3	C	3
	Trumpet	B	2	–	–
	Basic II	B	3	B–	3
	Harmony II	A	2	A–	2
	Counterpoint I	A	2	A–	2
	English I	C	3	C	3
	Band	B	1	B	1
	Flute	–	–	C	3

CONSERVATORY RECORD (Cont'd)

Year	Subject	1st Sem. Grade	1st Sem. Credit	2nd Sem. Grade	2nd Sem. Credit
1949–50	Piano	B–	2	B–	2
	Recital Class	#	#	#	#
	Analysis	C✓	2	C✓	2
	Counterpoint II	B	2	B✓	2
	Composition I	A	2	A	2
	Instrumentation I	A–	1	B✓	1
	Psychology	C	2	D	2
	Band	B	1	B	1
1950–51	Piano	C✓	2		
	Composition II	A	6		
	Instrumentation II	A	3		
	Fine Arts	B–	2		
	History of Music	C–	2		
	Conducting	B	1		
	Chorus	A	1		
1951–52	Violin	–	–	B	2
	Composition Ib	–	–	B	6
	Instrumentation Ib	–	–	B	3
	Fine Arts Ib	–	–	C	1
	History of Music Ib	–	–	D	2
	History of Education	–	–	C	2
	Conducting Ib	–	–	B✓	1
	Chorus	–	–	A	1

Total sem. hrs. 124

transcript sent to Grice 2/27/63
transcript sent to Grice 9/12/52
transcript to Grice 7/28/52

A—Excellent   B—Good   C—Fair   D—Low   E—Fail
X—Absent from Examination   W—Withdrew from Course

This is a correct copy

James V. Vitagliano   10-20-98
RECORDER REGISTRAR.

Transcript of Gryce's grades at the Boston Conservatory

While in Boston, Gryce came in contact with local musicians including Sabby Lewis and also continued to associate with the larger names in bebop such as Howard McGhee and Thelonious Monk.[12] There were plenty of opportunities for both groups of players. Trumpeter and former Berklee College of Music professor Herb Pomeroy describes the Boston jazz scene:

In the 1950s and early 1960s there was a great deal of activity. The level of the local players was very high. The clubs divided it in half as far as using local people and traveling names. There was a very rich jazz scene. The band singers of the 1940s were individual stars in the 1950s. The dance bands as such were on the way down so it was pretty much the jazz musicians and the singers. I primarily played at the Jazz Workshop. The original Workshop was located right where the Westin Hotel is now. A good amount of the audience were college students. Now these people were probably not able to understand everything we were doing but a majority of the audience went out enough to develop a sense of taste. When I play these days, I observe the audience, and I do not see the listening intensity. In the mid to late 1950s there were ten clubs. Five in Copley Square and five around the Mass. Ave./Columbus Ave. corner. Copley Square was the white area and Mass. Ave. was the black area. The audiences didn't overlap as much as one would have hoped for. Storyville would bring in the major contemporary names such as Basie, Ellington, Ella Fitzgerald, Sarah Vaughan, George Shearing, Erroll Garner, etc. Downstairs from Storyville there was Mahogany Hall, which would bring in the major Dixieland players like Pee Wee Russell, Vic Dickenson, and Doc Cheatham. Those two clubs were in the Copley Square Hotel. Then there was a club called the Five O'Clock on Huntington Avenue. The Downbeat Club was on Boylston Street across from the Public Gardens. On the corner of Mass. Ave. and Columbus there was the Hi-Hat, which brought in names like Miles Davis and Charlie Parker. About a half block from the Hi-Hat on Mass. Ave. was the Savoy, which featured big names from the 1930s and 1940s. Wally's was there, but it was across the street from where it is now. There was a club called Eddie Levine's that was right next to where Wally's is now. Also, the 411 Club, which was on Columbus.

Except for the Hi-Hat and Storyville, all of them at times were hiring local musicians. As a musician, you could go from one club to the other. We had some wonderful experiences at the Jazz Workshop with musicians coming across the street from Storyville. Anytime there was a big band like Dizzy or Basie or Ellington, on our breaks we would go over and see them play. On their breaks they would come and dig us.[13]

It is known that Gryce played in many of these local clubs. With regard to the local/name musician situation, pianist Cecil Taylor commented that:

People like Gigi Gryce were not working in places that the big-name people from New York, like Bud and Stan Getz and Oscar Peterson, were working at, but these were the cats known to the local musicians.[14]

Gryce did get the opportunity to work with the name musicians from New York and played at the Hi-Hat with Thelonious Monk in 1949, during the period of inactivity when the pianist was not recording.[15] Monk was a hero to Gryce, as Emery Smith attests:

Yeah, he talked about Monk's writing and Monk's playing. In fact, when he talked about Monk, it was like he was on cloud nine. In fact, he used to stutter when he talked about Monk's music, trying to explain what Monk's music was like. We didn't know, like we were trying to find out what Monk's music was about anyway. He would kind of stammer because he was in awe of Thelonious. He loved his music. He said, "Now there's a guy who should do nothing but compose and if he wants to play, play." But he said, "But the system won't allow that." And at that time, Monk was—well, he didn't have a cabaret card. They took that cabaret card from him. (ES)

Saxophonist Sam Rivers recalled how Gryce was enthralled:

He sat in with Monk and he got the job. After he went to New York, he got the job with Monk right away and it was interesting, I mean, the way he talked about it. He said, "Monk is the first guy I've played with that anything I play is right." He said, "Whatever I play, I mean, Monk hits a chord and I'm—it sounds right." I never forgot when he said that. He said, "You've got to play with Monk, Sam." He said, "You can do anything with Monk and it comes out like it's right, you know. If you make a mistake, Monk is listening and he will make it sound right." That's what he said. Monk was one of his... One of the most amazing things about Monk, you know.: you could really almost play free with Monk and he would make it sound right. (SR)

Informal recordings from an all-star jam session at Christy's restaurant featuring Oscar Pettiford on cello, bassist Tommy Potter, trumpeter Howard McGhee, and vibraphonist Joe Roland, among others, reveal Gryce in a formative stage. The influence of Charlie Parker is obvious and Gryce's characteristic style which would be apparent only a few years later is not yet evident.

Certainly one of the most memorable experiences that Gryce had in Boston was spending time with Parker himself.

He was a frequent visitor to my place in Boston, where I was studying at the Boston Conservatory of Music. I knew him as a gentleman, a scholar, a person aware of everything around him. He was generous to an extreme. I wasn't eating too steady in those days, and whenever Charlie came around, I knew I could stoke up and be ahead a little. Not only me, but he would treat large parties of friends, paying checks up to a hundred dollars.[16]

Sam Rivers remembers these visits and indicates that many other jazz giants jammed in the basement of the house at 13 Rutland Square where he and his brother Martin, Jaki Byard, Gryce, the Perry brothers (drummer Bay, violinist/saxophonist Ray, and saxophonist Joe) and other musicians lived. It is interesting to note that many of the Boston musicians, because of their solid educational backgrounds, were not intimidated by their better-known New York counterparts:

Charlie Parker was a good friend of ours. He came over to our house when he was there in Boston and jammed with us all night long in the basement. Clark Terry came through there, Zoot Sims, all those people, Stan Getz. They would come down there. We would invite them down and they'd come down and jam. And the union too. The union was open for jam sessions, you know. We'd have jam sessions there. And then there was a club outside of town where we went out to jam sessions. Miles Davis, when he came there, he played in that club. It was pretty fairly close-knit. All the musicians in New York knew about the musicians in Boston and vice versa. I would say, more harmonically grounded. Boston musicians, I mean, had a better musical education than New York musicians. We sort of looked down on the musical knowledge of the New York musicians because they were all there before they were ready. We all knew that. They got the on-the-job training. We waited and got ourselves together first and then we went to New York. (SR)

I had a job every night, downtown at a place called Ort's Grill. He was one of the early rumrunners that went legal. So he had this place. He hired all the musicians. It was across the street from the RKO. They brought in bands like Duke Ellington, Count Basie, Stan Kenton, Woody Herman, bands like that came in and across the street was the restaurant where the musicians played, the local musicians played. They would come across from stage entrance where the club was, so they just came across the street from the stage entrance and the musicians were playing there, pretty much starting at noon... Twelve hours of music. Quincy Jones was in the band across the street. Charlie Mariano was hired from there by Stan Kenton. Jaki Byard was playing there... There were a lot of musicians who were hired, [leaders] came over and listened to musicians and [local musicians] got jobs with the band that was coming in, travelling bands like that. There was another place over there where we played, too, that Gigi and I played where Farrakhan was in the band. (SR)

Louis Farrakhan, a classically trained violinist, was Louis Walcott at the time and a student at Boston Latin School. This was years before he was recruited into the Nation of Islam (in 1955).

Sam Rivers was among the Boston musicians that Gryce respected most, according to Emery Smith.

He talked about Sam Rivers all the time. Yeah, and I didn't know who the hell Sam Rivers was until years later. He talked about this guy Sam Rivers and he talked about a guy that years later I played with, a trumpet player named Joe Gordon. Yeah, and they all went to the Boston Conservatory. They were all there. He talked about Sam Rivers who I didn't know and he was saying that Sam Rivers's family had a great history in classical music and that Sam was interested in opera and finally, years later, I met Sam Rivers and he was the director of the Harlem Opera Company I think... So that's who he talked about. (ES)

The leader of the Modern Jazz Quartet, John Lewis, was also one of the musicians that Gryce was following.

Well, John Lewis for one. He's a great piano player. And Jaki Byard. He's another pianist; comes from Boston. Yes, a lot of good people come from Boston.[17]

Boston players, including drummer Roy Haynes, put forth Gryce's name alongside Lewis's as a significant force in jazz.[18] Sam Rivers has also pointed out similarities between Gryce and Anthony Braxton, the Chicago-born avant-garde saxophonist and composer. Rivers felt these two great musicians shared a very serious and dedicated approach to music.

The two of them sort of remind me, real close character-wise, music-wise, the way they talk, the way they think about music. I mean, I'm comparing the two. Braxton and Gigi Gryce, they come to my mind together. I was on good terms with Gigi and I'm on good terms with Braxton and they always remind me of each other. (SR)

Pianist William Sebastian "Sabby" Lewis (1914–1994) led a band in Boston that was one of the finest in the area. It was a musical incubator for many fine players including Paul Gonsalves, Big Nick Nicholas, Ray Perry, Roy Haynes, and Jaki Byard. Drummer Alan Dawson was first with the band in 1950–51 and remembered: "Working for Sabby was really a big deal, so many people started their careers with him."[19] Establishing credentials by playing with Lewis would likely have helped Gryce in his future endeavors.

Gryce was writing constantly while in Boston. In addition to arranging for local bands like those of Lewis, and trumpeter Phil Edmonds, he also produced quintet scores for saxophonist Bunky Emerson. In 1959 Gryce would organize an all-star, rehearsal big band in New York performing a repertoire of arrangements written, for the most part, during his years at the Conservatory.

Sometimes economics forced the forward-thinking young musicians to take jobs playing less-than-modern music. One place for such employment was in the society band of bassist Tasker Crosson. Alan Dawson got his start in Crosson's band and Sam Rivers remembered that

We were kind of amused with Tasker Crosson, old-school, you know, being young kids and Tasker was old-school, so we played with him sometimes and always made fun, we kind of ridiculed him. He had society jobs so he paid good money. It was just something. We didn't consider it... We didn't take his music seriously, kind of. It was older style, swing, you know. We took it seriously, but we thought it was kind of dated—we knew it was dated—so we didn't want to bother ourselves. He played places like society jobs, banquets, where nobody knew us. You didn't mind doing it. That kind of thing. If somebody saw us we'd be kind of embarrassed to be in the band. Yeah, Gigi was there. We played in the band together. It was a big joke. It was stock arrangements, you know. (SR)

Gryce and Rivers were much more receptive to another local Boston big band, that of Jimmy Martin, about which Rivers said, "That was a great band. We were known as the Boston Be-boppers. The BBB." (SR) "Martin led another provocative outfit that rehearsed at the black union hall and featured Jaki Byard (playing trombone), trombonist Hampton Reese, Sam Rivers, trumpeters Lennie Johnson and Joe Gordon, and drummer Bill "Baggy" Grant."[20] Gryce had considerable contact with the musicians in this band, and said:

My greatest influence in jazz in Boston was the meeting with two of the greatest minds in music that I know. They are Jaki Byard, and an unknown, underrated genius by the name of Hampton Reese.[21]

According to Sam Rivers, it was Byard who really ran this band and wrote all the arrangements. Martin was more a Count Basie-type piano player who fronted the unit.

Another forward-looking ensemble that Rivers recalls was a sextet composed of players who most certainly would have been considered Boston all-stars of the period:

We had a group: myself, Gigi Gryce, Joe Gordon, Jaki Byard, and Alan Dawson on drums, and the bass player was... I'm not sure who the bass player was at that time. We were playing around Boston quite a bit. (SR)

An important breakthrough for Gryce occurred in Boston when his composing abilities were brought to the attention of tenor saxophonist Stan Getz. By this time Getz had achieved substantial acclaim and recognition through his landmark recordings with Woody Herman and his own quartet. Fortuitously for Gryce, the tenor sax giant had recently hired an all-Hartford rhythm section, as Clifford Gunn recalls:

On some occasions because he [Silver] and Joe Calloway, a bassist, and Walter Bolden, I got them on another engagement—Joe left here and went with Stan Getz. Stan Getz came to town and asked me for some musicians to go with him. And so I recommended these fellows, who were eager to go. That was, in fact—I guess it was Horace's first away-from-home gig. (CG)

Horace Silver describes first meeting Gryce in Boston after joining the Getz band:

Gigi had left Hartford long before I ever got there. I met Gigi through my two buddies in Hartford, Walter Bolden, the drummer, and Joe Calloway, the bass player. Stan Getz heard us in Hartford and liked us and hired us to go on the road and play with him, you know. So they knew Gigi very well, Walter Bolden, drummer and Joe Calloway, bass player, and so they introduced me to Gigi, but Gigi was not living in Hartford by the time I got to Hartford, was living in Hartford, playing in Hartford. He had long left Hartford. He was in Boston or something—going to some music school or something in Boston. I met him in Boston through Joe Calloway and Walter Bolden and, you know, I had heard about him before then because they used to always talk about Hartford or whatever…

So when we were having a rehearsal, Gigi asked, you know, "I wonder if Stan would be interested in any of my tunes?" I asked Stan and he said tell him to come by and I'll try a couple of them out. That's how that happened.

It just so happened that when I met him [Gigi] in Boston that week, I was playing with Stan Getz, me and Walter Bolden and Joe Calloway, we were playing with Stan Getz at the Hi-Hat Club in Boston. And Stan called a rehearsal one day, during the week, during the daytime he called a rehearsal and so I was telling Stan that I met this guy and he's a writer and he's got a lot of tunes and would it be all right for him to come in and bring in some of his tunes to the rehearsal, and we try some of them out to see how he liked them, and he said, "Yeah, tell him to come by." So, we brought Gigi by and Gigi brought several of his tunes. We tried them out and Stan liked them and wound up recording several of them. (HS)

A total of six of Gryce's compositions were recorded by Stan Getz at three sessions: August 15, 1951 for the Roost label

("Melody Express," "Yvette," "Wildwood"); October 28, 1951 for Roost ("Mosquito Knees," and a blues later titled "Eleanor" included in the performance of "Jumpin' with Symphony Sid"); December 29, 1952 for the Norgran label ("Hymn to the Orient"). With the exception of the blues, these tunes are all 32-bar structures taken at medium to fast tempi, which Getz's talented quintets handle admirably. "Mosquito Knees" and "Melody Express" owe a debt to "Honeysuckle Rose," but have altered bridge harmonies. "Wildwood" and "Yvette" express Gryce's lyrical tendencies and, in fact, the former composition would emerge later as "Music in the Air," with lyrics by Jon Hendricks. The most interesting and original of this group of early Gryce compositions is "Hymn to the Orient" (sometimes mistitled "Hymn of the Orient") with its challenging and unusual chord changes. This song would be revisited in 1953 by the young trumpet sensation Clifford Brown on his first recording as a leader, a session that rapidly became a classic.

The Getz recordings were critically acclaimed (receiving either four or five stars in *Down Beat*) although Gryce had perhaps a more difficult time getting recognition. Nat Hentoff, when reviewing the later Clef Records issue of "Hymn to the Orient" wondered, "By the way, why no composer credits?"[22] Problems with attributions continued with subsequent releases.

The label strangely gives Getz composer credit for "Mosquito Knees." I beg to differ. When Gigi Gryce was in England he emphatically stated this to be one of the themes he wrote for Stan.[23]

During the Roost recording of "Jumpin' with Symphony Sid," live at Boston's Storyville, the Getz quintet interpolates the entirety of a Gigi Gryce 12-bar blues line later titled "Eleanor" (for Gryce's wife). No mention of this contribution to the session was ever made. Stan Getz used the same blues as his theme song for decades, performing it all over the world, and eventually Gryce's blues was listed on records and in print as "Stan's Blues." These difficulties must have been frustrating because, according to Emery Smith, Gryce desired recognition as a composer:

That's what his main thing was. It wasn't even playing. He said even without playing, he wanted to be a composer. And I guess one of the things I think he had that we talked about was doing studio work. But see, there wasn't many black cats doing that kind of stuff before, not unless you was writing in the background for some rhythm-and-blues band or something like that for some record company. Because I think he did that also. He was like a ghostwriter there for several things. (ES)

Smith was impressed with Gryce's compositional talent and felt he could have succeeded at jazz or classical writing. "Well, I know he was capable of doing it. He had that kind of a mind. He had a great sense of music all over the world." (ES) But at that time, the focus was on jazz.

No, we were too busy being involved with what Diz and Bird and Monk and them cats were doing. That was so far removed from European classical music. The only thing that anybody who was like Gigi and Clyde, they would practice out of those books, you know, which was based on the European tradition. (ES)

When asked specifically about the relationship between classical and jazz music, Gryce himself said:

I don't feel that my knowledge of European writing techniques has influenced my jazz writing. I do feel that it has played an important part in helping me to analyze the chords, rhythms, etc., that I hear while studying a new piece of music, either classical or jazz. My academic background has also helped considerably in writing for a large orchestra, rhythmically and contrapuntally. From imaginative and creative aspects though, I find only the experiences in life and natural ability helpful. I strongly believe that jazz music can only be played best by jazz-conscious musicians, and classical music performed best by classically trained musicians. I don't feel that classical music can be made to sound like jazz, nor jazz music made to sound classic. I'm sure that many classical forms, instruments, rhythms and effects can be used effectively in jazz music, however, and vice versa, *but with discretion.* I admire the experimenting musician whether he succeeds or fails. The art itself benefits from these experiments.[24]

Even as a student, Gryce's reputation was such that he was sometimes approached to provide private instruction. One of the young, aspiring musicians Gryce taught in Boston was saxophonist Ken McIntyre (1931–2001), who later went on to work with such luminaries as Cecil Taylor, Eric Dolphy, and Charlie Haden. Like Gryce, he also became a public-school teacher in New York City. In 1967, McIntyre became a college professor and shortly before his death had retired from The New School University in New York City, while continuing to record and perform.

Gigi was influenced by Bird. And I was greatly influenced by Bird. Gigi was an excellent teacher. He had me doing things that were quite intricate. He was a great teacher, fantastic. I was probably a good student because I took the position that I didn't know anything. Anything that any of my teachers suggested that I do, I did. I never questioned it.[25]

He had me doing things that were fantastic, that in my own teaching, I've not asked people, students to do it. He wanted me to learn the instrument. He would have me play maybe a major scale up and then play a harmonic minor scale down and then maybe a natural minor scale up and a melodic minor scale down. It may not have anything to do directly with each...the original scale I played. So it was very demanding. It was a brainbuster! (MKM)

McIntyre found that Gryce presented a striking contrast to Charlie Parker in personality and demeanor:

He was very secretive. He was not a loquacious person. I can say this in comparing him to my mentor, and I daresay *his* mentor. Charlie

Parker was a very outgoing person, a very loquacious person. Having sat with my feet on the bandstand many times, having walked around behind him when he came to the club in Boston, and listened to him talk, I knew his personality. Gigi was the opposite. You would never know…you wouldn't know, you wouldn't have a clue in terms of what was going on with him. That was very real. He was very mysterious that way. [Laughs] I'm laughing because he used to keep his scores in the refrigerator. He didn't have that much food, so the food would be on one side and the music would be, the scores and stuff would be in another part of the refrigerator. (MKM)

According to Cecil Taylor, Gryce also instructed the alto saxophonist Charlie Mariano.[26]

Gryce's ubiquitous presence in Boston brought him into contact with vocalist Margie Anderson, with whom he developed a significant relationship:

I was singing at a little club called Eddie Levine's with Jimmy Woode… And I met Gigi across the street from Eddie Levine's. It was called the Chicken Shack. You could get just delicious chicken in a basket for a musician's price which was… I'm saying that we were all very poor. The money wasn't good at all that we were making, but that's where I met Gigi. And we had kind of like a young lover's little thing going where every evening after I'd finish, he'd be over there and we'd sit and talk and he was so poor—until I couldn't see this going anywhere. He was so poor that he would be there waiting for me with his… He always wore this great big black overcoat, winter overcoat. And I found out why, because he had an alarm clock in the coat. (MA)

Anderson remembered Gryce's single-mindedness about music and how it overcame the difficult economic circumstances in which he found himself at that time:

[His apartment was] very sparse, very clean but just a chair, a table, a bed, I think a kitchenette. Nothing really. You could tell that this young man was struggling. He had nothing but I don't think it mattered to him. That wasn't important. Music was important. He was just into music. He would sit there and he's writing. The only thing we had in common was music, the love of music, and he more so than I. (MA)

When Anderson encountered Gryce three years later, after he had become established in New York, his fortunes had clearly improved:

I got booked into the Apollo again with Lucky Millinder. And I sang with Lucky and there was a hotel, the Alvin Hotel where we would stay, the musicians, especially the ones from Boston. If we didn't stay at the Theresa, we'd stay at the Alvin downtown And I'm getting out of cab, and I'm bending over picking up my luggage and it always knocked me out that he knew me from the back. He recognized me. And before I could turn around he said, "Porter, lady?" Which I thought was very cute. Anyway, I saw Gigi then.

But he did look good. He was all in brown. I'd never seen him look that good the whole time I knew him... Yeah, this was a completely different Gigi from Boston. He looked happy. The smile was so bright. He seemed like a very contented... He was at peace with himself. (MA)

An appearance by Anderson at the Apollo Theatre in New York with Sabby Lewis's band resulted in good reviews in *Variety* and ultimately, a recording contract with Columbia Records. In need of original material for the recording session, she enlisted Gryce, whose first experience in a recording studio was not an auspicious one:

So I went and told Gigi, I said, "Look, I've got a chance to record for Columbia but they want me to do something original." So he started writing... And when we went to New York to do the recording, we got there first. Well, first... I went a week ahead of time and Mary Lou Williams coached me on the tunes, the keys and the whole thing.

He [Gigi] didn't come with me. I don't know how he got there. I went by bus and all of a sudden, he tracked us down. I gave him no information at all. All he knew was that I was going to do his numbers. And he was not invited. In fact, they didn't know who he was and they didn't care.

Gigi kept getting put out of the recording session. He came in and I guess he was standing too close to the piano player and the musicians, making sure his music was done the way he wanted it to be. So they kept putting him out but he kept coming back. (MA)

This recording session took place around May of 1950 and produced two 78s. Only one of Gryce's compositions was recorded, the ballad "You'll Always Be the One I Love," which would be revisited five years later as part of his landmark sessions for the Signal label. But this early and now obscure Columbia issue represents the very first recorded example of a Gryce song.

In 1951, Gryce took two semesters off from school and tested the waters in New York and Europe before completing his undergraduate studies. It was probably during this time that he studied in Paris. "My wife and I took him down there and put him on the boat in New York," said Clifford Gunn (CG). While it is often written[27] that this was funded by a Fulbright scholarship, the U.S. State Department and other sources have no record of such an award.[28] Fulbright awards were not available to undergraduates and there is no record of Gryce's academic transcripts ever being sent for such a purpose. Sam Rivers says that Gryce was awarded a scholarship, but not a Fulbright. Ira Gitler wrote: "Through a competition held at the conservatory, Gigi was awarded a Fulbright scholarship to study in Paris. This he did in 1952, studying composition with Nadia Boulanger and orchestration with Arthur Honegger."[29] (Because records show that Gryce was a full-time student at Boston Conservatory during the first half of 1952, it seems likely that the correct year of foreign study, however funded, was 1951.)

Nadia Boulanger (1887–1979) was a renowned teacher of composition. She won the Prix de Rome in 1908. Over her long career she taught hundreds of students, among them jazz musicians Quincy Jones, Donald Byrd, and Egberto Gismonti. While better known as a pedagogue than a performer, Boulanger was also influential in reviving interest in the music of Claudio Monteverdi.

Perhaps unfairly remembered by many only for his work *Pacific 231* that was inspired by a steam engine, the Swiss composer Arthur Honegger (1892–1955) also composed large-scale pieces such as *Le Roi David* and several oratorios that combined Baroque elements with the influence of later composers such as Wagner. He was also affected by jazz music, as evidenced by his 1925 Piano Concertino. He lived in France for much of his life although he did visit America in the summer of 1947, just as Gryce was about to enter Boston Conservatory.

Gryce's professor at Boston Conservatory, Daniel Pinkham, wrote: "I had never heard of his working with Boulanger and Honegger (although *I* did). I recall no plans for European study, but that does not say this did not happen."[30] The lack of any recommendation by Pinkham diminishes the likelihood that this was a Fulbright award, which requires extensive paperwork and references.

During this period in France, it seems that Gryce was focused on his classical efforts and did not interact with the Parisian jazz community. The pianist Henri Renaud did not meet him at that time and record producer/publisher Louis-Victor Mialy said:

But, the thing is that nobody heard about him at that time. No jazz publication talked about it. No clubs remember him playing and he would have played before he left. He would have been invited to play. It's not impossible that he studied and with a humble type of attitude, you know, not showing up because he had no money, was very poor. It's possible but I can't remember that. He never mentioned that. No, I never heard about this guy. I was also going to clubs. I was reading jazz publications. I never—the first time I heard about Gigi was when he came to Algiers in 1953. But, like I said, it's not impossible that for a short time, for a short period of time, with a very humble attitude, and only coming to Paris to concentrate with his study with Nadia Boulanger, it's not impossible that he did that. But it would be very strange that nobody heard about that. (LM)

There is no question that study in Paris would have presented some formidable obstacles for Gryce. From all accounts, he was not fluent in French, a factor that would have severely hindered his ability to understand and benefit from Boulanger's classes. Furthermore, study with her was costly. Finally, without any apparent contacts and support system, he would have been extremely isolated and lonely. These factors alone could have placed him under severe stress. Perhaps it is not surprising then that Gryce returned prematurely, due to a nervous breakdown.[31]

Yeah, he told me that he did. He said he had been over there [Europe] before and that he came back to the States on a tramp steamer. He had a nervous breakdown. But he didn't really talk about that too much. (CS)

What is curious is how the stories of Gryce's time in Europe grew. A Fulbright scholarship, Nadia Boulanger, Arthur Honneger— by 1955 these were accepted facts and appeared in print. Neither Boulanger nor the Fulbright (nor, in fact, any earlier trip to Europe) is mentioned in an article from the French magazine *Jazz Hot* (November 1953, p. 17). This article does mention a nervous breakdown (*depression nerveuse*) that Gryce suffered in 1952 and says that, thanks to a grant, Gryce *intends* to study in Paris the *following* year; this raises the possibility that the trip *never* happened. (He was married within weeks of returning to America and his wife denies that any foreign travel occurred over the next decade.) Many of Gryce's associates do not recall mention of a Fulbright at all—although some do. It was apparently not a subject that was much discussed.

He never talked about it. He mentioned it in passing. I think he said, "Yeah, I studied in Paris a while. I think I'm gonna go back over there," or something like that. But it wasn't a lengthy discussion. Yeah, he was over there. But I don't know how long he stayed. I think at that particular point, it might have been a financial type of thing. And then I don't think he had studied French, the language. He mentioned something about the language. He never said anything to me about a scholarship. (JC)

When asked if Gryce ever mentioned a Fulbright scholarship, tenor saxophonist Clifford Solomon, a colleague in the 1953 Lionel Hampton band replied, "No, he never did. Gigi wasn't one to brag on his merits, you know." (CS)

Much confusion surrounds this period of Gryce's history, but the evidence available seems to best support the following scenario: He traveled by ship to Europe in 1951, the year he took off from Boston Conservatory. The trip was funded either through a scholarship he received from a competition held at the Conservatory (but most probably *not* a Fulbright), his own savings, financial support from his family, or a combination of all of these sources. He may have studied with Boulanger and Honegger in Paris formally or informally for an indefinite period of time, but these studies were terminated when he became ill with what he himself described to writer Raymond Horricks as a nervous breakdown.[32] It seems that during this excursion he was not involved in the Paris jazz scene. "No, in fact I played very little because my studies kept me more than busy—maybe an occasional jam session in Pigalle."[33]

The fact that Gryce had little to relate about the specifics of this European adventure to even his closest relatives and colleagues suggests that the memory was neither a source of pride nor pleasure for him. On the other hand, he was quite willing to accept and even exploit the prestige associated with an educational experience of the highest level. In years to come, nearly every set of album liner notes, every article, and ultimately, every obituary written about him would refer to this trip and the Fulbright scholarship with which it was supposedly funded. It became as much a part of his reputation and identity as the wonderful music he would create.

According to Tommy Gryce, two related events affecting his brother took place in Europe. The older sibling encountered a religious figure who influenced him to convert to the Muslim faith, taking the name Basheer Qusim (which he would later adopt completely), and, perhaps in conjunction with this, Gigi began to spell his surname with a 'y' instead of an 'i'. Reportedly, this was to separate the public performer from the private individual.

Apparently after returning from Europe, Gryce lived for a time in New York. He then returned to Boston and encouraged Sam Rivers to join him.

That's when he came back and he begged me to go to New York. He said, "I've got it set up now, Sam. You should come on and go with me." He begged me. We were sitting in the restaurant having lunch and he really, really begged. I'll never forget it, he begged me. He said, you know, "Come on, Sam. New York is ready for us. We can do it now." I said, "No…" My family was right there, I was pretty set in Boston. I said, "No, I'm going to wait." I was always planning to go to New York, but I didn't want to go that quick, you know. (SR)

Gryce returned to Boston Conservatory for two final semesters and on June 6, 1952, he was graduated, receiving a Bachelor of Music degree with a major in composition.[34] He remained in Boston for a few months after graduation before moving permanently to New York, where his career would soon blossom.

Notes

1. Rosenthal, David, *Hard Bop*, New York, Oxford University Press, 1992, p. 89, to name one. It also appeared in an October 19, 1955 *Down Beat* article by Nat Hentoff. This article may have supplied much of the information for the Leonard Feather *Encyclopedia of Jazz* entry.

2. Phone call to Registrar's office, University of Hartford, June 3, 1997; turned up no records under Gryce or Grice.

3. Demsey, David, "Chromatic Third Relations in the Music of John Coltrane," *Annual Review of Jazz Studies* 5, 1991.

4. This first appeared in the *Encyclopedia of Jazz* by Leonard Feather and was subsequently repeated by Ron Wynn in the 1994 edition of *The All Music Guide to Jazz*, which states (p. 299): "He presented a concert in Hartford with a 23-piece band that included Horace Silver."

5. Hovhaness, Alan, quoted by Allan Kozinn in *New York Times* obituary, June 23, 2000, p. A21.

6. Gryce, Gigi, quoted by *Melody Maker*, November 28, 1953, p. 7 (Mike Nevard).

7. Macero, Teo, "Modern Jazz at Cooper Union," *Metronome*, June, 1956, p. 21.

8. Hentoff, Nat, "A New Jazz Corporation—Gryce, Farmer," *Down Beat*, October 19, 1955, p. 11.

9. "Hovhaness, Alan," *The New Oxford Companion to Music*, Denis Arnold (ed.), New York, Oxford University Press, 1984, p. 431.

10. Parker, Charlie, quoted by James Patrick in the notes to *The Complete Charlie Parker Savoy Studio Sessions*, Savoy ZDS 5500, 1988.

11. Gryce, Gigi, quoted by Raymond Horricks in *These Jazzmen of Our Time*, Victor Gollancz, 1960, p. 188.

12. Hentoff, op. cit., p. 10.

13. Interview of Herb Pomeroy by Walter Gross, *Interlude*, Summer 1998, p. 8.

14. Taylor, Cecil, quoted by A. B. Spellman in *Four Lives in the Bebop Business*, Pantheon Books, 1966.

15. Gitler, Ira, liner notes to Gigi Gryce: *Orchestra/Quartet*, Signal 1201 and *Nica's Tempo*, Savoy MG12137.

16. Gryce, Gigi, quoted by Robert Reisner in *Bird: The Legend of Charlie Parker*, New York, Da Capo Press, 1979, p. 99.

17. Gryce, Gigi, quoted by Mike Nevard in *Melody Maker*, November 28, 1953, p. 7.

18. Haynes, Roy, quoted by Raymond Horricks in "Jazz on Parade," *Jazz Journal*, December 1954, p. 2. "John has the gifts of a composer. Gigi Gryce has too but John is the most serious."

19. Morgenstern, Dan, "The Poll Winner as Teacher," *Down Beat*, September 22, 1966, pp. 28–29.

20. Blumenthal, Bob, "Boston Blow Up: A Scene Expands," *Village Voice*, August 25, 1987, pp. 13–14.

21. Gryce, Gigi, quoted by Raymond Horricks in *These Jazzmen of Our Time*, pp. 189–90.

22. Hentoff, Nat, "Jazz Reviews," *Down Beat*, March 24, 1954, p. 15.

23. Horricks, Raymond, "The Month's Records," *Jazz Journal*, October 1954, p. 22.

24. Gryce, Gigi, quoted by Raymond Horricks in *These Jazzmen of Our Time*, p. 189.

25. Interview of Ken McIntyre by Bob Rusch, *Cadence*, November 1988, p. 6.

26. Spellman, A. B., *Four Lives in the Bebop Business*, Pantheon Books, 1966, p. 61.

27. Hentoff, Nat, "A New Jazz Corporation—Gryce, Farmer," *Down Beat*, October 19, 1955, p. 11: "He wanted to learn how to express

his ideas better so he applied for and won a Fulbright scholarship to study in Paris. For nearly a year he worked with Nadia Boulanger, who has taught many ranking American composers. Gigi also studied with composer Arthur Honegger. Illness cut short Gigi's stay in France, and he returned to Hartford."

28. Phone calls from N. Cohen to Effie Wingate, Programs Office, United States Information Agency, Washington, DC, January 9, 14, 1998: no record of Gigi Gryce (George General Grice, etc.) ever having been a Fulbright Scholar could be found in U.S.I.A. offices in Washington, Paris, or Fulbright Archive in Arkansas; cannot confirm but also, cannot completely deny that he was a Fulbright Scholar because "record keeping at that time was not so good." Phone call from N. Cohen to Walter Jackson, Institute of International Education, New York, NY, September 30, 1998: no records found under Grice, Gryce, or Qusim. Phone call from N. Cohen to the Fulbright Alumni Association, Washington, D.C.: no records found under Grice, Gryce, or Qusim. Letters from Alexandra Laederich, Fondation Internationale Nadia et Lily Boulanger, Paris, France, to Noal Cohen, February 24, 2000, April 4, 2000: no records found under Grice, Gryce, or Qusim.

29. Gitler, Ira, liner notes to Gigi Gryce: *Orchestra/Quartet*, Signal 1201.

30. Pinkham, Daniel, in fax letter to Noal Cohen, February 5, 1998.

31. None of the subjects interviewed on this topic were able to provide details concerning either the specific causes or effects of this crisis, although it appears to have been something known in general terms to many of Gryce's associates and family members. His activities do not seem to have been curtailed to any significant degree.

32. This scenario is bolstered by Benny Golson's recollection of first having met Gryce in 1951 and that Gryce "had experienced a nervous breakdown a few months prior to our meeting." See the Foreword to this book.

33. Horricks, Raymond, *These Jazzmen of Our Time*, p. 190.

34. Phone call to Kathy DeColla, Registrar's office, Boston Conservatory, April 15, 1997. Listed under Basheer Qusim with a "reference" to George Gryce.

manhattan blues

*B*OTH THE CONTACTS WITH VISITING JAZZMEN that Gryce encountered in Boston and his own occasional excursions to New York made for an easy transition when he moved to Manhattan during the latter part of 1952. Pianist Edwin Swanston remembers Gryce sitting in with tenor saxophonist Lucky Thompson's nine-piece band at the Savoy Ballroom around this time and flawlessly sight-reading the alto saxophone book. (ESw) By the spring of 1953, Gryce was recording with drummer Max Roach for the Debut label as part of a septet that also included trumpeter Idrees Sulieman and tenor saxophonist Hank Mobley. It was the commercial recording debut of Gryce.

Less than two years older than Gryce, Roach (1924–) had already been a part of the New York scene for over a decade, making important contributions to the development of bebop and participating in seminal recordings by Charlie Parker and Miles Davis. Along with a few other forward-looking percussionists including Kenny Clarke and Stan Levey, he was responsible for liberating the drum set from the limitations of the swing era and adapting it to the new music. It was indeed a tribute to Gryce's reputation, especially at this early stage in his career, that a figure as prestigious as the master drummer would invite him to a recording session.

Mobley did most of the writing for the date, but Gryce contributed a chart on the pop tune "Glow Worm." This arrangement begins with a pure bebop introduction (*à la* Dizzy Gillespie) and the simple counterlines behind Mobley's statement of the melody lead into a deceptive final chord that is reprised in a seven-bar coda making use of held tones over shifting harmonies.

On "Mobleyzation," Gryce solos uneasily, beginning with a quote of "Frankie and Johnny," one of his favorite melodies (he would record the tune in 1960). Although only a standard blues, the tempo (about 270 beats per minute) seems to be just ahead of his comfort zone at this point and he struggles to keep up during his two twelve-bar choruses.

While it must certainly have been an honor and privilege to make this first record with Roach, only four tracks were undertaken, and the opportunities to feature Gryce were not plentiful. A session with the legendary bebop trumpeter Howard McGhee (1918–1987) in the following month, however, provided ample room for showcasing Gryce, both as a soloist (on flute as well as alto) and as a composer in a fascinating sextet setting that also included pianist Horace Silver, guitarist Tal Farlow, bassist Percy Heath, and drummer Walter Bolden. Gryce knew McGhee, Silver, and Bolden from his time in Boston and Hartford but there appear to be no links either before or after this session with the talented Farlow. It was therefore fortuitous and historically significant that the guitarist was utilized on this date—presumably because of his presence in the Blue Note stable at the time.

Howard McGhee Volume Two, the Blue Note 10-inch album that was issued from this session, includes two of Gryce's tunes: "Futurity" and "Shabozz." The first is a "contrafact," or melody line based on existing chord changes, in this case those of "There Will Never Be Another You," and features two choruses by the alto saxophonist, culminating in a clever quotation of "Lazy Bones" in the last four bars of the second chorus. In line with the practice of many modern jazz soloists, Gryce would often interpolate quotations in his solos.

"Shabozz" is one of Gryce's most captivating and difficult compositions. While conventional in its 32-bar AABA form, the chord progression of this piece is labyrinthine and poses a substantial challenge for the soloist. Centered initially in E-flat minor, the A section involves a series of ii–V progressions ending a minor third away in F-sharp minor and necessitating an abrupt turnaround to the original key center. At the end of the second A section, a ii–V transition appears to be leading to G major but is, in fact, a tritone substitution, and the bridge actually begins with a D-flat major chord. From there, the structure journeys up a minor third to E major and another minor third to G major before another series of ii–Vs conclude the B section, again with a turnaround to E-flat minor. Despite the harmonic complexity with which Gryce endowed the piece, it does not sound contrived or pretentious. "Shabozz" is a unique and haunting theme and an overlooked gem in the hard bop repertoire.

The arrangement begins with an eight-bar introduction over a Latin rhythm. The theme is stated by Farlow's guitar with the horns playing a counterline. After an eight-bar interlude, Gryce enters on flute, changing key to B minor during a two-bar break before soloing rather weakly on that instrument for half a chorus. Farlow enters at the bridge (B section) and completes the chorus. McGhee then follows with a full chorus of his own before Gryce plays another on alto saxophone. This latter effort is clearly superior to his very uneven and tentative flute work in which he seems over-matched by his own chord changes. Following four measures of drums, the ensemble then plays a variation of the A section (shout chorus) back in the original key and Silver solos briefly on the bridge before the original theme and introduction as a coda complete the arrangement. The use of shout choruses to add variety would be a hallmark of Gryce's writing.

McGhee contributed two original works to this recording session. "Jarm" is a minor-keyed, 32-bar theme with an initial strain strongly reminiscent of "Dear Old Stockholm." Two takes of this tune were recorded, the alternative take being somewhat faster than the originally issued version. Gryce's alto solos on the two takes are remarkably similar, both kicking off with the same uncharacteristic double-time break, which clearly sounds practiced before-hand. The flute is also heard in the introduction and coda of this piece. Gryce does not solo on McGhee's exquisite and Monk-like ballad, "Tranquility," but his eloquent alto presence, especially in the introduction and coda, is very much in evidence and contributes greatly to the success of this moving performance.

Walter Bolden's "Ittapnna" (Patti Ann spelled backwards) is a fast 32-bar composition which harmonically seems to combine the standards "Fine and Dandy" and "Pennies from Heaven." Gryce's one-chorus solo is his most relaxed of the session despite the rapid tempo.

This early hard bop recording stands out because of the creative writing that went into it and the unusual combination of talented artists, both established and newly discovered, who comprised the sextet. It received a four-star review in *Down Beat* magazine and arguably represents one of McGhee's finest recorded efforts. It is regrettable that this ensemble left a legacy of only one 10-inch LP and never performed as a working band.

Remembered more for his composing and arranging than for his limited skills as a pianist, Tadd Dameron (1917–1965) was clearly one of Gigi Gryce's main influences. Dameron was an important contributor to the development of bebop, and in the 1940s had written for Billy Eckstine, Dizzy Gillespie, and Sarah Vaughan among many others. His compositions became some of the most enduring of the era and include "Our Delight," "Hot House," "If You Could See Me Now," "Lady Bird," "Good Bait," and "On a Misty Night." The groups he led were incubators for many highly regarded bebop musicians such as trumpeter Fats Navarro, tenor saxophonists Wardell Gray and Allen Eager, and drummer Kenny Clarke. Dameron's music was melodic, impressionistic, and lyrical—characteristics which would also apply to the work of Gryce and other composers of the hard bop genre including Benny Golson and Jimmy Heath. It is worth mentioning that, like Gryce, Dameron had studied the Schillinger System of composition.

When Dameron assembled a new band in the summer of 1953, it was indeed significant that Gryce and Golson were included in the nine-piece unit. This provided a unique opportunity for these up-and-coming artists to enjoy a close, working relationship with one of their acknowledged influences. Golson, who previously worked with the pianist in the Bull Moose Jackson band, has indicated that Dameron allowed him to copy scores as a means of studying arranging, and Gryce called Dameron "one of the greatest, most creative and exploring arrangers of our time."[1] This ensemble is most remembered, however, for the exposure it provided Clifford Brown, whose talent would soon lead him to become a legend among trumpet players.

Born in Wilmington, Delaware in 1930, Brown had attracted considerable attention around the Philadelphia area before joining Dameron. He would be the first in an impressive line of trumpet players to record with Gryce. With him he shared a passionate dedication to music along with an aversion to vices such as drugs and alcohol. Gifted with incredible technique honed by hours of practice, Brown, in his all-too-brief career, extended the legacy of the early bebop trumpeters, especially that of Fats Navarro, and rapidly became an enduring and influential voice on his instrument. In 1954 he and drummer Max Roach joined forces to form a quintet that would help define the hard bop ensemble approach. Brown's life was cut short in an automobile accident in 1956, extinguishing one of the brightest flames of the era.

On June 11, the Dameron band recorded in New York for Prestige Records. Trumpeter Idrees Sulieman who participated in this session recalled his first encounters with Brown:

We were there for about a week at a club in Philly and then the first night everyone said, "There's the little trumpet player that everyone is taking about." So I asked him, I said, "Hey, Clifford, you want to come up and play some?" and he said, "No, I want to listen to you." So I said, "OK." He didn't play that first night and that surprised me because I was sure that he was going to come and play and the second night he came in, he still said he wanted to listen. So I had the feeling that he was a little, you know, didn't want to play. Because see most of the time, guys just take their horn and come right up on the stand. So the third night he came and he said, "I got my horn tonight." So I said, "Well, come up and play." So he came and he played so fantastic that when I got back to New York, I called Tadd up and I said, "Hey Tadd, you got to hear this little trumpet player named Clifford Brown." So Tadd said, "Yeah, but I want to do you."

I said, "No, because you got to hear him first." So anyway, Tadd finally heard him and called me up, he said, "Good," he said, "I'm going to use both of you on the date."

So anyway, when the date came up, Tadd said Clifford would play all the solos and I'd play the lead trumpet which I was really kind of disgusted about that, you know. But I was happy because he was very nervous on the recording, which you cannot hear. Yeah, I had to keep saying to him—he kept saying to me, "I'm failing." And I said, "No, man, you're not failing. You're just playing so much, you can't understand it." [Laughs] So after about a week or two, he called me back and said, "I listened to them and I like it." So I felt much better then. And then, the fact that he died so quick, I'm glad I didn't [play the solos], you know—I would have had a bad feeling about that. (IS)

Any apprehension on the part of Brown is certainly not apparent. On only his second jazz recording (he had recorded for the Blue Note label two days earlier under alto saxophonist Lou Donaldson's leadership), he marches through this session with a confidence and assuredness that is truly astounding. His ideas flow with seemingly endless creativity, generating solos so beautifully structured that each could be considered a complete composition.

Four pieces were recorded, all written and arranged by Dameron. Gryce does not solo but his strong lead alto saxophone is very much in evidence. "Philly J.J." is a feature for drummer Philly Joe Jones and based on the same chord structure as Dizzy Gillespie's "Woody'n You." Brown takes two choruses followed by Golson for another two before Jones takes over. Although overshadowed by the spectacular Brown, Golson's style is worthy of comment. At this point, his first jazz exposure, his playing was anomalous in its close relationship to that of earlier-style saxophonists such as Coleman Hawkins, Ben Webster, and Don Byas, especially in sound and vibrato. But at the same time, his harmonic approach and conception were unquestionably modern. In the context of the early 1950s, he was an original and refreshing voice overlooked in the excitement over Brown. Golson's style has evolved greatly over the nearly fifty years since this recording was made and, still active, he remains a unique and creative force on the jazz scene.

The repertoire for this date shows an exceptional consideration for varying the available moods and colors. "Dial B for Beauty" is a romantic suite that interweaves Dameron's mostly rubato piano with the ensemble, exchanging lovely themes. Sulieman's lead trumpet is impressive here. "Theme of No Repeat" uses one harmonic structure for the theme and another ("I Got Rhythm") for the solos including a muted chorus by Brown and two by Dameron. Gryce would later employ this tactic in his own writing. Two takes of "Choose Now" have been issued. Harmonically, this tune is "I Got Rhythm" in the key of E-flat with a "Honeysuckle Rose" bridge. A highlight of the originally issued take is a nearly seven-bar stream of continuous sixteenth notes by Brown at the end of the bridge of his second chorus. After a chorus by Dameron, Golson plays one and a half, building the intensity until the ensemble returns at the bridge. A few reed squeaks that can be heard from Gryce on the first take are not present in this clearly superior retake, which is nearly a minute and a half longer due to the insertion of the piano solo. The 10-inch LP *A Study in Dameronia* did not receive glowing reviews at the time of its issue, with most of the critics' praise being reserved for the solo contributions of Clifford Brown.

After the record session, Dameron's band worked the summer at the Paradise Club in Atlantic City, New Jersey. Brown, Gryce, Golson, and Jones were present for most of the engagement while other band members came and went. Personnel was drawn in part from the Philadelphia area (Golson was from there and Brown from nearby Wilmington, Delaware) and sometimes included

Johnny Coles on trumpet, Herb Mullins, Don Cole, and Steve
Pulliam on trombone, Percy Heath and Jymie Merritt on bass,
and Oscar Estelle, Cecil Payne, and Kellice Swaggerty on baritone
saxophone. In view of this wealth of talent, it was unfortunate
that the role of the band was to back performers in a variety show
rather than play their own material.

Benny Golson and Kellice Swaggerty recalled the experience:

Tadd wanted to come back to New York. He got a thing in Atlantic
City and we took that whole little group with us...Tadd, Philly Joe,
and as a trumpet player we took Johnny Coles who had also been
with Bull Moose [Jackson]. We added a second trumpet player. That
was Clifford Brown. We added a trombone and a baritone, and Gigi
Gryce played alto. It was basically a show band. After the show, we
would play dance music. No jazz... That was a hard job for $100 a
week. We had to play a breakfast show. We went to work at 9:00 on
Saturday night and didn't get out until something like 5:00 the next
morning. We had to play a breakfast show sometime well after
midnight.[2]

I think I remember we did two [shows] a night. The weekends were
something else. The weekend was like swinging, everybody get high,
feel good with the weekend off from work. Big crowd, but then there
would be like breakfast shows. Sammy Davis was in town, Dino,
Frank. They were over to the Jockey Club. Sammy and the trio, they
were at Skinny's 500 Club. So one breakfast show, Sammy came
over—well, breakfast show, you know, different artists come by.
Yeah, early Sunday morning. Sammy played the drums about a half-
hour. Played everything! (KS)

A primitive recording that Kellice Swaggerty made on his Pentron
tape machine shows that much of what the band was playing was
not adventurous jazz, but background music for the various acts,
in spite of the presence of the brilliant jazz soloists.

He [Clifford Brown] did exactly what we did. Played the show, played the dance music and almost no solos. We all did that! I mean, what a waste!

There was a young singer there who was just getting started when we were there in 1953. Her name then was Betty "Bebop" Carter. That's where I met Betty Carter.[3]

Swaggerty also remembered the routine:

[Paradise Club] had a pretty low ceiling. I remember that. It was considered one of the larger clubs, that and the Plantation, and the Club Harlem. Bob Bailey was the MC. He definitely was the MC. And I think they started off with Bobby Ephram for the taps and Anita Echols was like a comedienne. Now, I think Bobby Ephram opened. See, before they actually ran down the whole show, he gave a brief synopsis of where we're going, to be like a cruise. Then as he brings on all the acts, the acts begun to do their thing. So I think Bobby Ephram opened, then Anita. Janet Sayres… She was not exactly a chanteuse but she was a good-looking chick and she danced, sort of like interpretive dancing. All right, [Princess DePaure] was in one of the Caribbean scenes along with Joel Noble. She was just one of the featured actresses in this Caribbean scene. DePaure, Joel Noble—I knew him from high school. Gloria [Howard], she danced. She was pretty and she was built like a brick shithouse. She didn't have to do too much. There was another chick, I can't think of that girl's name. She was like the other sexual attraction. Stump and Stumpy, they were the headliners. They were like Abbott and Costello—yeah, Stump and Stumpy. And then, of course, Stump and Stumpy closed it. And at the closing, some nights they'd have different acts that would come out front to close with them. Other nights it'd just be the two of them and very few people in the joint and everybody was glad to go home. (KS)

Despite the frustrating limitations this gig imposed on the band members, their spirits and aspirations were not dampened, as Swaggerty recalled:

I thought all of them—they understood. They had the élan, the fervor going in their direction as far as approaching things from a different perspective. I remember Clifford telling us about how he saw he could play different things and he would just play wonderful. They all did. (KS)

Gryce and Golson provided assistance to Swaggerty but also had some fun at his expense:

He [Gigi] was very quiet. I think Gigi sat on the far end. I sat next to Benny. I suppose I was striving to play the way that they interpreted. You know I was like a misfit to their way of thinking. And it didn't take long... They had a certain way of phrasing, accents that were more identifiable, strictly with him [Tadd]. But Gigi and Benny both had an understanding of accenting, and how and where and it took me a while to understand. They would offer help.

After we'd get into the show, Tadd would come out front some time and he used to whisper under his breath: "Motherfucker, you're blowing too loud, you're blowing too loud!" But his back would be to the audience. So Tadd would turn and walk away or whatever. Gigi and Benny sat to my left and they said: "We can't hear you." [Laughs] (KS)

The opportunities to play jazz were very limited but were there. Gryce can be heard soloing briefly on the surviving recording.

We played stuff other than the show itself. In between the shows... The show charts as well as reading his charts in your book. This is what you're playing tonight in the show and this is what—you know, we're going to play such and such. Only as far as the shows were concerned. The band played the music. But then when the show was over, that's when we played "Our Delight," "Tadd's Delight"... I can still remember parts of "Tadd's Delight." (KS)

The Paradise Club engagement was not the only activity in which Gryce participated around this time. A special first meeting took place as the summer started. Trumpeter Art Farmer had been playing with Lionel Hampton since the fall of 1952 and was a regular recording artist for the Prestige label. On July 2, Farmer was scheduled to record as the leader of a septet made up of some of his colleagues from the Hampton orchestra. Gryce was invited to contribute a chart, perhaps on the recommendation of his Boston friend Quincy Jones. It was at this session that Farmer met Gryce. The two would continue their very fruitful musical partnership in various groups until late 1958.

It was myself, Gigi, James Cleveland, and our tenor player named Clifford Solomon and I think it was a baritone player named Oscar Estelle. I don't remember for sure. But I know that Gigi wrote some things for us because, let's see…we had one tune called "Up in Quincy's Place [Room]," yeah, that was Gigi's tune.[4]

Quincy Jones wrote three of the four pieces for the date and Clifford Solomon recalled some of that day's activities.

All guys from the Hampton band. One number on there called "Mau Mau" because they had the Mau Mau thing in Kenya at the time and so it was one of those get in the studio and mess around with some Afro-Cuban type stuff and then they decided to call it "Mau Mau." It was just messing around with different rhythms, polyrhythms and then the melody was a Quincy thing. He had everybody playing in a different key but it was all relative. It was weird [sings]. But everybody was playing in a different relative key. It sounded weird. (CS)

According to Prestige's Ira Gitler, Gryce was working late on the arrangement and hand-delivered it at the studio. Trombonist Jimmy Cleveland specifically remembered Gryce's presence there to clarify the charts for the musicians.

Yes, he was there. He just kind of conducted it and stuff, you know. He was like telling us what to play… Even though he might not have written but a page or something, an opening, he would be so involved that he would have had to—because there was always discussion about: "That chord, that note there, what chord is that?" And he'd have to explain why that note was there and what part it was playing in that particular chord relating to the arrangement. (JC)

"Up in Quincy's Room" is a striking tune that presages later developments in jazz composition. Its static harmony in two-bar segments has connections to the works of Herbie Hancock and Kenny Barron, and the introductory vamp features the horns voiced in fourths, again well before such techniques became commonplace in 1960s jazz.

One of the most curious of all recordings in Gigi Gryce's discography involved several members of the Lionel Hampton band recording under the name of the tenor saxophonist Clifford Solomon. The date was for the OKeh label, and for all intents and purposes appears to have been a rhythm-and-blues session. Four tracks were recorded on August 2.

This was just at the time when Gryce was joining Lionel Hampton and it seems that Quincy Jones and Gryce were in the process of reviving the association they had established in Boston.

Gigi and Quincy were friends and Quincy produced it and they did it together—I don't really know. Like I said before, I wasn't privy to all the back room—all I knew was that the date was done and I was on it. They did some other stuff so they put this one in my name. Quincy did that. (CS)

Gryce can be heard vocalizing on two of the four items from this session. The tunes have a somewhat comic slant, especially "But Officer," in which Gryce plays the role of a drunk protesting arrest—particularly ironic considering that Gryce himself did not drink. On this track, Gryce does not even play an instrument and can hardly be described as a "vocalist" in the usual sense, as Clifford Solomon remembered: "No, he *talked* it. 'But officer, that *is* my real name!'" (CS) Jimmy Cleveland was also surprised by the Gryce performance:

He was just the vocalist. Well, that's what floored me on the date. I never knew he was gonna sing until we got there. And I think it was kind of like a—it was a shock, especially to me. It was a shock that he was gonna sing "But Officer." I think it was supposed to be almost like comedy. To me it kind of sounded like comedy, but safer. Yeah. [Laughs] We couldn't figure out what was going on in the studio. "Do you think, has he turned his back on jazz?" The usual discussion when a guy jumps ship, you know. (JC)

Despite some confusion as to who was calling the shots on this session, the purpose of the date seems fairly clear: it was an attempt to cash in on the appeal of rhythm & blues.

Clifford Solomon had the exposure to that type of music. [He had worked with singer] Charles Brown—and his head was there and he also knew how much money that stuff could make. Cliff had never had a hit record or been associated with a hit record knowing about how much money was going to be coming in there of course. And he was with Charles Brown for *years*. So he was on the inside of the thing. And his idea was to do this and make a lot of money. (JC)

It was like somebody had a record date. We did it and got a few extra bucks but it wasn't like we were trying to play R&B either. We were just playing. It wasn't a stump-down jazz type thing. It was we were trying to do something commercial that would probably sell. As a matter of fact, that's one of the reasons that I didn't get no action with Columbia because they couldn't decide, well, they said I couldn't decide whether I wanted to be a stump-down jazz player or a rhythm & blues player. This was 1953. Later on, later on through the years there were other guys that were thinking the same way just like Junior Walker and people of that ilk that became big. That was my idea way back then. So all these other guys twenty years later that made it big. Because then, you had to be this or that. You had to be a jazz player or a honker. There was nothing in between—one or the other. (CS)

While this occurred early in the recording career of Gigi Gryce, it is odd that the drummer is Max Roach, who was well established as a leading jazz percussionist ever since his first session with

Charlie Parker in 1945. This foray into the world of the commercial was done just before Roach moved to California. Success was
not achieved, however. Solomon remembered the fate of the two
78s that were issued from this session: "Yeah, I think my mother
bought one. Quincy's mother bought one. They didn't sell, man."
(CS)

Also present on the OKeh session was vocalist Ernestine Anderson who was with Hampton at the time. She can be heard on the
Jones/Gryce collaborations "Li'l Daddee" and "Square Dance
Boogie"—certainly two of the least memorable compositions in
the legacies of both of these great talents.

As early as the end of spring in 1953, Lionel Hampton was planning a European tour. A front-page announcement in the June 3
issue of *Down Beat* included the following:

Associated Booking Corp. is now arranging dates that will enable
Hamp to take his entire orchestra across the Atlantic in late September and to cover France, Belgium, Holland, Scandinavia, etc., before
flyin' home around the end of November. It will be Hamp's first
venture overseas.[5]

It is of interest to note that the end of the tour was already scheduled as late November. It seems that the success in France and
other locations did not unexpectedly add time to the tour, as is
sometimes suggested, but was already tentatively planned. Some
legs of the tour were more uncertain, and even after they were in
Europe there was question about performing in North Africa and
Israel. It may have been that trouble in Israel forced the band to
return to Europe for a second set of performances.

I was going there this time and we were to donate our receipts from
concerts there to underprivileged children, but the Jordan–Israeli
incidents prevented our going.[6]

The incidents that Hampton refers to stem from difficulties in negotiating treaties relating to the Jordan River.

The tour did not schedule performances in Italy, nor in England, though there was considerable interest in both countries. At that time, the British Musicians' Union had a very controversial ban on foreign performers, and British publications such as *Melody Maker* were forced to report on Hampton concerts in Paris.

On July 6, the Hampton band began a two-week engagement at the Surf Club on the Jersey shore. The proximity to Atlantic City led to a very fortuitous change in personnel, instigated by Hampton trumpeter Quincy Jones:

> In the summer of 1953, while I was working with the Lionel Hampton band in Wildwood, New Jersey, I begged Hamp to hire three of the musicians from Tadd Dameron's band, which was nearing the end of its Atlantic City engagement—Gigi Gryce, Benny Golson, and Clifford Brown. They were all hired and then began an association that I'll always be grateful to Lionel for.[7]

In fact, Golson's tenure in the Hampton band started late and ended early. Brown and Gryce were able to join immediately, but Golson had to remain for a time.

> They wanted me too. The show was coming to an end. As a matter of fact, Clifford and Gigi left about three weeks before the season ended. But they wouldn't let them go unless I stayed to make sure their replacements learned the music. So I had to stay. Then I left and joined Lionel Hampton. I joined them in Greenville, South Carolina. I didn't stay with them very long.[8]

The band at the time consisted of: Anthony Ortega and Gryce, altos; Clifford Solomon and Clifford Scott, tenors; Oscar Estelle, baritone; Walter Williams, Art Farmer, Clifford Brown, Quincy Jones, trumpets; Al Hayse, Jimmy Cleveland, George "Buster" Cooper, trombones; Oscar Dennard, piano; William "Monk"

Montgomery, electric bass; Alan Dawson, drums. Additionally, singer Ernestine Anderson, blues shouter Sonny Parker, and show drummer and dancer Curley Hamner performed selections with the orchestra. Ortega recalled his first encounter with Gryce:

Actually, I met him when he joined Lionel Hampton, you know. And that was a little bit before we had gone to Europe. And so, in that case, he joined the band and we were doing, you know, the usual thing, one-niters in locations here and there and shortly thereafter Clifford Brown joined the band and they were very good friends, you know. Clifford and Gigi were very good friends. So then, pretty soon after that, then we had gone to make the first European trip there. (AO)

The money paid the musicians in the Hampton band was not very good, and it was this fact that opened the door for Gryce's participation in the European tour. According to Benny Golson, the pay was only nineteen dollars a night.

And they'd agreed to pay me more! You see, they'd agreed to pay me $25 a night. Then Lionel's wife met the band in Columbia, South Carolina and she said, "Oh no! We'll have none of that! We're not going to pay him $25 a night." ...Oh no? Goodbye![9]

Jimmy Cleveland concurred:

That's about right. That's just about right. Bobby [Plater] wasn't gonna go over there for the money that Hamp was gonna pay. And those of us that went over there shouldn't have gone. [Laughs] ...We weren't making any money. [Laughs] My God, that was one of the greatest and strangest experiences. (JC)

When Plater left the band, Gryce was hired. Several other Hampton band members left around the same time including trumpeter Benny Bailey (who was replaced by Clifford Brown), and the legendary pianist Oscar Dennard.

Oscar was with the band when I joined. But the band was in the U.S.

for two weeks before it went to Europe. He and a few others decided not to go to Europe because the bread was not that good. Most of the rest of us, including Lionel, had not been to Europe and were anxious to get a chance to go. George Wallington went, Annie Ross replaced Ernestine Anderson, who didn't go.[10]

The orchestra played various engagements in America: "Back east, you know, like say Massachusetts, like Holyoke, Massachusetts and some other cities around the east coast, maybe even a few southern cities." (AO)

They traveled down to Norfolk, Virginia where they were joined by Gryce's Boston colleague Alan Dawson on August 13 (one day after his discharge from the military) and then, beginning on August 18 and lasting until just before their departure for Europe, the Hampton band played for two weeks to very receptive crowds at the Band Box, in New York City. One of the most amusing pictures of this engagement was painted by Quincy Jones:

I remember playing with Lionel Hampton—who was really the first rock & roll bandleader, even though he had a jazz background—and we were at the Bandbox in New York City, which was next door to Birdland. Clifford Brown, Art Farmer and I were in the trumpet section. We had to wear Bermuda shorts with purple jackets and Tyrolean hats, man, and when we played "Flying Home," Hamp marched the band outside. You have to imagine this—I was 19 years old, so hip it was pitiful, and didn't want to know about anything that was *close* to being commercial. So Hamp would be in front of the sax section, and beating the drum sticks all over the awning, and soon he had most of the band behind him. But Brownie and I would stop to tie our shoes or do something so we wouldn't have to go outside, because next door was Birdland and there was Monk and Dizzy and Bud Powell, all the bebop idols standing in front at intermission saying, "What is this shit?" You'd do *anything* to get away.[11]

Gryce's future wife Eleanor Sears and his section mate Clifford

Solomon recall that these kind of antics were anathema to Gryce, and he refused to participate:

They were playing at the Apollo in Harlem and I went to see the show. Hamp had the guys play and then when they got to a certain part, they had to get off the stage and march up and down the aisles with their instruments, all except the pianist of course, and only one person was still standing on the stage playing his saxophone. He refused to walk up and down the [aisles]—and that was Gigi! (EG1).

No, no, that was beneath his dignity. Oh yeah, he was very dignified. But then, too, he was about three or four years older than the rest of us. We were like just out of our teens. So we had that exuberance and energy whereas Gigi was more a mature man of the world. So that was his dignity. Three or four years later, I don't think any of us would have done it, you know. It was a thing where everybody that worked with Lionel Hampton could expect that type of thing. (CS)

Jimmy Cleveland, who joined the Hampton band in 1950, well remembered the displays put on for the audiences:

Oh definitely. That was "Flying Home" or "When the Saints Go Marching In". "When the Saints Go Marching In"—sometimes he would do it on "Flying Home" if he could get the audience really excited you know, to the point of breaking seats and stuff. You know I've seen them do that. Yeah, they start tearing up seats and to make it even worse, he'd have us march off the stand and march all around theaters and clubs. [Laughs] He'd really get them worked up. No, Gigi wouldn't come off the stand to march in the aisles all through the place. And I thought that was rather funny, you know. Gigi started by looking at Hamp and Hamp was throwing daggers at Gigi. Oh, *strange!* (JC)

Gryce felt that music should be respected and not used as a gimmick—not cheapened to elicit an audience response.

Well, he liked the band when they were really playing but he disliked what Hamp was doing to the music. When Hamp would come on, it would all be "Hamp's Boogie Woogie" and that sort of stuff. He detested that. He didn't like that. (JC)

Fortunately, one of the audience members at the Band Box was Bob Weinstock, the owner of Prestige Records.

OK, let me tell you how I first got to hear Gigi. As you know, I sort of discovered Art Farmer when he was in California. I authorized this recording session with Wardell Gray. And they did "Farmer's Market" and stuff like that. And I immediately knew he was a great player. I could hear these players, you know. So then I arranged to sign Art to a contract and he said he wanted to come east anyway. So I signed him to a contract and I was very impressed with him and his brother, what fine people they were, very unusual for musicians you know, very intelligent, clean-cut, and very good musicians naturally. So I got friendly with Art and we were recording different things and one night, he said, "We're playing in a club." It may have been Birdland or some club. I don't even remember the club. But I know it was on Broadway in Manhattan. He said the band, the Hampton band was playing down there. See he was the in the Hampton band with Clifford. And he said, "There's some people I want you hear." And I said, "Well, do you guys play solos?" He said, "Yeah, they'll play solos later in the night. We'll stretch out."

So I said I'd be happy to come down and that was before I stopped going out late you know. I used to go out really late, hang out. And I stopped later but not then. So I went down there and the club was basically empty. And Hamp was sort of pissed. And it was sort of like an unannounced thing. No one knew about it, you know. So finally, towards later in the evening, Hamp just split and the band kept playing. And that's when I heard Clifford and Art. They stretched out and he said when I came in that he wanted me to hear Clifford Solomon and Gigi and Brownie. And so all the guys were taking long solos, whoever was left in the band. And that's when I heard Gigi, the first time. (RW)

Weinstock would prove to be a great supporter of Gryce and recorded him numerous times between 1954 and 1960 for his

Prestige and New Jazz labels. While the crowd that night may have been small, soon the word spread, as can be seen by the following accounts in *Metronome* magazine:

Lionel Hampton's recent two-week stand at New York's Band Box was the most sensational show that that club has had since its inception. Aside from the screaming and yelling, the nightly parade through the audience and the space helmets which Hamp distributed, the biggest and happiest news, to the owners at least, was that every night was like an opening night. Shoehorns had to be applied several times to fit in the huge crowds. After many years off Broadway, Lionel proved again that he is one of the greatest crowd-pleasers in the business.[12]

Lionel Hampton and his orchestra means just that, for this night, as every other night, it was Hampton the showman—bubbling and infectious—surrounded by a whole corps of entertainers, some good, some fair and some with only noise quality. He was the motor for the whole unwieldy vehicle, as well as the radiator, wheels and anything else you might want to imagine.

Much of the rest was sloppy and undisciplined stuff, but it had its humorous and exciting moments. With dancer Curley Hornser [Hamner], Lionel did a drum duet that had to be repeated for the hysterical audience. Attractive vocalist Ernestine Anderson showed a fine voice, although on one number, "Moonlight in Vermont," she had a background that featured at least three quarters of that proverbial kitchen sink. Sonny Parker is a bluesy blues singer in the wildest tradition.[13]

On August 28, just days before they departed via plane for Scandinavia, the newest additions to the Hampton band made a record session for Blue Note in New York. It was Clifford Brown's debut as a leader and he was assisted greatly by his close friends Quincy Jones and Gryce who both composed, while Gryce also played alto and flute. Other members of the sextet were tenor saxophonist Charlie Rouse, pianist John Lewis, bassist Percy Heath and drummer Art Blakey. Rouse was a Dameron alumnus and would eventually spend many years with Thelonious Monk, while Lewis and Heath would soon combine forces to achieve fame and fortune as one half of the Modern Jazz Quartet. Blakey (1919–1990), whose dynamic percussion style had already made its mark through recordings with Billy Eckstine, Buddy DeFranco, and Miles Davis, was about a year away from assembling his first Jazz Messengers co-op band with Horace Silver.

This was a landmark recording date for Clifford Brown, and Gryce's contribution is a major factor in its success. The burning "Hymn to the Orient" is a challenging line and Brownie's solo on it (the master take) has been singled out for praise.

The second and third choruses of this minor-key work illustrate strikingly Brownie's capacity for creating long, flowing phrases and executing them impeccably. This passage, 65 seconds long, was to us a major highlight of the entire LP.[14]

Mostly employing descending dominant seventh chords in the A section and a sequence of major seventh chords in the first half of the bridge, "Hymn to the Orient" moves away from standard ii–V progressions, only reverting to them in the second half of the bridge. The A-section melody is structured around the shifting relationship of the common tones between the chords, while the bridge melody persistently centers on the major seventh of the major chords in the first four bars before moving into a syncopated line over the ii–V chords in the latter four.

The tune had been recorded previously by Stan Getz, but it is the Clifford Brown version that stands out as a classic. After a six-bar piano introduction followed by a two-bar drum break, the band is off and running at a fast tempo. The 32-bar theme is stated by Brown with background from the saxophones. A four-bar interlude precedes Brown's famous two-chorus solo during which the

saxes provide background on chorus number two. He negotiates
the complex chord changes with incredible ease, spurred on by
the explosive but supportive drumming of Blakey. Rouse and
Gryce split the next chorus with the alto taking over at the bridge.
Lewis then takes an entire chorus before Brown and Blakey trade
fours for another. In typical Gryce fashion, the last chorus begins
with a shout variation on the A sections before returning to the
original theme at the bridge. The alternative take of "Hymn to
the Orient" is similar in routine but clearly inferior overall with
Blakey missing the ending.

Another classic that this session produced is the warhorse "Cherokee." A timeworn, up-tempo bebop vehicle, this 64-bar tune was
inscribed in modern jazz history through Charlie Parker's legendary recording (as "Koko") in 1945, and the successful negotiation
of its chord changes remains a crucial test for the aspiring musician. Brown passes his exam with flying colors. The entire ensemble is heard only in the eight-bar introduction, which is then
repeated as a coda. At a tempo of 300 beats per minute, Brown
immediately begins soloing while Lewis plays the melody during
the first chorus and continues for another amazingly fluent chorus being pushed constantly by the ebullient Blakey. Brown's thematic development at this tempo is astounding. Drums and trumpet then trade fours for a chorus and a half before the track ends
as it began. The alternative take of "Cherokee" is somewhat slower
and Brown's solo takes a while to develop to the level and fluency
of the master version. With "Cherokee" and "Hymn to the Orient" alone, Brown had elevated himself to the highest echelon of
jazz trumpet players.

But this session offers other gems, although not at the same strato-
spheric level of achievement. "Wail Bait" is a catchy Quincy Jones
melody taken at medium tempo. The six-bar introduction over a

Latin rhythm contrasts with the feel of the tune but the transition is eased by Lewis's two-bar piano break. The 32-bar theme is stated in unison but harmonized at the bridge. Piano and alto saxophone split a chorus with Gryce entering at the bridge spurred on by a Blakey press roll. The introduction is then reprised as an interlude whereupon Brown enters with a two-bar break followed by a beautifully constructed chorus. Constrained by the time limitations of the 10-inch LP, liberties are now taken with the form as Rouse enters at the bridge for sixteen bars. A harmonized shout chorus is then followed by eight bars of Brown at the bridge, and a return to the original melody completes the last chorus.

"Minor Mood" is a minor blues penned by Clifford Brown. Lewis provides an appropriately melancholy introduction for this rhythmically and harmonically interesting theme. Brown takes three steadily building choruses followed by Gryce for two, his most relaxed and well-constructed solo effort of the session. Rouse adds two choruses and Lewis one before the track concludes with a different theme than was stated initially.

Two ballads were recorded at this session, the standard "Easy Living" and "Brownie Eyes," composed by Quincy Jones. Gryce plays flute on both and contributes a characteristically lyrical alto saxophone solo on the latter.

Clifford Brown's debut as a leader was an auspicious one indeed, and cemented his status as the new trumpet voice of the period. While overshadowed by Brown's incredible virtuosity, Gryce and Jones would also benefit from the acclaim this recording and their contributions to it received.

Despite the fact that Hampton had a reputation for underpaying his band members, Gryce's younger brother recalled that, "One of the reasons that Gigi went to Paris is to pay off my mother's mortgage,"[15] and Clifford Solomon felt that Gryce may have merited extra money.

I don't know what Gigi made but Gigi was smart. And so he probably negotiated some decent money to even go to Europe. You know what I mean? And then they had a setup where the straw boss would make more, the lead, the first trumpet, the first trombone, all the lead players would make a little more. Then the soloists would make a little more than that and then regular sidemen wouldn't make as much. Fortunately, I was a soloist so what I made was a little bit under the lead players. And then the straw boss made the most. I know Bobby Plater did but I don't know if Gigi, whether he got straw boss money or lead alto money or just negotiated his own understanding with Hamp because Hamp knew him and respected him. That's why he got him on the band so he might have made Gigi an offer and Gigi said, "Well, that's not enough." So he went, so they must have reached a happy medium. (CS)

Jimmy Cleveland recalled Gryce sending money back home:

He mentioned something about he was helping his family. He put it to me like that. He didn't say it was his mother or sisters or whatever. We would go to Western Union a lot of times together to send money back. (JC)

The chance for international travel and the opportunity to spend time with several like-minded young musicians including his old friend Quincy Jones probably made the trip more enticing than the typical big-band gig.

Unfortunately, not everything was rosy within the ranks of the orchestra. There remained several of Hampton's old-time sidemen and a friction developed between the younger players, including Gryce, and these veterans who tried to assert dominance. It was noticed by outsiders, whether journalists or fans who spent time with the band.

You could tell right away—I could see that there was two type of musicians, two clans, one conservative people around Lionel Hampton, people like Billy Mackel, Al Hayse, Sonny Parker, the singer, Curley Hamner and so forth—and the moderns. The leader of the moderns was, of course, a good friend, Quincy Jones. And they were, you know, the bebop musicians. There was Clifford Brown and Art Farmer, Jimmy Cleveland, Anthony Ortega, Alan Dawson, the drummer, William Montgomery on bass... (LM)

He [Curley Hamner] was a good drummer. He was doing duets with Lionel Hampton. And he was not a bebop drummer. He was a kind of a showtime or show drummer. He could play with the band, but Alan Dawson was a much greater drummer than he was. So, there was, in the band, some malaise. You could tell that—you know, those two groups of different people, different musical mentalities. (LM)

The younger musicians were very much of the same mind. They were looking to advance music, rather than rest content with the hackneyed riffs and pounding backbeat that characterized the swing hits that made Hampton's reputation ever since he was with Benny Goodman in the 1930s. The friendships that had developed between Gryce and Brown in the Dameron band continued to blossom, and with Bostonians like Alan Dawson and Quincy Jones joining Hamptonians of similar bent like Art Farmer and Jimmy Cleveland, the orchestra's balance of power became a little too unstable.

I guess that was the clique that Hamp referred to—"You and your clique." Because we were thinking kind of in the same direction, musically. We really didn't care too much about what Hamp was doing. Not that he didn't have some good charts. Hamp had some excellent charts written by a lot of good people, tough writers. But those things he hardly ever played.

Hamp would play three or four things on his vibes and then we'd go into "Hamp's Boogie" and, of course, we'd end up by playing "Flying Home" and marching all over the people's stadiums and clubs and stuff.

Every musician that has ever worked or will ever work with Lionel Hampton will be limited. Some more than others. He's just not gonna let you play.[16]

Cleveland recalled that there were times when Hampton gave performance time to the charts by the young arrangers such as Gryce and Jones, but the support was less than one hundred percent, with the leader attempting to strong-arm the modern pieces into a swing style.

Oh yeah. We were ready to change things. He [Hampton] really didn't want to play the music and he would try to have the drummer play the backbeat through the opener and that other fast [Sings]... "Smoke Signal," yeah. And we *played* it too, man! [Laughs] We liked Gigi's music. And the band would jump on his music and it sounded like a different band. Gol-ly! Regardless of what Hamp said when we would come to Gigi's music the band would get away from the backbeat. He would try to get the drummer to play backbeat. (JC)

The stylistic and conceptual differences between the younger band members and Hampton were substantial. It is interesting to note, however, that despite this, Gryce greatly admired Hampton's ability as a vibraphonist and would marvel at the leader's virtuosity on many solo efforts during concerts.[17]

At the last minute, Hampton added two stars of the bebop scene to his ensemble.

Only 24 hours before the Lionel Hampton orchestra departed via plane on the first leg of a two-month overseas tour, Annie Ross and George Wallington signed up as vocalist and pianist with the Hamptonians.

The surprise move was the result of a two-week engagement played by Annie and George opposite Hamp at the Band Box. Annie, recently honored in the *Down Beat* critics' poll, has never before worked with a name band. Wallington's experience too, has been almost exclusively with small combos.[18]

It seems that Hampton wanted to reach the fans of more modern music and made the late additions of Ross and Wallington to his personnel in hopes of attracting a more progressive audience. This two-pronged attack, attempting to appeal to both swing and be-bop sensibilities, was a success, but would also create serious problems.

Notes

1. Gigi Gryce, quoted by Raymond Horricks in *These Jazzmen of Our Time*, Gollancz, London, 1959, p. 191.
2. Benny Golson, interviewed by Paul B. Matthews in *Cadence*, September 1996.
3. Benny Golson, interviewed by Paul B. Matthews in *Cadence*, September 1996.
4. Art Farmer, interviewed by Tyrone Ward, 1987.
5. *Down Beat*, June 3, 1953, p. 1.
6. *Down Beat*, January 27, 1954, p. 1
7. Jones, Quincy, "A Tribute to Brownie," *Down Beat*, August 22, 1956, p. 10.
8. Benny Golson, interviewed by Paul B. Matthews in *Cadence*, September 1996, p. 21.
9. Benny Golson, interviewed by Paul B. Matthews in *Cadence*, September 1996, p. 21.
10. Dawson, Alan, interviewed by Stu Vandermark in *Cadence*, December 1983, p. 8.
11. Quincy Jones, quoted by Zan Stewart in "The Quincy Jones Interview," *Down Beat*, April 1985, p. 17.
12. *Metronome*, September 1953, p. 8.
13. Coss, Bill, *Metronome*, September 1953, p. 18.
14. Leonard Feather, liner notes to Blue Note BLP 5032—Clifford Brown Sextet: *New Star on the Horizon.*
15. Tommy Gryce, interviewed by Phil Schaap on WKCR-FM, New York, July 2, 1997.

16. Jimmy Cleveland, interviewed by Bob Rusch in *Cadence*, January 1991, p. 19.

17. Personal communication from Dan Morgenstern to Noal Cohen.

18. *Down Beat*, October 7, 1953, p. 1.

paris the beautiful

*T*HE HAMPTON ENTOURAGE departed from New York by plane on September 2 bound for Norway.

We toured Norway, like Oslo, and then we toured...Stockholm and Göteborg and about four or five other cities in Sweden, and we came down and played in Brussels. We played Copenhagen, Brussels, Paris, another city in France called Mentz. And then in Germany, we played Berlin, Stuttgart, Frankfurt, and Hamburg. We even went to North Africa. We played in Tunis, Algiers, and Morocco. And that was supposed to be the end of the tour, but the tour had been so successful that without even coming back to the United States, we just started right over at the beginning. We started the whole thing all over.[1]

The tour ultimately lasted about twelve weeks. The Norway performances provided the first portent of the warm reception the band would receive throughout the tour. They also would result in a meeting of special importance to alto saxophonist Anthony Ortega:

Oslo, Norway was our first stop and that sticks out in my mind because that's where I met my wife. That was our first stop and then—well, the first thing I have to say about it is that none of us, myself included, could believe the acceptance that we got, you know. Of course, this was 1953 also which was a new era for jazz musicians from America to go over there, but we just couldn't believe it, like the standing ovations and the crowds that were going crazy. Because, you know, we were accepted in the States fine but not like that! And that just happened in every city we went to. I think it was because of Hampton was so well known. But, of course, after they heard these guys, and I guess they were like all fired up about it—but Hampton was the biggest name and everybody went to see him but then after hearing the band and the soloists and, of course, Hampton himself, and the whole thing, you know, they went wild. (AO)

After-concert jam sessions in local clubs were common on the tour and while Gryce was not the most outgoing of the musicians, he definitely did participate in several such events. "A couple of times, on occasion, yes on occasion, not a big partygoer but on occasion he would." (AO)

Yeah, he might have been there that night when there was a jam session with Clifford Brown. Yeah, I think we were all there. When I say all, not the entire Hampton band but there were so many players. They were really that, jam sessions. You'd sit around and wait and wait and wait and you'd go up and play...because the places were small and all the guys couldn't get up there at the same time. Oh yeah, yeah, little basement-type things. We always were partying you know. (JC)

Any chance we got, man, we would go out. There was a club in Paris called The Ringside. It was George Gainford's, who was Sugar Ray Robinson's manager. And there was the Mars Club, and one of those two places, it probably was the Mars Club that Don Byas was working. This was in Paris. Don Byas was such a tiger on that horn. The musicians would just flock in. He was a beautiful cat, man: "Come on up and play. I need some help." Even though he was *the* Don Byas, the musicians were always welcome to come play. As a matter of fact, young guys at the time, that was the way we would learn, by listening to the old established saxophone players. And I was the type of guy that, being a saxophone player, I didn't just limit my listening to saxophone players. I'd listen to trumpet players, trombone players, guitar players, piano players, whoever had something to say. You know like Clifford Brown was an influence on me playing trumpet. Gigi was a big influence when he played alto. I played tenor but he played alto. But he was an influence just like Charlie Parker was. (CS)

Perhaps more than jamming, Gryce was interested in the possibility of making some money by recording—his alto playing, but more importantly his compositions and arrangements. Though it began in Stockholm, this became particularly evident when the band arrived in Paris.

They were in one of the most exciting cities in the world, OK? And they had small salaries, so they needed the money. And, of course, they took advantage of the circumstances to play new compositions and do something different. So it was a dual type of goal. You have two goals but the first one was necessity, was money. (LM)

Ever since the Swedish Metronome label was founded in 1949, its practice of recording visiting Americans had been well established. James Moody was the first, in October of that year. Over the next four years, Metronome would record artists such as Zoot Sims and Stan Getz. The Swedish baritone saxophonist Lars Gullin was the leader of a date on August 25, 1953 featuring Lee Konitz, Zoot Sims, Conte Candoli, Frank Rosolino, Don Bagley, and Stan Levey out of the Stan Kenton Orchestra, which toured Europe just prior to Lionel Hampton. It is conceivable that Gryce's work was known to some of the Swedish musicians, particularly Bengt Hallberg, Gunnar Johnson, and Jack Norén, because Stan Getz had recorded with them while visiting in March 1951, around the time that Horace Silver had joined his band and Gryce had submitted compositions to Getz.

The leaders for the first of a dozen sessions (not counting concert broadcasts and jam sessions) that took place during the Lionel Hampton tour were the newest additions to the group, Annie Ross and George Wallington. Gryce arranged two pieces for the singer and Quincy Jones arranged two for the pianist. Though some of the later recorded material was borrowed from the library of the Hampton band, or included tunes written by Gryce and Jones before joining the band, the charts for the September 14 date were last-minute affairs.

He [Jones] went with Gigi Gryce to one of the Swedish sessions, and their scores were unfinished. The studio contained only one piano. Gigi immediately sat down at it to finish his scores. Quincy sat down in the far corner and despite the crash of experimental piano chords going on about his ears, and the talking and tuning up by the other musicians as they arrived, he finished his work on a few scraps of manuscript.[2]

Back in the U.S., Benny Golson became aware that his former Hampton bandmates were supplementing their meager pay by doing these sessions.

I said to myself, "Why are they going to Europe for that little bit of money?" Quincy sent me a letter from Stockholm: "We just did two record dates today, outside the band." Then I got another card: "We made an album last week. Sure wish you'd made it." They made more money on the side than they did with the band.[3]

The records were well received by the press, particularly Ross's rendition of "The Song Is You," which was performed at an unusually slow tempo for this tune.

Altoist Gigi Gryce arranged and directed each side. Scottish-born Miss Ross sings the beautiful Jerome Kern tune in a most arresting manner with exemplary vibrato control (notable in her sustained notes). Her phrasing is reminiscent of Sarah Vaughan at times while Gryce's background is sympathetic and extremely interesting.[4]

This reception, however, was not extended by the Hampton organization. As was fairly common at that time, touring sidemen were forbidden to make records away from the group.

What happened was when we recorded in Stockholm, there was a pianist by the name of George Wallington. He had just come in the band and he was kind of naive and he didn't know what kind of guy Hamp was. So he just happened to tell Hamp one day that he had just made a record and Hamp hit the ceiling and you know, with this slave mentality, and said, "I brought you guys over here and you are not supposed to do any other work other than work for me," you know, but we were not going to buy this, but knowing him, we just said OK and then we had one more date scheduled to do in Stockholm and we would sneak out the back door of the hotel and went and played the date after we had played the concert that night, and had to take a train to Göteborg and when we got there, some of the guys in the band said, "Hey, Hamp wants to see you guys right away." So we went to his dressing room and he said, "Hey, what happened to you guys last night?" We said, "Hey man, you should have been with us. We ran into some real tough chicks…You know, some real tough blondes." We said, "I'm real sorry you weren't with us." Hamp said, "Yeah well, look, from now on, when the train leaves, everybody leaves." We all said OK.[5]

The situation reached a flash point when it was learned that the star trumpeter Clifford Brown had recorded for Metronome one day after the Ross and Wallington session. Lionel Hampton became furious and threatened to fire Brown, who was very well liked by the band members for both his extraordinary playing and his warm personality. Gigi Grycc and Jimmy Cleveland played significant roles in resolving the situation.

See, we would have to sneak out of the hotel. We had to slip out and in one incident, we had to push Clifford Brown through a—his big ass through a small window. [Laughs] That was funny when I see this picture. Here we are pushing this guy through so we can all go out.

Well, he had George Hart who was supposed to be the manager in charge, and Leroy, I don't know what his last name was, a couple of thugs. I think they're dead now so I'll make that statement. I'll call them thugs. [Laughs] So they were supposed to be on watch because, rumors, those kind of rumors gotta get out—the musicians getting very antsy after they know the job is over, they're down in the lobby, hangin' out in the lobby too long or they're coming down periodically. Then all of a sudden someone goes, "I saw him with the horn last night." You know, that happens two or three times and all of a sudden they get the idea that, hey, they're recording. And see he actually found out from some of his friends in the city there that— when I say he, Lionel Hampton—that the band was recording. Quincy Jones, Gigi Gryce, Clifford Brown, Jimmy Cleveland, Clifford Solomon, Art Farmer, they called all the names. All these guys are making records all over the city. This was in Sweden and Paris. [Laughs] And man, this dude was *furious!* So I said, "Well, Gigi, I'm going to call Gladys." So Gladys started to sound really weird. She said, "Well, Jimmy, you hurry up and come over to the hotel. I want to talk to you." I said OK.

So I think Gigi Gryce and I got in the cab. But first, before I went over there I said, "Gigi, I'm gonna call Hy Jaffe in New York." So I called Hy Jaffe. Jaffe says, "Man, whatever they do, the Union will send all of your money if they don't want to pay it. If they want to get real nasty and we'll just let him play the jobs, the rest of the jobs with the trio and when he gets back here we're going to fine him and we're going to pay you all the money that he owes you for the entire tour. So that's what we're gonna do." Now, armed with this information, Gigi Gryce and I went to this hotel and went to Gladys's suite. And we're sitting there. [Gladys:] "Now, Jimmy, relate this to me." I said, "Well, we've been making records. And we don't have a contract with you stating that we cannot make records. I mean, we all have careers and we're trying to enhance our careers. We're trying to further our careers just like you guys have been doing all this time. And, thankfully, we're all here together at this particular moment in life. So, I will tell you this, the news that I received last night or early this morning was that you're going to fire Clifford Brown. And when you fire Clifford Brown..." [Gladys:] "Who's going to fire Clifford Brown?" I said, "OK, your husband." [Gladys:] "Hamp, come in here!" They had a big suite. It took him a half an hour to come out the back to face us. [Laughs] He didn't want to face us. When he gets out there—[Hamp:] I tell you, man, uh, uh, uh, these guys been sneakin' out with my job. I paid these guys' transportation over here and..."

I said, "I'll tell you what, Hamp. Sure enough you're paying our transportation and all that stuff over here," I said, "but you're supposed to be paying much more than what you're paying. I mean, you're supposed to be paying much more food than just one measly little breakfast. The talk to entice us to come out here to Europe was that we would be treated much better. My gracious, playing all these shows. Anyway, I spoke with Hy Jaffe. And Jaffe says if you fire anyone out of this band based on this not making records for anyone else or any other record company in or throughout Europe, you will have to pay us for the rest of the tour and they will send all of us money and tickets to come back to New York immediately." Boy, you should have seen him dancing. [Laughs] Oh, it was really, really weird. What happened was a statement was made that well, we don't want Hamp. We want you guys. And that's what ticked him off. (JC)

Neither Brown nor any other member of the band was terminated at this point although the remainder of the tour was fraught with tension and difficulties.

Over the next few days the band traveled from Sweden to Denmark, the Netherlands, and on to Belgium. Annie Ross was reportedly heckled at a concert in Brussels on September 20, and a review of that concert commented that Ross "had more good intentions than talent." It was also intimated that Hampton was influenced by more traditional-minded outsiders such as Hugues Panassié in not allowing Ross to perform in The Hague and firing her before the band came to Paris. Wallington left in a show of support, and the remainder of the tour was done without a pianist. Jimmy Cleveland recalled this unfortunate episode.

I think they got angry and came back home. Well, they weren't treated right. I'll tell you that right now. You know I've seen prejudices. I mean I'm from Tennessee, man. I know it. I know the insignia. I just smell it. I can taste it. I know what it is. They were definitely not treated as they should have been treated! Not [by] all, just some of the other musicians. Not the younger guys, you know, the older guys. (JC)

On September 24, the band played a concert at Kongresshaus in Zurich, Switzerland and one the following night in Basel at the Mustermesse. The pace of the tour was demanding and taxed the strength of the musicians.

The band tore it up in Europe. It really did. It was something like what you hear about the reaction that rock groups get. The places would be mobbed with people. We spent a lot of time in Scandinavia. This was in the fall of the year. In Scandinavia in September and October it's pretty brisk, and we were doing outdoor concerts. We would do two outdoor concerts in two different cities. We would do one from seven to nine. Of course, we would never get through at nine. As long as people have enough strength to put two hands together, he's [Lionel Hampton] not going to go off the bandstand. So, we'd be scheduled to be in another city—maybe 15 to 20 miles away—to play a concert from 10 to 12. Well, we'd be just about packing up at 10 o'clock. So, the next concert would start at about 11:30 and we'd finish at about 1:30 in the morning. But all these places were mobbed, and people didn't leave. In fact they would keep clapping and keep clapping. And we'd keep playing and keep playing. And we'd all be cursing. [Laughter][6]

At the first French concerts at the Palais de Chaillot on September 26 and 27, the reviewer from *Jazz Hot* noticed that the young players were being slighted, and singled out Gryce as one of the better musicians.

This group seems impoverished in soloists of class, more especially as the good soloists were those whom one heard less. One has the curious and slightly depressing impression that the orchestra is composed of two very distinct clans: the ancients and the moderns... As for the saxophonists, none appeared particularly brilliant to me, except perhaps G.G. Gryce, a classy alto saxophonist and a brilliant arranger.[7]

Clifford Solomon was aware of the dissension that existed in the audience as well as in the Hampton band.

And so when we played Paris, we played the Palais de Chaillot and there was two factions. Hugues Panassié with the *Hot Club of France* was traditional jazz and then there was Delaunay who had *Le Jazz Hot*, which was more like bebop type. And so we were playing this gig and talk about political parties battling, man, they were—pretty soon there was a riot going on and Panassié walked with a cane. And I remember looking up and he had this cane in there and he was trying to hit Charles Delaunay with it. And they were tussling around and it was a riot, man! This was at a Hampton concert. The reason was is that Hamp's band was so versatile in different types of music that both were claiming Lionel Hampton for their own, you know. And that was what the riot was about. They said, "He played our...", "No, he played our..." Because Hamp was doing everything! He played everything! (CS)

According to Panassié's publication, *Bulletin du Hot Club de France*, the fighting did not stop there.

At the concert of Saturday, October 10 (matinee), Hugues Panassié was struck and pushed down by three boppers, probably excited by the heinous and defamatory campaign organized by the "zazotteux" [Le Jazz Hot adherents; modernists] against the President of the HCF. We hope that such incidents will not be repeated.[8]

The clandestine Paris recording sessions were organized on very short notice. The Hampton orchestra first set foot in Paris on September 26 after playing the previous days in Switzerland and that they were recording immediately after their very first night in the City of Light is remarkable. It also shows how important a cultural event the tour was for European jazz fans and musicians. Several French fans traveled to Brussels to hear the band earlier in September and Léon Kaba and Charles Delaunay of Vogue Records may have had advance notice regarding the presence of new bebop-minded jazz musicians in the sections, which could have first suggested the possibility of documenting these players who were underexposed during the concerts.

Someone had been talking to someone. Well, now, they knew. One thing I can say about the European people, they knew the ones that are playing and those are the ones they're gonna try to get on record. And they'd go out and hear Hamp but see, one thing that Hamp could not do was take out all the solos—people like…Clifford Brown and Art Farmer and Gigi and you can't take those soloists out. If you do, he'd end up playing all the solos himself and it would be his particular instrument on each and every selection. So they knew how to pick the people that they wanted to record. And they'd go around and ask, "Would you record? Will you record?" They'd come and ask you if you'd record you know. I think the way we started recording especially after the first or second engagement over there—it started happening that quickly. And we hadn't played that many places in Europe. I think some of it—either Quincy or Gigi Gryce knew someone already over there or hooked it up through some recording companies here some type of way. I don't know how closely they had been connected. (JC)

French players were already aware of Gryce through his compositions, according to pianist Henri Renaud.

Gigi went to the Tabou, where my quartet was playing an impressive number of his compositions; needless to say, he was stupefied! Stan Getz had lent the charts to Sacha Distel in New York a year earlier, having discovered them in Boston."[9]

The ex-Hampton pianist George Wallington in fact, had recorded in Paris on September 24, just two days prior to the orchestra's arrival, with bassist Pierre Michelot and drummer Jean-Louis Viale who would soon be in the studio with Gryce and company. He could have alerted the Parisians also.

Gigi was involved in organizing the Paris things. Quincy and I— actually, it was more me than Quincy—were involved in the Prestige things in Stockholm because, by that time, I had already signed a contract with Prestige and there was a Swedish man over here working for some record company or something and we worked out a deal between Metronome Records and Prestige Records to record while we were in Sweden. But Gigi worked out a deal to record while we were in France. (AF)

The sessions done by the Hampton musicians in France were not unique. Henri Renaud had already served as a musical liaison for American musicians in Paris as early as 1951 when he recorded with tenor saxophonist Sandy Mosse. A little over a week before the Hampton band arrived, on September 17, 1953, Renaud recorded with Lee Konitz and used guitarist Jimmy Gourley on the date. Both Renaud and Gourley would reprise these roles at a November 18 Paris session led by Zoot Sims.

The pieces recorded by an octet at the first of the Paris sessions on September 26 were mostly features for the soloists, as opposed to ensemble works, standards, or jam-type material. Anthony Ortega took a slightly avant-garde approach to Quincy Jones's ballad "Purple Shades." Jimmy Cleveland was spotlighted playing his traditional solo with the Hampton band, George Gershwin's "Summertime," but in a new guise devised by Jones called "La Rose Noire" (the name of a club in Brussels). The only soloist on this piece besides Cleveland, Gryce plays two choruses, opening with a phrase he would include in his own composition "Salute to the Band Box" (see example) and moving into some fluent double-time passages at the end of his first chorus.

Excerpt from Gryce's solo on "La Rose Noire"

Most of his phrasing lies well behind the beat and is very relaxed, in contrast to some other Paris performances. The coda of this tune features a short flute cadenza that has been credited to Anthony Ortega, but may well be Gryce. Instrumentation and personnel are partly uncertain on these performances and have often been incorrectly listed. The baritone saxophone of William Boucaya is prominent on all these tracks.

Gryce featured himself on his composition "Paris the Beautiful." This ballad in AABCA form is 64 measures long and while the sixteen-bar A sections are in F major, the eight-bar B section played as a flute (unquestionably Ortega here) and trombone duet is in A major, moving into C-sharp minor for the eight-bar C section, before the final A section reappears after a surprising resolution. This use of tonal centers a third apart would become a major feature of John Coltrane's playing later in the decade. The arrangement is simple but effective with a thick three-saxophones-plus-trombone horn cushion backing Gryce as he paraphrases his own melody line, winding back and forth, building the intensity into spectacular double-time runs in the final section before gently concluding. The model is clearly Charlie Parker.

For the second of the Paris sessions the musicians became a bit more ambitious and the seldom-played modern charts from the Hampton library were featured. These September 28 big band sessions presented a slight problem in that it was predominantly the younger players who were involved and this did not constitute a full instrumentation for those charts that were borrowed.

I would say that since there were only twelve of us that was into the thing, and if it was a big band [arrangement]… So if it was three saxophones, they would have to get another two. If there was two trumpets, they would have to get another two or three. You know what I'm saying? And so if the chart was for four trumpets, and we had three—well two, because Quincy didn't play, he was directing or whatever. So they would say well we'll get a couple of French guys to fill the section. (CS)

Henri Renaud was a key figure in finding these supplementary Parisian players, and although a language barrier existed, it did not present any difficulties.

Yeah, they spoke English. They spoke a little, enough to make their way, make themselves understood. Yeah, they could speak English. Henri Renaud, yeah, he spoke good English. (JC)

There would be somebody there that could interpret. And then music is an international language. Anybody that had a jazz feeling— you know, it wasn't a problem, we couldn't speak the same language but we spoke the same language. And it was no problem. If I remember right we would hang out and drink and have a good time. We couldn't communicate language-wise but we could in other ways. (CS)

Anthony Ortega felt that Gryce's talent, training, and dedication were what allowed him to take a leadership role while in Paris.

Well, I would say a lot of it was due to his ability to write these arrangements because neither I nor a lot of these other guys could arrange. We just were soloists, so to speak. So that was his foothold there, I would say because he was educated very good in all this scholastic stuff, you know, plus being a soloist.

I think he was always concentrating on music. He was very, not studious, but very, what do you say, conscientious. I used to see him writing a lot, jotting down things. On the train or on the airplane, he would be concentrating on his music. You know, he was thinking about that all the time. That's basically, I think, all his pastime was, you know. (AO)

Even the French jazz writers were aware of Gryce's dedication and intensity:

Gigi lives only for the music, often writing during several days without eating, nor sleeping. Let us hope that his arrangements and compositions, which will be released very soon on Vogue, will find many fans, and will make him more famous in France, where, thanks to a grant, he intends to come next year to study classical music.[10]

There is no evidence that Gryce ever followed through on his plan for European study in 1954.

Although some of the material recorded at the Paris sessions was already available, many of the arrangements were written during the tour.

Well, I would venture to think that Quincy and Gigi would stay up all night writing. I don't think this stuff was done beforehand because this stuff was put together when we got there. These record dates were put together once we got there. (CS)

Yeah, they were written over there. You know what? It's like Clifford Brown and Gigi and Quincy, they would always be working on something, even on the bus or on the plane. Clifford Brown—most of us would be trying to get some rest so we could get up and get back on the plane or get on a bus and ride half the day on a bus. Clifford Brown would still be practicing on his trumpet like at six o'clock in the morning. We didn't get in till maybe twelve or one in some of those places. Now, those dates were all arranged whether we were gonna have a long trip you understand, like one of them nine-hour trips. Basically, when you're doing it by bus everything is nine hours in Europe. But the whole thing is, yes, they would count their own tunes off. And they worked pretty closely together. (JC)

One of the masterpieces in the legacies of both Clifford Brown and Gigi Gryce, "Brown Skins," is a jazz concerto for trumpet. Of all the Paris recordings, it has received the most recognition— primarily after the fact, but to a certain extent at the time of its original issue also. One particular champion of Gryce as a composer was the British writer Raymond Horricks, who in speaking of Gigi Gryce and John Lewis wrote: "Not since I made my first acquaintance with the work of Duke Ellington have I met such concentrated intelligence in jazz composition."[11] It was "Brown Skins" that held special significance for Horricks among the large ensemble works recorded in Paris.

The best of these I find is "Brown Skins." As the title implies, this six-minute work is a feature for trumpeter Clifford Brown. The idea hails from Bill Russo's "Portrait of a Count" with a slow-tempo opening chorus followed by a sequence of fast, swinging music.[12]

It might also be suggested that both Russo and Gryce were updating the traditional two-part "French Overture" (slow, fast) form that goes back to the Baroque period and was so favored by Gryce. Brown's brilliant improvisations sometimes overshadow Gryce's composition and intricate arrangement, but this work is considerably more than just a blowing vehicle. While the solo changes are borrowed from "Cherokee," there is an original set of chords for the slow opening (which is a full 32-measure tune, preceded by a dramatic five-measure introduction) and there is also a strong melody played by the saxophones underneath Brown's first uptempo chorus. A half-chorus ensemble and various background figures complete the package. Thankfully, drummer Alan Dawson, who was experienced with these arrangements, made the session and was able to provide a solid, unhesitant backing for the ensemble.

More than a decade later, when Art Farmer listened to a recording of Brown playing "Cherokee," he confirmed that the Hampton band performed the Gryce chart.

He sounded fine on this, but I heard him play the tune ["Cherokee"] so many times. We used to play it together in Hamp's band—we had an arrangement by Gigi Gryce, with the same chords; it was called "Brownskin" [sic].[13]

Clifford Solomon remembered how the piece entered the repertoire:

Well, you know it was remarkable when Gigi wrote that chart, and we did it, we ran it down. I believe it was—well I don't remember exactly where it was, somewhere in Scandinavia. I don't remember if it was Copenhagen or Stockholm but it was somewhere and Gigi brought that chart. We had a rehearsal, we ran it down and Cliff was back playing the part, you know, in the trumpet section. He was reading the part. And it started off slow and it gradually until it wound up flying, right? So that night, when we played it, Cliff came out front and played it like he had been playing it for months. It was so remarkable. Everybody was so impressed. Although thinking back over it, I'd say that Gigi and Cliff were very, very close. Yeah, they probably collaborated where Cliff knew exactly what was to be and it was the changes to "Cherokee" so after he got through the initial—it was Cliff playing the little melody. But it was an ad-lib melody and so Gigi was directing so Clifford was playing the lead but it was directed by Gigi. We played it at a Hampton concert. We recorded that too. So I think the tune stayed in the book. We did it at other concerts too. (CS)

One of those concerts was in Brussels. A review mentions Clifford Brown being featured on "an extremely interesting interpretation on 'Cherokee'."[14]

While "Brown Skins" featured Clifford Brown, the reverse-titled "Deltitnu" (in the tradition of Dizzy Gillespie's "Emanon" from 1946) showcased Gryce. Like so many bebop-era pieces, the harmonic basis is "I Got Rhythm" and the treatment is very much in the tradition of the Gillespie big band, with powerfully syncopated brass punches contrasting with the smooth saxophone riff melody.

Compositionally, both of Gryce's pieces are quite adventurous compared to the contribution of Quincy Jones, "Keeping up with Jonesy," which is a laid-back foursquare number. (It would later resurface as "Muttnik" on a 1959 Count Basie album). Both takes of this tune feature solos by Renaud, Cleveland, Ortega, and Solomon.

On the next date, with Gryce and Brown fronting a sextet, Gryce debuted his composition "Blue Concept" (some issues list it as "Conception," though it has no relation to the George Shearing tune of that name). This is a simple line that allows for Gryce, guitarist Jimmy Gourley, Brown, and Renaud to blow on a variant of the reharmonized blues progression popularized by Charlie Parker and Bud Powell. Gryce's solos are well constructed methodically on the changes, using primarily long lines of his behind-the-beat eighth notes with limited syncopated figures. Later recordings of this tune would up the tempo but would use traditional blues changes. The two takes show the ending of the piece was somewhat in flux, but the solos more than make up for this indecisiveness.

In their performance of "All the Things You Are," Brown and Gryce dispense with the hackneyed eight-bar introduction taken from the famous 1945 Dizzy Gillespie–Charlie Parker recording in favor of Jerome Kern's original verse, played by Gourley. Building on each chord's guide tones, Gryce improvises a clever counterline to Brown's melody statement and the two make for very compatible partners here. Due to some unclear labeling, what is often called the first take is probably the first choice, but second take. What is probably the earlier take has some uncertainty toward the close of the arrangement, with Gryce and Brown trading fours for half a chorus instead of a piano solo, before Gryce (not Brown, as on the other take) begins to lead the group out. The slightly faster take with the piano solo is tighter, better organized, and Clifford Brown's solo is one of his very best from this period. It begins with the same "Band Box" figure that Gryce played on his opening of "La Rose Noire," which was certainly in the air around this time.

As the session progressed, the performances became looser and looser. "I Cover the Waterfront" is an off-the-cuff version, with Brown and Gryce each taking a chorus—no arrangement, no backing, just blowing on a standard. "Goofin' with Me" does have an arranged introduction, but proceeds quickly into a string of solos on "Back Home Again in Indiana," which was a popular favorite at the various jam sessions during the tour. Gryce sounds very comfortable on this, using some side-slipping (temporarily stepping into another key) in his first chorus and generally being Bird-like, though at times a bit out of tune in the high register.

The unauthorized recording activity in Paris again precipitated a crisis within the Hampton band. But solidarity among the young Turks, coupled with a realization of their importance to the success of the tour, averted any firings, as Art Farmer remembers:

So then we went down to Paris and we had all this activity going on. They have this jazz club down there like the Hot Jazz Club. Membership clubs. And somebody saw Brownie in the studio one day and went and told Hamp. You know, just casually. It was not like they were trying to be a stool pigeon or anything, but they figured it was OK. Hamp found out and called a meeting and said, "I heard you guys been recording again and I told you not to do it." Now, in Sweden he told us, he said, "If I hear about anybody doing any recording, I'm gonna fire you. I'm gonna take your passport and have you thrown out of the union." Now, he can't do all that stuff. He could fire us, but that was as far as he could do and he didn't have no reason to fire us.

Then he found out what was happening in Paris. He found that Brownie had recorded and he said, "If Brownie recorded, I'm sending Brownie home," and Gigi said, "Well, if you send him home, you should send me home too because I recorded this and this and this and this and this," and he ran down a whole string of things he recorded and the next thing, the other guys start saying, "Me too" and "Me too" and "Me too," and so he said, "Well, the hell with it. I'll cancel the whole tour then. I am not going to have the tail waggin' the dog." And Gladys said, "Oh, shut up, Lionel," because the tour was very successful and what he was talking about was just non-sense.[15]

Between September 30 and October 4, the Hampton band performed concerts in Germany: Düsseldorf followed by Munich, Frankfurt, Hamburg, and Berlin. An unscheduled jam session took place in Baden-Baden on October 5 when disc jockey Joachim Berendt learned that the musicians would be staying at a local hotel after their performance in Berlin prior to traveling to Strasbourg, France. Berendt hastily organized some musicians from the Kurt Edelhagen big band in the Tannenhof Club, part of the Südwestfunk radio station. Although they arrived at the hotel at nearly midnight, Hampton, along with Clifford Brown, Al Hayse, and Gryce, played for four hours, and the proceedings were recorded by Berendt for later broadcast on his radio program. As was the case with most of the jam sessions that took place occasionally throughout the tour, the repertoire was very straightforward. Tunes such as "Tenderly," "Perdido," "How High the Moon," and "Star Dust" were the order of the day. Berendt reported that one extraordinary part of this particular session was a multifaceted demonstration by Clifford Brown. "Brownie shared the piano with Werner Drechsler. The devilish lad played everything: trumpet, bass, trumpet, piano, trumpet, clarinet, trumpet, drums, trumpet, vibraphone, trumpet...trumpet...trumpet."[16] Gryce traded fours as part of an alto trio with Franz von Klenck and Helmut Reinhardt.

Henri Renaud and the other local French musicians had been keeping busy while the Hampton band was touring. The rhythm section of the Gryce–Brown sextet sessions recorded as a quartet on October 5. When the band returned to Paris two days later to play a five-night engagement, Gryce was prepared with material for another sextet date on October 8. All four of the compositions are his and this is a very well-balanced set, possibly reflecting the time he had to plan, in contrast to the hastily organized September sessions. Three of the four would be recorded by Art Blakey in a few months, but "Baby" was never recorded by Gryce again. This dedication to his old Pensacola girlfriend Evelyn DuBose contains A sections based on "Perdido," but a new bridge with no written melody, though it does present a challenging sequences of ii–V chords that Brown improvises on during the melody statements. It was later revised by Gryce when he published it in 1955. He composed a line for the bridge and adjusted some of the harmony parts. For some reason, one of the takes (again, probably the earlier one, though often labeled as take two) fades out as Brown returns after a bass solo, possibly due to performance difficulties in ending the piece.

The other tunes include the first recordings of what would become Gryce's best known and most performed composition, "Minority," taken at a relatively slow pace (though the chosen take is the brightest). Also recorded was "Salute to the Band Box," Gryce's line on "I'll Remember April" chord changes that is also known both as "Salute to Birdland" and as "Reunion." The performances on both suffer somewhat from lack of rehearsal. Brown misses entrances toward the end of each. The rhythm section is also somewhat non-committal, particularly when set against later versions with drummers such as Art Blakey and Max Roach. Comparing Gryce's solos on the two takes of "Band Box" reveals that his basic framework remains the same from take to take, even to the point of playing identical lines in identical locations. It does not seem that this construction was strictly determined beforehand but was more of a tendency in his improvising.

Offsetting the three up-tempo pieces is "Strictly Romantic," another beautiful ballad that gives Clifford Brown a chance to shine in the opening statement, followed by the composer. The tonal center cleverly vacillates between A-flat major and G major (as does the bridge of "Baby"), and after a reprise of the introductory material finishes with a startling E major. This kind of adventurous harmony was a trademark of Gryce and he was obviously concerned with stretching the boundaries of jazz tonality while remaining firmly footed in the idiom, using the ubiquitous ii–V progressions in new ways and maintaining a solid swinging 4/4 meter.

The critical response to the Paris recordings was mixed. Alun Morgan of the British *Jazz Journal* was positive, writing, "Don't pass up this LP just because the names are new; Hampton's discoveries shine powerfully here and I hope Vogue will let us have more Gryce before long."[17] An unidentified reviewer for the same magazine, however, came away with a rather different impression:

Clifford Brown and Gigi Gryce on Vogue LDE048 quite failed to please. That these two should have found themselves in a tough, jumping band like Hamp's is pretty strange. They provide further evidence of the current passion for overpraising promise rather than awaiting achievement. Chicagoan Jimmy Gourley plays some pleasant guitar, otherwise nothing emerges except the already familiar and ugly contemporary sounds. Prominent amongst these sounds is that of the trumpet. If that kind of playing is to be taken seriously it cannot be called jazz. If it is to be called jazz, then it cannot be taken seriously. Line up about fifty of these legit-conscious pip-squeakers and Basie's four-piece trumpet section could blast them out of any hall. Their metabolism must be damned low.[18]

The October 9 date was used to record two big band pieces: Gryce's "Quick Step" and "Bum's Rush" by Quincy Jones. Both are fairly conventional arrangements and the Jones piece is very much in a Woody Herman vein. Gryce's arrangement has the sound of something hastily put together. The tune itself, with its tricky bridge, would be revived later as "Steppin' Out" with the Jazz Lab group. On "Bum's Rush," Gryce solos rather tentatively in a weak outing but plays somewhat better on the take labeled two. The ensembles are raucous and out of tune, and the absence of Alan Dawson is felt here. Viale is overbearing in his kicks.

A version of Gryce's "Anne Marie" was recorded at the same session. This is a simple but pleasing 32-bar tune that apparently began life as a ballad entitled "I Need You So." No guitar can be heard on this, as opposed to an earlier rendition that has Jimmy Gourley on hand. Several breakdown performances exist and the commonly issued take ends clumsily. The date for the version issued in recent years is in dispute. All versions have Gryce playing strong choruses at a moderately fast tempo, not nearly as far behind the beat as in other examples from the period. It should be mentioned that these sessions finished well into the wee hours of the morning after the American participants had played grueling concerts at 6:30 and 9:30 at the Théatre de Paris.

When evaluating these Paris recordings as a whole, it must be borne in mind that they were done when the participants were both fatigued and under the stress of trying to evade detection by Hampton. Lack of rehearsal time was another problem contributing to the obvious flaws. That the sessions achieved the level that they did under the circumstances is testimony to the dedication and musicianship of Gryce, Jones, and their colleagues. In reflecting on the recordings some four and a half decades later, Jimmy Cleveland felt they were good, but were not ideal representations of the players at that time in their development, due to the odd conditions under which they were produced.

Some of the recordings are very tense because you don't know if someone is—they're gonna come over there—if Hamp and his henchmen were going to come over there and make bad trouble, you know. (JC)

They had to sight read everything, you know—zippo, just go on down and do it and hope that it's right, hope that it comes out. There was one thing I really didn't like about European recording—well, it's OK but to be recording under those conditions. OK so like you run something and just because the Swedish or the French or whatever people don't hear exactly what is supposed to really happen, to them it all sounds right to a certain extent. [Laughs] It all sounds right— and some of the players could be playing some of the stuff wrong. But they didn't want to spend the time to back the tape up or put on another tape and do it correctly. And having that thing over your head about: OK, I gotta sneak out then I gotta sneak back in. I wonder if the hotel guards are gonna be, you know… We got in without any problems because most of the hotels we stayed in were big, nice hotels, of course. But in some places they closed it up so they would make arrangements and I would always tell them again I want a sandwich when I come in. Please have it by my door. And I think that was one of the other ways that they found out that—hey, it's too many sandwiches being left here for that many people out of the band. And they can't all be partying. So what is all this? That's probably one of the ways this kind of leaked out that we were doing something and then they got wise after a period of time and asked did they have their horns. [Laughs] Of course we did. You know they couldn't say—well they could have but they didn't. Yeah, there was tension, a certain amount of tension. The way I felt about it, I found it kind of exciting you know, because I'm doing this because that's what I want to do and so far I've gotten away with it. And not because I'm trying to be sneaky or anything, it's just something I want to do. Why shouldn't I make records, you know? That was my attitude. We were going to and we didn't care what Hamp said! (JC)

But under the circumstances, I think that we did a wonderful job on it with the music being as complicated as some of it was. After doing two or three shows a day and then going in and playing jazz at night that late, sneaking out of a hotel. I mean just picture that. It's sort of ridiculous, you know. (JC)

At the October 10 and 11 sessions Gryce alone was featured on two ballads: Quincy Jones's "Evening in Paris" and his own "Hello." The former is a lovely, evocative minor theme, which Gryce plays expressively with a beautiful vibrato. He improvises on the eight-bar bridge only before returning to the A-section theme. The "Band Box" lick once again makes an appearance, this time in the coda, before a whole-tone flourish concludes the performance. Quincy Jones himself plays piano, though Cleveland remarked that "I could very easily understand that he was not a Hank Jones [Laughs]." (JC)

With the title in mind, the recurring two-note motif of "Hello" immediately suggests a lyric, but none has ever been discovered. With the A sections in E-flat major and the bridge moving from

E-flat minor to its relative major of G-flat, the tune is a textbook example of traditional song form, and the melody is full of colorful upper intervals (9ths, 11ths, 13ths). Gryce plays the tune with a warm vibrato and takes a solo of just over half a chorus in a double-time feel. During the bridge and final A section he reprises the theme and at times casts a bluesy sound across the chords before reaching with a strained, yearning tone up toward the top of the saxophone's range, hitting a high concert G-natural during the last A section before concluding with a short flourish. Though functional, the three-horn accompaniment is basic and might well have been sketched in haste.

The release of "No Start, No End" was only made to present one more opportunity to hear Clifford Brown's genius, and originally all that was available was a four-minute excerpt of just his solo. Subsequently, the entire take (a rehearsal for "Chez Moi," a pop tune recorded earlier that same year by Django Reinhardt) which is nearly twelve minutes long, was issued, giving a more complete view of the proceedings (including some background conversation)—though there is still neither start nor end. It opens in the middle of Gryce's solo, fades during Clifford Solomon's, and gives a good representation of a jam session setting where the musicians are not constrained in terms of choruses. Brown and Cleveland each take six here, while on the master take of "Chez Moi" each is limited to two. There, Gryce's solo is full of energy and it could be that he also wrote the arrangement of the melody of this tune, though it is very simplistic compared to his other work.

At the October 11 date, Clifford Brown was afforded a chance to demonstrate his writing talents with a tune that Anthony Ortega entitled "All Weird." Three takes of this ambitious composition were released, one being a much slower, incomplete version consisting of only Brown's solo during what appears to be a rehearsal.

The two complete takes sound very tentative, as if the tune had not been mastered. Of all the soloists, Brown seems the most at ease. It is unfortunate that this engaging piece was a casualty of the rushed and tense circumstances under which it was recorded, and that it was never revisited.

The recordings in which Gryce participated were reported on in *Jazz Hot* October 1953 as follows:

Many recording sessions were taped during the short visit of Lionel Hampton. They allow us to hear the excellent soloists: Gigi Gryce, Clifford Brown, and [Jimmy] Cleveland, whose solos were extremely rare during concerts.[19]

These were featured on R.T.F. radio on November 22 and again on December 9.

The future music, television and movie producer Louis-Victor Mialy spent a good deal of time with members of the Hampton band during their trip to North Africa. His recollections give a wonderful personal view of their visit.

I met Gigi in Algiers, Algeria, probably during the last two weeks of October in 1953. He was at the time traveling with the Lionel Hampton Orchestra and the band gave four concerts in Algiers—the Sallebordes [theater] and the Majestic Theater—and two at the Empire Cinema in Oran, which is about 350 miles west of Algiers. I stayed with them, I stayed with some of the musicians like Gigi and Clifford Brown and so forth during the eight days, and I went with them also for a two-day trip to Oran when they performed two concerts. In Algiers, they were staying at Hotel Aletti which is downtown, beautiful hotel and one of the best of Algiers, overlooking the harbor and the bay of Algiers. Gigi was sharing his hotel room with Clifford Brown.

At that time, Algiers was the second largest city of France, when the French were there. Right after Paris, Algiers was the city, was fantastic, was a beautiful city, clean, well organized, and the musicians loved the city. You know, there was no segregation or anything like that. Like I said, right after Paris it was probably the most exciting city of France. And they stayed there—the band was supposed to play only two concerts but by public demand they stayed the whole week. So I spent much time with them, as much as I could. You know, I had a very bad schedule with IBM, but I managed to go to their hotel as soon as I was free, during my free time and stayed with them late at night. This means that I had to get up early in the morning.

In Algiers, what did we do? Mostly I was spending my time with Clifford Brown because I heard about him. Everybody—I had calls from Paris where they heard him and they recorded him and also my good friend from Vogue Records, Charles Delaunay, told me that this was a great trumpet player.

Early in the afternoon when I could manage, I used to go to the hotel, their hotel room that Gigi shared with Clifford Brown. One day, I brought them some cooked quail. I had somebody from my family who cooked quail and they never had quail before. So, right there, in the hotel room, on the bed, they ate the quails and they loved it! As a matter of fact, you will see in the letter that he sent me that he said: "Those birds that you brought to the hotel were really good." [Laughs]

OK, also what I used to bring to their hotel room was my portable phonograph and a bunch of LPs, most of them were 10 inches. He was with Clifford Brown, they were, the two of them, laying on the bed and the phonograph was on the little table next to one of the beds, and they were listening intensely to the music, you know, my records. They were playing over and over again a Blue Note recording of Miles Davis with J.J. Johnson, Oscar Pettiford, Jackie McLean, the title was "Dear Old Stockholm," and, at the time, he wanted to put the needle back to the beginning of the record and he scratched my copy by accident. So Gigi said, "Oh, I'm sorry, Lou" [Laughs]. I still have this record, scratched by Gigi Gryce. (LM)

Apart from visiting them in their hotel rooms, Mialy was able to spend time sightseeing with Gryce and others during their stay in Algiers.

We used to take strolls on a beautiful street of Algiers and there are parks and Art Farmer took pictures and so forth. They really enjoyed their stay there. The weather for October was *wonderful*, sunshine all the time, no rain. The city was alive with restaurants. It was nice to live in Algiers at that time. Anyway, another thing I noticed besides their poor clothes and no cameras and things like that, they didn't have any money. So, I took Clifford Brown and Gigi Gryce, I took them to several French restaurants. And for the first time, they had couscous. Yeah, they loved it! They were coming for the first time to Africa, most of them. My goodness, The Casbah! Algiers, the mystery of all this! It was the food, the smell, the sky, the color, the people, the way they dressed. So they were excited.

He [Gigi] was, like most of the musicians in the band, his clothes were poor and shabby, and you could see that the musicians were not paid very much in the band. Two musicians were well dressed, had nice clothes—Art Farmer and Quincy Jones—but most of the musicians had poor clothes. In spite of their personality, you could see that he [Hampton] never lent them money and the clothes he was wearing were old. He [Gigi] had a beret that he bought, probably in Paris, and he kept that beret [on] under the sun all the time, you know. (LM)

Even with his limited finances, Gryce continued to pursue his interest in classical music while in Europe and purchased many scores to study. He was proud of his acquisitions and showed them to Mialy.

So anyway, in his suitcase, when I was in the room, the suitcases most of the time were open on the bed, and Clifford Brown's suitcase had all shoes, nice shoes [Laughs]. The suitcase of Gigi Gryce was full with musical scores. And he used to go through them and show them to me and there was no Beethoven, no Mozart, no Bach. He needed to talk about this because to him, it was like gold, you know. But, to my surprise, those scores, like I say, were not from the three B's: Brahms, Bach, or Beethoven, but they were from important Baroque composers, you know, chamber music type like Francois Couperin,

1113 Washington avenue
Apartment 4
Bronx 57 New York

Dear Lou,

I spoke to Quincy Jones by telephone and he gave to me your address in Alger.

Congratulations to you for getting married. I was very sad to hear about your illness, I hope you are very healthy and strong now.

Please write to me at once and tell me how the recordings are being accepted by the jazz fans (lovers) in Africa.

I would like to tour Europe with an orchestra sometimes in the future. Do you think it can be arranged?

What size orchestra is best for the tour? Please write to me all possible information and also tell me much about the records, I have not heard any of the records and they are not sold as yet in America.

I wish for you and your wife much success. I often think about our wonderful friendship in Africa and the food (bird) we ate in my hotel room.

I hope to received a letter from you soon because I must find another apartment before 9, April

Best of Luck and blessings

Your Friend
Gigi Gryce

Letter from Gryce to Louis-Victor Mialy. 1954 (courtesy Mr. Mialy)

Handel, Scarlatti, Corelli, and the string quartet of Boccherini. Well, the Boccherini Quartet at the time was seldom performed. And I was surprised because I was at the Conservatory and we used to talk about Boccherini. Two musicians we would talk about that were not given the proper exposure—one was Boccherini and in the modern, Mahler. He bought them in Paris. He didn't buy them in Italy because he didn't go to Italy at that time. (LM)

Mialy remembered attending concerts in Algiers and heard Gryce's music played by the Hampton orchestra.

And they played one of his compositions, I can't remember when. Lionel Hampton, you know, gave them an opportunity, I think it was a quintet or a sextet, and he played one of his compositions, which title I can't remember. I know Hampton said Gigi Gryce composition. They would play this during the concert, probably the second part. (LM)

But most of this concert I was backstage with them. As a matter of fact, they used to open, Quincy Jones used to open a door backstage so I could get in. I was a young man, you know, and not having a lot of money so he was getting me inside the hall, and I was staying backstage, and watched them from there. And Lionel Hampton, before every concert, used to chew them out. You know, they were all very silent, very quiet and he would give them a lecture, a very violent lecture. I don't know, he had some ideas that they recorded in Paris without his permission and he knew that something was going on. But, like I told you previously, there was a malaise in the band. OK, but going back to Gigi playing, I think he was influenced by Jackie McLean and also by Lee Konitz. He was not exactly blowing the notes, he was *sliding* them. He was like gliding the notes. What a great composer! He was a fine composer. You could feel that this guy was living for music. (LM)

There were also after-hours jam sessions in Algiers with local musicians:

Now, in this hotel there was jam session at night, at the Aletti Hotel, in the lobby and, of course, with Gigi Gryce, Art Farmer, and

Clifford Brown doing duets and some jazz men from Algiers, Guy Combes on piano and Lucky Starway on tenor, some very good jazz men from Algiers, French musicians. (LM)

In Algiers Mialy was a witness to a disheartening episode of violence involving Clifford Brown, which fortunately did not end in tragedy, but which was the culmination of the tensions within Hampton's band:

One of the turning points, one of the highlights of the stay of Lionel Hampton in Algiers was a terrible street fight with razors between Clifford Brown and the road manager of Hampton [George Hart].

One afternoon, I was going, early afternoon, I was rushing to the hotel, must have been maybe 2 PM or something like that, and I see in the street adjacent to the hotel all the musicians. You could see these black guys, you know, there was screaming and everything and here I go and Clifford Brown is on his ass—on the floor and people are screaming and I don't know, personally, what's going on but Quincy Jones said, "Hey Lou! Help! Help!" So, we take Clifford Brown to Quincy Jones's room and Clifford Brown had a fight with (because I told you about that malaise) the Hampton people, dedicated to Hampton, they didn't like to see those new, modern guys getting all the glamour and success and things like that. So there was a great malaise on the band. And, I was told after, because when I arrived, I didn't see the beginning of the fight but I saw the end of it, when I was told that the guy insulted Clifford Brown and provoked him and they went outside and there was a razor out of his pocket, you know, the guy, the road manager, a tall guy and Clifford Brown fought. But he [Clifford Brown] had previously a car accident on his shoulder and in the fight, he pulled out something and something happened to his shoulder.

So, we took Clifford Brown—he was in pain, had tears in his eyes, he was screaming in pain. It was terrible. And they asked me to call a doctor. So, I pick up the phone and I ask for a doctor. It took forty-five minutes before the doctor came. In the meantime, what Quincy was doing, he took Clifford Brown's arm and slowly started moving it, you know, like going around, circles, kind of and put back the shoulder, OK? He put back the shoulder, the bone…

And the same night, Clifford Brown was blowing trumpet like never before. But anyway, they were all in the room. That was like twenty people in that small hotel room and they were looking, they didn't know what was going on or what was going to happen because this was the summit, the accumulation of the tensions, the fight within the band. And I remember the face of Gigi Gryce and Art Farmer and Jimmy Cleveland. They were looking at what was going on, you know, when Quincy Jones was trying to put back the shoulder together, they were totally defeated. They couldn't talk. Art Farmer could confirm all this, you know. He was very, very pale. It's funny but they never talk about that thing anymore. I produced a record with Art Farmer in New York about fifteen years ago and I said, "Do you remember that fight, Art?" and he said, "Oh yes, I did." He [Farmer] looked terrible. He looked terrible. (LM)

That evening Brown played as if nothing had happened, but the incident surely widened the gap between the young and old players beyond hope of reconciliation.

Back in Paris, Henri Renaud recorded a complete album of Gryce's compositions on November 2, demonstrating the high esteem in which the American was held during his European visit. Renaud has stated that the inspiration for his group with tenor saxophonist Bobby Jaspar was the Stan Getz quartet with Al Haig, and the supervising presence of Gryce, whose compositions "Mosquito Knees" and "Eleanor" had been recorded by Getz with Haig a few years earlier, must have lent authority to the proceedings. Some of the selections were older, established works ("Eleanor," "Capri," "Shabozz," "Up in Quincy's Room") from the Getz, J.J. Johnson, McGhee, and Farmer dates, but Gryce also composed "Au Tabou" (later retitled "Stupendous-Lee" in dedication to his wife, Eleanor

"Lee" Sears), "Expansion," and possibly also "Consultation" and "Simplicity" expressly for this session. All four make their debuts at this date and "Expansion" and "Consultation" were never subsequently recorded by Gryce. The album, which features perhaps the best-rehearsed and least-harried performances of all the European dates, was icing on the cake for the critics and fans following Gryce's blossoming career. And it serves as important historical documentation that Gryce's activity in Paris outside of the Hampton band was not limited to the Vogue sessions on which he performed. Raymond Horrick's review was glowing:

> The tunes themselves are excellent and those already familiar with Gigi's work will know what to expect. "Capri" is beautiful, "Eleanor" (a blues) logical and swinging, "Au Tabou" has an extremely attractive theme, the remaining five equally good and cram full of interest.

> For many of us the most important jazz event of late has been the emergence of Gryce as a composer and arranger. This LP gives more than an insight into their talents to say nothing of the excellent musicianship displayed by Henri's group.[20]

In early November there were further sessions in Stockholm in which Gryce did not participate but did feature members of the Hampton orchestra (Alan Dawson on November 6, and Dawson, Art Farmer, Jimmy Cleveland, and Quincy Jones on November 10). Both dates included the baritone saxophonist Lars Gullin, who would record "Yvette," one of Gryce's earliest compositions, on December 1 in Helsinki, after the Hampton band had returned to America, as part of a group led by drummer Jack Norén.

The November 28 *Melody Maker* reported:

> Sixteen members of the Lionel Hampton Band spent eight hours in or over Britain on Tuesday last. They were passing through London and Glasgow on their flight from Paris to New York at the conclusion of their European tour.

Apart from Hampton himself, the whole band, including singer Sonny Parker, was at London Airport, where MM staffmen greeted them.

Hampton and his wife are returning to America by sea.[21]

The "Tuesday last" mentioned would seem to be November 24, 1953. The band would then have arrived back in the USA on November 25, 1953. Lionel and Gladys Hampton did not leave until December 4. During these last days in Paris, Hampton recorded for Barclay Records on both November 30 and December 3, mostly in the company of traditional-jazz clarinetist Mezz Mezzrow.

In spite of the apparent success of the "triumphant" tour with its great publicity and acclaim, the sidemen were not compensated by Hampton upon their return to the United States.

We got shafted with the money again. He would always do that. He would always find some way to not pay your salary. He'd take money from you. I think what happened on that, we filed charges, some of us filed charges, the ones that were not going to go back with that band. I stayed in New York.[22]

Cleveland soon became recognized as one of the top jazz trombonists in New York and frequently crossed paths with Gryce throughout the 1950s.

The sidemen were not the only ones with thoughts of legal action. The following article from *Melody Maker* presents Hampton's side of the story.

When Lionel and his wife stepped off the *Liberté* on December 10 (the bandsmen had returned two weeks earlier by plane), he told this reporter [Leonard Feather] that he would file charges with the AFM against altoist Gigi Gryce and seven other Hamptonians for recording in Paris, and using arrangements from the Hampton library, without his permission.

Lionel is furious, he says, since it was expressly understood that none of the sidemen would do any outside work during the European tour without his consent.

He is even angrier because, he claims, the men received only $12.50, where he normally pays them four times that amount for a record session.

All the offenders are being dropped from the band, which means a wholesale personnel shift before Hamp reorganizes next week. He is seeking modern jazzmen and hopes to get Horace Silver and Art Blakey, among others.[23]

Of the musicians who made the trip to Europe, Walter Williams, George Cooper, Al Hayse, Oscar Estelle, Billy Mackel, and Curley Hamner—the "old-timers"—remained with the Hampton orchestra. Apparently undeterred by the tribulations of the 1953 tour, Hampton continued to hire young bebop musicians to fill the ranks of his band, which played in Philadelphia's Rendezvous Room just before the new year. Hampton never managed to hire Silver and Blakey, but in late 1953 a contingent of Gryce's old Boston colleagues joined Hampton: Herb Pomeroy, Dick Twardzik, and "Floogie" Williams. Alan Dawson went back to Boston and rejoined the Sabby Lewis band. Gryce himself maintained his union membership in the Boston Musicians' Association until mid-September 1954, possibly a sign that he was hedging his bets about making it in New York.

Hampton's argument that he paid musicians more for record sessions most likely held little water with the younger players since no official Hampton recordings were made in the entire year of 1952, and many of Hampton's record dates frequently used all-star personnel in small-group configurations (the last big band recording was made in October 1951 and the next would not be until July 1954). Hampton did use band members for the recordings he did in Paris, but younger musicians such as Gryce, Farmer, Brown, Jones, Ortega, and Dawson were not invited to participate. Since these musicians were being featured neither in concerts nor in recordings, it should have been expected that they would take advantage of every opportunity. Later, in his autobiography, Lionel Hampton admitted as much:

> Now, the press says I was annoyed when I found out about it later on, and maybe I was at the time (I know Gladys must have been). After all, we were paying for their travel and hotel rooms and everything. But looking back, I realize that they were just trying to get over, make a name for themselves, just like I did when I was playing with Benny Goodman and making all those small-band sides. I don't harbor any grudges about it.[24]

The Hampton musicians were fortunate to experience foreign travel and Quincy Jones was appreciative of this chance. "Over here [in America], we had the racial hassles and the sociological trips, but over there it was really free by comparison. It was great to get that positive input at 19 years old."[25] As Alan Dawson put it, "It was a very successful tour. We worked like mad and made very little money, but I did get to see Europe and made some valuable contacts."[26] Over the next two decades a number of American jazz musicians left the United States in search of better conditions.

Notes

1. Art Farmer, interviewed by Tyrone Ward, 1987.
2. Horricks, Raymond, *Quincy Jones*, Hippocrene Books, New York, 1985, p. 19.
3. Benny Golson, quoted by Gene Lees in *Gene Lees Jazzletter*, Vol. 10 No. 6, June 1991, p. 3.
4. Morgan, Alun, "The Month's Records," *Jazz Journal*, March 1954, p. 9.

5. Art Farmer, interviewed by Tyrone Ward, 1987.

6. Dawson, Alan, interviewed by Stu Vandermark in *Cadence*, December 1983, p. 9.

7. Vermont, Jackie, "Lionel Hampton au Palais de Chaillot," *Jazz Hot*, October 1953, pp. 16–18.

8. *Bulletin du Hot Club de France*, October 1953, pp. 24–25 (translation by M. Fitzgerald).

9. Henri Renaud, quoted by Jerome Cotillon in notes to "Bobby Jaspar/ Henri Renaud" Vogue CD 74321 40937-2 (translation by Victoria Rummler).

10. Fleiss, Marcel and N. Remy, *Jazz Hot*, November 1953, p. 17.

11. Horricks, Raymond, "The Search for Orchestral Progression," in *Jazzbook*, p. 32.

12. Horricks, Raymond, "The Month's Records," *Jazz Journal*, September 1954, p. 18.

13. Art Farmer, quoted by Leonard Feather in "Blindfold Test," *Down Beat*, January 28, 1965, p. 30.

14. De Radzitsky, Carlos, "Lionel Hampton in Brussels," *Jazz Hot*, October 1953, pp. 36–37.

15. Art Farmer, interviewed by Tyrone Ward, 1987.

16. Berendt, Joachim E., "Hamp-Session in Baden-Baden," *Jazz Podium*, November 1953, pp. 3–4 (translation by M. Fitzgerald).

17. Morgan, Alun, "The Month's Records," *Jazz Journal*, March 1954, p. 11.

18. "Contemporary Clichés and Modern Music," *Jazz Journal*, June 1954, p. 13.

19. *Jazz Hot*, October 1953, p. 21 (translation by M. Fitzgerald).

20. Horricks, Raymond, "The Month's Records," *Jazz Journal*, December 1954, p. 29.

21. Nevard, Mike, *Melody Maker*, November 28, 1953, p. 1.

22. Jimmy Cleveland, interviewed by Bob Rusch in *Cadence*, January 1991, p.18.

23. Feather, Leonard, *Melody Maker*, December 19, 1953, p. 12.

24. Hampton, Lionel with James Haskins, *Hamp: An Autobiography*, 1989, Warner Books, New York, p. 100.

25. Quincy Jones, quoted by Lee Underwood in "Q Lives," *Down Beat*, October 23, 1975, p. 14.

26. Alan Dawson, quoted by Dan Morgenstern in "The Poll Winner as Teacher," *Down Beat*, September 22, 1966, pp. 28–29.

laying the foundation

WHEN GRYCE AND HIS HAMPTON COLLEAGUES returned from Europe, the New York jazz scene was poised for innovation. These young and gifted artists seemed destined to lead the charge as bebop evolved through the cool jazz of the early 1950s into what would become known as the hard bop era. As the dust of the bebop revolution settled, hard bop emerged as a more groove-oriented, swinging style that drew upon influences with broader appeal such as the blues, gospel music, and the structured arrangements of the big bands. It should not be assumed, however, that this change was mainly commercially motivated. In fact, the new style allowed all of the freedom of bebop, but its presentation was more cohesive and less frantic.

One of the more prescient of jazz writers, Nat Hentoff, noted early on the intelligent and serious nature of Gryce and company and suggested the important role they would play in defining the music of the next decade:

Fortunately, there are more and more young jazzmen who have seen the frightening deterioration of once promising talents because of dope, and these younger men will have nothing to do with it. All of which brings me to a group of such men who have not been written up in *Time* magazine, who are not being glamorized as members of any "school," but who are increasingly well known and respected in Europe though still almost unknown in this country.

The easy way out would be to call them members of a new eastern school of jazz, since they often work in the east together and have discussed seriously among themselves the future of jazz and their place in it. Not being a labelist, however, I can best tell you the individual names of some: Quincy Jones, Clifford Brown, Gigi Gryce, Art Farmer, and the perhaps somewhat more familiar Lou Donaldson, Horace Silver, and Percy Heath.

These musicians are building their own way, and in the process are helping build a better prospect for jazz.[1]

But one of the first orders of business which Gryce attended to after his return involved a very important personal matter. After meeting the Hampton band at their stopover in Britain, Mike Nevard of *Melody Maker* reported, "I offered Gigi a cigarette; found he didn't smoke or drink, but was contemplating marriage."[2] A few weeks later, on December 20, 1953, Gryce married Eleanor Sears. It was trumpeter Idrees Sulieman who introduced Gigi and Eleanor in early 1953. Sulieman was seeing Eleanor's older sister Betty at the time. Eleanor did not normally attend jazz performances, but made an exception.

I never went to anything except that my sister, one day, said, "Come go with us," and that's when I met Gigi and Idrees and we became an item! But, I never went to clubs or gigs or anything prior to that. (EG2)

While she went by the name of Eleanor Gryce, her maiden name lived on. "Lee Sears" was the *nom de plume* used by Gryce for several of his compositions: "Batland," "Exhibit A," "Transfiguration," "Wolf Talk," and "Wake Up." Years later, she explained.

Lee Sears was an official of Melotone or Totem [Gryce's two publishing companies]. I had a stamp that I signed [used]. I was the "Lee
Sears"! And long after we had separated... I had an aunt and uncle
that lived in Connecticut...and I established their address as Lee
Sears's address, residence, and I used to get, periodically, a check
from BMI for tunes that he wrote under the name of "Lee Sears."
(EG1)

The wedding of Gigi and Eleanor was a modest affair, taking
place in a mosque in Brooklyn. Only Eleanor's sister and brother-
in-law and a Muslim friend of Gryce's attended the ceremony and
luncheon that followed. That very night, Gryce was off to an out-
of-town gig.

A native New Yorker, Eleanor was employed as an infant and
child nurse at the time she first met Gryce. Because of the time
demands this career imposed, she instead secured a job working
in data entry with the Social Security Administration soon after
the wedding—a position she held until becoming pregnant with
the couple's first child in 1957—which allowed her more time at
home. Their first residence was a shared apartment in the Bronx,
but they soon moved to a place of their own on the west side of
Manhattan at 411 West 52nd Street. It was an area populated by
many musicians and a hub of musical activity.

Curiously enough, Gryce's first recording after returning from
Europe was another meeting with Henri Renaud. The French pianist was in New York for three months, and during this time made
a number of recordings for the Vogue label with all-star American groups. Gryce participated in one of these on February 28,
1954, playing section baritone saxophone in a front line that included trumpeter Jerry Lloyd, tenor saxophonist Al Cohn, and
trombonist J.J. Johnson. His playing is solid, but he is not featured
as an improvising soloist on any of the four tracks.

Very soon after this, Gryce formed a quintet with his former Hampton bandmate, trumpeter Art Farmer. Born in Council Bluffs, Iowa, Farmer (1928–1999) was raised in Phoenix, Arizona and cut his musical teeth in the active Los Angeles scene of the late 1940s. Before his Hampton experience, he had gained some notoriety through recordings under the leadership of tenor saxophone legend Wardell Gray in 1952 for the Prestige label, among which was his own blues, "Farmer's Market."

The quintet's first engagement was at the Tijuana Club in Baltimore in late March of 1954. Compositions performed there were later used for the Prestige record dates resulting in the album *When Farmer Met Gryce*. The pairing was a mutually beneficial one and the two shared similar approaches, complementing each other beautifully and emphasizing structure and lyricism in their solo efforts. Farmer was perhaps the most compatible front-line partner Gryce would ever have. On a practical level, Farmer benefited from their association in that he composed only rarely and was always in need of new material. Gryce, on the other hand, felt that a day in which he did not compose a song was a day wasted.

You know Farmer, he knew he needed help. Art wanted to be a leader and he was always getting work. Because, you know, people liked him and they came to see him. But he knew his limitations for material. And that's why he linked up with Gigi, you know, to get the material. (RW)

What had happened was that I had already gotten this contract with

Prestige but, knowing Gigi, and really admiring him, and respecting him, and knowing what he could do, and we had played a couple of gigs together so I said, "Well, why don't we organize the group and call it the Art Farmer–Gigi Gryce Quintet?" And that's the way it happened. So, we made some recordings for Prestige under that name.

We played live gigs, like in Birdland. I don't remember, yes, I think we did play a week there, and we played a lot of Monday nights. Monday night was the off night. And we played in Baltimore and, I think, we played in Boston. We were supposed to go to Chicago to play [at the Bee Hive] but, something happened and Gigi didn't make that. We worked in a place called "Tony's" [in Brooklyn] that's where he got [the name for] this tune, "A Night at Tony's." We worked around this area [New York City] mostly. (AF)

The Farmer–Gryce partnership made its first date for Prestige Records on May 19, recording four selections that were originally released as a 10-inch album, *Art Farmer Quintet*. For these tracks, the two were supported by the excellent house rhythm section of pianist Horace Silver, bassist Percy Heath, and drummer Kenny Clarke. Perhaps due to Prestige's penchant for quickly prepared and recorded sessions, the compositions are fairly conventional and the arrangements simple, allowing this particular aggregation to do what it does best: the rhythm section swings irresistibly, providing a buoyant lift that inspires the soloists. "A Night at Tony's" is an appealing line based on the chord sequence of Charlie Parker's classic "Yardbird Suite" and taken at a medium-up tempo. The title refers to a rather special 1954 encounter with four be-bop giants:

"A Night at Tony's" dates back to a gig played by Gigi a few years ago at a club by that name in Brooklyn, in the company of the four M's—Miles, Max, Mingus, and Monk. "I sat at the piano during intermission and picked out this melody. At first I was going to call it "The Four M's."[3]

The remaining three were recorded in Paris by various aggrega-
tions—"Blue Concept," "Deltitnu," and the very lyrical "Stupendous-Lee," recorded by the Henri Renaud Quintet in 1953 as "Au
Tabou." Only the last tune is based on an original harmonic structure.

Bob Weinstock reflected on how this rhythm section came together and how a Prestige recording session usually proceeded:

I used to interject my own tastes a lot because I was very close to the
music. I was always listening to records, mine and otherwise, and I
just knew that Percy Heath was the greatest at that time until he went
away to the MJQ. Kenny Clarke was a pleasure to work with but then
he went away to Paris. And Horace, then he started to work with his
group finally. I mean those guys worked well together and the thing is
I tried—whenever I had a group put together, I'd always want people
that were like good personalities. Like Horace and Percy and Klook,
they just were happy people and they were an asset to a recording.
And it was pleasure to work with them and it was like a team effort,
you know everybody cared. And that's why I used them a lot on
Miles's things and everything. But unfortunately, as I say, they went
away, all three of them.

Prestige never had rehearsals that I knew of. Blue Note always had
rehearsals and Prestige never had unless the musicians did it on their
own. Yeah, in fact a lot of times they didn't even run them [the
charts] down. They'd just play it. We'd record it and go on to the next
one. That was my style of recording. I'd say ready, OK, and then—
see there was one big asset we had was Rudy Van Gelder. Because
Rudy loved jazz, he still loves jazz. And he goes back like I do to the
swing era and before and once I'd say who's coming, he knew where
to put the microphones before they even got there. So they could
come and unpack and start to record immediately. So they'd just
come in and I'd say, "OK, what do you want to do?" And they'd play
it and I'd say, "How was it? You like it?" and they'd say, "Yeah,
good—next." Ninety percent of the time we didn't even listen to

playbacks. Don't forget, these were world-class players. They knew when they were good or not. (RW)

Art Farmer appreciated the freedom that Weinstock offered and said, "We did what we wanted to do. We would have chosen the material and had at least a couple of rehearsals before we got into the recording studio."[4]

The four tracks recorded at this session are notable for the long lines that the soloists weave, abetted by the strength and coherence of the rhythm section. Both "Blue Concept" and "Deltitnu" are taken at faster tempi and performed with much more confidence, energy, and assuredness than the versions recorded in Paris. Gryce cleverly inserts a reference to "Ol' Man River" at the beginning of his third chorus on the fast-paced "Deltitnu." (Themes from Jerome Kern's *Show Boat* seem to have been particular favorites of Gryce's, possibly due to the influence of the film version released in 1951.) When Gryce and Farmer exchange fours, it is as if one person were playing two instruments, their conceptions are so alike. Horace Silver's comping (accompaniment) is superlative and the recording demonstrates perfectly how he could light a fire under a soloist.

On the very next day, Art Blakey recorded seven Gryce compositions ("Minority," "Salute to Birdland," "Eleanor," "Futurity," "Simplicity," "Strictly Romantic," and "Hello") on a date for EmArcy Records which featured a front line of Gryce and trumpeter Joe Gordon, and a rhythm section of pianist Walter Bishop, Jr., bassist Bernie Griggs, and Blakey. On one track, "Futurity," this Boston-heavy group was joined by an unnamed conga player, possibly Sabu Martinez, who had worked with a similar aggregation at club engagements. The one selection not written by Gryce was Horace Silver's "Mayreh," a variation on "All God's Children

Got Rhythm." It is doubly remarkable—that a new composer on the jazz scene would be given such extensive space and that every single one of these compositions had been previously recorded.

When compared to the recordings of those pieces done earlier in Paris, there is a striking difference in the rhythm section concept. The time settles in much more comfortably and pieces such as "Minority" do not sound tentative at all. This relatively early document of Blakey as a leader shows him establishing the approach that would make him a top jazz artist for the next thirty-five years. Solos are short, however, limited by the 10-inch LP format, and the routines are fairly unsophisticated, not typical of the direction that Gryce would take over the next few years. In "Salute to Birdland," Gryce does present a melodic idea that would reappear in his later improvisations.

Excerpt from Gryce's solo on "Salute to Birdland"

Around this time, Gryce prepared the publication of two music folios of his works. Titled *Modern Sounds* vol. 1 and 2, they were issued by the B. F. Wood Company of Boston in 1955. Several compositions ("Futurity," "Simplicity," "Baby," "Expansion," Quick Step," "Deltitnu," "Strictly Romantic," Eleanor," and "Consultation") were taken from the various recordings by Getz, McGhee, and Blakey, as well as from the Paris sessions. Some never-recorded tunes ("Trolly Tracks," "Since You've Come To Me," "Lover's Mood," "Wishing," and "Mood in Blue") were also included.[5] The folios were advertised as "The Music of Tomorrow—Today!" and Gryce's introduction offers some insight into his orientation and goals as a jazz composer at this point in his career:

Like all art forms that remain alive, jazz has evolved considerably during this swift half-century. The original compositions contained in this volume represent several aspects of what is generally termed "modern jazz"—a way of creating in the jazz idiom that has its roots in the traditional jazz language but which incorporates all of the advances in jazz theory and practice that have been made in the past ten years.

"Modern Jazz," then, is a continuation of and an extension of the older forms of Jazz. New chord patterns are formed by altering the basic chords. New melodic structures take shape from the sounds of those altered chords and from the subtle rhythmic variations that are also part of the "modern jazz" approach.

For several years, modern jazz musicians have utilized their transforming skills on "standard" compositions but there has been an increasing need for new works that are more immediately in the modern jazz context. The compositions presented here are an attempt to fill part of that need. The melodic, rhythmic and harmonic profiles of these songs come from within this writer's experience—an experience gained by many years of writing for and playing in modern jazz units. It is my hope that they may become "Modern Jazz Standards."[6]

Each composition was presented as a piano arrangement with separate transpositions of the melody line and chord symbols for both B-flat and E-flat instruments. Oddly, better-known pieces such as "Hymn to the Orient" were not included, although evidence suggests that "Salute to the Band Box" was considered.

The biographical section, which includes a photograph of a nattily attired Gryce writing music, perpetuates the Fulbright story, stating: "After having received a degree in musical composition Gryce was awarded a State Department Fulbright Scholarship to study in Paris. His studies were interrupted by illness and Gryce returned to his home in Hartford, Connecticut." It must be assumed that Gryce himself was responsible for providing this information.

At a June 1954 session, Art Farmer revisited the septet instrumentation that had first introduced him to Gryce the year before. For this date, again for Prestige, the alto saxophonist's role was only as composer/arranger. He brought a new arrangement of "Wildwood," one of his earliest compositions written when he was in Boston, and a recent Afro-Cuban number, "Tijuana," named for the club in Baltimore where he and the trumpeter worked with their quintet. The new piece, in C minor (one of Gryce's favorite keys), uses strong ostinato-like figures behind the entirety of Farmer's solo, breaking the mood with an interlude sequence of descending seventh chords with raised ninths, strongly reminiscent of Duke Ellington, before returning to the melody.

Jimmy Cleveland, who participated in both of the septet sessions, recalled Gryce and his role in the New York scene at that time:

I got to see Gigi, oh, quite often. I would see Gigi two or three times a week you know, like on the scene, different clubs and stuff. We worked a lot of little gigs and stuff around New York. Well, some places that I worked with Gigi were just going out and playing, you know, just to experiment, kind of. We use to go down to Café Bohemia. We would go down there and that was one of the hangouts. Yeah, mid-fifties. There was another place over on the east side but I can't think of the name of that little place. It didn't last too long just like most clubs. They open then all of a sudden they're gone. And we would go up to Harlem—there was a place—breakfast type jam session, some place up there that had good food and stuff for breakfast, you know. You'd stay there playing until the wee hours of the morning. We'd be up there some mornings.

Gigi, he was sometimes on the night scene. He was kind of a loner. He was kind of—he was just a wonderful person, kind of laid-back and easygoing. I thought he should have been a little more aggressive. But everyone can't be the aggressor. His music spoke for him, man. I mean his music was just, it was just really kickin'. You know the stuff that he would put down was just so right on. And he scared a lot of people with his music. (JC)

On October 30, 1954, Gryce had an opportunity to share the bill with his hero and primary influence, Charlie Parker:

Charlie Parker, although still not completely recovered, showed up at a concert at Town Hall with Sonny Rollins, Thelonious Monk, Art Farmer, Horace Silver, Jimmy Raney, Gigi Gryce, and Wynton Kelly. The concert was organized by the Record Collector's Shop in the person of Rob Reisner, "professor of jazz" at Brooklyn College and assistant of Marshall Stearns.[7]

During this period, Parker was a frequent visitor to the Gryce home and would benefit in many ways from the relationship. Eleanor Gryce remembered her husband's admiration of Bird.

Parker was very close to Gigi in that—I don't know why, but oftentimes Charlie didn't have his horn, not horn, they called it his "axe." So, he would borrow Gigi's. So, when Gigi lent it willingly, he went to work with Parker because he cherished his instrument and he used it. I know Gigi and Charlie were very close and Gigi always spoke very warmly and sympathetically about Charlie. (EG2)

Of course, the usual reason that Parker was without his saxophone was because he had pawned it for drug money. Gryce reported that "Bird used to borrow my horn. I always got it back. After a job, he would slip me some money, saying, 'Here's a taste, man. I'm sorry it's not more.' "[8] Producer Don Schlitten recalled another example of Gryce's relationship with Parker:

Well, I did see him once at the Open Door when Bird was playing. The Open Door didn't have a stage. It was just like a restaurant, really, and in the back of the restaurant was a piano and they had drums set up so when the cats played they were on the same level as you were. And there was no stage, no curtain, there was nothing like that. And Bird had gotten too high and he pulled a chair out in the middle of the floor, sat down and passed out. And everybody was screaming, "Where's Bird? Bird play!" Bird was working with Brew Moore and Brew Moore kept saying, "Oh, fuck him, fuck him," while walking around the chair. And Gigi was running around with a wet towel trying to wake Bird up. And eventually Bird got up and played. But Gigi was very, very nervous about it and he was like a mother hen trying to take care of her baby. (DSch)

On March 7, 1955, Gryce was involved with one of the very first play-along records of the type that have now become ubiquitous learning tools for students of jazz. The recordings were the first to be issued on the newly established Signal label, and introduced the "Jazz Laboratory" name that Gryce would later appropriate for his own groups. Under the supervision of Signal co-founder Jules Colomby, Gryce played along with an all-star rhythm section made up of pianist Duke Jordan, bassist Oscar Pettiford, and drummer Kenny Clarke—but he was not himself recorded at the time. This was done to ensure that the rhythm backing would sound inspired and realistic. The issued alto solos were overdubbed after the backing tracks were completed. Don Schlitten, one of the founders of Signal Records, credits the success of the idea to the wizardry of engineer Rudy Van Gelder. Both sides of the original Signal LP were identical but for the addition of the alto overdubs on one side. The LPs also came with a book containing instructions, lead sheets, and even solo transcriptions with analyses— again, prototypical of teaching materials commonplace today.

Four tunes were done at this session: two standards, "Sometimes I'm Happy" and the ballad "Embraceable You," a blues by Pettiford entitled "Oh Yeah," and Jordan's "Jordu," which would soon become established in the hard bop repertoire. This session very much shows the soft side of Gryce. His sound is ironically similar in many respects to that of Paul Desmond, the alto saxophonist with the Dave Brubeck Quartet, a group stylistically quite different from the incipient hard bop school with which Gryce was associated. On "Sometimes I'm Happy," Gryce produces a nicely constructed three-chorus solo during which he quotes at the top of his choruses both "(He's Just My) Bill" (another *Show Boat* tune) and "And the Angels Sing," and makes extensive use of melodic sequence. He also thrice employs a substitution (F-sharp minor to B7 into B-flat) that creates a striking effect. The end result is an excellent model for the aspiring musician to emulate. Similarly on "Jordu," Gryce's two choruses demonstrate how to nimbly negotiate the challenging chord changes which this composition poses, particularly the circle-of-fifths sequence that makes up the bridge. Interestingly, he interpolates his own "Hymn to the Orient" at the beginning of his second solo chorus. While both pieces are in the key of C minor, the chords are very different, and when necessary Gryce mutates his melody line to fit Jordan's harmonies. On the ballad he provides a lesson in how a gifted soloist can reach into the harmonic resources of song to mine pure gold. A transcription of the second chorus of his solo on this track was included in the booklet which came with the LP. Gryce's treatment of the melody is influenced by the style of Charlie Parker, but is not imitative of Parker's classic 1947 versions of the Gershwin tune (which also featured Duke Jordan on piano). Where Parker creates a powerful new opening melody to replace Gershwin's, Gryce stays closer to the original line before gradually moving away through variation and embellishment, eventually arriving at a lightly syncopated double-time swing in his last sixteen bars.

In comparing Gryce's work with that of Phil Woods, who did the other Signal play-along recorded a month earlier (the material from both sessions has often been issued together, and in *Down Beat* magazine the two alto saxophonists were neck-and-neck in that year's Readers' Poll), it is apparent that Woods's sound is much bigger and more in the hard bop tradition. But Gryce's ideas and way of negotiating chord changes are more interesting, even though less forcefully presented. The absence of detailed arrangements and of any of his original compositions allows him to be seen in a very different light, and Gryce sounds very relaxed in this unusual quartet setting. There are rare isolated instances of him returning to this format, but it seemed more often to be his choice to emphasize his writing and arranging for quintet or larger groups, downplaying his performance as a saxophonist on more conventional pieces. His work on this session clearly shows that he was a more-than-capable soloist in the less structured format.

Less than a week later, on March 12, 1955, Charlie Parker died in New York. This was a crushing blow to all of jazz, even more so to those who knew the man personally. On March 21, Gryce attended the funeral at Abyssinian Baptist Church on 138th Street in Harlem, as Don Schlitten remembers:

Nobody had a car in those days and Jules Colomby had access to one. And we all met on 47th Street. That was Jules, Ira Gitler, Herbie Mann, Herbie Lovelle, Gigi Gryce, myself, and Art and Addison Farmer. And we all got in the same car to go uptown to the church, to Bird's funeral. (DSch)

In speaking with writer Robert Reisner, Gryce said, "I've still not gotten over his death. I want to do the best I can for the art that such a man dedicated his life to."[9]

The trumpeter Kenny Dorham recorded "Basheer's Dream" on March 29 in an octet arrangement that Gryce wrote. This offers one of the earliest appearances of Gryce's Muslim name, Basheer Qusim, which he would use exclusively after he left the music business. The piece, in the Afro-Cuban style, starts with an intro-duction that harks back to "Shabozz" and "Up in Quincy's Room," with the interval of the fourth predominant in the horn voicings. The A section bears a strong harmonic similarity to the earlier "Hymn to the Orient," but the bridge employs a chromatic root motion that the soloists (Dorham, Hank Mobley, J.J. Johnson) use to good advantage. On the Dorham recording (the only recorded version), an unnamed additional percussionist is on hand, playing clavés alongside Blakey on drums and Carlos "Patato" Valdes on congas. Richie Goldberg has been suggested, but the execution is less than perfect and it may well be Gryce himself, who was prob-ably in the studio.

On May 26, the Farmer–Gryce quintet recorded a second 10-inch album for Prestige.

We would just get into the studio… All the recording took place out at Hackensack, in New Jersey out at Rudy Van Gelder's studio. I think we usually did the thing in one day, two days at the most, but in those days we most likely took one day. Usually we would just go in and start one tune and we did it until you got it to the point where you feel you can't get it any better, and then you go on to the next one. He [Gigi] brought most of the material.[10]

A major difference in this second session was the use of the work-ing band, with the rhythm section of Freddie Redd on piano, Art Farmer's twin brother Addison on bass, and on drums, Art Tay-lor, who was a favorite of Prestige's Bob Weinstock.

Arthur Taylor was the drummer on over eighty Prestige LPs. And why? Because he was a great musician, but beside that he was a comedian, he was a happy-go-lucky guy and whatever the musicians would say they wanted, in two seconds he knew what to do. So he was an asset, you know and that's really important in making records. (RW)

These musicians had more opportunity to rehearse and perform the arrangements, which are much more involved than those done a year earlier. At this session Gryce began to introduce the subtly innovative compositions that developed and expanded the concept of form in jazz. Whereas the first quintet session was split three to one in favor of "contrafacts" or tunes based on existing chord changes, here only the minor blues "Blue Lights" is not based on an original harmonic structure. Both "Social Call" and "Capri" are 36-bar themes, though the improvisations on this version of "Social Call" are in 32-bar choruses. Instead of just a theme bookending a string of solos, all the pieces here have arranged introductions and also send-offs, interludes, and shout choruses, that help to lend coherence to the performance as a whole. While Charlie Parker was a great influence on Gryce's alto playing, his method of composing and arranging—quickly writing an eight-bar A section and improvising a bridge, with mostly unison for trumpet and alto—was almost never employed by Gryce. His studies in composition may have steered him towards thematic development, and his familiarity with the Schillinger System allowed him to generate quantities of material, all stemming from a single musical kernel.

One of the tunes done at this session was a ballad entitled "The Infant's Song." This simple but beautiful melody has, inexplicably, never been recorded again. It could not have been better suited to the talents of Farmer whose work is touching and exactly in line with the context of the composition, which was titled to honor the birth of Bob Weinstock's son.

Yeah, it was very nice of him. And in fact, Gigi said, "I heard you had your first son and everything. Art told me. I heard it from Art." And I said, "Yeah, it's something else, man, being a papa." And he said, "Well, I think I'll name this song "The Infant's Song." "Gee, that's very nice of you." And you know, my older son today is a lawyer. He's a little over forty years old. He never forgot that, that a song was named for him. I felt it was very nice. (RW)

This track exemplifies Farmer's exceptional taste and uncanny ability for choosing only the perfect notes to play in every setting.

The Farmer–Gryce band with Freddie Redd and Addison Farmer played at the Berkshire Music Barn in Lenox, Massachusetts on July 10, minus the scheduled drummer, Art Taylor. The group performed as a quartet, and later in the program were joined by the dancers Al Minns and Leon James. These two were favorites of the pioneering jazz scholar Marshall Stearns and it was certainly his influence that brought the performers together. Prior to the evening's show, the members of the quartet spent some leisure time on the beautiful grounds. Photographs show Gryce and Farmer having a go at archery.

It appears that the *Down Beat* report[11] of a late July session for the Bethlehem label with Gryce alongside Herbie Mann, Frank Wess, Sam Most, Jerome Richardson, and Hal McKusick playing multiple woodwinds, with arrangements written by Wess, Quincy Jones, and Gryce, was inaccurate. If such a session actually took place, the results were never issued. However, some of the participants named did share an involvement with bassist Oscar Pettiford around this time.

Although Gryce's association with Pettiford would blossom more significantly a year later, the two participated in a memorable octet recording session for Bethlehem in August of 1955 under the bassist's leadership. Three years older than Gryce, Pettiford (1922–1960) was present at the birth of bebop, co-leading with Dizzy Gillespie one of the first groups of that genre at the Onyx Club on 52nd Street in the 1940s. By the mid-1950s, he had established

himself as one of the most highly respected and influential bassists in jazz and, as early as 1950, had also begun experimenting
with pizzicato cello as a solo instrument.

The octet was made up of two trumpets (Ernie Royal and Donald
Byrd), valve trombone (Bob Brookmeyer), reeds (Gryce and
Jerome Richardson), the much overlooked Don Abney on piano,
Osie Johnson on drums, and Pettiford on bass and overdubbed
cello. Arrangements were provided by Gryce, Quincy Jones, Ernie
Wilkins, Tom Whaley, and Tom Talbert. Clearly the finest talent
available at the time had been tapped to participate in this session.

"Another One" is Jones's contrafact based on "Between the Devil
and the Deep Blue Sea" to which Gryce contributes half a chorus, beginning rather tentatively but perking up as the solo
progresses. He is also heard briefly on Johnson's "Minor Seventh
Heaven" and Pettiford's blues, "Kamman's A'Comin'." But his best
solo effort is found on Pettiford's "Bohemia after Dark," a minor-keyed opus with an unusual modal bridge, where he begins
with a repeated triplet motif and quotes "My Man" during his
nicely formulated one-chorus outing. Gryce's clarinet, rarely heard
on record, is featured on Tom Whaley's arrangement of Mary
Lou Williams's "Scorpio" suite. His one arrangement credit on
the LP is "Oscalypso," a minor-keyed Latin vamp by Pettiford.
This short track demonstrates Gryce's effective use of dynamics,
as the horns punch and shout interactively around and behind
piano, drum, and trumpet solos.

The Pettiford band performed at Birdland in September of 1955
with modified personnel. Gryce, Richardson, and Johnson were
the only holdovers from the recording session, as Byrd and Royal
were replaced by Art Farmer and Joe Wilder, Brookmeyer by Eddie
Bert, Abney by Hank Jones, while Danny Bank was added on

baritone saxophone. In addition to the recorded material, the ensemble performed other arrangements by Quincy Jones and Ralph Burns, as well as Gryce's "Smoke Signal," which the composer would soon record himself. Leonard Feather, in a *Down Beat* review, lamented the fact that the band's personnel were in such demand that it was unlikely to have a very long existence. While this was true, a more interesting Pettiford organization would emerge the following year, in which Gryce would play an even more important part.

A September 12 big band session with Dizzy Gillespie does not feature Gryce as a composer, arranger, or soloist at all and he serves only as a section saxophonist. However, Gillespie surely must have kept him in mind. Two years later, Gryce would be called upon to provide half an album's worth of material for the trumpeter, and he would be included in the octet that recorded his arrangements for Verve.

In the summer of 1955, Gryce founded Melotone Music, affiliated with BMI and the first of three publishing companies to handle rights and royalties for his own compositions as well as the works of other jazz composers. In view of the problems Gryce would eventually encounter as a result of his bold and provocative publishing efforts, it is curious that the attorney who assisted in setting up the corporation was none other than William M. Kunstler. Kunstler was not yet the radical firebrand and defender of revolutionaries he would become in just a few years, but was occupied with rather mundane legal matters, teaching and writing at that point in his career. Although it could be assumed this was an important connection that affected Gryce's future, there is no evidence that Gryce and Kunstler ever interacted significantly again.

The first copyright registrations were dated August 4 and included the four new pieces taken from the Kenny Dorham Octet date and the May 26 Art Farmer Prestige session as well as three that would be important in the coming months entitled "Sans Souci," "Gina," and "Playhouse," the latter two much better known as "Evening in Casablanca" and "Nica's Tempo," respectively. Another inclusion in this first batch was a contrafact on "Pennies from Heaven" called "You're Not the Kind," which would not be recorded until the end of 1958 by Benny Golson.

Golson was a partner in Melotone, which was headquartered at Gryce's apartment on West 52nd Street. Later, a second company called Totem would be established and Gryce would sublet an office from the lawyer (now retired judge) Bruce Wright to run the companies. As a manager for several jazz musicians, Wright knew quite a bit about the music business.

One of the reasons he was setting up Melotone and Totem with Benny was that he felt that black jazz musicians were being cheated by record companies, by producers. For example, he showed a great deal of emotion when I told him about a jazz concert at Carnegie Hall once: The producer came around to me because I was representing Max Roach and Art Blakey. He said, "Here's fifty dollars, give twenty-five to Max and twenty-five to Art to have a drum war." Of course, I was insulted and he [Gryce] was insulted just hearing that and one of the reasons he established these publishing companies was to become an honest broker in a field where musicians believed they were being cheated in large part. So he was stalwart, upright and wanted everything to be kosher. (BW)

In his autobiography, David Amram made it clear that there was a definite need for change in the publishing area at this time.

Morris [fictitious name] told me this particular A&R man had his own publishing company. What Morris didn't tell me was that it was a common procedure for original tunes to be illegally taken by the publishing company of the A&R man, who then wouldn't report record sales but kept the composer's, as well as the publisher's, royalty.[12]

Often the musicians were their own worst enemies regarding royalties:

A lot of black musicians in those days used to say, "Well, let me play the gig, let me make the record date, give me my money and screw the rest of it. Let somebody else handle the business part of it." They didn't attend to their business affairs, you know. They just get their money and go out and get high or get drunk or something, you know, and party, and, consequently, they were getting screwed business-wise and they didn't even know it—didn't even try to look after their business interests. You know, they had no lawyer to go to or nothing—to examine a contract—they'd sign anything that somebody puts in front of them—or somebody hands them some cash money, they'll sign it. (HS)

Gryce's influence on other jazz musicians in the area of publishing remains a lasting legacy. Horace Silver is often regarded as a prime exponent of the self-sufficient jazzman with his publishing company Ecaroh Music and record label Silveto, but he first learned of this from Gryce.

Gigi was not an overly aggressive guy but Gigi was a good businessman. I gotta say this: Gigi was a good friend of mine, we became good friends and Gigi was responsible for turning me on to music publishing. Because, in those days, very few musicians, well, not any that I knew of anyway—of course, I didn't know a hell of a lot of musicians in those days because I was just getting started in New York—but, I didn't know of any musicians who had their own publishing company, you know, especially black musicians who had their own publishing company. And the only ones I knew were Gigi and Lucky Thompson. They were the only two black guys I knew who had their own publishing. And Gigi turned me on to it, you know. Before then, I had my tunes with Leonard Feather's publishing. I had some tunes with Mills Music.

Yeah, he [Gigi] had some there [with Mills Music] too for a while. A lot of the black guys who were writing went and put their tunes with Mills Music simply because Duke's tunes were there. We all respected Duke [Ellington]—well, gee, if Duke had his tunes there it must be cool. Let's put our tunes there too. But anyway, he turned me on to publishing. He taught me how to set it up. He told me to go see a lawyer. He taught me what to do and whenever I had a problem, publishing-wise, I would always call Gigi on the phone and he would try to straighten it out for me or explain what I should do about it. (HS)

You see now in the beginning, guys were putting their tunes with big publishers like Mills Music and other big publishers, you know, putting our tunes there with these people. Then, the record companies, all of a sudden, got hip: "Well, we're gonna start our own publishing because when we do that, we can have them put their tunes with us, then we only have to pay them half the [mechanical] royalty instead of the whole royalty." In other words if I had my tunes with Mills Music, and I did something for Blue Note, they would have to pay Mills Music 100% royalty, you know. And then Mills Music would take 50% and give me 50%. But now, if Blue Note started their own publishing, and they get me to put my tunes with them, that means they save 50% because they pay themselves 50%. They only pay me 50%. You understand what I mean? So all the record companies started getting hip as to starting their own publishing. Blue Note in the beginning never had a publishing company. Some of the early things I made with Blue Note, we just signed a little written [royalty] agreement saying that they would pay me a penny per tune, you know, my original compositions, a penny or two cents, whatever it was at that time, and let it go at that. But then, when I put stuff in Mills, they had to pay Mills. Now, say they were paying me a penny per tune according to this little written agreement we had, then if I put tunes in Mills, they'd have to pay Mills two cents because two cents was the going rate. So then, Mills would keep a penny and give me a penny. So that's what the record companies did because they were saving money by having their own publishing.

Plus, they get their hands on the copyright, that's good for them too 'cause if somebody else records it on some other label, they issue a license for it and they get half of that. So, that's when people like Gigi and Lucky Thompson and myself started to get our own publishing because we could not only control our music 100%, own the copyright 100%, but also get 100% of the money rather than 50% of the money. (HS)

As might be expected, the music business establishment did not look favorably on these efforts.

They'd let you get just so far, then they're afraid that you're going to get too much and get more than they're getting and they don't like that. So, they want to keep their thumb down on you just to let you go so far and then hold you back. (HS)

Bob Weinstock of Prestige Records confirms that this was the situation. While Gryce frequently recorded for Prestige, at no time were any of his compositions published by the Prestige Music Company.

In the record industry, most of the people that ran the companies or in charge, whether they owned it or not, they thought musicians basically were stupid and not businesslike and were on something and they just wanted immediate money. And they screwed them basically. They took the songs away. A lot of times they put their own names on them even if on the record it said the writer of the song was correct, the song contract was not in the writer's name. It was in the producer's name. And this is notorious, going back, way back to the early King Oliver, Jelly Roll Morton era. But anyway, they sort of would resent a person like Gigi Gryce that knew the publishing business and took care of business and made his reputation as a writer of songs, you know. He probably just wanted what was coming to him, a publishing contract, you know, that he should publish his own songs because of the vast amount of material that he turned out. It was a profession with him to be a songwriter and an arranger.

To me, I never cared whether I got—whether Prestige Music Company got the publishing or the writer got it, or had their own publishing, because I always felt it's their right. And if they didn't have a publishing company, I explained to them that if they did publish with me, that they would get money from all over the world because my company was respected and people requested licenses from everywhere. And I'd collect the money and pay it to them in their statements besides my own records. And Prestige was a very unique company. Right from the beginning, the company was vastly profitable, vastly profitable. You know, I had big seller after big seller. And being a jazz company, when you come up with a King Pleasure "Moody's Mood for Love," which was a smash hit in all markets, R&B, pop, jazz, everywhere, the money for a small company like mine with low overhead—no overhead, I owned my own building eventually—money didn't mean anything. So I ran the company as what I thought was fair. So when a Gigi Gryce came, more power to him that he should keep his songs in his own publishing company. I had no animosity. I can see a lot of these other people—you know I knew what went on. I wasn't square, you know. (RW)

The saxophonist Harold Ousley and the singer Jon Hendricks (among many others—see Appendix B) also availed themselves of Gryce's publishing knowledge, registering compositions in his companies and establishing companies of their own.

Yeah, he was a forerunner in that he had a concept that could change things and benefit musicians and he was doing it at a time when it wasn't favorable to do that. Nowadays, being an independent now is the way that most artists are going and that's the way to go but at that time, it was an open door. (HO)

Well now, almost every jazz musician, white or black, worth his salt, has his own publishing company. And that's due to the pioneering efforts of Gigi Gryce and people like him. Benny Golson has his. I have mine. Well, I had mine when I met Gigi. I was a contemporary of Gigi. I had my firm—my firm is forty-five years old. I've been in ASCAP a long time. We were thinking along the same lines is what it was. Gigi and I were thinking along the same lines. (JH)

After about a six-month hiatus, the Signal record label began working on new recordings in the middle of October. One of the first sessions in their new (non-play-along) series was a quartet date led by Gryce that featured one of his musical idols, Thelonious Monk, in a rare sideman role along with Percy Heath on bass and Art Blakey on drums.

They first met in Boston in 1949 when they played together at the Hi Hat. Since then they have stayed in touch musically and socially. Charlie Parker, Dizzy Gillespie and Monk, the trinity of modern jazz, mean more to Gigi than any other jazz musicians. He recounts learning many things in their company. All were first academic and orthodox and then creative and unorthodox, paralleling greats in any art form. Combining with Monk here led Gigi to his freest and most sparkling solos on record.

Gigi describes this as one of the most relaxed recording sessions in which he has ever played. After setting up the themes, everything was spontaneous even to the length of the solos. There is much to be gleaned, as always, from Monk's originals and the one which Gigi contributed is up to his usual high standard.[13]

The presence of three Monk compositions, coupled with the pianist's exalted standing in the history of jazz, has sometimes led this to be called a Thelonious Monk outing, but Don Schlitten of Signal adamantly asserts that it was Gryce's date. It seems that Gryce would naturally defer to Monk with regard to repertoire—what a coup to be able to debut three new tunes! But there was a price to be paid for this collaboration.

Even the sounds of the horns become different in his work and you have to get exactly those sounds that he wants out of your instrument somehow if you want to keep working with him. He wrote a part for me once that was impossible. I was playing melody and at the same time was playing harmony to his part. In addition, the intervals between the notes were very wide. I told him I couldn't do it. "You have an instrument, don't you?" he said. "Either play it or throw it away." And he left me. Finally, I was able to play it.[14]

The piece Gryce refers to is "Gallop's Gallop," a composition so challenging that Monk never again recorded it, though he did attempt it in performance.[15] Gryce's old Hartford friend Emery Smith recalled hearing the legendary quartet that included John Coltrane struggling with this difficult line.

He [Gryce] did a thing with Monk called "Gallop's Gallop." You know, I haven't heard nobody play that tune that well. I heard Trane trying to play it with Monk at the Five Spot. It sounded terrible, you know, because Trane was learning on the job because when he went with Monk, he was asking for rehearsal. Monk said, "No, man, you rehearse every time you play your horn." Boy, you should have seen that shit that first month or so. [Laughs] Trane scuffling with them tunes, "Little Rootie Tootie" and "Four in One" and all of them. (ES)

A visitor to the rehearsal for this session, bassist Julian Euell presents insight into how the musicians prepared and the high level of esteem in which Monk held Gryce.

I attended that thing with Colomby records when Gigi recorded with Thelonious. This was Signal. Remember Colomby, Jules Colomby? I went to a rehearsal and Jules's brother Harry was handling, beginning to try to handle Monk and manage Thelonious. And Colomby was actually managing Monk. This is Harry Colomby. Jules had the record company. And he was the one who wanted to record people that Prestige and all these people weren't recording and that included Monk—Ernestine Anderson, people like that, Cecil Payne. Anyway, I went to the rehearsal and Gigi and Thelonious—there was no one else there—were going over the tunes that they were going to do, that they were going to record.

And they went over the tunes just to familiarize Gigi with the tunes that Monk was going to record. And Gigi never looked at a note of music and Thelonious never said anything, never told him anything. They talked you know. You know how Thelonious would sort of talk and mumble. He played the intro and they would discuss it, Gigi would play it.

Gigi was a very knowledgeable musician. I think his knowledge exceeded his technical ability, not his technical ability but his ability on the horn. I don't think he concentrated on that part of it. But he could play anything that Thelonious put up to play. Well, when I say Gigi's ability, you know he didn't reach his level, let's say, with his tone and maybe speed or whatever, you know, saxophone technique. But as far music goes, you couldn't play anything that he couldn't, that he didn't know.

At the time, I just recall Monk's tunes. It was a long time ago man. And I was sitting there. Jules had asked me to come along. Now, Jules Colomby was a friend of mine. And we were pretty good friends during that period. In fact, they offered me the gig with Thelonious and to this day man, I could kill myself but I had been working at the Five Spot a lot with other groups but when Thelonious came in there, you know I had the opportunity to get that gig. And I went with Phineas. You know—big error! But I had the inside—so I was hanging out with Jules and he used to ask me to come sit in on some of these jam sessions—not jam sessions, rehearsals. And this was one of them. And he knew that I knew Gigi and whatever. I'll never forget it because anything with Thelonious was memorable and to see Gigi handle that very difficult music like bam!

They had gone through four or five tunes or so they were going to record. Gigi did not have any music because Thelonious didn't write anything down. He'd say, "You'll hear it." And so he would play and say, "Yeah, man, check this out, baby." And he'd play it for you. Now, maybe Gigi saw this sometime or heard it before. I don't know. But I didn't see him with no sheet music up there. And Thelonious, at the end of the date, complimented him and turned in his usual way and said: "Now, there's a musician." You know how Thelonious used to mumble, you know, he said, "Now, dig it, didn't need no music, nothing. You dig? That's a musician, man." (JE)

The issued material is ragged at times, particularly in Gryce's "Nica's Tempo" (named for the Baroness Pannonica de Koenigswarter, a close friend and supporter of Monk, Charlie Parker, and many other jazz musicians of the time), taken at a very fast tempo, where Monk's somewhat rambling solo (which is little more than chords) is broken off by Gryce, who begins an exchange of fours with Art Blakey. But overall, Gryce's playing is strong and inspired with a more hard-edged tone than exhibited on the Duke Jordan play-along. He had clearly mastered Monk's material and made it his own. It is regrettable that these two great talents collaborated so seldom during their careers.

By the time of their third session as co-leaders of a quintet on October 21, Art Farmer and Gigi Gryce had perfected their group conception. Of the Gryce originals on this album, most feature non-standard forms and the arrangements are adventurous, though solidly within the hard bop idiom. The presence of Philly Joe Jones on drums adds a new sound and Farmer and Gryce make good use of the exceptional drummer, who less than a month earlier had joined the Miles Davis quintet, which was in residence at Birdland at the time of this date. The pianist was Duke Jordan, who also contributed the tune "Forecast."

The Latin-flavored "Sans Souci," named for an island in the Gulf of Mexico near Pensacola, Florida, is based on "Out of Nowhere" and finds Gryce using the same harmonies that his idol Tadd Dameron had reworked into "Casbah." (Gryce himself would write a completely unrelated tune entitled "The Casbah" four years later, in 1959.)

Perhaps dissatisfied with the previous week's outcome of "Nica's Tempo," Gryce returned to the tune in a somewhat slower rendition. This composition, one of Gryce's best, has a 44-bar, AABA structure (12+12+8+12) in which the first six bars of the A sections are reminiscent of Dizzy Gillespie's "Woody'n You" in their downward movement. The performance is much more secure than the Signal session and the players solo over slightly different A-section chord changes with a V13 chord with flatted fifth in place of the ii–V progressions used in the first recording. This type of subtle change can be found in many of the compositions that Gryce recorded more than once. The treatment of "Shabozz," in its third recorded version, is another example of this approach. Gone are the interlude and modulation that appeared in the Howard McGhee recording, leaving the piece more streamlined while retaining the essential elements.

"Evening in Casablanca" is a beautiful ballad in F minor whose only reference to geographic exoticism is in the introduction and interlude. The main form of the 46-bar tune (10+14+8+14 measures) is divided between Farmer and Gryce, with each horn player paraphrasing the melody without ever stating it outright. This piece must somehow have been heard by trumpeter Lee Morgan, as the A section of his 1963 composition "Carolyn" recorded by Hank Mobley on the Blue Note LP *No Room for Squares* has a shocking similarity.

The highlight of this session is the intricate "Satellite," which, like the earlier "Brown Skins," borrows from the harmonies of "Cherokee," but uses this as only one part in a multifaceted piece, here described by the composer:

It's rhythmic in structure, in that the melody is syncopated; there are triplets and while there's a long melodic line, it's not characterized by long duration of whole notes and half notes. It's a 32-bar piece with a four-bar tag. Another element of the song is that the improvised blowing is on a different set of changes than those of the theme. I feel this sort of thing should be done more often because a new set of chords provides fresher materials for blowing and allows for a change of tone color. You know, although you can change your dynamics by playing louder or softer, you can also change them by altering the tone color, as we do here. In this case, the tune is written in D-flat and then there's a modulation going to C, and it's in C that the two horns blow their improvised choruses. It works this way: the statement of 32 bars is followed by a four-bar modulation and then there are 64 [actually 56] bars of blowing on a new set of chords. The new set of changes is related to the basic feeling of the tune although it is not related to the chords of the theme. Another modulation leads to the piano solo, the two horns play a variation of the theme in 3/4 against the 4/4 of the rhythm section, and then finally the horns merge with the rhythm and swing out.[16]

Begun one day after the quintet session, the next project Gryce led involved an expanded group, a nonet using French horn (Julius Watkins or Gunther Schuller), tuba (Bill Barber), trombone (Eddie Bert or Jimmy Cleveland), and trumpet (Art Farmer) as the brass section, and just alto and baritone saxophones (Cecil Payne or Danny Bank) as the reeds. The personnel shifted slightly over the two dates that this ensemble recorded for the Signal label, but the pianist for both was Horace Silver, who contributed an arrangement of his own composition "Speculation." This altered blues was a favorite of Gryce, who would record the tune in several other settings in the years to come.

Obviously it was inspired by the Miles Davis "Birth of the Cool" group, you know, and I think it was the first recording that I ever did a semi-big band chart on. Most of my writing was for quintet. But, it was the first thing I ever put on record that was written or orchestrated for more than a quintet, you know, like a semi-big band. (HS)

Davis, along with the composers/arrangers Gil Evans, Gerry Mulligan, and John Lewis, had selected this particular instrumental configuration in an attempt to distill the unique sound of the Claude Thornhill orchestra into a small group. And on the West

Coast, Shorty Rogers had used a similar instrumentation in his famous "Giants" recordings in the early 1950s for the Capitol and RCA Victor labels.

Gigi felt that this instrumentation should not be neglected because of its tremendous possibilities of different tonal colors, dynamics, ranges, and voicings. He wanted to get away from the brassy sound of the usual jazz band of this size.[17]

Even Davis himself was impressed with Gryce's compositional skills. In a 1955 *Down Beat* article, he included Gryce alongside two of his own "Birth of the Cool" colleagues.

My favorite writer has been Gil Evans. He's doing commercial things now, but if you remember, he did the ensemble on "Boplicity" and several other fine things around that time...

Other writers I like are Gigi Gryce—there were several nice things in the last date he did with Art Farmer—and Gerry Mulligan is a great writer, one of my favorites.[18]

Gryce wanted the date to contrast with what was popular in the jazz market at the time. There were instrumental considerations of balance to be made. Trombonist Jimmy Cleveland who recorded with the nonet at the second session recalled Gryce's instructions to the players.

I think I heard him say, "This is going to be a different kind of sound. So you guys kind of got to get ready for it. It's going to be a different kind of sound. Some of the steps might be played—you know we got a tuba so we have to be sympathetic for the tuba. Of course, he can play loud but some of this stuff has got to be played almost like it's subtones on the saxophone." (JC)

Bassist Chris White, who first met Gryce as a struggling newcomer to the New York scene, recalled hearing this album and being impressed by the novel approach.

Definitely innovative, off beat, I thought the textures were interesting. Again, like you've got to remember I was like listening to all these tenor kind of things. So here these guys were using French horns like you would use a saxophone section, essentially, voicing for horns and tuba like you would voice for four saxophones and a bari [baritone saxophone]. And I thought that was interesting because the French horn came off sounding—how can I say this—the saxophones had more punch, more body. And so the French horn and the tuba provided the same notes but it was wrapping the package in a lighter, it's almost like wrapping it in cellophane instead of like brown paper bags. And it was interesting because later on in my career I ended up working in Dizzy's band and Lalo [Schifrin] wrote a lot like that. But he would write for *four* French horns and tuba, you know. And got a chance to explore why I felt the way I felt when I first heard it like in Gigi's thing. But when I heard it with Gigi, it was like, *what* is that? (CW)

Cleveland recalled that Gryce had a strong mental concept of the result he was after and was reluctant to adjust his idea to make it easier for the players.

We stopped a couple of times because he kicked it off at the tempo where it was gonna be played. And there were some people who said, "Now, wait a minute. Let's take it just a little bit slower. We don't have to take it real slow but take it a little bit slower," but he wanted that certain type of sound. That sound was what he was looking for. (JC)

The trombonist was featured on the ballad "In a Meditating Mood," initially titled "Autumn Serenade." It was retitled later, possibly after lyrics by Gryce and Jon Hendricks were written. These lyrics remain unrecorded to this day, though Cleveland's playing of the melody follows them precisely.

"In a Meditating Mood" is a very descriptive title, for Gigi's original is just that. He describes it as "sitting in a dark room with your mind wandering from thought to thought."[19]

This song has a 56-bar, AABA form (16+16+8+16) and a highlight of Gryce's arrangement is an interlude featuring meter shifts and counterpoint utilized, as always, in an unpretentious and contextually appropriate manner.

"Social Call" was written at the home of trumpeter Idrees Sulieman, who had played with Gryce in the Tadd Dameron band of 1953 and on the Max Roach session that same year. In his liner notes, Ira Gitler reported:

"Social Call," a Gryce composition, was originally performed in its instrumental form by Art Farmer and Gigi with their quintet. Jon Hendricks, the talented lyricist–jazz vocalist, heard it and wrote a set of words which fit both the idea and the mood of the melody. It is sung here by Ernestine Anderson, a singer of husky-voiced warmth whose work Gigi has had great admiration for since they were in Lionel Hampton's band together.[20]

The lyricist elaborated on how the collaboration came about.

Gigi was working with Art Farmer very closely at that time and Art was married to Ernestine Anderson and she was going to have a baby in about seven months, you know, she was about two months pregnant. She was doing a record date and he thought that "Social Call" would be a good thing to lyricize. (JH)

This job opened doors for Hendricks and he ended up writing several sets of lyrics for Gryce compositions.

After I started to do "Social Call" and things like that, I was just kind of on hand and I became a part of the quartet of Art Farmer, Benny Golson, Gigi, and myself. I'd be at the house every day and whenever anything needed a lyric they'd say, "Hey, Jon, here's one," you know, "You can do that," and I would just lyricize it without any problem. We didn't deal so much like other business people did. We treated everything like it was an artistic work, you know, casually and, "Hey, try your hand at this one," like that. It wasn't, "I hereby commission you to lyricize this song." [Laughs] It was, "Hey, Jon, this one needs a lyric. See what you can do with that." (JH)

The other vocal selection included in this recording session was the ballad "(You'll Always Be) The One I Love" written several years earlier in Boston, for Margie Anderson's Columbia Records debut. Gryce's rich arrangement features the French horn prominently in the ensemble backing for Ernestine Anderson's sensitive interpretation of this lovely melody.[21] As with "The Infant's Song," it seems incomprehensible that this engaging song was never again recorded.

The instrumental nonet session for Signal of October 30 was notable for the first recording of Gryce's "Smoke Signal," an up-tempo contrafact based loosely on "Lover," in which a connection to the Rodgers and Hart waltz is provided by a meter change to 3/4 for the first half of the bridge. Basically a drum feature, this arrangement also offers brief but strong solos from Gryce, Farmer, and Silver. The demanding tuba part is skillfully executed by Barber. Setting up Kenny Clarke's chorus-long drum solo is a swirling, atonal eight-bar ensemble interlude demonstrating Gryce's ability to draw upon his classical training in a manner that rendered his writing varied and original. Also of interest is his selection of "Kerry Dance," a traditional Irish melody, as a rather unlikely jazz vehicle. The result is a swinging romp with the theme stated initially by baritone sax, tuba, and bass in unison. The leader also contributes a solo chorus blowing on modified "I Got Rhythm" chord changes.

Any doubts that Gryce was a major figure in jazz of the mid-1950s were dispelled by these Signal recordings, which, along with his Art Farmer collaborations for Prestige, showed him to be a composer and arranger of great individuality, as well as an alto saxophonist who had fashioned his own sound and conception out of the Charlie Parker legacy. Gryce's success on the very competitive New York scene was something of a surprise to those who had known him only as a youngster in Pensacola, such as

Donald Shirley:

[I came to New York in] 1954. George had been probably on the scene before I got to New York. But I know that on one of the occasions when I was playing there I said who's around and they said Gigi. I said, "Gigi? Who is Gigi?" And they said Gigi Gryce. I said, "What, that's George Grice." That's how he got the name Gigi. And I recall during one of my breaks going around and I saw him. It was a great thing greeting him and seeing him now that we were both grown people.

When I saw that he was here headlining at Birdland—wow, that was something! In my mind I said, "George Grice?" It was one of those kinds of things. And I went to hear George play. I don't know where this was. I think it was at Birdland because I rarely went in there. But I did hear him play with a group. I presume it was his group. Well, George was playing at Birdland, that I'm sure. I went over to see him and say hello. But again, George Grice, it was a shock to me that George had amassed that much notoriety, even to the point of playing at Birdland. I was very happy for him, of course. (DS)

The notoriety Gryce had achieved in New York had not gone unnoticed back home in Pensacola. It was during this period that he and Eleanor made their only visit to the Florida city and she was impressed by the reception he received.

That was my first plane trip, the first time I had ever gotten on a plane and I was petrified! That was my first experience there and I was just amazed at how everybody greeted him. But of course they were the guys that he grew up with. And we went to a game…I guess the high school… They played football. It was a big game. And after it they had a dance some place and Gigi played. And oh, he was just so… I said, boy he's really famous [at] home, you know. They followed him everywhere. (EG7)

Gryce himself was fearful of air travel throughout his life and must have summoned considerable courage to make the trip, which would turn out to be his last visit to Pensacola until 1983, shortly before his death.

As Gryce became better known, another aspect of his professional talents and development began to assert itself. In contrast to many of his peers, he often assumed the role of mentor and teacher to younger players still involved in the learning process. Bassist Chris White recalled his own experiences:

I ran into Gigi as a young musician. I was living in Brooklyn. My home was Brooklyn but I would come to sessions in Manhattan and I ran into him, I used to see him a lot at a session at the Baby Grand and I was introduced to him by Ben Riley, the drummer. And I was like graduated from high school in 1953. So, yeah, it was like right around that time. I was running, of course, sneaking out, going hanging out. I shouldn't have been but—from 1953, so I think I ran into him more like 1954–55, in that period, someplace between getting out of high school and my first couple of years in college. And I used to see him at sessions and like I said, Ben Riley was the connection there. But, I mean, he was the connection insofar as that he was in the house rhythm section.

Yeah, the Baby Grand, it was on 125th right off of Lenox. And he was pointed out to me because I was a young guy and I was amazed—of course at that time, being at that age, I was amazed by everybody who could play. But everybody pointed out to me that's Gigi Gryce. And then I started buying his records, you know. He had a record called "Social Call," I think. And I bought that immediately. That was the first thing I bought of his and started listening to him. And then I would overhear conversations because at that time, you know, I was really learning how to play. So I was very reticent to approach him. He was like a god. But I overheard conversations of him telling people, "Have you published this or copyrighted this?" So he was very much into advocating controlling your own music. And I tell you, my thoughts of him sort of blur into this person who was *that* tight on top of *that* aspect of the music industry.

…If you had a modicum of talent he would talk to you. But when he spoke, it was either of something technical, musical, you know, what are the notes in this chord? What are the notes in this chord? "It's a C7 but I hear you playing something else. What is that?" I would say, we would say that to him. "You know, the notes are C, E, G, B-flat, and I'm hearing other notes. What are those notes? Why are you doing that?" And he would be very open to talk to you about that kind of stuff whereas a lot of the other players, at that time, were not... Gigi would at least point out, "That was another scale. I'm doing something else and this is what it is." And he was very much into sharing musical knowledge.

And he was also encouraging everybody to continue school. That was another thing with him, very much on that. And it would sort of all meld in, you know. The conversation would inevitably start around music and then talk about, continue to study and, by the way, when you write, protect yourself. I mean that was the overall message, you know, a real mentor kind of figure. But at the same time, not terribly outgoing, so he'd be sort of withdrawn, but if you approached him, he had something to say to you. (CW)

By the end of 1955, Gryce had become a respected member of the elite New York jazz scene through his recording, performing, and publishing endeavors. It was now time to build on his achievements.

Notes

1. Hentoff, Nat, "Counterpoint," *Down Beat*, April 7, 1954, p. 6.

2. Nevard, Mike, *Melody Maker*, November 28, 1953, p. 7.

3. Gigi Gryce, quoted by Leonard Feather in liner notes to Dizzy Gillespie: *The Greatest Trumpet of Them All*, Verve MGV 8352, 1960.

4. Art Farmer, interviewed by Tyrone Ward, 1987.

5. No evidence has been found of an Earl Bostic recording of "Mood in Blue" even though one is mentioned in the folio.

6. Foreword to Gigi Gryce, *Modern Sounds for Piano, Eb Horns and Bb Horns*, B.F. Wood Music Co., Inc., Boston, 1955.

7. Feather, Leonard, "Nouvelles d'Amerique," *Jazz Hot*, December 1954,

p. 24 (translation by M. Fitzgerald).

8. Gigi Gryce, quoted by Robert Reisner in *Bird: The Legend of Charlie Parker*, London, Quartet Books Ltd., 1977, p. 100.

9. Gigi Gryce, quoted by Robert Reisner in *Bird: The Legend of Charlie Parker*, London, Quartet Books Ltd., 1977, p. 100.

10. Art Farmer, interviewed by Tyrone Ward, 1987.

11. "Bethlehem Slates Woodwindy Jazz," *Down Beat*, June 15, 1955, p. 15.

12. Amram, David, *Vibrations*, New York, The Macmillan Company, 1968, p. 265.

13. Ira Gitler, liner notes to Gigi Gryce: *Orchestra/Quartet*, Signal 1201 and *Nica's Tempo*, Savoy MG12137.

14. Gigi Gryce, quoted by Williams, Martin, "The Private World of Thelonious Monk," *Esquire's World of Jazz*, New York, Thomas Y. Crowell Co., 1975, p. 125. This is also paraphrased slightly differently by Nat Hentoff in *Jazz Is*, 1984, p. 210.

15. A 1964 performance by the Monk quartet from the It Club which was posthumously released does contain the piece, but while Monk later produced studio recordings of the other two, there is no record of him revisiting "Gallop's Gallop" in a studio session intended for issue.

16. Gigi Gryce, quoted by Nat Hentoff in liner notes to *Modern Jazz Perspective*, Columbia CL1058.

17. Ira Gitler, liner notes to Gigi Gryce: *Orchestra/Quartet*, Signal 1201 and *Nica's Tempo*, Savoy MG12137.

18. Miles Davis, quoted by Nat Hentoff in "Miles," *Down Beat*, November 2, 1955, p. 14.

19. Ira Gitler, liner notes to Gigi Gryce: *Orchestra/Quartet*, Signal 1201 and *Nica's Tempo*, Savoy MG12137.

20. Ira Gitler, liner notes to Gigi Gryce: *Orchestra/Quartet*, Signal 1201 and *Nica's Tempo*, Savoy MG12137.

21. It is curious to note that the only recorded versions of this song were performed by vocalists named Anderson. And the pianist backing Margie Anderson on the 1950 Columbia session was very probably Duke Anderson. There is no evidence that any of the Andersons were related and their association with Gryce and this ballad appears to be purely coincidental.

on the cutting edge

*A*LTHOUGH HE CONTINUED HIS SMALL GROUP WORK with Art Farmer, beginning in 1956 Gryce spent time with two large ensembles that spanned a wide range of music, from avant-garde experimentalism to more traditional swing. The players involved in both the Teddy Charles Tentet and the Oscar Pettiford Orchestra were of the highest caliber, and through these contacts Gryce was able to solidify his position as a fixture on the highly competitive New York scene.

Gryce's association with the Teddy Charles Tentet was a brief but significant one. One of the early bebop vibraphonists, Charles (Theodore Charles Cohen, 1928–) was also noted for his dedication to expanding the jazz vocabulary through composition. He had been deeply influenced in this direction through studies with pianist/composer Hall Overton (1920–1972) at the Juilliard School of Music in the 1940s. Between 1952 and 1955, Charles led a series of groundbreaking and highly regarded recording sessions for the Prestige record label entitled *New Directions, Vol. 1–5*, which involved many notable musicians from both the East and West Coasts including saxophonists Jimmy Giuffre and J.R. Monterose,

guitarist Jimmy Raney, trumpeter Shorty Rogers, valve trombonist Bob Brookmeyer, bassists Charles Mingus and Curtis Counce,
drummers Shelly Manne and Ed Shaughnessy, as well as Overton
himself.

Given the interest in composition and experimentation evinced
by Charles, it was not at all surprising that he should cross paths
with Gryce at some point. They first met in Charles Mingus's Jazz
Composers Workshop.

I came back from the West Coast in 1953. That's when we started
with the Jazz Composers Workshop. Art Farmer was there. I believe
Gigi was there, if not all the time, a good deal of the time. (TC1)

The Workshop was a collective made up of New York musicians
who shared an interest in innovative composition and a willing-
ness to take the time to rehearse their own works and those of
others.

Yeah, that was a great thing. When I came back from the West Coast,
you know, all gung-ho, flushed with success and everything, I joined
the Workshop, I guess through Bill Coss, the editor of *Metronome*
magazine. I guess that's the first time I met Teo [Macero] and I
already knew Mingus from his playing with Red Norvo. And they
were all involved with this Composers Workshop. So they invited me
to participate. I don't remember if it was Bill Coss who influenced
that. Ed Shaughnessy was playing drums I guess. So at any rate, the
idea of this was various guys would write compositions and bring it
into this thing and then we'd rehearse it and try to play it and so
forth. Mal Waldron was involved early, Gigi and so forth and it was
great because everybody was off in their own directions, doing their
own thing and though experimental, it was very rewarding. Everybody opened up each other's minds and ears to other things. It led to
those things with David Broekman later at Cooper Union and
Newport which were very successful. (TC2)

In that environment, anybody could compose anything. The idea was

only a few musicians, about ten or twelve to rehearse and compose.
Other writers were invited. And if you want the names: Don
Butterfield was the tuba player, and I think Wally Cirillo was the
piano at some time. Mal Waldron was the piano at other times; John
LaPorta on clarinet, George Barrow, baritone saxophone, and Eddie
Bert on trombone. And Mingus used to bring some of his pieces in.
And this is a little aside, but Mingus brought in a piece, a bunch of
older pieces, like a lot of us, who sometimes get caught short for
time and use the music you already had around. So he brought this
stuff in and we sort of laughed about it because it sounded like his
Glenn Miller period. If you can believe that—Mingus wrote some
arrangements when he still lived on the West Coast that sounded like
Glenn Miller. Mingus was not—he wasn't embarrassed about it but
he thought it was almost funny that he wrote like that. And you know
what he wrote like in his later years! So that was a moment of
amusement for all of us. And then there was Teo who was *really* way
out. He was the first guy to play chords on a saxophone, years before
Ornette—not to take anything away from Ornette. But Teo was
around doing that stuff, pretty wild you know, free improvising. He
was studying informally at Juilliard with Henry Brant, very avant-
garde. So let's see. Who else was in there now—Jimmy Raney used to
come down there, Billy Bauer, Hall Overton.

We went down to this basement studio and rehearsed, bring in the
music and rehearsed. Nobody got paid for anything. We just chipped
in to pay the studio time. (TC1)

An outgrowth of the Composers Workshop, the Teddy Charles
Tentet was a rather unusual ensemble made up of three saxophones, trumpet, tuba, guitar, vibraphone, and rhythm section.
Charles engaged several like-minded writers for the band, many
of whom were great talents worthy of wider exposure at the time.

Well, you know the idea of the Tentet when I got the chance to do
it... I knew all these jazz composers that were almost completely
forgotten, Gil Evans, George Russell, Giuffre, Gigi. They were
unknown to the new audience. Mal nobody ever heard of anyway. I

said, "Here's guys that can really write. I'm gonna give them a shot." And that was the idea. Instead of just my writing, get all these guys involved in it. And it did a lot for Evans and George Russell. It brought them back out of total obscurity, you know. Most jazz people didn't even knew who they were at that time, in the 1950s. (TC2)

Tubist Don Butterfield (1923–), whose long and distinguished career has spanned many musical styles, was an important member of the Tentet. Many years later, he recalled the ensemble's innovative character:

That was one of the most adventuresome groups around and there were some wonderful things done there with that. Jon Eardley played trumpet in it… Art Farmer, of course. My God, I mean it was unbelievable who was there at that time. And these were—they were pointing the way for everybody else, those records, you know. (DB)

The unit first recorded in January of 1956 for the Atlantic record label employing new compositions and/or arrangements contributed by Waldron ("Vibrations"), Russell ("Lydian M-1"), Evans ("You Go to My Head"), Giuffre ("The Quiet Time"), Bob Brookmeyer ("Show Time") and Charles himself ("The Emperor," "Nature Boy," "Green Blues"). Gryce's close friend and associate Art Farmer was present (listed in the liner notes as "Peter Urban" because of contractual obligations) as were Raney and Monterose who, along with Charles, are responsible for most of the improvised solos.

Unquestionably the culmination of Charles's compositional approach, the music produced at these sessions is challenging, unconventional, and remains as fresh today as it was when first released forty-four years ago. But this is neither "free jazz" which radically reinterprets the traditional structural elements of music, nor a fusion of jazz with classical music along the lines of the "third stream" experiments of Gunther Schuller, John Lewis, and others, that would soon gain much attention. Instead, the Charles/ Overton manifesto required that the compositions prescribe boundaries and contexts designed not to limit but rather to liberate the soloist, thus inspiring unhackneyed creative efforts. Charles explained:

After studies with Hall Overton, it's always been my personal theory of jazz composition that the composition itself should generate an environment that makes the creative musician play compositionally instead of just going into a bag of tricks one right after another. And all the successful jazz composers I think do that. Certainly Duke [Ellington] did that as the greatest example. (TC1)

[We] used the idea of the form and more cohesive compositional techniques so that the piece actually made musical sense as you improvised. It wasn't just throw away the first chorus and then play forty minutes of how good I am, every trick in the book. That's what many players ended up doing after Coltrane. Play the first chorus and then it all became, "OK, I got the next twenty minutes and this is every trick I know." I couldn't stand that stuff. These pieces were done in such a way you couldn't do that. You got your two choruses or your four choruses and it was in the context of the music. Mal Waldron was particularly good at writing for that kind of thing. He made you play the way he wanted it to come out. So did Gigi. (TC2)

Gryce solos on two of the Tentet tracks, both recorded at the January 17, 1956 session. "The Emperor" is Charles's adventurous update of "Sweet Georgia Brown" taken at a fast tempo with rhythms alternating between a Charleston-like vamp and straightforward swing. Interspersed among the solos are four- or eight-bar sendoffs having a three-against-four feeling, even sections sounding like free improvisation. Gryce is the first of seven soloists and acquits himself well, gliding through the altered chord changes for one chorus, mostly over drummer Joe Harris's tom-toms.

About Mal Waldron's "Vibrations," Charles wrote in the LP liner notes: "You'd swear this was written for Gigi. Just beautiful!" Beautiful indeed, Waldron's composition is a complex and ever-shifting piece of music that begins with an eighteen-bar section of drum figures having an almost military quality. This gives way to an initial fast theme stated by the ensemble. Next, tenor and baritone saxes introduce a vamp at slower tempo, over which Gryce states a new 32-bar minor theme in a most evocative manner. He then solos for sixteen bars, achieving exactly the contextual unity of improvised solo and composition that Charles was seeking. Jimmy Raney also solos effectively on the same form, before the original tempo returns and Charles presents his contribution. The enduring beauty and musicality of Gryce's brief solo was not lost on others who performed this composition, as Charles recalled:

I remember Mal's piece, "Vibrations" that Gigi played on so beautifully. You know what's interesting about that—a little aside here. We did that on the Tentet and Gigi played this beautiful solo. Yeah, it's a work of art. And then, was it thirty years later, I did a concert with Teo's group, a ten or twelve piece band at the Cooper Union—some kind of thing that Joe Papp was producing. And Teo had the band and I brought out the same piece. And damned if Teo's solo didn't sound almost like Gigi's. The music as a composition was so powerful that Teo had to play it the way that Gigi had played it on my record of 1956. That's kind of interesting you know. That, to me, is successful jazz composing when the composition generates a tonal and musical environment that the soloist improvises from instead of just going into the usual bag of tricks which mostly everybody does. (TC1)

The Teddy Charles Tentet was more than just a recording unit, and the group played a landmark concert at New York's Cooper Union in the spring of 1956. The musical director was composer/conductor David Broekman (1899–1958) best known for his affiliation with Universal motion pictures. Other participants included Gunther Schuller, John Lewis, Oscar Pettiford, Art Farmer, Bill Russo, and George Russell. Gryce contributed to the Tentet repertoire although none of his works was recorded and, as mentioned in Chapter 2, his "Al Gashiya" was performed at this concert. Teo Macero's review in *Metronome* magazine was very favorable:

The spokesman of Progressive Jazz, as John Lewis is sometimes called, had to take the back seat to Teddy Charles and Gigi Gryce whose talents shone with blinding brightness their capacity to compose great jazz pieces.

"Lydian M-1" was by George Russell. This is my first association with his work. I felt that this composition did not come up to the level of Gryce's or Charles's compositions, but that it was a work well worth hearing. He has great potential as a composer but needs more of a "classical" approach in developing his musical ideas.[1]

Throughout 1956, the Tentet performed at various concerts including one on April 27 at a New York junior high school on 93rd Street where bass giant Charles Mingus was part of the ensemble.

More than 300 quietly intent high school and college students attended a recent Teddy Charles Tentet concert in the Joan of Arc Junior High School auditorium, sponsored by the two jazz clubs of City College of New York. Musically and programmatically, the concert was one of the best modern jazz evenings held in New York in the last few years.

The musicians were Charles, Art Farmer, Gigi Gryce, Hal Stein, Teo Macero, Don Butterfield, Jimmy Raney, Hall Overton, Charlie Mingus, and Rudy Nichols. A large percentage of the concert consisted of numbers from Charles's recent Atlantic LP for the same instrumentation and with five of the same men.

Among the more immediately effective performances were Mal Waldron's "Vibrations," Jimmy Giuffre's "The Quiet Time," Charles's arrangement of "Nature Boy" and his own "The Emperor," Bobby Brookmeyer's "Show Time" (not on the LP), George Russell's "Lydian M-1," improvisations on "Night in Tunisia," and Butterfield's surprisingly flexible tuba performance on "Sunday Kind of Love."[2]

On Saturday afternoon, July 7, the Tentet made a high profile appearance at the Newport Jazz Festival along with the Phineas Newborn Quartet and Friedrich Gulda's ensemble. The concert was later broadcast worldwide on the Voice of America's *Music USA* program. Gryce and tubist Don Butterfield were the only holdovers from the January recording session.

The Teddy Charles Tentet, comprising Hall Overton, piano; Gigi Gryce, alto; Hal Stein, tenor; Jon Eardley, trumpet; Don Butterfield, tuba; George Barrow, baritone; Addison Farmer, bass; Barry Galbraith, guitar, and Ed Shaughnessy, drums, was welcomed by a yipping reception from Teddy's ringside cronies, Bill Coss and Charlie Mingus, who sounded the Charles battle cry.

Bob Brookmeyer's "Show Time" preceded the lovely Jim Giuffre composition, "Quiet Time," which was beautifully performed and highlighted Teddy's vibes in a solo that fairly sung. Charles has cast away much of his earlier flashiness and has become a ranking jazzman.

Gil Evans's haunting "You Go to My Head," Teddy's "Green Blues" and "The Emperor" (an atonal "Georgia Brown") brought out the almost unbelievable work of Butterfield and drumming of Ed Shaughnessy, who was playing at every moment for the group instead of for himself.

"Word from Bird," by Charles, closed the set and though not very well played (a hampering wind was blowing the music about), deserves to remain as a part of the group's repertoire.[3]

Charles remembered the Newport appearance and this unfortunate encounter with Mother Nature during the performance of one of his most difficult pieces, which David Broekman had been enlisted to conduct.

We get up there and we're playing hard at the Tentet music and I had Broekman specifically to conduct the "Word from Bird." It was a great honor for me to get a guy like that willing to get up and conduct my music. The wind starts blowing. The trumpet music blew away—catastrophic! But it still came off quite well—retrieved the music and so forth. (TC2)

You can't win 'em all. That's really improvising man. Suddenly the music is blown away and you gotta go for it. (TC1)

The surviving recording proves that the ensemble acquitted itself admirably. Gryce is heard soloing on "Show Time," "The Emperor," and "Word from Bird," and the band is propelled by Shaughnessy's driving percussion.

The Tentet recording on Atlantic received a five-star review in *Down Beat* and was also mentioned in *Metronome* as one of the best records of 1956. But despite critical acclaim for both its recordings and live performances, especially the Newport appearance, the band had little commercial potential. Charles rebuffed any attempts to broaden the ensemble's appeal and opportunities for appearances dried up. By 1957, the Tentet was history, only occasionally revived in the years to come.

The Tentet at Newport in 1956 got a hell of a write-up in the *Times*. For me that's always been the kiss of death. Whenever I get some very high accolade or something like that, or notice, a big article in the *New York Times* talking about us as if Duke Ellington was second on the program compared to us, it seems to kill my momentum. So Willard Alexander was gonna represent me and put me out on the road. He said, "You've got to get a dance library together." I said: "This is not a dance band!" "Well, why don't you get a dance library together?" I said nah. So we never got a gig out of it after the [*New York Times*] write-up and all that stuff. That was the end of the Tentet—my greatest success.

It was too good. You know, it was too advanced, too good—all those great musicians—you know unless you had real money for them they were gonna go their own way, which Art Farmer, Gigi, and Raney did. (TC2)

As far as Charles is concerned, the Tentet and the Atlantic recordings represent the epitome of what he was striving for in jazz: "And I say the Tentet was exceptional. If you want to hear what I was really doing, *that's* the record. That was the real stuff." (TC2) While short-lived, the Tentet experience benefited everyone involved. Charles solidified his position as one of the major innovators in modern jazz while Gryce, Farmer, Waldron and other sidemen considerably enhanced their visibility and reputations through their contributions to this unique and forward-looking ensemble.

Further evidence of Gryce's ascendance to the highest echelons of the New York jazz scene was provided by his inclusion in a project initiated by Creed Taylor of ABC-Paramount Records called *Know Your Jazz*. Other participants tapped by Taylor were Billy Taylor (piano), Jimmy Cleveland (trombone), Oscar Pettiford (bass), Kenny Clarke (drums), Tony Scott (clarinet), Al Cohn (baritone saxophone), Joe Roland (vibraphone), Charlie Rouse (tenor saxophone), Mundell Lowe (guitar) and Donald Byrd (trumpet)—clearly a stellar collection of musicians of the time and many with whom Gryce had already had or would have significant interactions. The producer laid out the goals of this recording series:

A primary purpose of the *Know Your Jazz* series is to give some sort of direction to the new jazz fan. Volume I (ABC-115) is a series of improvised solos on the major instruments used in jazz. The musicians who participated were selected according to their activity and importance on the current jazz scene.[4]

Gryce is heard on two tracks from this LP recorded on March 1, 1956. "In a Mellotone" is a feature for Kenny Clarke in which the alto saxophonist, clarinetist Scott, and guitarist Lowe exchange two-, four-, and eight-bar phrases with the drummer. Gryce again chooses to express his softer side on his own feature, the ballad "Come Rain or Come Shine." Billy Taylor's analysis of this track in the LP's liner notes is insightful:

Gigi Gryce demonstrates various contrasting shadings of tone in the melody. There is a subtle lyric quality—with thoughtful harmonic variations. Gigi's style on this piece sharply contrasts with the "peck" style on Charlie Rouse's recording. Gigi intimates the double-time feeling which is so characteristic of the "peck." One might say that Gigi is speaking the same language as Charlie Rouse, but in a quieter, less emphatic manner. Another important player in the introspective alto school is Paul Desmond with Dave Brubeck's Quartet.[5]

The very next day, Gryce was in the studio again, recording with Earl Coleman. This was a major event in the singer's career. Coleman (1925–1995) had recorded with Charlie Parker on one of the saxophonist's best-selling records, "This Is Always," in early 1947, and had gigged with Bird in California around the same time. But he had not recorded at all after 1948 until being reunited with Gene Ammons on two dates for Prestige in 1955. A few months later, Bob Weinstock offered Coleman the opportunity to make his first record as a leader and suggested that he pair up with Gigi Gryce.

I felt Earl would need somebody of a higher musical level to work with him. A lot of times I did that because a lot of times the leader or the featured player would need some help. And Earl Coleman was a great singer, no question about it, but he needed some help, really. And I felt Gigi could give it to him. Those were good sides. Earl Coleman's another singer that didn't make it. He could have but he didn't. Look how long it took Johnny Hartman to make it. We did a lot of stuff, Earl and Gene Ammons. Gene Ammons loved him, boy. (RW)

Weinstock felt that Gryce was someone who could bring stability as well as musical expertise to a session.

The first date involved three standards: "No Love, No Nothing," "It's You or No One," and "Come Rain or Come Shine." It is conceivable that Gryce was responsible for suggesting the last title as he had recorded it just the day before. The quintet, including Art Farmer and Hank Jones, provides gentle but sure backing for Coleman's deep baritone. Gryce does not play on the second session on June 8, which included two of Gryce's tunes that had been "lyricized" by Jon Hendricks: "Social Call" and "Reminiscing." While the former was recorded several times under Gryce's supervision, the latter is preserved as a vocal version only on this LP.

Reports of a later session by Coleman for a record label that Gryce had founded appear to be false. The musicians were supposedly Harry "Sweets" Edison, Tommy Flanagan, Reggie Workman, and Gus Johnson.[6] Neither Workman nor Eleanor Gryce recalls anything about the session or the existence of such a record label.

Around this time, Gryce and Farmer were working in the quintet of bassist Oscar Pettiford, and in March of 1956 this group joined forces to record with the Dutch accordion player Mat Mathews (1924–) for the Dawn label. Pianist Dick Katz remembered that there were some technical difficulties on this session.

Well, for one thing, we did it in Carl Fischer Hall, which is a small hall opposite Carnegie Hall, not really a recording studio *per se* but a small concert hall. The engineer, whose name escapes me, was a classical engineer, and he wanted to record the band like a classical ensemble, with one microphone overhead, rather than the usual setup of having one mike for each instrument. And Oscar Pettiford threw a fit! He certainly didn't want that and he insisted on a mike for his bass, which I think he finally got. The engineer was shaking his head. I wrote a piece especially for that called "Knights at the Castle," and if you listen to the piano sound on that, it sounds far away, like in a hall, which was not the way jazz records were done in those days, usually miked very close. He [Gigi] was terrific on that date. He played the music. There was no problem. Oscar was the one. I mean that's a separate hour long TV program [laughs]. Once Oscar got straight it was OK. But I remember the date and I love the way he [Gigi] played on it. He had his own sound—very individual. (DK)

Besides Katz's original, Gryce also appears on Mathews's "Not So Sleepy," an attractive 56-bar theme which would resurface in the book of Oscar Pettiford's orchestra later that year.

In addition to all of these studio sessions, Farmer and Gryce's own quintet continued to perform and mature. In November of 1955 they had headlined at Chicago's Bee Hive for three weeks, then in the spring played extended engagements at New York's Birdland in March and the Café Bohemia in April. Nat Hentoff reported on the Birdland appearance:

As their series of Prestige albums have increasingly indicated, Art Farmer and Gigi Gryce enjoy a mutually growing, creative partnership which should be sustained for the good of modern jazz as well as for their own careers. During their Birdland stand, they were excellently complemented by pianist Duke Jordan, bassist Addison Farmer, and drummer Art Taylor.

Since the quintet has not been working for nearly as long an uninterrupted period as the Modern Jazz Quartet, it does not have the constant substructure of interdependent assurance the MJQ has achieved. But like the MJQ, this is not only a blowing unit. The strong skeletal framework of the quintet is in the generally fresh, melodic, and personal originals and arrangements of Gryce. These encompass a variety of directly expressed feelings, from the sensitive but not sentimental "Infant's Song" to the drivingly angular "Nica's Tempo." Also more durable than too many other's modern jazz "originals" are Gigi's "Social Call," "Satellite," "Wake Up," and several others.

Gigi, too, has become a considerably improved altoist in the past couple of years. He is no less emotionally powerful than he has always been, but he has disciplined his passion into consistent idea patterns that strengthen the communicative channels of his emotion.[7]

While Gryce's role in the Teddy Charles Tentet was largely as a sideman, his involvement with the Oscar Pettiford Orchestra around the same time was much more substantial. The band that Pettiford assembled in 1956 was, like that of Charles, quite unusual in terms of instrumentation. Basically a modified big band, the brass section was composed of two trumpets, two French horns, and trombone, while the reeds included alto, two tenor (one doubling flute), and baritone saxophones. In a novel move, Pettiford augmented the nine horns and rhythm section with a harp, and it would be the combinations afforded by the harp, his amplified cello, and the French horns that would provide the ensemble with a most appealing and easily identifiable sound. In order to play cello and keep the rhythm section intact during live performances, Pettiford utilized a second bassist, usually Whitey Mitchell but sometimes Paul Chambers.

Pettiford enlisted Gryce and tenor saxophonist Eli "Lucky" Thompson as the primary arrangers and key sidemen for his new ensemble. Thompson (1924–) was a ubiquitous presence on the New York scene at this time and, like Gryce, would eventually leave the music world in bitterness and disillusionment. A gifted soloist with an original style that, like that of Benny Golson, had evolved more from Don Byas than Charlie Parker, Thompson's insufficiently appreciated abilities as a composer and arranger were never better showcased than during his association with Pettiford.

Composer/French horn player David Amram recalled the beginnings of the Pettiford band:

The following weekend at Ken's [Kenneth Karpe] jam session, Oscar Pettiford announced he was going to form a band. We had a nucleus that came every week to play and Oscar decided this group of superenthusiasts could make a great new sound in jazz. He hired Julius Watkins, the brilliant French hornist, and myself; a harpist, Betty Glamman; a flute and saxophone player, Jerome Richardson; Gigi Gryce, who did most of the arrangements as well as played a superlative saxophone; Sahib Shihab, who was a mainstay at Ken Karpe's sessions and had a quintet of his own for a while that featured Tommy Flanagan, a pianist who also was in Oscar's band. J.R. Monterose also played saxophone and the trumpets were Art Farmer and Ernie Royal. Jimmy Cleveland played trombone and Osie Johnson was the drummer. Needless to say it was some band![8]

The challenges to an arranger posed by the unusual instrumentation were noted by Gryce, and David Amram's comments touch on the subject from the performer's point of view:

It was quite an interesting but difficult group to write for, especially in blending the two French horns and trumpets as one trumpet section, in which the sound of the trumpets is naturally much stronger and creates a balance difficulty. I think this could have been one of the major bands of our time if only Oscar could have secured enough work for it. But he faced the same longstanding problem.[9]

If something got messed up, we could usually figure out what was wrong. And Oscar himself could hear everything and if something, anything sounded mysterious, he would suddenly in the middle turn around from his bass while he was playing and sing one of the inner voices, or sing one of the French horn parts, or even the harp part, whatever it was. And with Gigi's arrangements and a lot of the other ones, Julius and I were way up high and kind of picking notes out of the air that were very often a raised eleventh of a chord or something like that where you really had to be able to hear everything to be able to play it. Oscar could hear everything that everybody was doing all the time. And so could Gigi, of course. (DA)

In contrast to the Charles Tentet's experimental and sometimes inaccessible repertoire, the Pettiford band was a hard-swinging unit that could excite an audience in the best big band tradition despite the somewhat unorthodox instrumentation. Jimmy Cleveland recalled:

Well, the Oscar Pettiford band was one of those *baaaad* swinging bands. We had a lot of Gigi's music in there. Yeah, we had a bunch of stuff in there by Gigi, and all of it was swinging right on man. It was just a joy to go to work—Birdland and then we went down to Bohemia. We worked all around. Oh yeah, Gigi was…he was playing, fantastic solos too. Sometimes he'd play his alto and then pick up his flute and play his flute. Yeah, he was inspired with that band. We all were because Oscar was such a great leader. (JC)

The band debuted at an Easter Sunday Jazz Festival at New York's Town Hall produced by Ken Karpe. Other acts on the bill included the Farmer–Gryce Quintet, the Thelonious Monk Trio, and singer Morgana King. Headliners and sidemen assumed multiple roles at this event as Farmer and Gryce also played in Pettiford's band, and the bassist backed Monk. David Amram remembered the concert as a much more creative than commercial achievement.

The concert was a great success artistically, even though Kenny lost his shirt financially. He didn't care. The concert was so beautiful that he felt he had made a great contribution to music and to all his friends who had come and played at his house so many times.[10]

Burt Korall's review of the concert in *Metronome* magazine, however, suggested that the Pettiford band had not yet mastered its repertoire.

Ken Karpe (an old personal friend) produced his first jazz concert at Town Hall recently… It had some compelling moments.

The Art Farmer–Gigi Gryce Quintet were the most swinging this night with Art and pianist Duke Jordan literally sparkling. Oscar Pettiford and his large orchestra featured an unusual instrumentation—two trumpets, one trombone, two French horns, three reeds, and four rhythm, some fair to middling scores, but seemed to suffer from insufficient rehearsal time. With further preparation, this band could be quite interesting. Trombonist Jimmy Cleveland and Oscar figured as most fruitful soloists in the large band segments of the program.[11]

In June of 1956, the orchestra made the first of two memorable recordings produced by Creed Taylor for the ABC-Paramount Label. Six of the ten tracks were arranged by Gryce. "Nica's Tempo," in its third version in two years, is taken at a relatively slow tempo. The main theme is stated by the saxes adorned with brass punches and countermelodies. Using the ii–V harmonic variation of this composition, pianist Tommy Flanagan takes a full 44-bar chorus followed by Farmer for two A sections. Gryce enters at the bridge, completing the chorus with a solo exhibiting very nice rhythmic variety and construction. The powerful shout chorus features Ernie Royal's dynamic high-note work.

Another return from the earlier Signal date is "Smoke Signal." In this version Gryce introduces the theme with rubato piano and harp before the rhythm section sets the fast tempo. The melody is stated by the brass up to the bridge where the saxes take over led by Gryce's steady alto. Whereas on the earlier version the bridge was done in 3/4 time, on this session straight 4/4 is maintained throughout the introductory chorus. Gryce's one chorus solo is very fluent and punctuated with orchestral background kicks. Osie Johnson's four-bar drum breaks bracket an ensemble interlude very similar to that employed on the Signal nonet session, but with a more Native American character befitting the tune's title. Farmer, Thompson, and Cleveland each take brief solos, then

Johnson returns to the spotlight for 32 bars before altering the meter to 3/4 at the bridge of the concluding chorus.

Composed by Pettiford but arranged by Gryce, "Sunrise–Sunset" is a Latin-flavored, minor theme with effective use of woodwinds, piano, tom-toms, and harp to create the desired mood. This track offers no improvised solos and impresses one as possibly having a commercial motive.

Mat Mathews's "Not So Sleepy" is reprised from the composer's date earlier in the year on which both Gryce and Pettiford partici-pated. The tempo and routine are similar to the small group ver-sion and Gryce employs the band's unusual instrumentation to great effect, enhancing the exotic beauty of the theme. French horn is used to state the melody for eight bars, followed by reeds and harp for the next eight bars of the 16-bar A sections, with embellishment from Pettiford's overdubbed cello. Brass enter at the bridge dramatically changing the mood. Pettiford on cello and Lucky Thompson are the soloists on this track.

The only blues of the session, Horace Silver's "Speculation" is yet another holdover from Gryce's Signal nonet date of a year earlier and the arrangement largely adheres to the pianist's version, re-formatted by Gryce for the larger ensemble. Pettiford kicks things off with two choruses on cello before the theme is stated. Other soloists include Cleveland and Richardson who blow on conven-tional blues changes, while Farmer and Flanagan use an alternate progression based on the circle of fifths.

Gryce's last contribution to this recording session is a flag-waver featuring the two horn players and aptly entitled "Two French Fries." The 32-bar theme is based on the chord changes of "I Got Rhythm" with a bridge taken from "Broadway." Julius Watkins and Amram exchange choruses and fours in spirited fashion, both demonstrating great facility on a very difficult instrument.

Among the highlights of Lucky Thompson's arrangements for this recording session are his exquisite ballad "Deep Passion" on which he is also featured, and an update of the classic "Perdido" serving as a showcase for Pettiford on both cello and bass.

The album was enthusiastically received by the jazz critics. *Down Beat* awarded the album five stars (highest rating) and in his review, Ralph J. Gleason said:

When I first heard this album, I wanted to stand up and cheer. It represents exactly what should be the ideal in large group recordings. The arrangements—all originals by Pettiford, Mat Matthews, Horace Silver, Gigi Gryce and Thompson—are tight but loose enough for creative blowing, the solos are all clean, the ideas provocative and frequently exciting.

The performance, by the soloists and by the orchestra as a whole, is crisp, swinging, and yet earthy and vital. This easily could be a lasting LP.

One of the best things about it is the more you play it, the better it sounds. There is depth here, and a greater perspective in writing than most new large group scores. Total color is not neglected for strength, and there is a continual churning of ideas and effects throughout almost every number. This is the sort of performance that can be carried off only by a group that has melded together over a period of time or by an assembly of top-notch musicians with an instinctive feeling of oneness both with each other and with the music.[12]

Admiration for Pettiford as well as the excellent repertoire the band was noted for always made it possible to secure top-level musicians to play gigs with the band, and to maintain high morale in the face of often daunting economic conditions. In addition to the musicians mentioned above, the sections were filled at various times with people like Kenny Dorham, Ray Copeland, and Donald

Byrd on trumpet, Al Grey on trombone, Ed London and Jim Buffington on French horn, saxophonists Benny Golson, Gene Quill, Danny Bank, and Dave Kurtzer, pianists Dick Katz and Hank Jones, and drummers Shadow Wilson and Gus Johnson. The brief Pettiford experience remains a very pleasant memory for at least two of its surviving participants.

I usually got a pretty fair price for playing, even as a sideman, especially with people like Oscar Pettiford. One of the highlights of my life was that Oscar Pettiford band, and it was tough and I love that band. We just loved each other. Oscar and I were very good friends.[13]

Oh, the people loved it! Oscar himself was such an extraordinary personality and he was such a wonderful speaker when he would lead the band and such a sensational player that everybody in the band would just sit there eating up all of his solos on the bass and the cello. And everybody in the band was such a good player. I think at one point in the band, every single band member had a record out under their own name, had their own little bands and all loved each other's playing. So there was this tremendous collective energy that just made it irresistible. And when we would play at Birdland, the entire area by the bar (called the bullpen), which is the place you can get in without paying a cover charge, was jammed with musicians and music fans. It was tremendously exciting every night, every time we ever did it. And making the recordings, everything that we ever did was an adventure. It wasn't anything resembling a job. And we all worked tremendously hard. I mean you couldn't pay people for what we did. And you also couldn't pay to have the great time that we had being together. It was something I'll be grateful and proud to have been a part of every day of my life. (DA)

Occasionally the band would venture outside of New York for appearances.

Oh yeah, we took one tour that I described in my book, *Vibrations*, to Tallahassee, Florida, Florida A&M. And how we ever made it there was a miracle. One time we had a tour that was supposed to be an

Gigi Gryce in Navy uniform playing clarinet. c. 1946 (courtesy Valerie Grice Claiborne)

Gigi Gryce and mother. Pensacola FL. 1950s (courtesy Valerie Grice Claiborne)

Howard McGhee and Gryce at the Howard McGhee Sextet. Vol. 2 *session. May 20, 1953. WOR Studios, New York (Francis Wolff © Mosaic Images)*

Gryce. Tal Farlow, and Walter Bolden, same session (Francis Wolff © Mosaic Images)

Charlie Rouse, Clifford Brown, and Gryce at the Clifford Brown Sextet session, August 28, 1953, Audio-Video Studios, New York

Gryce rehearsing the Hampton Band, Autumn 1953 (© Ernest Zwonicek)

Lionel Hampton Band at railroad station, Basel, Switzerland, Autumn 1953 (© Ernest Zwonicek

Lionel Hampton, Clifford Solomon, and Gryce at Hampton Band rehearsal. Autumn 1953 (© Ernest Zwonicek)

Gryce, Anthony Ortega, Quincy Jones, Louis-Victor Mialy, and Clifford Brown. Algiers, Autumn 1953 (courtesy Louis-Victor Mialy © Louis-Victor Mialy)

Gryce and Quincy Jones, Autumn 1953 (courtesy of Louis-Victor Mialy © Louis-Victor Mialy

Gryce and Art Farmer at Birdland, New York City, February 17, 1955 (© Carole Reiff Photo Archive)

Gryce practicing on flute, Music Barn, Lenox MA, July 10, 1955 (photo by Bob Parent © Dale Parent)

Art Farmer and Gryce (with bow and arrow), Music Barn, Lenox MA, July 10, 1955 (photo by Bob Parent © Dale Parent)

The Oscar Pettiford
Band at Birdland,
New York City, 1955
(© Carole Reiff
Photo Archive)

Gryce and Jerome Richardson at the Ken Karpe Easter Concert, Town
Hall, New York City, March 26, 1956 (© Carole Reiff Photo Archive)

Gryce with the Teddy Charles Tentet at Cooper Union. 1956
(photo by Bob Parent © Dale Parent)

Gryce, Art Farmer, Teddy Kotick, Don Butterfield at the Teddy Charles Tentet Atlantic recording session, Coastal Studios, New York, January 17, 1956 (© Carole Reiff Archive)

Gryce, Idrees Suleiman, Julian Euell at the Pad, New York City, late 1956 (photo by Don Schlitten)

Jimmy Flanagan, Thad Jones, and Gryce, rehearsing for The Magnificent Thad Jones Vol. 3 session, late January 1957 (photo by Francis Wolff © Mosaic Images)

Thad Jones, Benny Powell, and Gryce at the same session, February 2, 1957, Rudy Van Gelder Studio, Hackensack NJ (photo by Francis Wolff © Mosaic Images)

Lee Morgan, Gryce, and Benny Golson, at the Lee Morgan, Vol. 3 session, March 24, 1957 Rudy Van Gelder Studio Hackensack NJ (photo by Francis Wolff © Mosaic Images)

Gryce, Cecil Payne, Wendell Marshall, Duke Jordan, Art Taylor at the Golden Thread Room, New Yorker Hotel, New York City, June 24, 1957 (photo by Don Schlitten)

Gryce blowing at the Lee Morgan, Vol. 3 *session, March 24, 1957, Rudy Van Gelder Studio, Hackensack NJ (photo by Francis Wolff © Mosaic Images)*

Gryce, Donald Byrd, Wendell Marshall at The 2nd New York Jazz Festival, Randall's Island, New York, August 24, 1957 (© Jerry Dantzic Archives)

Gryce directing at the Rich vs. Roach *session (Phil Woods and Stanley Turrentine in background), April 7-8, 1959, Fine Sound Studio, New York (© Chuck Stewart)*

Gryce and Max Roach at the Rich vs. Roach *session, April 7-8, 1959, Fine Sound Studio, New York (© Chuck Stewart)*

Gryce with tenor, Sahib Shihab, Jerome Richardson, and Budd Johnson at the Randy Weston Uhuru Afrika *session, November 16-18, 1960, Capitol Recording Studio, New York (© Raymond Ross)*

Gigi Gryce with his children Leila and Bashir, early 1960s (© Chuck Stewart)

hour and a half away. After we'd been on the bus about ten hours, Gigi said, "Man, we're in Ohio." [Laughs] And we went to the Springfield armory on a bill with Dinah Washington and only a handful of people showed up. The promoter, I guess, had disappeared with everything and there was no—there was Dinah Washington and Oscar Pettiford's band in the Springfield armory in Massachusetts. We just about outnumbered the audience. We stayed all night and played and Oscar just paid out of his pocket whatever he could—just an understanding that the married guys with the most children would do the best and most of us that were single would just get maybe carfare. In fact, Oscar finally went broke. He put his life savings into the band as so many bandleaders did. (DA)

The band continued to perform and record well into 1957 before economic realities forced its dissolution. What Pettiford, Gryce, and Thompson had created was a unique musical organization that encompassed all the best qualities of big bands while presenting them freshly and in a manner that was engaging and enjoyable for members and listeners alike. In this sense, it prefigured the Thad Jones–Mel Lewis Orchestra of the next decade.

Gryce's association with vocalists continued with his participation as arranger and conductor on a Betty Carter recording session for the Epic label. While she would eventually evolve into one of the most influential and highly respected jazz singers, at this point in her career Carter (1930–1998) was still seeking exposure. Four tracks were produced—"Frenesi," "Run Away," "Let's Fall in Love," and another version of "Social Call." The writing is competent and the accompaniment by a virtual all-star big band excellent, but this session offers little new or inventive relative to other contexts in which Gryce found himself during this period. Unfortunately, the album was never completed and Carter was dropped by the label later in the year. This music was not available until it was finally issued nearly thirty years later.

During the month of September, Gryce kept busy both as a side-man and with the quintet he co-led with Art Farmer. At the start of the month, he performed with Thelonious Monk at St. John's Recreation Center in Brooklyn.

The program picked up sharply with the arrival of Thelonious and his group. Gigi Gryce, alto, Wilbur Ware, bass, and Ron Jefferson, drums, combined with an obviously pleased Monk to produce a most thoroughly rewarding program of modern jazz.

Jefferson, an able and powerful percussionist, demonstrated plenty of talent—and, intriguingly enough, an engaging stage personality. Ware continued to indicate great promise and flexibility. Gryce, somewhat hampered by inadequate mike pick-up, was a stirring and ever-swinging soloist. Thelonious' hands still showed that amazing harmonic approach, especially on "Intermission Riff" and "Round Midnight."[14]

This free concert was the kick-off event for Jazz, Unlimited, a nonprofit organization that ran jam sessions and concerts and, in addition to presenting established artists like Monk, also played a significant role in starting the careers of saxophonist George Braith and tubist Ray Draper.

The week (September 14–20) that the Farmer–Gryce quintet spent at the Continental nightclub in Norfolk, Virginia must have been one of the last engagements for this band. Gryce decided not to make a job booked in Chicago and very soon thereafter Farmer joined the Horace Silver quintet.[15] It could well have been that traumatic effect of the sudden death of Clifford Brown on June 26 while en route to a Chicago club that forced Gryce to reconsider making the trip. The two men had been very close and Gryce was godfather to Clifford Brown, Jr., now a jazz disc jockey. Tommy Gryce reports that ever since Brown's death, Gigi had a fear of long car trips.

With Farmer out of the picture, Gryce sought other collaborators. Given their similar backgrounds in formal training and their mutual passion for composition, it was inevitable that Gryce and pianist Mal Waldron (1926–) would join forces at some point. They first worked together in the Teddy Charles Tentet and their approaches and writing talents were complementary. In the latter part of 1956, the first incarnation of the Jazz Lab Quintet appeared as a cooperative unit made up of these two along with trumpeter Idrees Sulieman, bassist Julian Euell, and drummer Arthur Edgehill. The band played at a New York club called The Pad (with Richie Goldberg replacing Edgehill), utilizing a repertoire made up of original compositions and cleverly reworked standards, the well-balanced mix being a hallmark of ensembles that Gryce would lead or co-lead in the years to come. The emphasis was on organization, form, and the avoidance of a casual, jam-session approach.

On November 9, the band recorded for Prestige Records under the nominal leadership of Waldron. Reflecting on this session, which produced the LP *Mal-1*, Bob Weinstock said:

It was probably a fusion of two people that were great jazz writers, Mal and Gigi. And there's one difference though. Mal could really cook. You know he was up there in the scheme of things with piano players. And Gigi, unfortunately, as I mentioned, wasn't right up there near the top as a player. But that they played well together and Idrees to me was another—we're talking about all these uncredited geniuses. Idrees Sulieman to me was a *great* player. He just never got any acclamation. He's like a virtual unknown today when he was really right there, you know. He could play anything. And I used him a lot because whatever we had to do he could knock it off right away. See, that was a very musical band, that *Mal-1*. (RW)

Four of the six tunes recorded were composed by band members. Gryce's contribution is "Transfiguration," based on the chord changes of "Gone with the Wind" and credited in the liner notes to Lee Sears. The composer offers a fluent and relaxed solo on this track and engages in two-bar exchanges with Sulieman in which the horn men cleverly play off each other's ideas. Waldron's up-tempo "Bud Study" is a fascinating and well-disguised variation of the standard "I'll Remember April," described by the composer as "an attempt to combine a classical flavor with jazz, something I heard in Bud Powell in 'Glass Enclosure'."[16] The other Waldron original is the multifaceted "Dee's Dilemma," a 36-bar opus built upon blues elements, in which the meter shifts from 4/4 to 3/4 in certain sections, even during the solos. The pianist also arranged Jerome Kern's "Yesterdays" yielding a compelling version of this evergreen, in which Euell's bass plays a prominent role in creating the mood. Gryce is up to the challenge of Waldron's adventurous writing, playing with confidence and swinging throughout.

Benny Golson, Gryce's music publishing partner, is represented by his "Stablemates," debuted by the Miles Davis Quintet almost exactly one year earlier. This 36-bar melody has a rather unusual ABA (14+8+14) structure that leads to some confusion during the four-bar exchanges between Gryce and Sulieman, marring an otherwise excellent performance. The program is rounded out by the trumpeter's contribution to the date, a blues entitled "Shome."

While the preponderance of Gryce's musical activities involved jazz, his musicianship and versatility provided him with the tools to participate in commercial recording sessions. He certainly must have done this from time to time in order to generate income, even though he was not prone to compromise his musical standards and few documented examples placing him in such a setting have been discovered. But less that two weeks after the Waldron session, Gryce was present in the Columbia Records studio on E. 30th Street in Manhattan as part of a band backing the pop singer Johnnie Ray. Ray Conniff was conductor and Mitch Miller producer of the date, which contributed three tracks to Ray's LP titled *The Big Beat*. Other jazz notables in the ensemble included trumpeters Clark Terry and Jimmy Nottingham, trombonist J.J. Johnson, and drummer Ed Shaughnessy. Gryce must have been considered among the top New York studio players to have been called for a session such as this.

Gryce's last recording activity for 1956, extending into early 1957, involved a series of big band dates for RCA led by clarinetist Tony Scott. His only solo on the sessions is a short outing on "Just One of Those Things," sandwiched between the trumpet of Clark Terry and the piano of Bill Evans, but his alto leads the saxophone section (unconventionally made up of a single alto, two tenors, and two baritones). While produced with a view towards the dancing audience, the LP (*The Complete Tony Scott*) does have some very strong jazz moments thanks to the talented cast of characters present. Nonetheless, 1956, which began with such interesting and creative associations, was ending on a relatively mundane note.

As the year wound down, there was some important recognition for Gryce (and several of his close associates) in the jazz press.

Metronome magazine recognized Gigi Gryce, Mal Waldron, and Donald Byrd as "New Stars for 1956." It also named Art Farmer and Jimmy Giuffre as two of the "Musicians of the Year." Both were associated with the Teddy Charles Tentet during 1956. Farmer was again named as a "Musician of the Year" in 1959. The Teddy Charles Tentet record on Atlantic was also mentioned as one of the best records of 1956.[17]

Gryce had worked with all but one of those artists in the Teddy Charles Tentet during the course of 1956 and while he had recorded with the Detroit trumpeter on the Oscar Pettiford octet album, the partnership of Gryce and Donald Byrd would come to the attention of the jazz community through numerous recordings and performances in 1957.

Notes

1. "Modern Jazz at Cooper Union," *Metronome*, June 1956, pp. 21, 30 (Teo Macero).

2. Hentoff, Nat, "Caught in the Act," *Down Beat*, June 13, 1956, p. 8.

3. Tracy, Jack, "Newport Festival—Afternoons: Panels and Music," *Down Beat*, August 8, 1956, p. 18.

4. Taylor, Creed, "Record Survey," *Metronome*, August 1956, p. 13.

5. Billy Taylor, Liner notes to *Know Your Jazz*, ABC-Paramount LP, ABC-115.

6. "Strictly Ad Lib," *Down Beat*, November 10, 1960, p. 48.

7. Hentoff, Nat, "Caught in the Act," *Down Beat*, May 2, 1956, p. 8.

8. Amram, David, *Vibrations*, New York, The Macmillan Company, 1968, pp. 233–234.

9. Gigi Gryce, quoted by Raymond Horricks in *These Jazzmen of Our Time*, p. 195.

10. Amram, David, *Vibrations*, New York, The Macmillan Company, 1968, pp. 234–235.

11. Korall, Burt, *Metronome*, June 1956, p. 8.

12. *Down Beat* Jazz Reviews 1957.

13. Jimmy Cleveland, interviewed by Bob Rusch in *Cadence*, January 1991.

14. Feehan, Gene, "Jazz Unlimited: New Club Is Formed," *Metronome*, November 1956, pp. 17, 41.

15. The new Horace Silver lineup was reported in *Down Beat* October 17, 1956, p. 6.

16. Ira Gitler, Liner notes to *Mal-1*, Prestige PRLP-7090.

17. Metronome Year Book, 1956, p. 29; Metronome Year Book, 1959, p. 15.

in the laboratory

BY THE MEASURE OF RECORDING ACTIVITY, at least, Gryce's jazz career peaked in 1957. This would be his most productive period not only as a leader, but as a sideman and writer on several recording sessions of high quality and great importance. It was at this time also that he would solidify his group conception of jazz, utilizing as a unifying element his series of recordings as co-leader of a quintet with Donald Byrd. And having entered the elite group of New York musicians capable of filling roles in a variety of settings, he was now getting sufficient work to ensure financial security.

Eleanor Gryce remembers this time as a relatively happy one for the couple despite the pressures imposed by a jazz musician's career. While passionately devoted to music, Gryce did have other interests, in particular motion pictures, and the two would attend the theater weekly if schedules allowed. He was a great admirer of fine drama. Orson Welles was his favorite actor and *Citizen Kane* his favorite film.

Occasionally the couple would take long weekends in Connecticut to visit Gryce's sister Harriet in Hartford or Eleanor's family

in Fairfield. But because of the demands of Gryce's chosen profession, Eleanor was frequently alone. She had been a member of
a social club before she was married but this caused a bit of a
problem after the marriage.

It was very boring after we got married for me because I either went
to where he worked or we went to the movies. And he was just so
serious like I think that sometimes I liked to go out and just be
with... Oh yes, he did go to a couple of dances with me because
before I married him, I belonged to a social club that used to give
dances once a year, give a dance annually. And because there were
other social clubs at that time, in the years that Gigi and I were
married, there were clubs. There was the Renaissance, the Savoy and
all those and somebody's social club was giving a dance either Friday,
Saturday, or Sunday. Cocktail sips—those things were very prominent
in those days. And because I belonged to the social club, you really
had to patronize other social clubs so that they would come to yours
and you would go to theirs and whatever. So when I got married to
him, he was really my father: "You can't do this anymore. You can't
go to these social clubs. You have to get out of your club." But it
didn't happen in the first couple of years but after about two or three
years, I had to get out. But when we were together he would occasionally go with me to these particular clubs. (EG5)

Musically, the year began with one of two sideman sessions for
Savoy Records where Gryce played Ernie Wilkins arrangements
behind the blues singer Big Maybelle. Although the band was made
up of jazz players, there was little room for stretching out. Another session at the end of the month would produce four more
tracks.

A very important event occurred in early 1957 when Gryce and
Donald Byrd decided to join forces and co-lead the Jazz Lab ensemble. Seven years Gryce's junior, Byrd (1932–) relocated from
his native Detroit to New York permanently in 1955, and soon
thereafter was ensconced in the jazz scene, working and record-

ing with nearly all of the hard bop stalwarts including Jackie McLean, John Coltrane, George Wallington, Art Blakey, and Horace Silver. He shared with Gryce a formal musical training, having received a Bachelor of Music degree from Wayne State University in 1954. Byrd also studied in Paris with Nadia Boulanger (1963) and later became an educator, obtaining advanced degrees from Manhattan School of Music and Columbia University. He currently teaches at Delaware State University as a distinguished artist-in-residence.

Fluent and lyrical, Byrd's style, like that of Art Farmer before him, fit beautifully with the conception of Gryce, spinning long, graceful lines in his solos. His facility at very fast tempi was notable, and in general his approach was somewhat more aggressive than that of Farmer, but not to the extent that it conflicted with or overshadowed that of Gryce. Furthermore, Byrd had an interest in writing and would contribute both originals and arrangements of standard tunes to the group's repertoire.

The name "Jazz Lab" might suggest an esoteric or academic approach to ensemble performance, but in reality the music the band offered was most accessible. It consisted of original compositions (many taken from Gryce's publishing company) and cleverly reworked standards. Blues were an important component of the repertoire. Gryce, who appeared to be the more dominant musical force of the two co-leaders, summed up the philosophy the band espoused:

The Modern Jazz Quartet will come to a club or concert and play very soft subtle music and then Blakey will come around like thunder. We're trying to do both, and a few other things besides. Insofar as I can generalize, our originals and arrangements concentrate on imaginative use of dynamics and very strong rhythmic and melodic lines. We try to both give the listener something of substance that he can feel and understand and also indicate to the oriented that we're trying to work in more challenging musical forms and to expand the language in other ways.

One advantage, we hope, of the varied nature of our library, which is now over a hundred originals and arrangements, is that in the course of a set, almost any listener can become fulfilled. If he doesn't dig one, he may well dig the next because it will often be considerably different. Several people write for us in addition to Donald Byrd, myself and others within the group. We have scores by Benny Golson, Ray Bryant, and several more.

A point I'm eager to emphasize is that the title, Jazz Lab, isn't meant to connote that we're entirely experimental in direction. We try to explore all aspects of modern jazz—standards, originals, blues, hard swing, anything that can be filled and transmuted with jazz feeling. Even our experimentations are quite practical; they're not exercises for their own sake. They have to communicate feeling. For example, if we use devices like counterpoint, we utilize them from inside jazz. We don't go into Bach, pick up an invention or an idea for one, and then come back into jazz. It all stays within jazz in feeling and rhythmic flow and syncopation. In any of our work in form, you don't get the feeling of a classical piece. This is one of the lessons I absorbed from Charlie Parker. I believe that one of the best—and still fresh—examples of jazz counterpoint is what Charlie did on "Chasing the Bird."

We want to show how deep the language is; in addition to working with new forms, we want to go back into the language, show the different ways the older material can be formed and re-formed. We want to have everything covered. My two favorite musicians among the younger players may give a further idea of what I believe. Sonny Rollins and Benny Golson are not playing the clichés, and they play as if they have listened with feeling and respect to the older men like Herschel Evans, Chu Berry and Coleman Hawkins. They're not just hip, flashy moderns.[1]

In its brief existence of barely a year, the Jazz Lab quintet utilized some of the finest rhythm section accompanists available: pianists Tommy Flanagan, Wynton Kelly, Hank Jones, and the underappreciated Wade Legge (1934–1963), a great talent who passed away at the age of only 29; bassists Wendell Marshall and Paul Chambers; and drummers Art Taylor and Osie Johnson. During this period, the Jazz Lab recorded for no fewer than five different labels, at fourteen sessions, producing a total of six LPs, all of which helped to establish a high standard for ensemble per-

1957 Jazz Lab Recording Sessions

Date	Format	Label	Rhythm Section
January 13	nonet	Columbia	Legge, Marshall, Taylor
February 4	nonet	Columbia	Flanagan, Marshall, Taylor
February 27	quintet	Riverside	Legge, Marshall, Taylor
March 7	quintet	Riverside	Legge, Marshall, Taylor
March 13	quintet	Columbia	Legge, Marshall, Taylor
July 5	quintet *	Verve	Jones, Marshall, Johnson
July 30	quintet	RCA	Jones, Chambers, Taylor
July 31	quintet	RCA	Jones, Chambers, Taylor
August 1	quintet	RCA	Jones, Chambers, Taylor
August 9	quintet	Jubilee	Jones, Chambers, Taylor
August 30	quintet	Columbia	Kelly, Marshall, Taylor
September 3	quintet **	Columbia	Kelly, Marshall, Taylor
September 5	nonet	Columbia	Kelly, Marshall, Taylor

Live Performance   **Vocalist Jackie Paris added*

formance within the hard bop genre.[2]

Between the two Big Maybelle dates in January 1957, a landmark jazz recording took place, the debut of the Donald Byrd–Gigi Gryce Jazz Lab on Columbia Records, the most prestigious label in the business. At this time it was the label of Dave Brubeck, Miles Davis, and Duke Ellington. The Jazz Lab was signed just after Columbia dropped Art Blakey's Jazz Messengers upon completion of three albums, the first of which Byrd had partici-

pated in. Gryce returned to the nonet instrumentation (the working Jazz Lab quintet augmented by four additional horns) to record the very first version of Benny Golson's touching tribute to Clifford Brown, "I Remember Clifford," arranged by the composer, as well as the waltz by Randy Weston, "Little Niles," dedicated to Weston's son. Gryce's playing on all the Colum-

bia sessions is especially robust and consistent, and his solo on the Weston piece displays his most soulful traits. Jimmy Cleveland has a special fondness for these Columbia sessions:

Yeah, they're great. I thought they were just out of sight. The personnel was great, you know. That's the other thing too. He made sure he got the right kind of guys to really work together great, you know, and get the concept that he's looking for. (JC)

The early days of February were exceptionally busy for Gryce. He recorded four times for three different albums. Trumpeter Thad Jones (1923–1986), a longtime mainstay in the Count Basie Orchestra was another fine soloist with an interest in and talent for writing. He enlisted Gryce and his Basie bandmate trombonist Benny Powell to form the frontline of a sextet that recorded for the Blue Note label on February 2, a session that produced *The Magnificent Thad Jones, Volume 3*. Except for the standard, "Ill Wind," all of the compositions are by Jones. Gryce distinguishes himself on "Let's," a fast, minor-keyed 32-bar tune with sections reminiscent of Thelonious Monk's "Evidence," in that the melody line occurs as isolated notes distributed rhythmically at odd places. Gryce builds off the diminished scale repeatedly in his exuberant solo, which employs extended ideas stitched together most cleverly. About this solo Leonard Feather stated in the LP liner notes, "Gigi has three choruses that rank among his best recorded work, more like Gigi Gryce and less a shadow of Charlie Parker as are so many modern altos."[3]

Two days later the Jazz Lab nonet returned to the Columbia studio to reprise three compositions from earlier sessions. The fledgling Signal label on which Gryce had recorded in 1955 would soon be history, and Gryce was apparently hoping to capitalize on the distribution and publicity advantages now available through his association with a large, well-established record company. To this end, "Speculation" was recorded for the third time in two years in very much the same format as the original version but with some modifications in the solo patterns. Now Byrd, Gryce, and pianist Tommy Flanagan each take an introductory chorus to begin the proceedings, but Gryce's solo following the theme is only two choruses as opposed to four in the earlier version. This is unfortunate since his playing is now more assertive and developed, although still very much in the Charlie Parker mold in this blues setting. In general, solo space on the nonet tracks is limited, probably because of Gryce's desire to include as much material as possible.

"Smoke Signal" is also performed using the same basic arrangement as on the Signal date but in a slightly shorter version wherein Gryce and Byrd split a chorus, the piano solo is omitted, and Art Taylor's drum feature is only a half chorus versus Kenny Clarke's earlier full-chorus outing. This track was not released with the original LP, *Don Byrd–Gigi Gryce Jazz Lab*, but appeared for the first and only time on a Columbia anthology entitled *Jazz Omnibus* along with selections from many other artists associated with that label, including Louis Armstrong, Dave Brubeck, J.J. Johnson, Erroll Garner, Miles Davis, and Art Blakey.

Gryce's fourth recording of "Nica's Tempo" borrows elements from the Oscar Pettiford chart but features a new and attractively voiced introduction. The soloists, who again take only one chorus each, are the composer (in fine form), Byrd, Flanagan, and Taylor.

The very next day the quintet recorded two tracks, again for Columbia. Gryce's arrangement of "Over the Rainbow" is typical of the Jazz Lab approach to standards, fresh yet accessible. This 1939 chestnut is transformed from a ballad into a swinging medium-tempo piece in which the melody has been reformulated rhythmically and embellished harmonically to provide a very appealing and memorable frame for the improvisations. Byrd, Gryce, and Flanagan each provide two choruses, while bassist Wendell Marshall plays one. In the same lyrical vein, a second version of "Sans Souci" was recorded, this time at a faster tempo than in 1955 and now featuring Flanagan's celeste in the introduction and coda. Gryce utilized this instrument more and more during 1957 sessions for a different orchestral color (it was probably only available at the better recording studios). The pianist lays out or "strolls" during the first of Gryce's two solo choruses, a practice commonly employed by hard bop ensembles of this period to offer some variety and tension to performances. The routine conforms to the 1955 Prestige version with Byrd and Flanagan each taking two choruses, and the same shout variation leads to Marshall's solo which continues for another chorus. The final track of the first Columbia Jazz Lab LP was recorded a few weeks later and was yet another return to earlier material, this time "Blue Concept," in its third incarnation. Wade Legge was back on piano in the quintet. Always conscious of form and eager to avoid a haphazard jam-session approach, Gryce updated the Prestige version with shout figures behind the horn soloists and an interlude incorporating "The Hymn," made famous by Charlie Parker.[4]

Quincy Jones had founded his own publishing company, Silhouette Music Corp., and in early 1957 released a group of five quintet arrangements edited by Gryce called the *Jazz Messenger Series*. The compositions and arrangements were all written by Horace Silver and had been recorded by the early Jazz Messengers cooperative for the Blue Note label. Some of the tunes such as "The Preacher" and "Doodlin'" would achieve the status of jazz standards and remain shining examples of the hard bop repertoire. Each folio contained an arrangement transcribed from the recording with parts for trumpet, tenor saxophone, piano, bass, and drums and sold for $1.00. Except for the price, these folios appear very similar to published materials common today which allow students to recreate notable recordings and professional bandleaders to expand their libraries with high-quality and recognizable charts. Presumably Gryce's role as editor was to ensure that the transcriptions were true to the recordings from which they were taken.

Around this time, Gryce's compositions were being documented by several other jazz artists. The greatest advocate was Art Blakey, who by recording eight versions of Gryce tunes over the course of a few months continued the endorsement he had begun in

1954. These were debuts of several pieces ("Exhibit A" and "Wake Up") and, in the case of "Casino," the Blakey rendition remains the only recording. Other musicians were interested in Gryce's work as well. The minor blues "Blue Lights" was recorded twice within a few days, first by the pair of Chicago tenor saxophonists John Gilmore and Clifford Jordan, then by the father of the tenor saxophone, Coleman Hawkins, on his Riverside album *The Hawk Flies High*. Gryce would have an opportunity to work closely with

Hawkins three months later, again for the Riverside label, which was showing interest in Gryce's own group during this same period.

Apparently the contract that Gryce and Byrd signed with Columbia was not exclusive, as the Jazz Lab recorded for four other labels in the course of 1957. Their next studio activity was for Riverside. Donald Byrd's arrangement of Cole Porter's "Love for Sale" is interesting in that it uses several different tempi and a 6/8 rhythmic background on the A sections in the melody statement. This predates Freddie Hubbard's 1963 arrangement of "Caravan" for Art Blakey, which is very similar in style. Gryce solos first, then Byrd, then Wade Legge, each taking one chorus, all in straight-ahead up-tempo swing. Gryce and Byrd then trade fours with Art Taylor before Taylor takes an extended solo and then reintroduces the 6/8 feel.

"Zing! Went the Strings of My Heart" is not a song performed much by jazz groups, but one that was rediscovered by the Jazz Lab in the form of an arrangement contributed by Byrd. Again, considerable liberties are taken with the rhythmic features of this tune and a shout variation is added on the last chorus. Trumpet, alto saxophone, and piano each take a 56-bar chorus and then the horns trade fours with Taylor. Legge's ballad "Geraldine" features Byrd and Gryce splitting a chorus with both employing a double-time feel.

In an attempt to promote his own compositions, Gryce was recording them frequently. "Minority" would become his best known and most often performed piece. At the Riverside session, it is given its third exposure and taken at a medium-up tempo with the standard introduction being played in a swing pedal-point style (a later version places this in an Afro-Cuban context). Gryce solos first, taking five 16-bar choruses and quoting the old torch song "My Man" on the third. Byrd follows with four. After a piano solo, Byrd and Gryce trade fours. Halfway through, Art Taylor jumps into the sequence unexpectedly, leading to a bit of confusion.

This session produced the only recording of Gryce's "Straight Ahead," a slow, funky blues, as well as a second version of "Wake Up," a medium-fast "I Got Rhythm" variation. "Lee Sears" is credited as the composer of both of these tunes.

By this time, Benny Golson was a member of Dizzy Gillespie's big band, as was fellow Philadelphian Lee Morgan. Morgan's third Blue Note date used a rhythm section that brought together Wynton Kelly and Charli Persip of the Gillespie band with Blue Note house bassist Paul Chambers. This was the first recorded encounter of Kelly and Chambers, who in a few years would work together extensively in and outside of the Miles Davis group. Although this is the first meeting of Morgan and Gryce, the trumpeter did record Gryce's "Wildwood" (probably due to the influence of Golson) a month earlier in Los Angeles as part of an "East Meets West" session on Liberty Records.

The tunes and arrangements are all by Golson, who convincingly demonstrated his writing abilities with this album. Gryce plays flute on "Hasaan's Dream," taking the melody on this minor blues. His flute playing here is mediocre, obviously the work of a doubler, but his alto solo is impressive, beginning with a clipped quarter-note motif to which he returns at the end of his four-chorus solo (see example). He also includes a reference to "It Ain't Necessarily So," along with some blues-tinged lines amongst the bebop.

Excerpt from Gryce's solo on "Hasaan's Dream"

Of particular note is his work on "Domingo," a fast-paced 56-bar theme. Here Gryce has the unenviable task of following a fiery Lee Morgan solo and for his first chorus is somewhat overshadowed. However, in the second chorus, Gryce comes on strong and is able to stand on his own, launching some very well conceived extended patterns. In this context, he seems steeped in the harder-edged alto saxophone approach in favor at the time, as exemplified by artists like Jackie McLean, and has moved away from the softer sound in evidence on the recordings of two years earlier. The example shown is a highly chromatic line that is heard several times during the solo.

Excerpt from Gryce's solo on "Domingo"

The most unusual tune of the date is "Mesabi Chant," a 34-bar opus with a challenging ABA, 13+8+13 structure. Gryce again follows Morgan and uses a half-step pattern while negotiating a potential minefield with ease. On the final track, "Tip-Toeing," a blues heard in two takes, Gryce at last has the opportunity to precede Morgan and he plays very well on his short two-chorus solos. Interestingly, the solos Gryce plays on the two takes of this tune are very similar. On both he begins with an authoritative blues lick (somewhat similar to his opening of "Hasaan's Dream"), moving into triplets. On the master take (which immediately followed the issued alternate), he ends with some double-time playing. This does not occur in the alternative take.

Gillespie's band was packed with talent and Art Blakey borrowed Morgan and Kelly as well as the trombonist Melba Liston to augment his Jazz Messengers quintet for an RCA recording session in April. Saxophonists Sahib Shihab and Cecil Payne were also added. This grouping recorded two compositions arranged by Gryce: "A Night at Tony's" and "Social Call." It will never be known whether this was to be the start of another album of Blakey's dominated by Gryce compositions, but it is fortunate that the session was issued, albeit nearly thirty years after the fact. It is also Lee Morgan's first recording with his future boss, Art Blakey.

Others in the business were interested in availing themselves of Gryce's talents. A few weeks later, he wrote for a Herbie Mann recording session on Epic that included his sectionmate from the Hampton band, Anthony Ortega, as well as associates Hank Jones, Oscar Pettiford, and Philly Joe Jones. His charts on Randy Weston's "Little Niles" and Mann's own "Song for Ruth" beautifully balance the exotic and the mainstream.

Throughout their collaboration, both Byrd and Gryce were performing in situations other than the Jazz Lab. One was the Oscar Pettiford Orchestra, which was nearing the end of its existence but still active. Frequently featured at Birdland, the band was preserved on tape through the recording of a CBS radio broadcast from that club in late May, and both the trumpeter and alto saxophonist were present. Three of Gryce's arrangements were performed, "Nica's Tempo," on which both he and Byrd solo, "Two French Fries," the French horn feature, and "Smoke Signal" taken at a blistering tempo. On the latter, Gryce struggles to keep up at the beginning of his one-chorus solo but is burning in the best bebop tradition by the time he reaches the bridge. Sometimes a bit ragged, the band nevertheless swings powerfully with its fires stoked by drummer Shadow Wilson and the leader. The tracks are short because of the radio format, and the sound quality poor, but the recording gives a good sampling of the excitement this aggregation could generate in a live setting.

The trumpeter Kenny Dorham asked Gryce to arrange two compositions for his Riverside *Jazz Contrasts* date. One was the standard "My Old Flame," and the other, known sometimes as "Tribute to Brownie," has a curious background. It was first recorded by Louis Smith (February 4, 1957) and credited to Smith's friend from Atlanta, Duke Pearson, but on this date was titled "LaRue" and attributed to Clifford Brown.

The last gasp of Signal Records turned out to be a unique occasion for Gryce and involved a nationally broadcast television appearance, as Don Schlitten recalled:

> When we started the company we were kids with dreams as we all have and none of us very business-oriented and we got involved in the recession and ran out of money and, of course, went out of business. It began with the Jazz Laboratory series and actually it ended with, believe it or not, I don't think too many people know this, an appearance by Gigi and Cecil Payne and Duke Jordan and Wendell Marshall and Arthur Taylor on *The Tonight Show*. (DSch)

This was not a working band but one assembled for the occasion from musicians associated with Signal.

Tonight! America after Dark was a version of *The Tonight Show* that aired on NBC between January 28 and July 26, 1957, during a period of transition after host Steve Allen had left the program but before Jack Paar had become his permanent replacement. The Signal quintet was broadcast on June 24 on location at the Golden Thread Room of the New Yorker Hotel, with Hugh Downs as moderator, starting around 11:30 PM. Other performers featured that evening included the Johnny Guarnieri quartet and ventriloquist Shari Lewis. Broadcast records indicate that the quintet's material involved a mixture of standards, as well as two original compositions by baritone saxophonist Cecil Payne and one by pianist Duke Jordan, which were published by Melotone Music; however, none of Gryce's music was included. In between selections, Marshall Stearns, professor of music at Hunter College and a noted jazz authority at the time, was interviewed by Downs. Although neither Schlitten nor Payne remembers who served as the quintet's leader, the on-air dialogue between host Al "Jazzbeaux" Collins and Downs suggests it was Gryce:

> Right now there's some mighty sound music emanating from the

Golden Thread Café in the Hotel New Yorker. So let's join Hugh Downs and listen to the sound of Gigi Gryce and his group. To you, Hugh.

Thank you, Al. Here at the Golden Thread Café of the Hotel New Yorker the sound is what is known as modern.

Tonight we are celebrating a signal event… By that we mean the group you are hearing has just completed an album for Signal Records. This is the first time they have been heard on the air.[5]

Unfortunately, Signal Records was defunct before the LP mentioned could be issued and neither the tapes from that recording nor the live broadcast seem to have been preserved.

When Gryce and Thelonious Monk joined forces for their second and final recording session, the result would be an LP of lasting importance and one that demonstrates how genius can overcome adversity. The septet which Monk and Riverside Records producer Orrin Keepnews had assembled on June 25, the day after Gryce's TV appearance, was rich in talent and included two tenor saxophone giants of different eras, John Coltrane and Coleman Hawkins, trumpeter Ray Copeland, bassist Wilbur Ware, and drummer Art Blakey. Some accounts suggest that Gryce assisted Monk in the preparation of the horn parts for this session but this has never been verified.

Things got off to an unpromising start. Keepnews remembers Monk being on time for the session but Blakey arriving an hour late, initiating a downward spiral that would result in Monk's inability to continue. Before it got to that point, however, two takes of the pianist's very difficult new composition "Crepuscule with Nellie" were attempted, one not completely unsuccessful as the producer would observe many years later.[6] But subsequently events completely deteriorated and Keepnews could not get Monk to continue to participate. In order to salvage something from the

disastrous situation and utilize the wealth of talent on hand, Keepnews commissioned a blues to be performed by a pianoless sextet. What resulted was "Blues for Tomorrow," an over-thirteen-
minute track featuring extended solos by all participants. Gryce,
who is credited with composing the simple blues line, is the first
soloist and the most concise, taking only three choruses and participating in the exchanges of fours with Blakey later in the performance. This track was not included in the LP *Monk's Music*, but
issued later as part of an anthology also titled *Blues for Tomorrow*,
which might imply something more futuristic than practical. Riverside was not concerned with momentous events but was simply
hoping that the following day would be more fruitful.

The next day the session continued with Monk restored to a productive state but Keepnews now under pressure to complete the
album in one evening or risk losing band members whose all-star
status required them to meet other commitments. As with most
Monk recordings, the material is all from the pen of the leader
except for the hymn "Abide with Me," a most unexpected 53-
second-long sketch for the four horns alone. On the rest of the
tracks, the arrangements are minimal and provide extended space
for solos by all participants. At times there is obvious confusion
about who should be playing when and some of the ensemble
sections are ragged. But what is most fascinating about this session is the inventive and contrasting work of the tenor saxophonists, who delve deeply into the challenging Monk tunes in their
own, most distinctive styles.

Gryce solos on "Epistrophy" following Coltrane and Copeland,
taking two choruses while Monk lays out, and interpolating Tadd
Dameron's "If You Could See Me Now" just before the bridge of
the first chorus. On "Well, You Needn't," he follows Hawkins,

inserting a reference to Oscar Pettiford's "Swinging Till the Girls Come Home" on the bridge of his first chorus. Both quotes allude to employers of Gryce at one time or another.

The *Monk's Music* LP resulting from this session is not without its flaws, which, under the circumstances, were unavoidable. That the recording assumed the classic status it did (including a five-star *Down Beat* review) is testimony to the genius and creativity of all involved.

A demonstration of the status that Gryce had achieved by 1957 is provided by his inclusion in advertisements in *Down Beat* for Vibrator saxophone and clarinet reeds manufactured by the H. Chiron Company. The full-page ad shows a segmented wheel of six "Top Soloists and Recording Artists who use Vibrator Reeds," along with their photographs. Joining Gryce are Lucky Thompson, Tony Scott, Zoot Sims, Jerome Richardson, and Danny Bank, an impressive aggregation to be sure. His biographical description reads: "Gigi Gryce...Alto Sax. One of the best jazz composers and soloist on alto sax...Band Leader of his own orchestra!"[7] Eleanor recalls that the compensation for endorsing these products was not very substantial.

I don't think he got any money. He just got free reeds. [Laughs] I can't remember any funds coming in for it. Just, you know, the popularity... In those days, they didn't pay like they would now. They took your picture and you got free reeds. (EG2)

On July 5, 1957, the Jazz Lab participated in the fourth annual Newport Jazz Festival, produced by George Wein. The quintet appeared as part of a "Future Jazz Greats" series of afternoon concerts that also included Gryce associates Mat Mathews, Tony Scott, Eddie Costa, Oscar Pettiford, Horace Silver, and Jackie Paris. While Gryce's name was not immediately recognizable to the general public, headliners at the 1957 festival with a Gryce link included Lionel Hampton, Dizzy Gillespie, Stan Getz, Coleman Hawkins, and Gerry Mulligan—all among the biggest names in jazz.

The set of three tunes performed by the Jazz Lab was recorded by Verve Records. For this appearance, the rhythm section comprised Hank Jones, Wendell Marshall, and Osie Johnson. Willis Conover, the master of ceremonies, observed that one would expect to see Milt Hinton on bass because he, Jones, and Johnson formed a trio whose presence was ubiquitous on the New York scene at that time. Marshall was, however, the bassist of choice for Byrd and Gryce. The introduction continues with the comment that Byrd is one of the "new" trumpeters, last with the Jazz Messengers, and that Gryce is "continuing to write freshly and interestingly." At this point, Gryce takes the microphone and states with a hint of annoyance, "We're only going to be on the stand about 25 minutes so we'd like to save time by announcing the numbers immediately after we finish." He then proceeds to announce each tune *before* its performance.

The set begins with an up-tempo piece by pianist Ray Bryant entitled "Ray's Way" wherein Gryce seems more at ease with the expansive chord changes of this 56-bar theme than does Byrd. He opens his solo with a repeated note figure using false fingerings that was a pet lick of his (it also returns later in the improvisation). Next up is Gryce's blues, "Batland," which had just been recorded by Art Taylor's Wailers, and would shortly be recorded in the studio by the composer as well. The saxophonist's four-chorus solo on this track is very strong, alternating double-time runs with down-home, funky passages, resulting in a varied but cohesive presentation. The shout section of this performance is actually another Gryce composition appropriately titled "Blues Shout," which he would use in other contexts in the years to come. Completing the Jazz Lab's brief Newport program was a reprise of "Love for Sale" done as on the Riverside recording of four months earlier. The rhythm section is stiff on the Afro-Cuban sections, particularly when Johnson is compared to Art Taylor, drummer on the studio version of February 27, whose absence from the festival was unfortunate. Gryce is buoyant and energetic on his solo and the band swings hard during the improvisations.

The quintet's performance overall was competent but less than stellar, and reviews were lukewarm. Furthermore, when issued on LP, this short set was oddly paired with one by the Cecil Taylor Quartet from July 6 and the reaction to the avant-garde pianist's exploratory and provocative approach greatly overshadowed that generated by the Jazz Lab. Nonetheless, Newport 1957 provided a high-profile exposure which Byrd and Gryce attempted to exploit with another burst of recording activity in the second half of the year, and which began to bear fruit when Donald Byrd was voted "New Star" on trumpet in the 1957 *Down Beat* Critics Poll in August.

In rapid succession, the band did sessions for the Vik (RCA) and Jubilee labels. If the Columbia Jazz Lab sessions would feature the expanded instrumentation and more involved arrangements that Gryce favored, the Vik and Jubilee sessions would spotlight other facets of the group. These dates can be viewed together, as they share identical personnel, but seem to be two sides of the coin, with the Vik album addressing the kind of structured material for which Gryce was known, while the Jubilee album gives a more informal picture. All the sessions utilized an excellent and very supportive rhythm section composed of Hank Jones, Paul

Chambers, and Art Taylor. This trio also recorded as a unit for Sahib Shihab on Savoy during this period and on Chambers' Blue Note debut, and was a well-integrated team. The presence of Chambers seems to influence the structure of the dates and he is featured as a soloist on nearly every title. This contrasts with the other Jazz Lab records, which have only occasional bass solos. Chambers' smoother, more horizontal walking style is also a change from the percussive approach of Wendell Marshall.

Done over a three-day period, the Vik sessions involved only originals, including the third version of Gryce's "Capri." The session began with an "I Got Rhythm" variation titled "Exhibit A" that had already been recorded twice by Art Blakey and once by Art Taylor earlier in the year. In addition to fleeting quotes of "Bye Bye Blackbird" (another favorite) and the "William Tell Overture" (harking back to Gryce's high-school days), this track makes blatant reference to the classic 1954 "Parisian Thoroughfare" recording of Clifford Brown and Max Roach, which begins with an agitated cut-time section evoking the sounds of a busy traffic intersection before moving into the forceful bebop melody line. Byrd was one of the trumpeters perceived as heir to Clifford Brown's crown, and "Thoroughfare" was a favorite of his that he performed and recorded several times during the 1950s. Art Taylor shines here in his one-chorus solo and in his accompaniment.

On the earlier take of "Ergo the Blues" (first issued on a French LP in 1982), Gryce begins thoughtfully, placing every note precisely and answering himself in a demonstration of jazz syllogism. In his next chorus he moves from a blues sound to a diminished color and back, before quoting and mutating "Carmen." His third chorus proceeds into double-time without any sense of haste, and winds up on a Charlie Parker motif, which he then

231

develops into his fourth chorus (see example) before handing off to Byrd. Apparently this tune was running a bit too long and the later take cuts the choruses back to three apiece. Gryce's improvisation here has some elements of John Coltrane's then current "sheets of sound" approach with strings of notes squeezed to fit the rhythm. When compared to the earlier attempt, however, this solo is not especially outstanding. The tune must have appealed to Gryce as three years later he reprised it under a new name, "Jones Bones," on an album for the New Jazz label.

Excerpt from Gryce's solo on "Ergo the Blues"

Another fine solo may be heard on "Byrd in Hand." This piece, written by Byrd's Detroit colleague, pianist Barry Harris, was also recorded twice by baritone saxophonist Pepper Adams under the title "High Step." It is a contrafact on "All God's Chillun Got Rhythm," and is taken at a medium two-beat tempo before the solos start up in a swinging four. Gryce solos third, after Byrd and Chambers, and makes a characteristic run to his high F, then double times, leaving room to digest before stacking ideas, using sequence as he winds into his final bars.

The track "Splittin' " was performed at Newport as "Ray's Way," and although not a blues, does bear some resemblance to Horace Silver's "Cookin' at the Continental." Compared to the Newport version, this rendition is much more flowing. Whereas Wendell Marshall and Osie Johnson play exaggerated hits on the fourth

beat of each bar in the A section, Taylor and Chambers are subtler in the accents. The introduction also is not as chaotic, and the
horns are voiced in more consonant thirds rather than tritones.
The result is a noticeable improvement.

The Vik album was not issued at the time, and in fact readers of
Down Beat were encouraged to write to RCA Victor to petition its
release.[8] It would have to wait years to be finally brought out on
LP by the Japanese division of RCA.

Just over a week later, the Jazz Lab recorded for the Jubilee label.
The tune selection and presentation were less adventurous, perhaps because Jubilee was a smaller company than either Columbia or RCA Victor. It was made clear that this album was to be
straightforward, using the "freer, less compositionally involved
scores in the Jazz Lab book."[9] That this album was completed in a
single session compared to three for the Vik album speaks volumes about the approach. The seven selections are easily catego-
rized: two standards as quartet features for the co-leaders, a blues,
and a piece in the minor mode each from Byrd and Gryce, and
finally a single up-tempo bebop line based on "I Got Rhythm" to
show the compositional talents of pianist Hank Jones. This last,
"Bangoon," was also recorded by Cannonball Adderley (belatedly
issued under the title "Allison's Uncle") and would be recalled by
Gryce for a session later that same year, again with Jones on piano.

The compositions of Donald Byrd show a strong connection to
the repertoire of the co-op Jazz Messenger group of 1954–1956,
which is understandable as Byrd was the last trumpeter in this
unit, having replaced Kenny Dorham in December 1955. His
"Onion Head" is a stop-time blues, and "Xtacy," a minor-key Latin
piece, is something of a cousin to Silver's "Nica's Dream." On the

latter track, Art Taylor borrows heavily from the distinctive sound and style of Art Blakey both in the mallet tom-tom work and during the swinging solo choruses. Although Blakey himself was recording Gryce pieces during this period, his own group was suffering, and the 1957 Jazz Lab group was superior in many ways. The Jazz Messengers would make a remarkable resurgence when Gryce's friend Benny Golson joined the band in 1958.

Byrd's take on "Isn't It Romantic" uses the cup mute, somewhat out of favor among hard bop trumpeters, who tended to prefer the Harmon mute popularized by Miles Davis. The treatment is more medium than the typical ballad and both Byrd and Jones spin long double-time lines. Gryce's alto playing on this session is relaxed and swinging, but occasionally fatigued. He double-times on virtually every solo, perhaps spurred on by Byrd, whose effortless use of the technique is notable in his work from this period. Gryce's feature on "Imagination" has good ideas but here and elsewhere on the session he suffers from intonation problems. "Batland" starts as a rather traditional blues and Gryce's solo is his best of the date. He makes use of altered chords and also fits substitutions on top of Hank Jones's comping, elevating the piece from the mundane to the sublime.

This burst of recording activity led up to the Jazz Lab's appearance at the second annual New York Jazz Festival at Randall's Island in mid-August. Also on the bill were Count Basie with Joe Williams, Dave Brubeck, Miles Davis, Billie Holiday, Gerry Mulligan, and Dizzy Gillespie. The event received great attention and August 15–21 was declared "New York Jazz Festival Week" by Mayor Robert Wagner.

In August, 1957 Gigi and Eleanor's son Bashir was born. Eleanor quit her job with the Social Security Administration and stayed at home as a full-time mother. Music was now the family's sole source of income. Gryce's abstinence from drugs and alcohol insured that these dependencies, which were ravaging the jazz community at the time, would not devastate his own family life, or negatively affect his earning power. In this regard, he was not quite unique; some of his closest friends and colleagues were also clean-living, well organized, and responsible in their approach to life (as Nat Hentoff had noted three years earlier[10]) including Benny Golson, Clifford Brown, and Horace Silver. But there is no question that temptations were everywhere and many of the musicians with whom Gryce was interacting both artistically and as a music publisher were plagued with serious and debilitating problems of addiction and the associated legal and health implications.

Religion became something of an issue in the household since Eleanor had not converted to Islam:

My family are very, very keen on Thanksgiving and Christmas and so either they came to my house or I went to theirs. But he [Gigi] didn't always participate. Leaning towards Islam, he crossed out Christmas altogether, which really broke my heart. It broke my heart simply for the children, so when Christmas time came, I was never in my house. I was always at a relative's house because we make a big to-do about Christmas. He'd come with me. He wouldn't have it at his house. (EG5)

Although he was a devout Muslim, Gryce's actual religious activities and participation were limited, as Eleanor recalled:

It wasn't obvious because the only thing he did was he faithfully read the Koran. He faithfully prohibited any kind of pork in the house. Other than that, he never went to any kind of a worship service. And I told him, you can be what you want to be, but we're not influencing these children into it because I was a Christian. I was going to stay a Christian. He wanted me to change my name. I said, "No, what's the point?"

He never went to a mosque as long as I know, while we were married. I understand he might have done it afterwards. (EG5)

Gryce gave Muslim names to several later compositions. (Specifics are included in Appendix A.)

Shortly after Bashir was born, the family moved from 52nd Street to a two-family house at 143-45 182nd Place in the Springfield Gardens section of Queens. They borrowed the money for the down payment from Eleanor's aunt and uncle in Fairfield, Connecticut. While this location was removed from the active Manhattan music scene, there was a Long Island Railroad station two blocks from their house that would take one to 34th Street in eighteen minutes. This was fortunate, because Gryce did not drive. He and Eleanor took lessons at one point but only she received a license.

The Springfield Gardens home was roomy enough to allow Gryce rehearsal space, with a piano in the basement where he worked with his groups. The basement also had office space for publishing-company activities; Gryce eventually installed a large photocopy machine there. He also gave private lessons to a small number of students, mostly from the neighborhood.

As the summer wound down, Gryce was busy on the second ABC-Paramount album by the Oscar Pettiford Orchestra and was simultaneously recording *Modern Jazz Perspective*, the second Columbia album by the Jazz Lab. In fact, he was booked for sessions for both on August 30.

This sequel to the 1956 Pettiford album is much better recorded in terms of sound, and Gryce plays very strongly as section leader and as soloist, offering statements that demonstrate his flexibility such as the impressive work at the end of "Sea Breeze." The material is an interesting, unique mix, from the blues of "Now See

How You Are" to the studio-orchestra treatment of "Laura." Although the arrangers for specific titles are not credited on the ABC-Paramount album, evidence suggests that Gryce was responsible for "Little Niles" and "Sea Breeze," and possibly also Ray Copeland's "Somewhere," which Gryce recorded the following year. The arrangement for the unissued "Two Basses" was by Gryce as well. There seems to be a better understanding of the sound of the ensemble and how to integrate some of the exotic elements (harp, cello, French horns) into the blended whole. Unfortunately, these sessions would be the band's last.

Between the Pettiford sessions, Gigi contributed a new piece to another Lee Morgan Blue Note date. Gryce's blues "Kin Folks" is heard in its only recording. It was arranged by Benny Golson, who described the tune's genesis:

Some of Gigi's relatives, including his mother, came to New York to visit him. As the time neared for their departure he became very melancholy. As a result, that morning, about 5:30 AM, he sat in a restaurant over a cup of coffee and began to sketch a melody on a napkin. If you listen closely you can feel the effects of his melancholy. I tried to set up an introduction, and a supplementary chorus after the opening theme that would keep the same flavor throughout. The stop-time was also Gigi's idea.[11]

The Jazz Lab did some traveling in September, playing for the Interracial Jazz Society in Baltimore, where they drew a crowd of 700. It was reported in Down Beat that the group would embark on a college tour. "Gigi Gryce, Donald Byrd and the Jazz Lab group are planning a music and lecture college circuit package in the fall. The group has a Columbia session due shortly, with a capsule jazz history featuring vocalist Jackie Paris."[12]

Apparently, the tour that is mentioned here did not take place. In the notes to the second Columbia Jazz Lab album, Nat Hentoff writes:

The idea of this album came from a projected college circuit tour by the Jazz Lab and Jackie Paris. It had been planned to devote the first half of each concert to a swift outline of some of the root channels of jazz with the blues as a primary linking element. The second half of the concert was to represent several of the "modern jazz perspectives" being worked out in the Don Byrd–Gigi Gryce Jazz Lab.[13]

Randy Weston did make a lecture tour with the same dancers who had appeared with Gryce and Art Farmer at Lenox in 1955.

We went to a lot of universities together, Marshall Stearns and myself. By this time I had two jazz dancers from the Savoy, Al Minns and Leon James. They gave a whole history of the dance, and we would play the music, and Marshall would do the lectures.[14]

This missed opportunity must have frustrated Gryce.

The opening track of the *Modern Jazz Perspective* album, entitled "Early Morning Blues," is an obvious remnant from this proposed tour. It treats the blues in different ways, more traditional at first with a gospel influence both in the call-and-response ideas and the use of secondary dominant chords, then moving into a swinging riff blues which is the "Lee Sears" composition "Now Don't You Know," and finishing with "Blues Shout," which is more in the Gillespie style (ending with a quote of "Salt Peanuts"). The banjo and vocals of Jackie Paris are heard here and on "Elgy," Byrd's take on "Honeysuckle Rose." The original LP was sequenced to move through an approximately chronological look at jazz evolution, although only on the first medley is there any attempt to play in an older style. Paris also appears on "Early Bird," a blues by Donald Byrd, and at the start of the trades Byrd quotes an as-yet unrecorded tune of Gryce's titled "Movin'," which was later renamed "Leila's Blues" for the Gryces' daughter, born in 1959.

The final Jazz Lab session was a nonet date, and the pieces recorded were Benny Golson's "Stablemates" and Gryce's "Steppin' Out." Contrary to what might be expected, the composers did not write the arrangements of their own works; Gryce and Golson each arranged the other's piece. "Steppin' Out" is an update of the tune "Quick Step" recorded with Clifford Brown in Paris.

When the album was issued, *Modern Jazz Perspective* was the first Columbia jazz album to feature striking cover art by the painter S. Neil Fujita. Associating jazz music with abstract visual art was popular, and two other classic Columbia releases followed this pattern: Dave Brubeck's *Time Out* and Charles Mingus's *Mingus Ah Um*.

As Gryce had invited Benny Golson to contribute material to the Jazz Lab recording, Golson returned the favor when the time came for his debut as a leader, *Benny Golson's New York Scene*, recorded in October on the Contemporary label.

Nat Hentoff approached me. We were pretty friendly back then and he approached me about doing an album for Lester Koenig. When he asked if I would be interested, I said, "Of course!" We all dreamed about doing our first record date. The money was almost non-existent. But it wasn't about the money. It was about the chance to do what I do and have some sort of voice in it. So I jumped at the chance.

I shared some of the writing with Gigi. I also got Ernie Wilkins to write something. Not that they needed it but because they were my friends. I said, "C'mon! This is a thing that's special for me. Come share in it!" So that's what we did.[15]

Working with a concept very similar to that used by the Jazz Lab on their Columbia records, Golson employed a nonet (with his own tenor saxophone instead of tuba) as well as a quintet on this album. Gryce wrote for both groups, arranging Ray Bryant's "Something in B-flat" and his own "B.G.'s Holiday" for the quintet and "Capri" for the larger ensemble. He also played alto and is heard as a soloist on all three nonet tracks.

The album opens with the Bryant tune, a "rhythm changes" flag-waver with catchy stop-time hits and a hint of gospel. It is not known whether Gryce or Bryant composed the short four-bar ensemble segments that precede the bass solo. In any event, the chart is not much, though the piece works marvelously with mostly unison playing and a simple arrangement.

On "Whisper Not," Gryce leads off the solos and packs his half chorus with music, double timing from the start. He splits a chorus with his old partner Art Farmer on "Just by Myself" and the magic is still there. For "Capri" Gryce wrote a striking new thirteen-bar introduction and radically alters the conception of what was a fairly straightforward piece. Both rhythmically and harmonically, the chart is the most advanced of the large ensemble pieces on this album. In the opening, which pits the ensemble against drummer Charli Persip, the shifting meters and accents create a strong sense of tension that is resolved as the melody, accompanied by a counterline, begins. On the repeat of the A section, however, the challenging unease returns as thick ambiguous diminished voicings predominate in the harmony, and the mind-boggling rhythmic scheme moves between 3/4, 4/4, and 5/4 before any sense of balance is regained. Golson is the first soloist and the ensemble backs him with punctuation on his second chorus. A development of the introductory material is used as an interlude, and Farmer takes a single chorus before passing the baton to the composer. A brief shout chorus reusing the metric juggling leads into the final melody statement and a quick denouement.

Unissued until the 1980s and even then misattributed to Benny Golson, the track "B.G.'s Holiday" is a little-known gem. Here again, Gryce uses metric modulation. Despite the strong soloists, it is understandable that this was not released at the time, as the performance is somewhat ragged and the tempo fluctuates. This is a pleasantly puzzling composition, having a long form (64 bars, AABA) with very little harmonic resolution and employing whole-step movement in both the A sections and the bridge.

It may seem odd that Gryce was chosen to work on Dizzy Gillespie's December session, issued in 1960 as *The Greatest Trumpet of Them All* since every other player on the recording was well established with the trumpeter at the time. In fact, Gryce was first choice for the alto chair in Gillespie's big band when it was organized by Quincy Jones for the State Department tour of 1956, but he declined the invitation. On this Verve album he again shared writing duties with Benny Golson who arranged three of the eight pieces (and received a front-cover credit). The tightness of the group is particularly welcome in light of the numerous times Gryce's music was rushed and underrehearsed on earlier occasions.

Soloing on only three tunes, Gryce plays well on "A Night at Tony's" and again takes a half-chorus on Golson's "Just by Myself," sounding a bit tired. But his writing for this date is stimulating. On his five scores, Gryce continues in the direction established by the "Capri" chart. He works with shifting time signatures, and makes free use of radical changes in instrumentation and feel. From the celeste, triangle, and woodblock heard on "Reminiscing," to the tambourine and gong on "Shabozz," Gryce searches for the unusual to express his music in different colors and textures.

"Reminiscing" starts with the ticking of a simulated clock and exotic parallel harmonies, then finds Gillespie stating the melody in rubato fashion, finally falling into a groove at the bridge with the other horns providing a lush cushion. Gryce takes over for the last eight bars of the form and finishes with a soulful blues line. During a newly composed interlude, the time feel doubles briefly before Ray Bryant takes over for an almost classical solo piano statement replete with right hand octaves and cascading arpeggios. After Gillespie reprises the theme, the piece ends as it began with Bryant's celeste and Persip's cymbal having the final say.

Larry Douglas's "Sea Breeze" is given its second treatment by Gryce (he would return to it once more the next year), and this is a short, beautiful atmospheric presentation with Persip using mallets on tom-toms and cymbals in a Latin feel during the first half, only briefly moving to a swinging four. Gillespie is the only soloist heard.

Gryce does not solo on his own "Shabozz," but Golson, Gillespie, and Bryant play beautifully on the difficult chord progression and the fresh arrangement now features meter changes in the opening melody statement and a new shout chorus.

"A Night at Tony's" uses many of the elements present in the April 1957 Art Blakey recording including the intro (which seems to have been borrowed from a Quincy Jones chart[16]) and shout chorus, but where the Blakey version pushes straight ahead for its duration, the Gillespie rendition is slower, and downshifts into a six feel during the bridge, something only hinted at by Blakey's polyrhythms. Gryce recycles the ensemble backgrounds from his "Capri" chart, which are reminiscent of the Miles Davis "Dear Old Stockholm" vamp. Overall, this is more of a big band than a combo arrangement and while there are a few minor slips, the performance is generally tight.

Apparently since he had utilized the meter-change technique already for this album, Gryce dispenses with the shift to 3/4 time on "Smoke Signal" that he had used when he recorded the tune for Signal Records, replacing it with an out-of-tempo piano solo. Thanks largely to the awe-inspiring work of Charli Persip, the band is on fire during this piece and all soloists are comfortable with the changes. (The "Dear Old Stockholm" vamp makes another appearance here). Gryce gives Golson some new chromatic chord substitutions and the tenor saxophonist devours them.

A few days later Gryce and Golson met once more to work on Golson's first Riverside album, which brought in a top-flight cast with several bebop pioneers.

As I look back in retrospect at that album, *The Modern Touch*, now...and I've talked with some of those guys since, like Kenny Dorham when he was still alive...here I was, a new boy in town, recording with Kenny Dorham, Max Roach, J.J. Johnson, Paul Chambers and Wynton Kelly! The one person people didn't know on there was me...the leader! I asked Max once, "Why did you agree to record with me? Nobody knew who I was. I mean, I had no reputation." He said, "Oh, there was just something about you. I had heard about you." Probably through Gigi, I'm sure, because he had been with Max.[17]

It seems Gryce was in the studio for the session and enjoyed having a chance to work with his old colleagues.

Benny also turned to one of his favorite writers, the talented Gigi Gryce, who contributed "Reunion" (named for "getting together with guys like J.J. and Kenny and Max—old friends I hadn't worked with for a long time").[18]

"Reunion" is actually "Salute to the Band Box" (or "Salute to Birdland"), retitled just for the occasion. Whatever the title, the soloists delight in the "I'll Remember April" chord changes. The version of "Hymn to the Orient" is very much the same as the classic Clifford Brown presentation although the shout chorus is modified. Throughout this performance, Max Roach is inspiring, but unfortunately Paul Chambers is buried in the mix (which is apparently mono only for the December 19 selections—these were early days for stereo recording in jazz). Likewise, the sound on the December 23 session presents Chambers' arco solo on "Reunion" as thin and scraping, and the bass is lost altogether during much of the proceedings.

The readers of *Down Beat* voted Gigi Gryce number 15 alto saxophonist, ahead of Willie Smith and Lou Donaldson. He was also voted number 22 composer, ahead of Marty Paich, Al Cohn, and Gil Evans. The next year would see far less of Gryce's performing presence on recordings and he would never again enjoy such exposure and recognition.

Notes

1. Gigi Gryce, quoted by Nat Hentoff in liner notes to Jubilee 1059.
2. There is no evidence of the Jazz Lab ever recording for ABC-Paramount, as incorrectly reported in *Down Beat*, March 21, 1957, p. 8. Another *Down Beat* mention of "a big band date for Epic and a string date for Signal" (June 27, 1957, p. 8) is also erroneous.
3. Leonard Feather, liner notes to *The Magnificent Thad Jones, Vol. 3*, Blue Note BLP 1546.

4. In the 1997 article "A Rare Bird," Max Harrison traces this theme back to Jay McShann's "Wichita Blues" from 1940 and also notes that it appears in the Miles Davis recording of "Trane's Blues." The article is included in *The Charlie Parker Companion*, Carl Woideck, ed., 1998, Schirmer Books, New York.

5. NBC broadcast documentation stored at the Library of Congress.

6. Orrin Keepnews, "The Thelonious Monk Sessions," liner notes to *Thelonious Monk: The Complete Riverside Recordings*, Riverside RCD-022-2.

7. Full-page ad in *Down Beat*, March 6, 1957.

8. "Strictly Ad Lib," *Down Beat*, December 11, 1958, p. 8.

9. Nat Hentoff in liner notes to Jubilee 1059.

10. See chapter five.

11. Benny Golson, quoted by Leonard Feather in notes to Blue Note 1575.

12. "Strictly Ad Lib," *Down Beat*, September 19, 1957, p. 8.

13. Nat Hentoff, liner notes to *Modern Jazz Perspective*, Columbia.

14. Randy Weston, quoted by Laurent Goddet in *Coda*, February 1, 1978 (159), p. 8.

15. Benny Golson, interviewed by Paul B. Matthews in *Cadence*, September 1996.

16. Quincy Jones's "The Little Bandmaster" is from the 1953 Art Farmer Septet LP on Prestige.

17. Benny Golson, interviewed by Paul B. Matthews in *Cadence*, October 1996.

18. Orrin Keepnews, liner notes to Benny Golson: *The Modern Touch*.

the out chorus

*B*Y THE END OF 1957, Gryce had made changes in his publishing arrangements. He transferred many of his works from
Melotone Music to Totem Music, the latter being located in Bruce
Wright's law offices at 120 East 56th Street. (Melotone had been
managed from Gryce's home on 52nd Street.) Like Melotone, Totem was a joint effort with Benny Golson. The difference between the companies was that Melotone was affiliated with BMI
while the new entity, Totem, was affiliated with ASCAP. At the
time, the older ASCAP was still the more prestigious of the two
rights organizations and it could have been that the change was
viewed as a step up.

His first recording activities of 1958 involved four tunes published by either Totem or Melotone, with Gryce assisting on two
dates for the more R&B-oriented Peacock label out of Texas.
Gryce's brother Tommy, who was attending Columbia Teacher's
College at the time, was also involved in the arranging, although
he was credited on the album as "Tommy Bryce." The star of the
dates was the singer Betty Carter, whom Gryce had been informally promoting for several years.

Although still among Carter's very first under her own name, these recordings would be her last for over two years and did not receive any special critical notice. After she returned to recording in 1960, her second effort would be a celebrated collaboration with Ray Charles that cemented her status as a major jazz vocalist once and for all. Carter would not forget the tunes from this early session, however, and returned to them later in her career. "I Can't Help It" is her own composition and her version of "Babe's Blues" preceded lyricist Jon Hendricks's (with Lambert, Hendricks, and Ross) by more than a year.

The performances on this date are short (many in the two-minute range) and very much focused on the vocalist. The small-band charts set up the tune, with short introductions, backgrounds, or occasional shout choruses. It is not known who was responsible for specific arrangements, with Ray Copeland and Melba Liston being collectively credited for all. Gryce directed the session for Carter, as he had in 1956. On the session with the larger band, Gryce's chores are split between conducting and playing some section alto. Vocalist/songwriter Norman Mapp was a frequent contributor to Gryce's repertoire, and it is likely that the arrangement of his "Foul Play" was done by Gryce. Tommy Gryce has claimed "Bluebird of Happiness" as his arrangement.

Donald Byrd left the Jazz Lab in early 1958, reuniting for a time with his friend from Detroit, Pepper Adams, before traveling to Europe in the summer and remaining there several months. Gryce tried to carry on with the group, using Ray Copeland in the front line. There was, however, little interest from record labels and this lineup never recorded. Gryce and Copeland worked at the Big George Restaurant in Corona, Queens, in February, and at the Café Bohemia in late May opposite pianist Eddie Costa's trio. Over a year later, Costa would join Gryce's band, playing not piano, but vibraphone, thus making it a sextet.

In early June, Gryce spent two days working on something of a follow-up to his Signal album with Duke Jordan. This time, instead of overdubbing himself playing just alto, he utilized a variety of woodwinds in everything from a quartet setting to a full reed section. Interestingly, Gryce's sectionmate from the Hampton band, Anthony Ortega, had recorded a similar album in 1955 for Herald Records, even using the same pianist, Hank Jones.[1] On bass and drums for this session were Milt Hilton and Osie Johnson, respectively, completing a great rhythm section that was one of the most popular on the New York scene. The record, titled only *Gigi Gryce*, was done for the MetroJazz subsidiary of MGM and was produced by Jack Lazare, who, in addition to writing the liner notes, also contributed the tunes "Rich and Creamy" and "Lullaby for Milkman" (Lazare was host of a radio show called "Milkman's Matinee" on WNEW).

Gryce took advantage of this opportunity to present himself on his doubles for three ballads: tenor for "In a Sentimental Mood," baritone (with strong vibrato) for "My Ideal," and clarinet for "Rich and Creamy." His approach to these instruments is not at all a strict duplication of his alto style and is more fluid, although the pieces he chose for his secondary instruments were not especially demanding. This is the only recorded documentation of Gryce soloing on these other woodwinds. Hank Jones is heard on celeste for the latter two selections but the effect seems lacking. When Jones returns to the piano for the coda of "My Ideal," the full sound is a welcome change.

Returning for his third go-round with it, Gryce treats "Sea Breeze" in full saxophone-section style with alto soaring above the other voices. Additional overdubbed percussion—clavés and maracas—add to the rhumba flavor. While the Larry Douglas tune was commonplace on Gryce's discography, another piece makes its recorded debut here. Benny Golson's "Blues March" has some curious aspects that would not be heard in later versions of the tune. Golson has stated that this piece was written specifically for Art Blakey, although the drummer would not record it until October 30, 1958. Gryce's version does not have the raw power that Blakey would bring to it, instead using elements such as the piccolo to bring a sense of the march to the proceedings. The piece is not played in what would be the normal key of B-flat, but rather in G for the opening and closing melody statements, with a modulation to E-flat for the piano solo and then F for the alto solo.

In addition to Golson, four more of Gryce's colleagues are represented with the compositions "Little Susan," "Bangoon," "Cold Breeze," and "Somewhere," most of which were published by Melotone Music. Recorded earlier with the Jazz Lab, "Bangoon" borrows rhythmic features of its introduction from that of the Miles Davis *Birth of the Cool* track "Budo" and spotlights the composer, Hank Jones, on piano. Gryce's buoyant solo follows, including his pet phrase (see the 1954 "Salute to Birdland" example) at the beginning of the bridge. After Hinton and Johnson do some trading, a powerful sax soli shout chorus leads into the short reprise of the melody. The adventurous "Cold Breeze," composed by Wade Legge, features two alto solos bracketing Hank Jones's contribution, as well as some woodwind soli interludes with Gryce playing clarinet and flute parts. The flute is the focus of "Little Susan," written by the modern jazz waltz king Randy Weston. Ray Copeland's lyrical "Somewhere" is revisited, with Gryce leading the reed section on clarinet, and soloing on both alto and tenor saxophones.

The fleet "Lullaby for Milkman" is a surprisingly complex piece to have been contributed by the session's producer, though it is true that Lazare had studied piano and worked with Herbie Fields before going into radio. If it is paradoxical to hear such an energetic lullaby, it is almost as odd to find Duke Ellington's "It Don't Mean a Thing" presented in a very laid-back setting. Here Gryce layers himself into a saxophone section featuring tenor lead. Hampered by a few reed squeaks, Gryce flies through his half-chorus solo in mostly double-time. The cha-cha-cha that appears in the final melody statement is another curiosity.

The sole original by Gryce on this date is "Baba's Blues," which is an affectionate reference to his son Bashir, not to be confused with "Babe's Blues," the Weston–Hendricks composition in the Totem Music catalog that Betty Carter recorded (though they were copyrighted together in the same collection!). As with all tracks on this album, there is really no room for stretching out and Gryce's solo on this blues is severely curtailed. The impression is that Gryce wanted to present himself in as many situations as possible and was reluctant to create extended tracks, preferring breadth to depth. This album is the rarest of all Gryce's commercially issued recordings, commanding top dollar when the occasional copy surfaces.

One of the most striking photo subjects in all of jazz was the August 13, 1958 gathering of musicians from all eras on the steps of a Harlem apartment building. It was shot for *Esquire* magazine by Art Kane and later commemorated in a documentary film by Jean Bach called *A Great Day in Harlem*. In the famous photograph, Gryce stands at the far left, alongside his friend Hank Jones. It is thoroughly characteristic that he appears there, on the fringe, with his dark suit and hat and a folio under his arm. He looks more like a businessman than a jazz musician.

Gryce played a role in getting Thelonious Monk to the shoot, as Robert Altschuler of Riverside Records explained:

On the appointed day, I learned that Gigi Gryce wanted to accompany us. So Gigi came to the office and then we proceeded to go up on the West Side and stop at Monk's home to pick him up. I was not on a big generous expense account and the meter kept running of course—you can never turn the meter off—and we kept waiting and waiting and finally after an hour and ten minutes—I was concerned we were going to miss the photograph—Thelonious Monk came out wearing a lovely sport jacket, made no explanation as to why he was late, and in fact, on the entire trip up to Harlem the only person he talked to was Gigi Gryce.

Later, I managed to pull Gigi Gryce aside and I found out why we had to wait so long. Apparently, knowing that so many people were going to be in a photograph, Monk wanted to ensure that he would be seen and he had to think about what he was going to wear and apparently he was trying on a lot of different combinations. He came to the conclusion that most people, since this was a special occasion, would probably wear a dark suit, so he elected to wear a light-colored jacket. And if you look at the photograph, he also, in his knowing way, decided to stand next to two lovely ladies—Marian McPartland and Mary Lou Williams.[2]

Another session to which Gryce contributed was the Art Farmer *Modern Art* date for United Artists. Recorded in mid-September, this album has been regarded as one of Farmer's finest and a hard bop gem among many from this rich period. Gryce arranged Wade Legge's "Cold Breeze" for a group involving Farmer, Benny Golson, Bill Evans, Addison Farmer, and Dave Bailey. In contrast to his own version earlier in the year, this one is Spartan with the melody stated in unison except for the last half of the final chorus. In a typical effort to add form and interest to a small-band arrangement, he separates trumpet and tenor saxophone solos with a 10-bar interlude.

That same month, an unfortunate accident occurred involving Gryce's 13 month-old son Bashir. Scheduled for minor surgery in a New York hospital, the child was required to undergo a preoperative diagnostic procedure wherein a radiocontrast agent[3] was injected intravenously. The physician performing the procedure missed the boy's tiny vein and the chemical caused severe burns to his arm which subsequently required skin grafts to repair. A medical malpractice suit was filed and after many years, long after Gryce and his wife had separated, an out-of-court settlement was reached. It has been suggested that Gryce's anger and frustration over the accident and slow pace of the attendant lawsuit contributed to a downward emotional spiral from which he never recovered.[4] However, this view of things is disputed by Eleanor, who recalls that, while she and her husband were understandably upset over the incident, he was not unusually depressed or agitated as a result of it and remained immersed in his many professional activities. Further evidence that the hospital incident was not one with lasting and devastating consequences for Gryce can be gained from the observation that his career and family life flourished for another four years, before unrelated problems emerged that *would* cause great turmoil.

But this was not the only family tragedy the Gryces experienced in 1958. Eleanor had become pregnant with their second child, but the boy, named Bilil, was born prematurely and died after only fifteen days. While the event was painful to both parents, Eleanor recalls that her husband was very supportive during this time of grief. In order to heal from the unfortunate incident, she chose to spend a month-long period of rest and recuperation at her aunt's home in Connecticut. Bashir accompanied her. Gryce again sought solace in his work and remained in New York.

Jazz was appearing on the fairly new medium of television, and Gryce was seen on a local program hosted by WNEW radio DJ Art Ford. *Art Ford's Jazz Party* was a show dedicated to musical performances, and for a brief shining moment scored some high points for arts broadcasting.

Following its most successful and exciting program—a show with the Gerry Mulligan group, singer Morgana King, and a modern group headed by Gigi Gryce and Jimmy Cleveland—the Jazz Party became the object of management pressure and seemed destined to start watering down what promised to be the most fortunate presentation of jazz on TV with some concessions to the commercial mind. Emcee Ford, whose role was one of organizer of the sessions and brief commentator on the action, did succeed in showing jazzmen at work in an uncluttered, ungimmicked manner. Musicians on the show chose their material and just blew.[5]

Gryce played on two *Jazz Party* shows a week apart. On November 13, 1958, Gerry Mulligan was featured and Gryce, Jimmy Cleveland, Kenny Burrell, Hank Jones, and Candido joined Mulligan's quartet to perform selections from the motion picture *I Want to Live*. The next week featured a jam session with several of the same players featured on a long version of "What Is This Thing Called Love." Earlier that same year, Gryce's "Blue Concept" was also played on a television show titled *The Subject Is Jazz*, though he himself did not perform.

Prior to departing for their European tour with Art Blakey's Jazz Messengers, Benny Golson and Lee Morgan recorded an album for United Artists with an all-Philadelphia group. The only recording of Gryce's composition "You're Not the Kind" (based on "Pennies from Heaven") appears and Gryce also arranged pianist Ray Bryant's "Calgary" for this date. Gryce's tune fits in well with the other selections, which include a brilliant arrangement of John Lewis's "Afternoon in Paris" and another version of Benny

Golson's breakthrough tune "Stablemates," the latter featuring exceptional work from Philly Joe Jones, who is a vital asset on this high-intensity session.

Jones also contributed to two important dates that would help to further Gryce's reputation as a composer. During 1958, "Minority" was recorded twice on Riverside records, by Bill Evans with bassist Sam Jones and, with the exact same rhythm section, by Cannonball Adderley. Both versions have become classics. It was the Evans version that really caught the ear of drummer Jack DeJohnette, who recorded the tune on piano in the 1970s.

You know, I did "Minority," a Gigi Gryce composition that I heard and was very impressed with on *Everybody Digs Bill Evans*. Came out with Sam Jones, Philly Joe. And Bill's version was really a classic version of that piece. Those voicings of his really opened it up, made it a lot more modern, contemporary.[6]

Partly by virtue of his position with the Miles Davis sextet (alongside Bill Evans), Cannonball Adderley was fast becoming the top alto player in jazz. He and Gryce had a chance to meet at an event on November 23, 1958.

The Jazz-Art society held a concert dubbed Alto Madness, and featured Cannonball Adderley, Jackie McLean, Gigi Gryce and Lou Donaldson, with Wynton Kelly, George Tucker and Charlie Persip among those participating.[7]

In attendance at this concert was saxophonist Bob Porcelli, who recalled:

Yeah, it was Cannonball, Lou Donaldson and Jackie McLean. And then there was also a little band that played before they played and maybe after they played, kind of young guys from the Bronx. And one of them was a wonderful alto player who died too young named Bobby Capers. He was also there but he wasn't playing *with* them. He was already making a little name for himself... Great player, you know. He was young at the time. He was probably not even…he was still a teen-ager at the time. But those four guys, Jackie McLean, I remember he played first because he had to leave and he even apologized because he was playing with Mingus down at the Half Note, I believe. I remember him getting on the mike saying… He played a couple of songs, then he was apologizing because he had to leave because he had to go down there and play with Mingus. And then I don't remember the order. But I remember Gigi because he came up and he had a funny way of speaking, maybe a little lisp. He's the one who acted more like the stereotypical jazz musician than the other three. He made this snide comment about Paul Desmond. He referred to Paul Desmond as like, I guess, the white guy who was making all the money, who played in a very effeminate style. You know, he made some kind of a little comment about, "You're not going to hear any of that Paul Desmond stuff here"—something like that. He was the only one who said something like that.

They each came up separately playing with the rhythm section. Whether they played all together at the end, I don't remember. Anyway, Jackie McLean left right away. I remember that Lou Donaldson played, I think it was "I Know That You Know," real fast. And he was the only one who played a real up-tempo, and I saw him and mentioned the concert to him at a later time and he said, "Yeah, they all got mad at me because I played that fast song." Like he was trying to show them up or something. (BP)

The power and facility of the other players overshadowed Gryce's subtler statements.

Maybe it was just my perception at the time being a young and impressionable guy, interested in hard bop and hard blowing. I already liked him. But in a certain way, the records he made with Art Farmer—the compositions—[had] a different kind of approach. But I had to feel it was not nearly as good as those other three guys. He didn't play the horn as well as they did and he certainly didn't come at you and hit you hard like they did. It was not the style of the day, you know, hard bop and hard swinging and he certainly wasn't like that. And technically he wasn't really as much on his horn as they were.

But then again, as I said, I used to listen to him on records and loved his playing because of the notes he would play and the creativity. (BP)

Porcelli considered Gryce a more intelligent player than the others.

Much more than those other three guys actually. I can't put Lou Donaldson down for any aspect of his playing and Cannonball was already pretty much formed by that time. Jackie is what he is. He's a real hard swinger and not very sophisticated harmonically or anything. And then I remember like he [Gryce] would sound to me like maybe someone who was doing so much writing that he's not practicing real hard. A lot of times he would attack a note and there'd be a little squeak. Things like that, sax players understand like that happens to anybody, but I remember it would be a little annoying sometimes. He didn't have a hard attack and a big sound. It was kind of, not ironic exactly, but of all people to be putting Paul Desmond down… [Laughs]

But, of course, it's the way you're using the sound and the notes you're playing. I more thought of him as sort of trying to take a little bit from the very soft Charlie Parker or the pretty—*Bird with Strings.* He played more like that. It was sort of like when Bird would play real soft but still swing. I thought of him more in that area. (BP)

The difference between the hard alto styles and that of Gryce was a topic of interest at the time, and remains so in the present day. Gryce's colleague from the Lionel Hampton band, Anthony Ortega, commented on how Gryce made himself different, even from his idol, Charlie Parker.

His style was pretty subdued, you know. It wasn't like fiery. However, if you listen to it very closely, there's a lot of his personality, very sensitive and very melodic and very sensible. All his notes made a lot of sense. Of course, you didn't hear him screaming up in the high register or honking any low notes for effect. But he would play his solo, [with an] almost ingenious kind of approach which, I think, for the general public, it went in one ear, so to speak, and out the other. For instance, Parker had his fiery thing. Of course everybody wanted to play like Parker anyway. And then, maybe also, he [Gigi] didn't have the business sense with the booking agents to be booked around enough to really be known by the general public also, you know. He was like the "in" guy. All the musicians knew him and respected him but it kind of ended there, you know, because the general public, a lot of people have never even heard of him.

Well, his sound, I'd say was along the same line, not fiery but it was distinctive. I would say it was a distinctive sound but it just didn't catch on with the general public, so to speak. I guess it didn't have enough fire or something. You had to listen very closely to it in order to be absorbed by it. And also, his ideas—I mean he was incredible as far as his voice on the instrument. When you look back now and listen to it, maybe a lot of people didn't realize it at the time, which they still don't. But when you stop to really concentrate and that was the thing—not enough people heard him or concentrated enough on him. Then he was into the other thing as far as the business end of it, struggling with the songs and publishing them and fighting with these different guys and he got involved with a lot of that where it held him back as far as presenting himself on his own instrument, I think. (AO)

Bob Weinstock, who recorded both Gryce and Jackie McLean extensively, saw the players' styles as extensions of their personalities and experiences.

Jackie grew up as a young kid and he was exposed to more raw music than Gigi. Gigi was schooled. And it came out in their playing as they matured: Jackie very down and funky and Gigi more schooled. Gigi was a great musician. I enjoyed—he used to go through the changes like they were nothing! (RW)

Bassist Bob Cranshaw agreed.

I think that was a difference because of being a prolific writer and composer and the studious thing, the studious aura that he had over him. You know people knew he could play but I don't think that he had the experiences—you know, you had to do a lot of hanging. You had to do other things. You knew it was clean. You knew it was good. And people accepted it. I mean the difference to me was such a welcome difference [from] all of the guys using the drugs and all the guys, the Jackies who came through another situation and saw a different thing. Gigi didn't see that. (BC)

Julian Euell supported the idea that there were other aspects of Gryce's musicianship that made him special.

I think his greatest strength was in his composing and arranging. He went beyond anything else. As a player he was good. A lot of people didn't like him because of the style then was to sound just like Bird. You know, and if you didn't have a Bird sound, then you weren't playing. I mean the guys imposed a lot of things on themselves and then the critics did the rest.

Yeah, you know his sound was softer and he didn't attack the horn like Cannonball. I had the feeling a lot of guys really liked Gigi and respected him because of his wig,[8] as they say. Heck man, they knew this dude was a musician. (JE)

The close of 1958 saw Gryce ranked number 18 in the *Down Beat* Readers Poll, beating out Ornette Coleman in the alto saxophone category, though the next year would see Coleman take the New York scene by storm. *Down Beat* also selected *Monk's Music* as one of the five best jazz LPs of the year. Gryce's showing is rather remarkable considering that his only recorded work as an alto saxophonist during that calendar year was one album for the small subsidiary MetroJazz, and some section playing for another obscure album by Betty Carter. Apparently he had remained in the public's eye and ear with his live performances, his earlier recorded work, and his writing.

According to bassist Reggie Workman, Gryce stayed involved in music without necessarily being a player. "A very large part of his activity in those days—he wasn't always performing. Sometimes he was directing or composing." (RWo) In fact, all of Gryce's work in the recording studios during 1959 involved his pen and not his saxophone. His good friend Jimmy Cleveland had a contract with Mercury Records and as Gryce and Benny Golson had used the trombonist on their dates, Cleveland now repaid the favor, although he did have to do some persuading.

I had the hardest time getting Mercury to agree with me to get Gigi Gryce *and* Benny Golson. I don't know who they had in mind. I don't know *what* they had in mind. I don't know why they objected so strongly against Gigi and Golson writing this date! (JC)

The record label was uncooperative in other respects as well.

I was going to give the album another name, but that title [*Rhythm Crazy*] was put on there against my will by Mercury Records. I don't know why they came to that conclusion. Yeah, in fact, they did all the mixing without telling me that they were going to mix it down. They really didn't know how to mix it down. There's a lot of stuff on there, some of the parts, that they didn't even put on the record. Some places the baritone is missing. Some places the saxophone is missing.[9]

Cleveland has reservations about many of his albums, but singled this one out as his finest effort.

Looking over the stuff that I've done, and the way it was done, and the conditions under which they were done, I don't think that we did them—one album, that *Rhythm Crazy* album, was getting close to the way I wanted the music to go. It was in the direction, but it didn't represent my best playing. I've done far better on other people's albums.

Well, I always feel better about my own work, my own albums. I think *Rhythm Crazy* was about the best one. That was pretty good.[10]

Gryce and Cleveland spent time discussing the approach for the album.

I wanted my music to be into that real hard, fiery—Gigi and I used to talk about that a lot. We want that rhythm to be fired up, I mean just really sizzling. That was one of the terms he used—"the sizzling rhythm, man!" Especially when you use it on those fast tunes—be sizzling. And when you're doing a ballad you want the rhythm to really be crisp and you know, like add feeling to the ballad. I don't know if that tune came off like that, but that's what he was looking for. But see, my feelings with the A&R guy—you know, if there is friction between the artist and the A&R guy, even though the other players don't realize it, it permeates, kind of. (JC)

The two also chose the repertoire.

I asked him what he had. He had another tune that he played for me. I don't know where we were but he played this tune or he sent me the music. I've forgotten how that went. I think he played it. I think we went up to Nola's and he played this on the piano, you know. "I think this would be great. I think it would be wise to put it in another key." That's what was discussed. Then he said, "'Reminiscing,' why don't you do that? I think you ought to do this." Now this is after we settled on—he got all of whatever straightened out with Mercury or EmArcy. And this is when we started trying to decide what tunes we were gonna do. And so that's how "Reminiscing" came in there. Then "Crazy Rhythm" was on there and so he did those two. (JC)

Contrary to what is implied in the liner notes, Cleveland has stated that it was Melba Liston who arranged her own composition, "We Never Kissed"—not Gryce. "Reminiscing" has elements which are similar to the Gillespie octet arrangement, with the celeste and ticking woodblock, but is not as extended a performance. "Crazy Rhythm" is an exciting look at the Gershwin standard, with buoyant contributions from Osie Johnson and a fresh rhythmic take on the melody. Typically, Gryce composed a shout chorus for this, and his arrangement makes this 1920s tune sound every bit as modern as the other pieces on the album.

The next project involved another trombonist, this time the Detroit-born Curtis Fuller (1934–), who at the time was frequently working with Benny Golson in a quintet. The first of the two arrangements that Gryce wrote for the March 9th date was of "Down Home," a Fuller composition. Both this and Fuller's "Bit of Heaven" were in the catalog of Totem Music. Regarding the gospel-flavored "Down Home," Gryce commented:

Curtis has a talent that he should develop. He should write more. He has very strong possibilities. This piece was very good to work with. It has a very interesting, very warm line and it created quite a mood in the studio. Its construction is sixteen and sixteen and the changes fall very naturally, not as if they were composed. It gets the feeling of the old-fashioned Church sound—it has a real vocal feeling.[11]

Gryce juxtaposes this with a very modern introduction that has the three horns voiced in fourths. The tune stayed on Gryce's mind and just over a year later, he recorded it with his own group, omitting the introduction, but keeping much of the arrangement the same. The other contribution was a chart on Jimmy Heath's "C.T.A.," the line based on "I Got Rhythm" chord changes that Heath recorded with Miles Davis for Blue Note in 1953. Gryce wrote some variations on the melody to act as a shout chorus, but the chart is simple, deviating only slightly from the original structure to include an interlude section before the trumpet solo.

If Gryce's input was minimal on the Fuller date, he more than made up for it the following month when he was specifically chosen by Max Roach to write all the arrangements for a battle of drums and bands between Roach's quintet and that of Buddy Rich. Producer Jack Tracy originally wanted only one band with two drummers but Roach was hesitant. "Max, a little dubious, said, 'Yeah, I'll do it, but I want to have my band on the date and Gigi Gryce has got to do the charts.'"[12] The relatively novel idea of stereo separation was employed, with the sound of each band emanating from a different speaker. Tracy said the charts would "utilize all the men as an ensemble, yet provide holes and jump-off points for the soloists. Each rhythm section would be responsible for its own soloists."[13] Gryce's scores are very even-handed and do not favor one band over the other, but instead make effective use of the available talents.

The repertoire is a hodge-podge, with Charlie Parker's "Big Foot" side by side with "Toot, Toot, Tootsie Goodbye." Gryce did manage to include one original piece, "The Casbah," which has never been recorded elsewhere.[14] This features two soloists from the Roach band, Julian Priester on trombone and Stanley Turrentine on tenor. Each takes half a chorus before the drummers move in to trade fours.

Louis Prima's "Sing, Sing, Sing" was attempted at two tempos, but either way the chart is simply an excuse for drum solos, as only eight bars of the melody are heard before Rich takes over, after which the same eight introduce Roach. Each drummer plays for dozens of measures, nearly 100 bars in one case. After the solos, the bridge and final A section are played to wrap up the performance. The other mainly percussion feature is "Toot, Toot, Tootsie Goodbye," which borrows the Brown–Roach introduction to "Take the 'A' Train" that Gryce would later graft onto his own arrangement of that tune.

The chart on Jerome Kern's "Yesterdays" is a much better representation of Gryce, and the basic arrangement was probably not conceived solely for this session, although the specific voicings for the horns certainly were. He would record a version similar to this on his final album. It is a powerhouse with, at times, a burning double-time swing feeling and at other times, a 6/8 Afro-Cuban groove. The marked difference between the style of the two bands is obvious here, and this arrangement is replete with the sort of characteristics that were Gryce's hallmarks dating back to his 1953 work with Art Farmer.

On "Big Foot," as with "Blues March" for MetroJazz, Gryce is not content to remain in one key during the performance but modulates from B-flat to E-flat when the solos begin. This track gives perhaps the clearest example of how the bands were dealt with for the session. The only exception to the solidarity of soloists and rhythm section is the piano, played by John Bunch of the Rich team, who sometimes accompanies the soloists from the Roach band (which was a piano-less group at the time). This straight-ahead blues is augmented with "Blues Shout," the line that Gryce had been using for several years as an uncredited concluding section for various blues pieces.

Another, even more subtle example of Gryce borrowing from himself is heard in "Sleep," the old Fred Waring big band theme, done here up-tempo with both drummers showing their brush technique. As the solos pass from Rich band to Roach band, there is an interlude of twenty measures that is taken from the arrangement Gryce wrote for the recording of "Capri" on *Benny Golson's New York Scene* over a year before.

Both drummers were masters of fast tempos, and "Limehouse Blues" is taken at breakneck speed (about 336 beats per minute). The soloists struggle to keep up at this frantic pace (which is amazingly surpassed on the improvised drum duet known as "Figure Eights"), with the Rich contingent coming off best.

Even though he was not recording instrumentally, Gryce kept up with his live performing. In the late summer, he was running the jam sessions on Thursday nights and Sunday afternoons at Copa City in Jamaica, Queens. The next turning point in his career occurred in the fall of that year. His newly formed quintet began work at the Five Spot at 5 Cooper Square, in Manhattan, on Wednesday, October 7. The hype in the press was that the five men in the band collectively played thirteen instruments, with Gryce on alto, tenor, baritone, flute, and clarinet; Richard Williams on trumpet and flugelhorn; Phil Wright on piano and vibes; Reggie Workman on bass, cello, and guitar; and Al Dreares on percussion. This was part of Gryce's master plan.

The expansion of jazz is unending and we as a group are working with that concept in mind. We have ideas for the future and one of these is to have each member of the quintet doubling on different instruments. We want to create and try to make everything we play listenable and exciting. Most of all, we want to play good jazz.[15]

Phil Wright, who had attended college with Tommy Gryce, remembered how he got the job and the education and experience he received during his short tenure with Gryce's quintet.

It was around 1959 because I got out of the Army in 1956 and I think I met Gigi through Tommy [Gryce]. And one of the reasons that I got to know him was that at the time I was living in Long Island, out in Jamaica. And he was living in Springfield Gardens. But he didn't drive. I got to know him by driving him around Long Island, going to the bank or to the store. So I got to know him and go by his house. He knew I was a piano player. And so I guess through that, you know, he started giving me a few little gigs and I got a chance to play with him on a few occasions. I never recorded with him but I worked with him at the Five Spot Café.

But I wasn't that experienced so he gave me hell and it's cool, he probably was supposed to give me hell because I was still learning. He wasn't nasty. He was just insistent about certain things. "You know you're playing that wrong—on the upbeat man. Hit the chord on the upbeat," or something like that. And frankly, he had his choice of piano players around New York who had reputations. And so he didn't really have to call me. I think he called me because, like I said, I used to drive him around and I was a friend of his brother's. But it was good for me because I got a chance to play with some really good players and I learned a lot. I learned all those tunes of his which some of them I still play. And when I left New York, I never saw him again anymore. (PW)

The Five Spot engagement lasted about a month and by November, the drum chair was occupied by Granville Roker, known as "Mickey," who had recently moved to the city from Philadelphia. This was his first gig in New York. Roker has fond memories of Gryce as a musician and a caring human being.

Back in those days, you had to have a police card. You had to go to the police station and register in order to play music. If you had any kind of a criminal record or anything, you couldn't play music in New York City. Thankfully for me, I didn't have any criminal record. Gigi took me to the Union and got my Union card and he got me my police card. I had two very small kids at the time. He would give me extra money, man, maybe five or ten dollars because he wanted to help me with my kids. So that's the kind of person I knew him as, a very generous person. He was a terrific musician, a great writer, and he was a very sensitive man. (MR)

Phil Wright named some of the other venues the band played.

I used to work with him out in Brooklyn at a place called the Turbo Village, a little bar with the bandstand over the bar. And then I worked with him, I think the last gig I did with him was in Pittsburgh at Crawford's Grill, up on the hill. And on that gig it was Gigi, Richard Williams, Reggie Workman, myself and Mickey Roker. (PW)

Workman (1937–), who would later be a member of John Coltrane's quartet and Art Blakey's Jazz Messengers, was another recent transplant from Philadelphia. Both he and Roker made their recording debuts on the Gigi Gryce album *Saying Somethin'!* in

March of 1960. Still a vital force in creative music four decades later, Workman recalled his first meeting with Gryce:

I think that when I first met Gigi I was working at the Turbo Village in Brooklyn, and it might have been with Kenny Dorham or one of those guys, and I know that's a place that Gigi used to hang out a lot. There are some other areas. I don't think that Gigi and I had any encounters in Philadelphia. It might have been through Freddy Cole because he's the one that I came out of Philadelphia to work with. Or, it might have been Jackie McLean. It's not really clear how that worked out but he asked me to work with his group.

We actually established a band very early on, about the first time I had come to New York. Gigi, let's see, somehow we hooked up a band with Richard Wyands, Richard Williams. That was the Prestige Records band and we were working together for a time with that band doing different things around New York. (RWo)

Gryce was also rehearsing a big band around this time, at the Club Ruby, not far from his home in Springfield Gardens, as Phil Wright recalled:

It was a popular spot at the time. It wasn't a jazz house, but he got the place to rehearse like during the morning. I can tell you some of the people in the band. My mind's a little fuzzy, but Jerome Richardson, Ray Copeland, Jimmy Nottingham... I mean it was an all-star band. I was overwhelmed because they were all much more advanced than I was, you know. And we rehearsed like every week for a while. I don't know how long but I mean the guys would come and it was like an eighteen-piece band, man, a full brass...like four trumpets, four trombones, five saxophones, and rhythm. And these were Gigi's charts. Now we never worked anywhere. (PW)

Interestingly, most of the arrangements were written years earlier in Boston.

He was like really very proud of his big band writing. He told me once, he said, "They don't know about my writing, man, my big band stuff. It's all like quintets." And then he went in his trunk and pulled out these scores and said, "Phil, Look at this man." I'm an arranger, an orchestrator and I was just starting out and that was one of the things that influenced me because his scores were so neat, meticulous. You could look at it and everything was symmetrical. So he was a very good arranger for big bands. I mean the only stuff that you probably heard is that stuff he did for Betty Carter but he wrote all this stuff when he was going to the Conservatory, a lot of it. He had them from up in Boston. (PW)

Like many other projects with which Gryce was associated, this ensemble never saw the light of day.

Just rehearsals. But it was a hell of a band. Never recorded and nobody knows about it except me and a few other people. It was something that was important to him. He really wanted to do something with a big band in New York. But as far as I know, he never did. (PW)

The last of an impressive list of trumpet players to share front-line duties with Gryce was Richard Williams. Williams (1931–1985) was born in Galveston, Texas and had studied music at Wiley College and served in the Air Force before touring Europe with Lionel Hampton's band almost exactly three years after Gryce had. After coming to New York, Williams played with Mingus at the 1959 Newport Jazz Festival and both he and Wyands were active with Mingus during the period they worked with Gryce. Williams was always eager to play, according to fellow trumpeter Lorenzo Greenwich.

Richard tended to play with anybody that would hire him. Richard was just a trumpet player. If you wanted him to play a show, if you wanted him to play this, you wanted him to play that, Richard would come with his trumpet. Richard just went to play. It didn't bother him which group he had to play with so long as it was something to read, or something to solo. It never bothered him. He tended to be a very easygoing person. (LG)

The trumpeter received high praise from Gryce, who said:

He is a student at the Manhattan School of Music. He has been with me for over a year. One of the sincerest musicians and individuals I know and I have the same regard for him as I had for Clifford Brown.

These boys had the sound and feeling I was looking for, the group has become a unit, one that is highly professional and has musical integrity. I think this is more important than looking for name value. A group made up of "names" doesn't necessarily mean they will work well together.[16]

Reggie Workman agreed with this assessment.

It's pretty clear in the people whom he chose to be in the band. I always say, even today, if you choose certain people in the band, it kind of gives an indication of what it is that you're trying to say and do, and once you choose that person, you expect that person to contribute whatever it is that you got him in the band for. Gigi was the same way. I learned those things from people like him. He would bring his music in. He would talk about the music. He would speak about what his idea is about a tune or whatever the case may be, but he'd give you the arrangement and you'd deal with it according to who you are. So, it wasn't that he was not in tune with being direct, it was that he was intelligent enough to understand that your direction comes from what you [as a leader] assemble and what you put down and what you ask the band to pursue musically.

We were working pretty often then. We were working a couple of times a month. Sometimes a gig like that would last for a week. In those days, you'd go in a club and stay in there the whole week. You might have a two-week engagement in one place then. That's when the music was allowed to grow, when it was happening every night like that or you work a whole weekend in one place. (RWo)

Compared to Workman and Roker, the group's new pianist, Richard Wyands, was a seasoned veteran. Born in Oakland in 1928, he had worked in California with Charles Mingus in the late 1940s and had served as accompanist to several great singers including Ella Fitzgerald. He moved to New York around January of 1958 and was introduced to Gryce by Richard Williams, whom he had known back in San Francisco. Wyands told *Cadence* magazine, "I'll say one thing, with Gigi I did get some freedom playing with him. We used to rehearse forever,"[17] and later elaborated:

Gigi was very serious, you know, about his music, and he wanted you to play it right too. That's why he rehearsed us so hard. He wanted perfection. He stressed dynamics. He wanted us to play in such a way that was loud when necessary, soft and so forth. We did a lot of rehearsing before we even played our first engagement, he had already rehearsed us pretty hard. It was almost like he had the whip out. Yeah, we used to go to his house in Springfield Gardens, in the basement, and we rehearsed quite a bit, I'll tell you!

He wrote no music for drums for Mickey [Roker]. But Mickey picked it up. We rehearsed enough, you know, that everyone could... In those days you had plenty of time to rehearse and you had time to rehearse on the job. You know, we would work some place for weeks at a time. That doesn't happen today. (RWy)

Art Farmer recalled how Gryce approached rehearsals.

I wouldn't say stern and he wouldn't be that casual to let something go by that he didn't like. He wasn't dogmatic but, when it came to music, I would say that he was more relaxed than unrelaxed because he was working with the people that he wanted to work with. He was working with people that he had respect for and, if you had to do two takes or ten takes, or whatever it took, he would go along with it. I never saw him say, "Gee, you guys are really sloppy," or never heard him make any kind of criticism like that of the people he was working with. (AF)

Gryce's high standards were also apparent to Benny Golson.

He was a stickler for perfection, and sometimes that drove people crazy. He would say gently, "Let's try it again," and give them another chance if he wasn't quite happy with something. He never tried to embarrass someone, but in the end he got what he wanted.[18]

But Julian Euell noted a clear distinction between Gryce and some other musicians who would make critical comments during performances or recordings.

See, some cats would say something to you while you were playing. But Gigi never turned around and said, "Hey, hey, hey," or whatever. At a recording, he never got nervous or excited with anyone if you missed the part. You know what I'm saying? He was very calm. He would try to figure it out. And he would say, "Let's try that again," or whatever. He was very understanding. *And* he would even say—a couple of times he asked, "What do you hear here? What do you hear there?" And you'd show him what you thought and he'd say, "Well, that's good. Let's leave that. That's cool." He wasn't so egocentric that you had to play every note—you know what I'm saying. He was willing to be flexible. He never criticized you on the bandstand. And we would play some stuff, arrangements, you know, we played music, not jammin'. We weren't jammin'. And I certainly wasn't up to his level in terms of musicianship and stuff like that. And I was struggling many times. But he would always say, "You got it. You can do it." (JE)

In an interview with Ron Eyre one day after the *Saying Somethin'* session for New Jazz/Prestige Records, Gryce made his plan clear.

We intend to integrate the sound of the group between straight jazz and commercial jazz. We want to play in clubs that have not previously had modern jazz units. The quintet will be capable of adapting their style to the atmosphere and requirements of the room and the listener. Our library consists of some 200 tunes and we have plenty of variety.[19]

Much of the extensive repertoire was drawn from Totem and Melotone material.

He did compositions of Horace Silver and singer/composer Norman Mapp, yeah. Gigi had a lot of his compositions in his publishing company, so he dipped out of it. He used a lot of tunes from different composers who… In those days, most of us didn't have our own publishing company. We didn't record many of them but we played them on the gig. (RWy)

The Gryce band was scheduled to play opposite the Ornette Coleman quartet when Coleman's group made its New York debut at the Five Spot in mid-November 1959, but this never happened. The large crowds—including many well-known musicians—who came to see "the shape of jazz to come" were treated to Art Farmer and Benny Golson's Jazztet instead. The Jazztet had better management and a higher profile at this time and these factors may have influenced the club's booking decisions.

A rare 33 1/3 demo disc by the Gryce quintet is stored in the collection of the Rutgers Institute of Jazz Studies. Donated from the collection of Willard Alexander, who booked the quintet, it bears a handwritten message from Gryce on the label: "A rushed demo, I hope it will be OK for your purpose. Gigi." It presents the band playing a variety of repertoire, but oddly includes not one of Gryce's own tunes. The arrangements of "Down Home," "Take the 'A' Train," and "Caravan" are virtually identical to those recorded for New Jazz and Mercury, and it may be that this was intended to attract label attention.

Of particular interest are the selections that exist only on this artifact since they tell something about the scope of Gryce's interests as a bandleader. "Sonor," a 30-measure composition by the pianist Gerald Wiggins, was recorded for Savoy in 1954 by Kenny Clarke while in California. It is associated primarily with the West Coast jazz scene (there were further California recordings by Curtis Counce and Les McCann), although Ray Bryant included it on a 1957 Prestige date. It may be that Bryant drew Gryce's attention to the tune, as they worked together shortly there-

Demo disc labels (Nola Studios), 1960. sides A and B

after. The same might apply to the ballad "I'll Walk Alone," recorded by Art Farmer in 1954 and Curtis Fuller in 1959, but it should be noted that this piece was also in the repertoire of Charlie Parker, who was documented playing it in Boston in 1953. "Stompin' at the Savoy," the classic from the 1930s Chick Webb and Benny Goodman big bands, shows that Gryce was searching for appealing repertoire from outside the normal hard bop sources.

The band played a week at Smalls' Paradise in early March and

during the time of this engagement also recorded their first album, *Saying Somethin'!*, for the New Jazz subsidiary of Bob Weinstock's Prestige label. Weinstock reflected on his earlier interactions with the Art Farmer–Gigi Gryce quintet and how Gryce had progressed as a musician:

I say he improved from the first sides with Art Farmer as a soloist to the Donald Byrd sides. I like them very much. I have them. I play them a lot.

And then I think by the time he recorded his own things, he really reached a good level of his playing. He was at the top of his playing. And that's why later on we did the three LPs of his group. Because I liked the man and I always believed as a writer he could really break through like a Horace Silver. See Prestige always, as I said before, we made a lot of money. So I could just—besides the Prestige label—I had the New Jazz label where I put newer talent. So that's why I did three LPs in one year with Gigi. It was like promotion to get him out there for the radio stations and the critics and everything. And unfortunately, it just didn't take. You know whatever a man plans doesn't always come true. And unfortunately, the only reason I can say he didn't make it is because maybe he just wasn't funky enough like Horace Silver. See funk was coming in with the organ players you know. (RW)

But Gryce made a definite move toward this soulful style of music, according to Richard Wyands:

Well, he just wanted it to be gospel, soul, funk. Those aren't his exact words but that's the way I would describe it. We had been playing these tunes on the job so we were quite familiar with it, felt comfortable. In fact I remember Mickey Roker used a tambourine on some of the things. He cut a hole in the tambourine right in the center, and put it on top of his hi-hat. (RWy)

The tune to which Wyands refers is "Let Me Know" by Hank Jones, which is a riff tune, a blues with a deceptive twist—a "hidden" 16-bar section that does not appear initially, but shows up in the 28-bar solo choruses and also at the end.

The other tracks on the LP *Saying Somethin'!* are similar in basic feel. Curtis Fuller's "Down Home" is reprised and "Back Breaker," a churchy, blues-drenched 12/8 number, features Gryce in an authoritative mode. His command of the idiom is remarkably convincing and his ornaments—grace notes, turns, and other filigrees—are perfectly placed and worthy of study. On this performance, Richard Williams is alternately restrained and rambunctious. His exciting open-horn solo is blaring and a bit sloppy, while his muted work adds the perfect effect to the piece. The tremolo shakes and touch of Erroll Garner that can be heard in Wyands's playing are simply icing on the cake.

"Blues in the Jungle" has another slight twist. At first listen it appears to be simply a minor blues in the tradition of Horace Silver's hit, "Señor Blues," but there are an additional four bars at the close of each section during the melody statements. The solos, however, are on the 12-bar minor blues form. On "Jones

Bones" (the retitled "Ergo the Blues"), Gryce plays a thought-fully restrained solo, with much use of across-the-barline phrases.

Excerpt from Gryce's solo on "Minority"

As John Coltrane became a larger influence on the jazz scene, similarities appeared in Gryce's playing. New elements such as a rhythmic complexity and symmetrical patterns, especially those taken from the diminished scale, show up more frequently. In his later solos on "Caravan" and "Minority," Gryce would make use of figures (such as in the example above) over extended domi-nant-seventh-chord harmonies.

Certainly, Gryce was already aware of the scale, as earlier solos show (see the excerpt from "Domingo" from 1957). And (as pre-viously mentioned) both Gryce and Coltrane were familiar with the Slonimsky *Thesaurus of Scales and Melodic Patterns*, which sys-tematically categorizes combinations of notes. It may be, how-ever, that Coltrane's explorations in this area affected Gryce, who during the 1950s had remained more of a disciple of Charlie Parker than had Coltrane, who was already developing a new style by the time he joined Miles Davis in 1955. The compositions Gryce re-corded in 1960 tended to be less adventurous than his mid-1950s works, but his improvisations moved further away from the be-bop mainstream. The idea of using patterns over chord changes entails an almost mathematical approach to music, searching for all possible solutions to a harmonic puzzle, rather than just the one readiest-to-hand. Gryce's experience with the *Schillinger Sys-*

tem of Musical Composition would have helped prepare him for these explorations. George Russell's *Lydian Chromatic Concept of Tonal Organization* was being studied by many musicians, and the categorization of scales that Russell advocated also puts emphasis on the symmetrical diminished scale as a useful color.

One example of Gryce taking chances in new territory is his long solo on "Leila's Blues," where instead of the five or six choruses that Williams and Wyands play, he goes for a full twelve choruses and seems to be digging, trying out new possibilities as they come to him rather than remaining in his comfort zone. Roker is especially stimulating at this fast tempo, spurring all the soloists on with his springy, on-top-of-the-beat approach. The title is an unfortunate misspelling of Laila, who was the Gryces's second child, a daughter, born in July of 1959. The piece itself existed at least as early as 1955, when it was copyrighted under the title "Movin'." Other blues figures find their way into this performance: "The Hymn" returns, and the shout chorus used by Clifford Brown and Max Roach on "The Blues Walk" is heard again. The latter tune also influences the trades towards the end of the piece, which become shorter and shorter.

Less than two months later, the band was back at Rudy Van Gelder's studio to record their next New Jazz album, *The Hap'nin's*. In total, Weinstock recorded and released three albums by the Gryce band, all done in the span of six months.

I really thought he would benefit from a lot of releases and a lot of exposure because I was really gambling on him breaking through as a real group like Horace Silver. And I felt at that time, the best way to do it was to get him a lot of exposure.

I think Esmond Edwards did the recording. The way we worked, I had a meeting with Esmond and I'd say, "Well, who's around?" and he'd tell me and he said "Gigi's got this and that and this and I think we could do some good stuff." And then I'd say, "OK, with who and what?" you know. And then I'd sort of give him the OK. And then each time, in another meeting he probably said, "What about Gigi? You said you wanted to really get behind him. Should we do him again?" I said, "Yeah, do him." And I think the contract was probably exclusive with three LPs or something. And so we just knocked them off all at once and put them out as fast as we could. (RW)

The first two albums seem to have been issued fairly soon after they were recorded, but the last of the three was released toward

the end of 1961 into 1962—well over a year after the session.

Each of the three albums has a slightly different flavor. *The Hap'nin's* includes more standard tunes and also presents Gryce's two best-known pieces in new settings. There is plenty of swinging, straight-ahead playing, and the sound has less of the stylized soul element than the first album.

"Frankie and Johnny" is an old tune from the 1920s that was in the book of the Duke Ellington orchestra throughout the 1940s. By 1960, it was almost exclusively the territory of traditional jazz groups, not beboppers, although George Wallington recorded a Quincy Jones arrangement of the piece in 1954, for the Blue Note label. The blues theme is stated in the key of B-flat by Gryce but recapitulated in E-flat by Williams. Gryce's routine places a heavy emphasis on dynamics, interludes, and shout choruses, all of which elevate and freshen the dated material.

In the late 1950s and early 1960s, it seemed that everyone had done a bit of *Porgy and Bess*. Miles Davis, Bill Potts, Hank Jones,

Rex Stewart, and Ella Fitzgerald and Louis Armstrong all devoted albums to the music from the opera, and many other jazz artists from Slide Hampton to Sun Ra were recording isolated tunes. "Summertime" begins and ends with a reference to another song from the show, "It Ain't Necessarily So," played in dramatic, rubato style by the alto over a tom-tom roll and strummed bass. Again, the use of interludes is key to the success and freshness of this performance of timeworn material. Gryce's two-chorus solo begins with one of his favorite interpolations, "My Man."

On *The Hap'nin's*, Gryce revisits "Minority" for the fourth time and "Nica's Tempo" for the seventh, using familiar routines and bright tempi on both compositions. The alto solos on these tracks demonstrate the change in Gryce's style. He makes use of the diminished scale in both, and reaches up into the altissimo register during the Latin-vamp section of "Minority."

"Don't Worry about Me" is taken at a moderate pace, with Williams muted and Roker on brushes throughout. The ensemble swings with restraint and both trumpet and alto solos offer inferences of "I Love You," a song which shares the prominent half-diminished chords. Perhaps the least interesting track on the album is the ballad, "Lover Man," marred by a hackneyed "Country Gardens" coda.

For whatever reason, Gryce played down his role as a soloist on this session, on several tracks taking only one chorus. Richard Williams plays more (often muted), but it is Richard Wyands who takes the longest solos on the album. Bob Cranshaw noticed this when he was working with the band.

Because he was such a great composer and writer, I think that overshadowed the playing because when you have a band and you let the other guys play, you kind of step back and you're playing less but you're hearing your music being played by guys that you enjoy. And that's how he got gratification: from watching the guys play his stuff. And we got off on playing his stuff and knowing that it was top level music. (BC)

During the time Gryce was actively recording the quintet, he also continued his work writing for others. In late May and again in late August, he contributed to a date by fellow alto saxophonist/flutist Leo Wright. The accompanying cast included Junior Mance on piano, Art Davis on bass, and Charli Persip on drums. On the May date, Richard Williams played trumpet, and in August violinist Harry Lookofsky appeared. At the time of this recording, Wright, Mance, and Davis were all members of Dizzy Gillespie's working band (Persip was an alumnus) and Gillespie's "A Night in Tunisia" is heard with the clever meter alterations that Gryce implemented. The introductory vamp is presented in six, the sendoff interlude in seven, and the rest in a fast 4/4.

West Coast pianist Russ Freeman's long-form ballad "The Wind," first recorded by Chet Baker in 1954, was in the repertoires of many bands including Ramsey Lewis, Chico Hamilton, Stan Kenton, and Slide Hampton. Gryce presents it in a dramatic setting, beginning with the high-note trumpet of Williams. Wright presents the beautifully simple theme on alto, backed by Persip, with the very interactive Davis commenting in counterpoint. Gradually the piano and trumpet join in to flesh out the sound. The bridge of the tune is replaced with a short piano interlude before Wright takes a bluesy solo with the rhythm section in double time, again with Davis prominent among the accompanists. A special aspect of this record is that Gryce's "Blues Shout" is finally presented as a stand-alone piece. The line is heard only at the conclusion of the track; it begins with the soloists each playing a few blues choruses.

Recorded at the second date, "Indian Summer" begins and ends as a beautiful duet between Wright's flute and the bass of Art Davis. In between, the bassist takes a strong solo, following Wright and Lookofsky. Throughout the two sessions, Davis is a wonder of creativity and taste. The arrangement of "Angel Eyes" involves little more than presentation of the tune in a somewhat exotic setting with a recurring bass figure, a written introduction and coda and a few harmonized lines for overdubbed violin. In late September, Wright would again en-counter Gryce's sidemen, Richard Williams, Richard Wyands, Reggie Workman, and drummer Bobby Thomas when Williams recorded his first (and only) album as a leader, *New Horn in Town*, for the Candid label.

The last album recorded for Pres-tige/New Jazz by the quintet (in June) was entitled *The Rat Race Blues*, and featured the compositions of only two writers: Gryce and Norman Mapp. Mapp had written several pieces in the Melotone catalog, and his two make up the LP's second side. The other three are by Gryce, although one of them is a collaboration with jazz journalist Ira Gitler, who re-called how he came up with "The Boxer's Blues":

I've written a lot of lyrics to already existing songs. The only one that's ever been recorded is "Filthy McNasty" by Horace Silver. And that's the way I've usually written, but I started writing these lyrics about a boxer and I finished them and showed them to Gigi, and he liked them so he wrote a tune to match the lyrics. Then he recorded the instrumental version for Prestige. (IG)

Not everyone was satisfied with the direction that Gryce had taken. Don Schlitten compared the band to the earlier Farmer–Gryce units.

See now, if you're a chef, you know how much pepper to use and how much salt to use to make the thing taste properly, OK? So when Art and Gigi played together, it was a proper amount of salt and pepper. When Gigi and Richard Williams played, there was too much salt. It didn't taste good. I don't know how else to describe it, I mean for me anyway. You know, somebody else might like a salty soup. (DSch)

Williams was a much more flamboyant player than Gryce (or Farmer, or Byrd), and this evidently bothered Schlitten. Nevertheless, *Down Beat* awarded the album four stars and reviewer Harvey Pekar's comments (below) are fairly accurate. It is worth noting that this album appeared as part of Prestige's New Jazz series, which leaned toward the adventurous (label-mates at the time included Eric Dolphy, Mal Waldron, Yusef Lateef, Steve Lacy, and Gryce's former student, Ken McIntyre, all of whom were stretching the boundaries of jazz).

Williams's playing generally is very good. A powerful trumpeter with a wide range, he seldom lapses into the bad taste that marred his work in the past.

But he still tends to play at one volume, and he is surely one of the loudest of trumpet players. On "Monday through Sunday," for instance, he "gets hot" too early, and most of his solo is anti-climactic. He builds intelligently from medium to high register, though, on "Strange Feelin'" and blows several lyrical passages on "Blues in Bloom." The quick tempo of "Rat Race Blues" doesn't phase him a bit; he never stalls—his solo is all meat.

Gryce takes an excellent solo on "Blues in Bloom," alternating pretty, melodic statements with double-time runs. Although he doesn't have the drive of some other alto men, he swings well and is inventive, as can be heard on "Rat Race Blues." But his solo on "Monday through Sunday" lacks continuity.[20]

On the title track, Gryce investigates such advanced musical concepts as bitonality (music in two keys at once). This can be heard in the interludes connecting the solos. Other jazz musicians investigating bitonality include Dave Brubeck and Slide Hampton, but the approach is common in classical music. Baritone saxophonist Pepper Adams noticed it in the music of composer Arthur Honegger, who was a favorite of Gryce's:

I love, particularly, the way he mixes keys. He'll have a beautiful melody going, and with a very strong accompaniment, but they could be, not the easy intervals, not necessarily the tritone interval or something like that, but be a minor third apart, or a second apart. It really gets fascinating.[21]

The melody of "Rat Race Blues" is not a blues at all but rather an eight-bar line which would later resurface as part of a film score; however, solos are based on the traditional twelve-bar blues structure but each in a different key: piano in A-flat, muted trumpet in F, and alto in B-flat, proceeding from the interlude where two of the tonalities are played simultaneously. During his rambling 14-chorus solo, Gryce touches on a modern-sounding figure based on fourths in the third chorus, but also falls into clichéd blues figures (and quotes of "Cottontail" and "Bye Bye Blackbird")— and is generally inconsistent, at times not articulating cleanly, and sounding confounded by the blazing tempo. The track concludes with Roker playing the melody on drums, another rather avant-garde device.

"Blues in Bloom" is not a blues either, but instead a modal composition, played in G minor with almost no chord changes. It could well be an attempt to imitate the jazz classic "So What" by

Miles Davis. The tempo and feel are identical. This track presents a rare glimpse of Gryce in a harmonic setting representative of the changes that bebop was undergoing at the time, and he sounds very comfortable, executing complex double-time runs with ease. This tune would be recorded by Mapp with lyrics on his debut album for the Epic label, *Jazz Ain't Nothin' But Soul*.

The slow 12/8 "Monday through Sunday" represents Gryce's most soulful showing on record. Mapp's minor-keyed composition has a 28-bar, AABA (8+8+4+8) form but, again, solos are based on a 12-bar blues structure, this time in C minor.

"Strange Feelin'" is another gospel-style opus, similar in feel to Curtis Fuller's "Down Home." The composer of this tune is listed as "Sam Finch," which may have been another of Gryce's aliases (as will be discussed later).

At the end of the month, Gryce traveled to Newport, RI where Charles Mingus was holding a "rebel festival" with many of his friends and compatriots. Those in attendance were Randy Weston, Kenny Dorham, Ornette Coleman, Roy Eldridge, Coleman Hawkins, Teddy Charles, and numerous others. Mingus, along with Max Roach and tenor saxophonist Allen Eager, had organized the festival in protest against the official Newport Jazz Festival, which was in chaos at that point. Mingus felt the artists should have more input and receive better compensation. The rebel festival was an artistic success. Unfortunately, no recordings were made of the proceedings and it has since entered the realm of legend. Toward the end of July, Gryce and his quintet played the Jazz Gallery, opposite the Thelonious Monk quartet.

Gryce's working ensemble was enlarged to a sextet in the fall of 1960 with the addition of vibraphonist Eddie Costa. An outstanding pianist and vibraphonist who, by this time, had established a reputation as an original and versatile musician, Costa (1930–1962) had been recognized as "new star" on both instruments in a 1957 *Down Beat* poll. He must have been familiar with Gryce's music, having recorded "Blue Lights" under the title "House of the Blue Lights" in early 1959, for the Dot record label. Costa would die in an automobile accident in 1962.

The new band was dubbed the Orch-tette by Gryce in an attempt to emphasize the various combinations its instrumentation afforded. He described his philosophy and aspirations regarding the unit to writer Martin Williams:

The fellows say to me, "Please, Gigi, let's keep this thing together. Let's stay on the scene with it." I think one way is for us to be flexible enough to take the group to places where jazz isn't ordinarily expected to go. To certain clubs and bars where they use music, but don't ask for jazz. Also, we can work fashion shows, for example. And on TV, radio, and movie soundtracks. We already have, in fact.

First of all, we want the fresh sound and blending I was speaking of. We are perfectly willing for the horns to play muted. If anything is happening, mutes won't stop it, and people will stop and listen to it too. Also, we want to keep a lot of things going on in the music. We want the background there all the time. For example, Eddie Costa will do comping for the horns solos with his vibrator turned off. And we want the drums there always, but never overbearing or obvious; "felt, but not heard," as they used to say.

All of the arrangements are new and in a definite style for this group. We want the band to provide a full-course meal and not just the same one or two dishes over and over—with discipline and subtlety, and also the jazz feeling. We also try to get a range and variety within each piece. We use lots of standards; they make friends with people. And blues. We use my own pieces, re-arranged for the group, some of Ray Bryant's things, and some of Norman Mapp's. Mapp writes nice, mellow things; he's a lyricist. I am also working on some of Duke's things and some of Monk's. I would like us to be able to play a complete set of pieces by each of them. Of course, there is also a feature piece for each of the men in the group.

We want to cover as much territory as possible with this "little band with the fresh big sound," as we are calling the group, with a wide range of tools. We also have a second repertory we will use for dancing.

The Orch-tette has also become a kind of seminar for us; there is always lots of discussion of music, about the best way to do things and the best way to reach different kinds of people with them. Of course, we always want to reach them with what we believe in and what we can do as jazz musicians, without being commercial about it.[22]

Bassist Bob Cranshaw recalled his experiences as a member of the ensemble:

We worked the Five Spot, the original Five Spot. That was the main place. We had maybe a regular Monday for—it seemed like a good while. I don't know whether Reggie [Workman] came back, you know, because we were kind of like musical chairs. It was guys in and out. But it might have been maybe two or three bass players who knew the deal. Yeah, Julian Euell was with him. It was kind of during the time when a lot of us were just kind of starting to get into various things. No groups were working all the time so you tried to fill in.

When I was there, it was always Richard Williams [on trumpet]. We called him "Notes." Everything that I did, I remember him being in the group. Richard Wyands on piano and I remember the times I played it was either Mickey Roker or...let's see, Walter [Perkins] might have done it a couple of times. It was mainly Mickey Roker and who else? It was [drummer] Al Dreares. Yeah, Eddie Costa [on vibes]... Most of the time I did it, it was a sextet.

Everybody was just there reading the music and kind of becoming part of the band. He had a bunch of guys who all knew his charts, which was nice because he was an employer and he was fairly busy. So we were all very happy with the deal we were doing. I just think that with the group that we had, you know, we were all very young and the energy was just very up and very happy.

I don't know whether he showed me, personally, whether he came to me and said do any certain things, but the music was well written. That I remember. And by being younger and watching guys like Eddie Costa who were already into the scene—I mean, Eddie Costa was one of the elder members of the band, probably. And all the rest of the guys—I mean, we were just starting. We were just getting into our shit and here we're playing with Gigi who was already a noted player. So for Reggie and Walter and all of us, we were young upstarts getting an opportunity to exhibit our playing through Gigi's music because we knew that any time we played with Gigi's band, it was a full house. The people came out to hear it and the music was good. People came out to hear the music because people knew that he was a great musician. And they knew he was a great writer. He allowed me to do what I do with the band and everybody seemed to have fun. I mean, I can remember nights when we couldn't wait to get back on the stand to play because it was so much fun. Everybody had so much fun!

He was such a great writer, I mean [the music] just played itself. We would finish late at night but nobody seemed tired. When you got through, we were still ready to play some more. Nobody ever looked at any watches and so forth. We just were delighted to play the music—because of Gigi's writing and because of the way Gigi was as a person. You had fun with the band. He gave everybody an opportunity—you know, you were still you within the things that he wrote. Yeah, he was a ball. I mean I know for Walter [Perkins], for the two of us that was the early years of our being here. So it was really very important to meet people like Gigi because these are people that I admired before I came to New York and had heard a lot about and would never have had a chance to meet when he would come to Chicago. I never met Gigi until New York and he was really a very brilliant guy. (BC)

Cranshaw did not attend the intensive rehearsals that Wyands did back in the days of the quintet.

We would rehearse on the gig. Yeah, I mean we could play something more than once a night and as you played it, you learned it. I don't remember how much rehearsing we really did. But we probably did some. The rehearsals, I guess for me, were probably like a gig. I never went to his house in Queens, see, so I never really knew a lot about his family thing. It was just a joy the nights we played. You know, I couldn't wait, Just like Walter [Perkins] said, we couldn't wait to get there because the music, we can handle it and it was uplifting to me. (BC)

Richard Wyands concurred:

Gigi was very elated about this particular group with the vibes added. It added a different dimension. He had written out things for Eddie Costa to play and Eddie was a good reader, you know, he could read very well. And we didn't necessarily have to rehearse that much, you know. A lot of that stuff was just sight-read on the bandstand. (RWy)

To drummer Walter Perkins, participation in the Orch-tette was an extraordinary experience:

Musically, it was—oh, oh it was so much fun! I'll never forget it. We had one night, we played there and it got so hot, I mean the music got so hot [Laughs], Gigi just said, "Stop, you can't go no farther. What can you play after that?" You know, after you play something so good, what can you do after it? You know, what can you play after something that's so good and hot, energy is up, everything is up, right? What can you follow behind that?

It was an honor to work with Gigi Gryce. I'll tell you, it was a very beautiful honor. I'm very thankful and very blessed to [have] had the opportunity to work with him. It was the most beautiful thing in my life as a creator—the same as workin' with Erroll Garner was a good time in my life, you know. A lot of the people I've worked with—I've been very thankful and very blessed to be able to work with all these different musicians. (WP)

The only commercial recording of the Orch-tette was done for Mercury, a major label. A record for Mercury was a privilege, a step up from Prestige and Riverside, as the more prominent label had better distribution and the larger budget allowed for more studio time. Reggie Workman, who returned to the band for one of the dates, suggested that Quincy Jones may have been involved in Gryce's being offered the deal.

Gigi and Quincy had done a lot of work in Europe together and they were pretty close and Quincy was involved with Mercury at that moment, so it's possible that it was like: "Hey, why don't you listen to Gigi Gryce?" or introduced him to the right people at the right time.

But, remember too that Gigi was always in the studio, he was always writing for somebody... Somebody probably liked what they heard and it's possible that they could have said, "Hey, why don't you come on and do something." Gigi was also in touch with a lot of the industry. (RWo)

Before going into the studio, Gryce and his band worked a week at the Showplace in New York, a club that had featured Charles Mingus for the previous ten months.

Recorded during three days in November of 1960, the LP *Reminiscin'* featured the sextet on five of the eight tracks, with Bobby Thomas on drums and either George Duvivier or Reggie Workman on bass. On the three quintet tracks, the bassist was Julian Euell and the drummer Walter Perkins. At the first session on November 7, two of Gryce's compositions, "In a Strange Mood" and "A Premonition of You," were recorded by the sextet, but they were never issued.

The Mercury sessions produced a really varied LP with all sorts of surprises. Mixing Ellington with originals and standards, Gryce seems to have gotten away from the bluesy, soulful, gospel-tinged material that dominated the New Jazz LPs earlier in the year. The arrangements are often complex with fast tempi, rhythmic and metric shifts, and subtle dynamics. Costa's presence provides an interesting new dimension to the band and the vibraphonist often comps behind the horns in place of the piano. Yet the LP proves disappointing in some respects, most notably in the brevity of the tracks, which, given the intricate arrangements, affords relatively little space for the talented members of the ensemble to stretch out in their solos. Again, it seems that Gryce was trying to exhibit as many facets of the band as possible, and the result is more of an appetizer than a main course. The listener is left wanting more.

About the title track, in the liner notes Gryce revealed that it was written in 1956 after re-encountering Evelyn DuBose when she visited New York.

I wrote it after visiting my childhood sweetheart. I hadn't seen her for ten years. Although life had led us apart, despite our youthful plans for marriage, we had managed to remain good friends. We sat and reviewed the wonderful times and things we did together.[23]

The piece, in its fifth recorded version, is approached in much the same manner as the earlier Gillespie and Cleveland renditions, with the woodblock that symbolizes "the relentless ticking of time" showing up at the close of the track.

Pianist Randy Weston, who had placed many of his outstanding compositions in Gryce's publishing companies, is also represented by one on the Mercury album.

"Gee Blues Gee" was composed especially for me by my dear friend Randy Weston. To me, Randy is one of the few great thinkers on the music scene today. Although he is extremely underrated and too often overlooked, his talent will one day shine.[24]

Weston's catchy composition, which would resurface as "Kucheza Blues" a week later, is a blues waltz with a four-bar tag performed by the quintet and the sixteen-bar form is followed by the soloists.

"A Night in Tunisia" is given a treatment very similar to that which Gryce utilized earlier on the Leo Wright session, with meter shifts between six and four and the famous interlude in 7/4. Polyrhythms are also an important feature of "Caravan." Yet another up-tempo burner, the Billy Strayhorn classic "Take the 'A' Train" utilizes an introduction and coda simulating a train, very much in the manner of the famous Clifford Brown–Max Roach recording. All three of these tracks, and "Yesterdays" as well, are taken at tempi above 250 beats per minute, although on the Jerome Kern standard the form of the tune is played at half the tempo of the rhythm section, creating interesting and at times dramatic effects.

Of the remaining quintet tracks, "Dearly Beloved" is stated in the key of D-flat but the solos are played in F, with very attractive transitions employed to effect the modulations. This piece also features a shout chorus with a strong resemblance to the bridge of Horace Silver's "Nica's Dream." In its third incarnation, the minor blues "Blue Lights" is given a treatment that adheres closely to the earlier recorded versions.

Throughout *Reminiscin'*, Gryce's playing is competent but not his best on record. Again, his arrangements and the sound of the Orch-tette seem to have been the features he was attempting to promote with this recording, not his prowess as a soloist.

However that may be, the album was well received by the press, being awarded four stars from *Down Beat*. Ira Gitler was the reviewer:

Gryce has organized a solid, unpretentious group that functions effectively as a small orchestra. Even when the material here is familiar, it is played with understanding and personal verve. Gryce is an arranger who fortifies a main theme without losing sight of its inherent qualities. He also finds new ways to present a piece, for instance, the refreshing vibes-with-bass-backing statement of Tunisia.

Gryce's playing has improved tremendously in the last few years. He sounds like no other alto man and has lost the stiffness which used to hamper him. Never strident, his strength is expressed by other means—his solo on Yesterdays is a good example.

Williams has often shown his capacity for explosive, confident, inventive playing in the Fats Navarro tradition, but rarely has he achieved it on record. Here he does. And his ensemble playing sounds like a whole trumpet section at times, as on Lights. Even his muted work on Yesterdays crackles.

Although better known as a pianist, Costa is a skilled vibist. He combines swinging and thinking effectively on Tunisia and Caravan. Wyands, a much underrated pianist, is fine throughout. His opening on Lights sets a good mood.

In this set, Gryce has achieved a balance between the blowing and arranged sections. The latter set off the former, investing the soloists' spots with greater interest and making the album a success.[25]

Recorded the next week, *Uhuru Afrika* was an all-star project conceived by pianist Randy Weston. It would turn out to be Gryce's final studio recording. His participation at this session, however, was mostly as a faceless section player. In fact, neither he nor any of the winds play at all on the first selection. Here, Gryce is most likely a member of the many-voiced choir responding to Tuntemeke Sanga's chanting. Photographs from this date show Gryce holding a tenor saxophone rather than his customary alto, although the record sleeve credits him with only alto and flute. His solo work on this album is limited to one tune, the finale

"Kucheza Blues," where he plays alto. This is only appropriate, as the piece is really Weston's dedication to him, "Gee Blues Gee," which was recorded just a week earlier for Mercury.

Gryce is not heard as a flute soloist (as the better-qualified Yusef Lateef and Les Spann are), but probably plays section flute on parts of "African Lady." Richard Williams, Gryce's bandmate at the time, is heard on "Bantu," the fourth part of the suite. On "Kucheza," Gryce begins his solo by establishing a motif against the percussion background. He then builds through the first chorus developing more and more momentum. When the piano enters at the second chorus, he moves more to traditional bebop-based lines. This rendition of the piece employs a 12-bar form rather than the 16-bar one that Gryce's version uses.

According to Jimmy Cleveland, as well as an album, there were also plans for a trip to Africa. Only Weston ended up going.

Well, it was different music because actually what was supposed to have happened, behind this, we were going to go to Africa with Randy. Me, Gigi, he had a group of guys that he was gonna take down there. What they did, they gave him a home near one of those cities down there and he was gonna go there to teach music and he wanted me, I think he also asked Les Spann about going over there. Gigi Gryce—he asked two or three people about going. Then something happened. They decided to fight and of course, we were not going. I think he went on anyway though. The music was great though, some really great music. The dates were always right on. (JC)

Weston's own recollections of the sessions were that they were exciting and groundbreaking.

So I got together with Melba Liston. I wanted to use a big band, and I wanted to use artists from Africa, and artists of African descent. Jazz musicians, cats from the Broadway shows, a classical singer, a guy from East Africa, a guy from West Africa. And all of a sudden, because a lot of the musicians said, "Uhuru Africa!" I didn't have to worry about the name. So Melba and I spent about a year together off and on, working on this music.

So it turned out that I had to do the recording two mornings in a row at nine o'clock in the morning. And every musician showed up on time! We had thirty-three artists altogether, including the narrators and so on, and everybody was on time. It was the most beautiful thing. We called it *Uhuru Afrika*, and it was in four movements. The first is "Uhuru Kwanza." At that time there were new African nations emerging. Africa was beginning to assert itself, and this was like a dedication to those various countries. The second was "African Lady," and it was dedicated to the African woman who has sacrificed much and produced much, and we wanted to honor her. The third was "Bantu," where we put all the drummers and all the other musicians together in one big thing, and the fourth was "Kucheza Blues," and that's the day when there's gonna be no more discrimination, man, it will not exist anymore. Everybody is together and everybody on earth is at love, you know; it's a big celebration. It's like a big fest; "Kucheza" in Swahili is like "dancing blues." The day when the African people will have their freedom and there will be none of these problems of discrimination. So this work is something fantastic.[26]

However, he also tells of some of the difficulties he encountered when the project was completed.

This particular album was packaged and put together in 1961. At the time it was a bit unpopular, especially with white people—even white people who were friendly to me. They would hear it once and they wouldn't want to hear it anymore. Especially the first part, where you have the poem. The other problem was with Roulette Records. They wanted to make some sort of a deal where I would be giving them power over my music. They promised to do a big promotion on me, but I have learned one lesson: Never sell a song. Never give the rights of a song. I don't care how sad you think it is. Never sell a tune! I refused, and therefore the album got buried. There was no publicity put behind it. So because of that and because of the message on the record, it was very hard to find.[27]

At about this time it was reported in *Metronome* that "Gigi Gryce has been hired by Finch Records to supervise its jazz dates."[28] This was not the first mention of the name Finch with regards to Gryce's activities. The August 6, 1959 issue of *Down Beat* magazine contained a brief and puzzling blurb: "Gigi Gryce, who got the band together for Owen Engel's ill-fated World Jazz Festival, is now A & R man for Finch Records."[29] Since a Sam Finch is credited with composing "Strange Feelin'," and because no one close to Gryce can remember such a person, it seems very likely that this was another of Gryce's aliases. No jazz records are known to have been issued by Finch Records (if indeed the company ever existed), although the following notice also appeared in *Down Beat*:

Vocalist Earl Coleman left for Paris after recording a date for Gigi Gryce's new record company, Gigi Records, accompanied by Harry Edison, trumpet; Tommy Flanagan, piano; Reggie Workman, bass; and Gus Johnson, drums.[30]

This session appears never to have been issued, and Reggie Workman has no recollection of the date or the label. If Gryce aspired to own his own record company, he did so privately because no one seems to recall discussions of either Finch Records or Gigi Records.

On Thursday, December 8, 1960, the Orch-tette participated in a benefit concert to raise money for the family of comedian and monologist Richard "Lord" Buckley who had passed away on November 12.

Gigi Gryce's new sextet came over from the Five Spot. With the alto saxophonist were Richard Williams, trumpet; Eddie Costa, vibes; Richard Wyands, piano; Bob Cranshaw, bass, and Walter Perkins, drums. The last two were on temporary leave from the MJT+3. Gryce's is an exciting group, but Williams, although obviously talented, should learn that playing loud is not everything. He also phrased very stiffly and, as a result, did not swing the way he had done in the Slide Hampton Band earlier in the year.[31]

On this same benefit were The Jazztet, Dizzy Reece, comedians Orson Bean and Larry Storch, and a group including Dizzy Gillespie and Ornette Coleman. The emcee of the event was disc jockey Mort Fega, who helped to organize the show.

Well, we got whoever was available. Between [Art] D'Lugoff reaching out and my reaching out we put together what I thought was a very top bill, an array of artists. You know, Buckley had a broad horizon of followers. Not even just friends but followers, a constituency if you would, because he was unique and he had an enormous attraction for people. And of course it was a busy night and I don't even remember all the particulars. (MF)

Fega particularly recalls the inclusion of Eddie Costa:

I was very friendly with Eddie. Eddie Costa was my ace you know. I was very tight with him. And it was really a dynamite band. And I do remember, yes. It was a *band*. It had an ensemble sound. It didn't have like two horns and a rhythm section. It wasn't that shit you know. It was a *band*. I always like to use that expression. (MF)

Apart from a week in January at the Jazz Gallery where a "battle of saxes" was booked between the bands of Gryce and Jimmy Giuffre, the Gryce sextet was ensconced at the Five Spot from December 1960 throughout the first half of 1961.

The Gigi Gryce Orch-tette, premiered in February at the Five Spot, consists of Gryce, alto sax; Richard Williams, trumpet; Eddie Costa, vibes; Richard Wyands, piano; Art Davis, bass; and Frank Dunlop, drums. Gryce explained that he was tired of formula modern jazz and hard bop, and wants to give the audience good, swinging jazz without gimmicks or hostility. We've noticed that groups led by Gigi always manage to be on the stand in time, and are neat and thoroughly professional in appearance and demeanor.[32]

Davis, who had just left Dizzy Gillespie's band when he joined the Orch-tette, went on to work with John Coltrane, who, like Gryce, was a particular champion of the bassist.

When I gave Gigi my notice, I felt very sorry especially since he thought I'd really stay because he said the group sounded better than any of his other groups. He was one of the very few people I hated to leave. Every moment was a gas with him and everyone in the group were excellent musicians and fine persons. We really had a happy group and many musicians and critics heard me to advantage and were amazed at what they heard. Gigi told critics that he always felt I was exceptional, and I feel that he is one of the most underrated arrangers around. Everyone was real friendly in the group, and we were all working together for improving the group. There was no friction or dissension.[33]

The personnel at the extended Five Spot gig continued to be fluid. Around March or April, after Art Davis left to tour England with Lena Horne, Eddie Costa was replaced by the Canadian vibraphonist Hagood Hardy. Costa would return to work with the band in later engagements. He died on July 28, 1962 in an early morning car accident on Manhattan's West Side Highway.

Drummer Frankie Dunlop was hired by Thelonious Monk and toured Europe in April and May of 1961. While Hardy was playing vibes, the rhythm section included Arthur Edgehill on drums and Addison Farmer on bass. Farmer himself would not live much longer. He died at Knickerbocker Hospital in New York on February 20, 1963 from a reaction to prescription medications.

The Orch-tette performed at Birdland in the summer and fall of 1961. One of the band's last documented appearances was at a benefit for the family of Booker Little. The trumpeter had died of uremia on October 5, 1961, and on October 31 a stellar gathering of musicians appeared at the Jazz Gallery to pay tribute: John Coltrane's quartet (with McCoy Tyner, Steve Davis, Elvin Jones), Duke Ellington, Thelonious Monk, Eddie Jefferson, Donald Byrd, Sonny Rollins, Philly Joe Jones, Jim Hall, Max Roach, Art Farmer, Benny Golson, Steve Lacy, Jerome Richardson, Roy Haynes, and John Ore. On this occasion, Gryce performed in the company of Art Davis.

During the Orch-tette period, Gryce became involved in a soundtrack project for a short dance film by director Fred Baker entitled *On the Sound*. The score for this work has been unearthed in the Library of Congress. It includes "Rat Race Blues" as a first portion. Scored for flute, alto, trumpet, vibes, piano, bass, and drums, it contains some of the most adventurous writing and playing of Gryce's career. The film's genesis and development were described by Baker.

Primarily, I'm a filmmaker/stage-director. My background comes out of stage acting and film acting and TV acting and directing in theater for about twenty years. And I got into films in the early sixties, actually, with the making of *On the Sound*. And, as a sort of a first trial run, to see if I could make some film, because I wanted very much— I was kind of a Bergman freak in those days, Kurosawa, you know. As a stage person, I was kind of very jealous of how expressive film could become for the *auteur* director or the director who considered himself more of a writer/director. So when I decided that I would try my hand at a film, basically *On the Sound* was the first thing.

And I was also an amateur or layman, avocational jazz musician, percussionist. So, I wanted to make a film that reflected that and I decided on a jazz dance film, like an eight-minute short jazz suite and dancers that would dance to the suite, therefore, the title, *On the Sound*. I wanted to do the sound first. The whole idea of *On the Sound* was to film the movie to an already recorded sound track, which involved bringing synchronous playback to the location so that it would be in absolute film time, you know, so when you cut the dance, almost like you were doing sync sound with dialogue, you know. It was kind of the music was playing for the dancers but it was playing on sprocketed tape, which meant there would be an exact sync to the tape.

So, I proceeded to try and get my most favorite jazz musician of those days. I was a very big Charlie Mingus freak and went to see Charlie Mingus at a club down in the Village and spoke to him and he said he would write an eight-minute piece for me and also record it with three or four other musicians [for] which I gave him some money, and he proceeded to do. I gave him very little money. I think I gave him three hundred bucks, which at that time was not that little but, you know, for an eight-minute suite I guess…

And when I went to kind of get the music, and get it all arranged about a month later, I had hired—well, actually, engaged some dancers from the Martha Graham Troupe, pretty well-known dancers, actually: Donald McKayle, Mary Hinkson, Matt Turney, who [were] kind of premier dancers at that time for Martha Graham, for the Martha Graham Company and they were also teachers as well. Donnie went on to become a top Broadway musical choreographer and Bunny was, for many years, the premiere ballerina for the Martha Graham Dance Company.

I went to see Charlie down at the club—Chantilly, the name of the club was Chantilly. It was on Waverly Place and Sixth Avenue or something like that, and he was sitting with Max Roach and he said, "Listen, Max is gonna sort of take care of my business here, you know? Before we make any further arrangements, Max wants to talk to you." And Max proceeded to be very salty and, you know, with the old—and I don't blame him because there were a lot of white guys exploiting black guys in jazz, in those days—almost all the managers were white—anyway, that was not my problem but it seemed to be Max's problem and he said he wanted me to come up with a thousand bucks right away.

And I left there kind of pretty depressed because I'd already given

Charlie three hundred bucks. I didn't have a thousand bucks to come up with just to cover the suite. I think I made the whole film for about twenty-six hundred dollars. That's total, you know, with paying the dancers, and paying an editor and all that kind of stuff, and all the post-production. So, there was no way I could put [out] that much money. Also there would have been the money to pay for the musicians and the recording session. So, I left there fairly depressed, but on my way out, Mingus came over to me and he and I kind of got along very nicely and he says, "Listen, I know you're very dissatisfied and I wrote something for you and it's not on paper yet, but let me get hold of somebody to call you and he'll take it from there because, well, you know, Max is trying to get my—I'm having a lot of trouble with my expenses." You know, he gave me the reason he needed Max to help him with [the] business part of his thing. I said, "Well, you know I'm very unhappy, Charlie, because I really wanted a Charlie Mingus score to this thing and I love your music," and all that stuff anyway. And he says, "Well, I wrote some good ideas," you know, because he knew the movements of the film. I gave him four movements like scherzo, adagio, you know, that kind of thing.

And, lo and behold, I got a call, not more than a day and a half, maybe even that night. I forget when I went home and I was depressed and I was talking with my wife and said, "Well, you know, Charlie Mingus pulled out and he's got my three hundred bucks and I don't know what to do about that but he told me he'll get me the music." So I said, "I wonder if I can kind of trust that he'll do that or just forget about it at this point." Nonetheless, I did get a call from Gigi and he said, "I'm Gigi Gryce," and I said, "Well, of course, I know who you are," and all that kind of stuff. I did have a pretty working knowledge of most of the people in the jazz world at the time.

I think I had heard Gigi play at the Five Spot, possibly down at Café Bohemia, a couple of times. You know, the old Bohemia on Grove Street and right around the corner from Louie's. That was a hot spot I used to go to and I think I heard Gigi maybe to sit in more than actually play, you know, play with his band. I didn't know him personally and I didn't know—I really didn't know almost all that much that he was as good a composer and arranger/conductor. And he said not to worry. He looked at some of the stuff Charlie had put down on a couple of lead sheets, some ideas, and he could take it and really embellish and work on it and get it into shape for me and that he would do it with, I think, five musicians. He would do the whole thing, recording session and all, on my budget which, I forget, at this point, I think maybe, at best, it was around—and I think he even mentioned that Mingus was going to give him some of the money. So, I think the fee base came to around, total of about seven hundred and fifty bucks. It was just one recording session, one three-hour or was it a five-hour recording session. Nonetheless, within not more than about a week to ten days, he came to my house in Manhattan and played me some tape recordings he had made, played me some of the ideas and I was absolutely delighted—just himself on piano.

So I told him, "Yeah, go ahead," and I think I gave him some money he needed to set up the arrangements. I think we recorded at Bell Sound. It was a place on 54th street. That was kind of a famous place for jazz recordings, small studio. And, we made a studio date and still hadn't shot a moment of footage. But he had, by that time, met the dancers. I had taken him over to see the dancers work and he had given them some basic idea of the rhythms and how the music would turn out. So they started rehearsing just basically what they would do and…I think he gave them kind of like that same tape that he had made. I don't exactly know because I didn't involve myself in that because it was their task to choreograph and get their thing together. I wasn't a dancer, you know. I was basically looking to see what they would give me on the set.

And we went into studio up at Bell Sound and it was a really wonderful feeling… Oh yeah, I mean, he gave his all. He wrote a beautiful piece of music. He made sure it was recorded well. He brought in top musicians. It turned out to be an all-star band.

But I knew from my own knowledge of the field that Gigi was a very well trained and very well studied musician. When he came into the recording session, I mean the charts were delineated, you know, per musician. You know, it was a pretty complicated little suite. And I was in awe at how fast they got it down. (FB)

Gryce orally explained the music to Mickey Roker, who couldn't read music at that point in his career.[34]

From that point on, once that day's recording was done, I left there with the disc, you know, a 33 1/3 disc and also, I think, a quarter-inch master copy. And, from that point on, it's just filmmaking. I know we shot sort of high summer up on the beach, or June, July, or August or something like that of '62. I think we shot for two days at my friend's house on the Sound, up on Long Island Sound. And it was a very successful shoot. We shot exactly what we needed. I mean, it wasn't like we shot fifteen to one or anything like that. We maybe did two or three takes on each piece, which were long, extended pieces at times because I wanted the continuity. I didn't break it down into little shots so we shot—well, we were so controlled by making it to the [music] that it was an easy shoot from that point of view except for the dancers who were dancing on pebbles on the beach. It was a stone beach. It wasn't really a sandy beach so they kept getting pebbles in their toes. It was kind of horrendous.

The whole idea was to shoot it in black-and-white using black dancers with white jump suits on, or actually white pedal pushers and white T-shirts. And also, the cameraman that I got was a guy named Richard Bagley who was a prize-winning cameraman. And his idea was to use Background X which was a very high contrast black-and-white film. And, hopefully, we would get some kind of a foggy day out there on Long Island. Another reason for the term "On the Sound" was that I had arranged with a friend of mine who had a beautiful estate up on Long Island, on Long Island Sound, up in Wading River. And there was this really beautiful kind of white-stone pebble beach which the dancers killed their feet dancing on but, nonetheless, we shot it so that the contrast between their skin tones and the white of the fog and the white of the sand and the white of their uniforms gave us a kind of a silhouette dancing effect, you know. A great deal of what I wanted in the suite, in the jazz suite was I wanted really defined, sharp, off-beat rhythms that I could cut to because I wanted to kind of innovate with a jazz cutting technique which, to that point, had really not been done. I wanted to do something new which was to cut on tempo, you know, so that if the thing was like be-dee, be-dee, ba-dah, ba-dah, ba-da-da-dah [sings], you know, I wanted those to be cut one, cut two, cut three, four cuts, you know, that kind of thing, so that it cut in the jazz tempo. (FB)

After the editing of the film was completed, there was a stir of interest in it.

One distributor who saw it wanted it immediately. There's a shorts distributor, Burstyn Enterprises. He was kind of famous for independent films in those days, in the sixties. His daughter ran the business. It was Burstyn. They picked it up for distribution. They got it submitted to almost all the art film festivals, three of which it won as best short. It then was submitted for a Cine Golden Eagle, United States Golden Eagle, which it won, and as a result of the Golden Eagle it got invited to [the] Edinburgh [and] Berlin film festivals of those years, which were very art-film minded in those days. Now it's all, you know, major films and that kind of stuff. It's not the same world in the film business anymore. In those days, if you made something small and artistic, you got lauded all over the world for having done so, you know? These days, they don't want to even know from you.

It won a first prize at Berlin. It went to the Venice Biennale. It went to Edinburgh. It went to a couple of other smaller film festivals. It came back here. When I came back from some of the festivals, we got [Manhattan theatre owner Donald] Rugoff—[he] opened it with a picture by Roman Polanski called *Two Men and a Wardrobe* at the Fifth Avenue Cinema. [It] got premiered pretty fast, along with a picture by Arnold Wesker called *The Kitchen*, and after that, I don't think it got very much at all of anything. I tried to get it into some dance film festivals and they were basically more interested in classical ballet, classical dance, than they were in modern dance.

I think the film cost a total of around three thousand bucks or thirty-five hundred bucks to make and I never made any money. I don't even think we had an arrangement where, if I did make money, I would recompensate him [Gryce] or give him a percentage. You know, it was the time in which filmmakers like myself were—you know, first-time-out filmmakers, certainly—had to make a short. They were kind of samples of your work. So, that was my entrée into becoming a filmmaker—from being, really, a young stage director/actor. (FB)

Baker recalled that the musicians involved were Gryce, doubling woodwinds, Richard Williams on trumpet, Eddie Costa on vibes, Richard Wyands on piano, Reggie Workman on bass, and Mickey Roker on drums.

I made the mistake of wanting to keep the credits down to a minimum and I didn't credit the players. I wasn't really thinking and I should have credited the players on the film. But I did credit music by Gigi Gryce. (FB)

The score contains elements of music that were found in Gryce's recordings, particularly in the two movements based on the blues, but also shows the influence of free music with an extended vibraphone solo over bass and drums with no pulse.

In addition to this film score, there were also some ads for the Pepsi-Cola Company that Gryce wrote involving the quintet. Had he wanted, this kind of work could have been a viable career choice for him, just as it was for his friends and colleagues Benny Golson, Quincy Jones, and J.J. Johnson.

As 1961 moved into 1962, Gryce's club playing tapered off. This inactivity was not forced upon him, however.

Well, he got work. I don't know about too much of the recording work, but he could get live work anytime he wanted. For a while, he was very busy with his publishing companies and we had the house in Queens and his was the first Xerox machine I had ever seen and he had, in the office, a Xerox machine and well, that's what he was most busy with. (EG2)

During this period, Gryce was growing more and more preoccu-
pied with the publishing companies, and the problems related to
those enterprises. In spite of the promise of his later groups, he
was unable to devote the necessary attention to performing and,
for all practical purposes, his career as a jazz musician was over.

Notes

1. "The rhythm section consisted of Hank Jones, Addison Farmer, and
   Ed Thigpen. Considerable multitracking was done on the date.
   Ortega played alto, tenor, baritone, bass clarinet, and flute." (*Down
   Beat*, December 14, 1955, p. 7.)
2. Robert Altschuler in *A Great Day in Harlem*, dir. Jean Bach, 1994.
3. A radiopaque substance (one through which x-rays cannot pass) used
   during an x-ray exam to provide visual contrast in the pictures of
   different tissues and organs. Such chemicals, also referred to as
   contrast dyes, allow enhancement of the anatomy demonstrable with
   conventional x-rays.
4. Wright, Bruce, *Black Justice in a White World*, Barricade Books, New
   York, 1996, p. 146.
5. "The East," *Music '59*, p. 25.
6. Jack DeJohnette, quoted in Ben Sidran, *Talking Jazz*, Da Capo Press,
   New York, 1995, p. 387.
7. "Strictly Ad Lib," *Down Beat*, December 25, 1958, p. 44.
8. Euell is referring to Gryce's intellect.
9. Jimmy Cleveland interviewed by Bob Rusch, *Cadence*, February 1991,
   pp. 20–21.
10. Jimmy Cleveland interviewed by Bob Rusch, *Cadence*, February 1991,
    pp. 20–21.
11. Levin, Robert, liner notes to *Sliding Easy*, United Artists UAS 5041.
12. Jack Tracy, quoted in liner notes to *The Complete Mercury Max Roach
    Plus Four Sessions*, Mosaic MD7-201.
13. Tracy, Jack, liner notes to *Rich Versus Roach*, Mercury SR60133.
14. Although, oddly enough, a leadsheet of this piece appeared in the

archives of the great alto saxophonist and composer Benny Carter. Carter had no recollection of how he came into possession of this and another Gryce composition, "In a Strange Mood."

15. Gigi Gryce, quoted by Ron Eyre in liner notes to *Saying Somethin'!*, New Jazz 8230.

16. Gigi Gryce, quoted by Ron Eyre in liner notes to *Saying Somethin'!*, New Jazz 8230.

17. Richard Wyands, interviewed by Bob Rusch in *Cadence*, May 1996.

18. Benny Golson, interviewed by David Griffith, June 8, 1997.

19. Gigi Gryce, quoted by Ron Eyre in liner notes to *Saying Somethin'!*, New Jazz 8230.

20. Harvey Pekar in *Down Beat*, August 16, 1962.

21. Pepper Adams, interviewed by Ben Sidran in *Talking Jazz*, Da Capo, 1995, p. 219.

22. Gigi Gryce, quoted by Martin Williams in "New Ears for Jazz: A Tal with Gigi Gryce," *Metronome*, June 1961, pp. 12–13.

23. Gigi Gryce, quoted by Don Gold in liner notes to *Reminiscin'*, Mercury MG 20628.

24. Gigi Gryce, quoted by Don Gold in liner notes to *Reminiscin'*, Mercury MG 20628.

25. Gitler, Ira, *Down Beat*, October 12, 1961, p. 29.

26. Randy Weston, quoted by Laurent Goddet in *Coda*, February 1, 1978 (159), p. 9.

27. Randy Weston, quoted by Art Taylor in *Notes and Tones*, 1982.

28. "Some of My Best Friends," *Metronome*, June 1960, p. 7.

29. "Strictly Ad Lib," *Down Beat*, August 6, 1959, p. 39.

30. "Strictly Ad Lib," *Down Beat*, November 10, 1960, p. 48.

31. Gitler, Ira, *Down Beat*, February 16, 1961, p. 47.

32. *Metronome*, June 1961, pp. 7, 46.

33. Art Davis, quoted by Valerie Wilmer in "Art Davis—A Struggle for Recognition," *Jazz Monthly*, 1962, p. 8.

34. According to Fred Baker, Gryce used phrases like "get to the wicket," borrowed from the lyrics Jon Hendricks wrote for the suite, *New York, NY* by George Russell. This rhythm appears prominently in both pieces.

metamorphosis

*T*HE LATER YEARS OF GIGI GRYCE are shrouded in obscurity and speculation. His exit from music was surprising and unexpected, and his reemergence from the depths of personal and professional devastation truly remarkable, though largely undocumented. A great deal of gossip and rumor concerning Gryce has spread through the jazz community, much of it unsubstantiated. But it can be said with some assurance that a number of factors played a role in his departure. These include psychological pressures, family troubles, and business difficulties relating to his publishing concerns.

As the 1960s progressed, things were changing both in Gryce's personal life and the music business. Clubs were closing and work was harder to obtain. Jazz itself was witnessing the early stages of a radical evolution as the hard bop genre of which Gryce was so much a part began to give way to experimentation led by individuals like John Coltrane, Ornette Coleman, and Eric Dolphy. The form and structure that Gryce favored in both his writing and playing was being set aside and replaced with freer and more purely emotional approaches to improvisation. Soon the civil-rights struggle and reaction to the war in Viet Nam would draw the music into the arena of protest and rebellion. This would be the decade that witnessed many fine jazz musicians leaving America for more hospitable conditions in Europe.

Gryce worked only sporadically in 1962. In fact, endorsements for King saxophones in *Down Beat* magazine featuring his photo provide the only evidence of his presence on the scene that year. Pianist Richard Wyands, who played with Gryce's last ensembles, remembers that the gigs just stopped—as did any form of communication.

The loss of income forced Eleanor to again seek employment and she secured a job with Chase Manhattan Bank working the night shift in data-entry. She commuted to Manhattan from their home in Springfield Gardens, Queens. This arrangement required Gryce to care for Bashir and Laila during the day. Eventually, he would work for a brief time as a short-order cook in a local department store luncheonette to help make ends meet. The situation was made even more complicated when Eleanor became pregnant with their third child, Lynette, born in February of 1963.

What was happening? How could someone of Gryce's stature and accomplishments suddenly terminate a career that had brought him to the highest level of New York jazz musicians, playing and writing the music he loved so dearly? Were outside forces preventing him from working? Without explanation, Gryce just appeared to have withdrawn completely from music and essentially cut himself off from all his former colleagues. This created a situation prone to the generation and perpetuation of rumors, many of which persist to this day. Eleanor remembers her husband during this period as a man beset with bitterness and fear, trying desperately and painfully to extricate himself from the music business. Richard Wyands noticed similar changes in Gryce.

I used to call him, phone him, you know, because I hadn't heard from him and I was wondering when our next job was. You know, all of a sudden, nothing is happening. So, he was afraid to answer the phone. That's how bad it was. His family was threatened. He, obviously, was quite frightened, to tell you the truth. (RWy)

He was always somewhat frail emotionally, dating back to his nervous breakdown in the early 1950s. By the early 1960s, Gryce was wearing many hats: musician, arranger, publisher, husband, and parent. This was a heavy and complicated load of responsibilities for anyone to bear. And there were some professional disappointments. The Orch-tette, while musically exceptional, never really caught on in terms of record sales or recognition. Furthermore, Gryce's reluctance to travel either by car or airplane severely restricted the band's ability to establish itself in other parts of the United States or in Europe. The death of his vibraphonist Eddie Costa in an automobile accident in July of 1962 must surely have reinforced those fears. But such factors alone should not have been sufficient to discourage him from continuing to perform and write. He was clearly gifted and versatile enough to pursue other alternatives in jazz even as things were changing, as long as they met his standards.

It appears to have been complications involving the publishing ventures that affected Gryce the most at this time. For years he had been quietly educating his colleagues to protect their compositions and insure that they would collect any royalties the works would generate. In this endeavor he was a role model to many composers, mostly black, who, out of ignorance or desperation, were routinely being stripped of their rights of ownership by record companies, in exchange for being recorded. When Gryce and Benny Golson founded Melotone and Totem, they were not unique; other musicians including Horace Silver, Hank and Thad Jones, and Quincy Jones had their own publishing companies. What was different about the Gryce–Golson ventures, however, was the goal of protecting not just their own music, but that of many others as well. If you were a black composer in New York with a desire to publish your work, Gryce was the person to see. It was the proselytizing, educating, and organizing aspects of the Gryce publishing approach that must have been viewed as a potential threat to at least some record company executives in a rather un-savory industry. And since the great preponderance of compos-ers in Melotone and Totem were black, there was an obvious ra-cial component to Gryce's efforts which were, in effect, very much in line with the incipient civil-rights revolution.

At their peak, Melotone and Totem had an impressive collection of compositions and composers (see appendix). But jazz tunes, in the context of the music business as a whole, generate relatively small royalties through sales of recordings and sheet music, and through performances. Nonetheless, Gryce had accomplished something significant, part of a trend that certainly must have been considered provocative and threatening to some elements in the recording industry.

Gryce was always very secretive and mistrustful by nature. The consequences of his publishing ventures must have aggravated these tendencies. Even his legal advisor, Bruce Wright, whose law office served as the headquarters of Totem Music, was not privy to details of the problems beginning to affect Gryce. At some point he apparently was warned that his efforts were not being received kindly in the recording industry, and he began to look over his shoulder for enemies out to hurt him and his family. This fear and paranoia would dog Gryce for the remainder of his life and, unfortunately, lead to the destruction of important personal and professional relationships. Gryce was clearly terrified, as both Eleanor and bassist Reggie Workman recalled:

My feeling is that he was pressured by somebody in the publishing field, in the music field, that either threatened him in some way that he became so paranoid that that's why I had to leave him because—not only that—well, I left him in 1963, the latter part of 1963. My baby was about ten months old. She was born in February. So, all I know is, he was petrified. (EG2)

He had become very secretive. He had become very introverted. He stayed to himself. I don't think he was trusting anybody because of the experiences that he had had and just went inside of himself and that was his way of protecting himself... And he'd be so nervous. He had this twitching nervousness that got worse and worse. (RWo)

It has been generally accepted by Gryce's colleagues that he was forced out of the music business by powerful interests, possibly with underworld connections, who were bent on the destruction of his publishing empire and the economic threat it represented. Stories abound that he and his family were harassed, threatened, and intimidated, but no evidence could be found to substantiate any of them. A rumor that the Gryce home in Queens was firebombed is denied by Eleanor, who recalls that the only harassment of any kind of which she was aware came from musicians demanding royalty money at all hours of the day and night, often driven by the need to fund drug dependencies.

But what was slowly happening was the withdrawal of musicians and their works from Melotone and Totem. By this time, Benny Golson had left with his music to start his own publishing company. According to Golson, this was prompted by Gryce's secretiveness:

Gigi was very insecure and, at that point, he wasn't trusting anybody. And it got to the point where he was very cryptic with me. When I'd ask to see certain things [files], he would get a razor blade and cut off this [text] and cut off that. My God, it [the document] looked like a paper towel and it just got very uncomfortable and then I just left.

…He was always that way, suspicious of people, very suspicious of people. And he would do what I thought was unnecessary things to assure himself of not being taken. And I went along with it but then after a while it just became overwhelming. And then when I resisted, it was like he didn't trust me. He was just protecting himself.

He was a nice enough guy. I mean he wasn't cruel or unkind to anybody. He was never that way. He was always courteous. He was hospitable and everything. But underneath he always had his hand of protection up to protect himself. No one would probably pick that up other than those who were closest to him, me and Eleanor. Only other people that would know about it is people that he dealt with, record companies and things like that, other people's attorneys. (BG)

Others were leaving because they were being told that having their music published by Melotone or Totem would prevent their ever having the opportunity to record the tunes. While Gryce encouraged his clients to take their music and start their own publishing companies, he was very hurt and embittered by those who left specifically because of these external threats.

They made lame excuses, saying among other things that Melotone and Totem were inexperienced, even though they had come to them because of Benny and Gigi's experience and their knowledge of the business. Because of their sense of brotherhood in being victims, I was ordered to release whatever was requested. We began an investigation. For years, if jazz musicians wanted their music recorded by established labels, the record companies would often insist that some stranger's name be added as co-composer. In that way, royalties would have to be split with someone unknown to them, usually a relative of an executive. If there was resistance, there would be no record date. Black musicians were being told that if they placed their music with Melotone or Totem, they need not expect any record dates in New York. Eventually, the Gryce–Golson firms were left without music to promote. I lost a sub-tenant and two clients.[1]

A few of the composers withdrew their works and registered them with the publishing companies of various record labels. This must have pained Gryce greatly.

That was one of the things that I know I heard him talk about a lot. Trying to get guys when they wrote tunes, to have the tunes published. They would leave the studio, everybody got paid but you never thought about doing the book work. So the record company ended up taking the publishing on the tune. You know, Gigi was really *totally* against that kind of thing happening. And he tried to let us know. (BC)

A significant problem was the collection of royalties, especially the mechanical royalties due the publishers of recorded tunes. Gryce was very astute concerning the protection of compositions through copyright registration as well as the establishment of publishing companies to receive and distribute royalties from the compositions. But the actual collection of royalties is quite another matter which, even today, requires substantial time and effort on the part of the publisher. It was not a forgone conclusion that all record companies could be relied upon to pay composers' royalties. This, in turn, would make it difficult for publishers to compensate the composers. Indeed, a number of composers indicated that they never received royalties from Melotone or Totem, and Eleanor Gryce confirmed that the business was not very profitable.

Our books would have been very free to audit because nothing came in hardly. I mean, it wasn't a real moneymaking thing because I can remember most of the royalties didn't come from the United States anyway, they came from Europe, and they were just a pittance. I mean, I can't remember anybody getting more than fifty or sixty dollars for whatever. (EG2)

From all accounts, Gryce had no staff to assist him in this aspect of his businesses. As a working musician, Gryce's time would have been limited and clearly insufficient to oversee the bookkeeping and promotion associated with hundreds of compositions present in Melotone and Totem. Furthermore, some record labels may have simply ignored Gryce's companies, challenging him to take costly and time-consuming legal action in order to force the acceptance and honoring of licensing agreements. Clearly, he was in way over his head. Eleanor remembered her husband's predicament.

He learned how to copyright the music and he learned how to set it up, I mean he did a fantastic job. But he needed a staff of professional people to run it and that's where he went wrong. Then he just panicked. He panicked and I don't know what happened. There was nobody there to advise him, especially me. I just said, "Oh, this guy, he's out of it and I've got these kids…" I was thinking too selfishly for myself and the children instead of trying to get help for him. (EG2)

Although the bulk of the Melotone/Totem holdings were of little commercial importance, by 1962 certain tunes had begun to get considerable attention and airplay. One was "Comin' Home Baby" by bassist Ben Tucker and pianist/vocalist Bob Dorough. This song had been recorded both by flutist Herbie Mann and vocalist Mel Torme on records that were accumulating substantial sales. The Mann version, as a single, rose to the top 30 on the pop charts, and the album *Herbie Mann Live at the Village Gate,* on which it appeared, sold over 500,000 copies. Another was "Moanin'" by pianist Bobby Timmons, which had become a jazz standard since its debut by the 1958 Art Blakey Jazz Messengers and was being recorded frequently. Both Tucker and Timmons felt that Gryce was not managing their property properly in terms of royalty receipts, and asked that the rights to the tunes be returned to them. Gryce agreed to do so in both cases and while the loss of this material did not, in and of itself, mark the end of the publishing companies, their future was sealed. Under pressure from several fronts, in January of 1963 Gryce decided to dissolve both Melotone and Totem. Handwritten letters similar to the following were sent to all the composers still having tunes in the companies. It is apparent from the uncertain legal language that by this time Gryce was no longer availing himself of the services of Bruce Wright or another representative.

January 16, 1963

Mr....

Dear...

I have been given permission to release your tunes to you by Melotone Music Inc. The Companies are disolving [sic]. This is to acknowledge that the contracts entered into between you and Melotone Music Inc. for your tunes [specific titles listed] be and the same hereby are terminated and cancelled and we do hereby transfer and assign to you all rights of Melotone Music Inc. including copyright.

Sincerely,
Gigi Gryce
Business Representative
Jazz Dept.

The publishing empire was history along with many of Gryce's dreams. Bruce Wright recalled the demise of Totem Music:

I do remember them disassembling all of the equipment that they had gone to such great lengths to put into the office space that I had leased to them. I mean, they spent a great deal of money putting in copying machines and so forth, and in those days, they were quite large, not as sophisticated as they are now. (BW)

The following year, in collaboration with his brother Tommy, his sister Harriet, and her husband Charles Combs, Gryce founded a new company, Jacogg Publications, Inc., to publish only his own music. Jacogg was run out of Harriet's home in Hartford, Connecticut, and still exists under the management of Harriet and Charles's son Kenneth.

The stresses that led to the end of Gryce's musical and publishing career were also taking a toll on his marriage. His behavior was becoming more and more bizarre and irrational.

He pulled the curtains closed. He double locked the doors. At the time, I was working at Chase Manhattan Bank at night and, when I came home at between one and two in the morning, I couldn't get in until he moved the stuff away from the door. And I had three babies! And I was afraid! And I even went to [the Community Service Society] where they help you.

At any rate, the lady that was working with me, when I was telling her what was happening at home, she said that I should bring my husband in too to talk to her. Of course, Gigi thought I was crazy! But anyway, this went on for quite a few months until one time… And he wouldn't have a phone in the house anymore, so I sneaked a phone in the house and I left in the closet, left it off the hook during the day when I wasn't home. (EG1)

There was also some tension over the naming of Lynette. Both Bashir and Laila were given Muslim names by Gryce, but in the case of their third child Eleanor made her wishes clear:

And, see, Gigi is the type that won't just touch on something, he gets really into it. And, I mean, he had a Koran which he cherished. He kept it covered. He washed his hands before he touched it, you know—really a dedicated Muslim. He tried very hard to get me into it, but I'm already set in my faith. I had mine and he had his.

Well, he tried it with—the children's names he wanted—my last one I said no, I will not have a Muslim name but my son is Bashir and my second child is Laila. These are Islamic names. So I said, "When I have this third child, if it's a boy you can name it, but if it's a girl I want to name it myself." And so he agreed, so my last child is Lynette. It has nothing to do with Islam. (EG2)

Apparently Gryce planned to name the girl Edthia had Eleanor not intervened.

But even at the nadir of his life, with his professional life in shambles and his marriage of almost ten years breaking up, Gryce evinced considerable strength, resiliency, and a survival instinct instilled in him as a child in Pensacola. He did not give up, fall prey to readily available crutches like drugs and alcohol, or undergo a complete emotional collapse. Instead, he began a second career that would ultimately last twice as long as the first one. In the fall of 1963, he applied for a position as a teacher with the New York Board of Education. "I came to Brooklyn and got the application and everything for him. He started teaching before I left him," recalled Eleanor. (EG1) Gryce began his teaching career as a substitute, teaching not music, but math, in junior high school. As this subject had never been one of his strong suits, Eleanor had to assist him with course preparation. Eventually he would teach music and do so very effectively.

Despite the promising professional turnaround, stresses on the marriage continued to build. Gryce's mistrust and paranoia began to be directed at Eleanor, and in November of 1963, on the advice of a counselor she had been seeing at the Community Service Center, she took the three children and left her husband for good.

…And I dealt with a social worker there. Well, anyway, when I went to tell her [what had happened], she told me, "I would suggest that you take your children out of that house or you're going to be a headline!" Because I had lost so much weight. I don't think I weighed 100 pounds, what with working and worrying about the children. So I left! (EG1)

For two months, Bashir and Laila were placed in foster care until Eleanor could find a place to live and get back on her feet, now as a single parent. Gryce saw his children only occasionally over the next twenty years and had little input regarding their upbringing. Relations between him and Eleanor were strained after she left, with child-support payments and religion being areas of contention. Gryce objected to being forced to contribute financially to the support of the children if he had no say in how they were being raised. The courts did not agree, however. It would not be until 1981, two years before his death, that the two would reestablish a cordial relationship.

Gryce was now bereft of his family, musical career, and publishing companies. But despite bitterness over what had happened, he found solace and new challenges as a teacher. He was employed by the Board of Education of the City of New York from October 1963 until his death in March of 1983, except for a brief period (from September 2 until December 16) at the end of 1976 when he was laid off temporarily. Rumors that he had relocated to Switzerland or Africa have no basis in fact. After serving as a regular substitute teacher or on a per diem basis for ten years, Gryce was appointed a regular teacher on September 10, 1974, and would hold that position for the remainder of his career. He taught at several schools in the boroughs of New York City, including Intermediate Schools 49 (The William J. Gaynor School) and 271 (The John M. Coleman School) in Brooklyn and, most notably, P.S. 53 in the Morrisania section of the Bronx.

It was in the 1960s that Gryce assumed a new identity by officially becoming Basheer Qusim. Gigi Gryce the musician was now history, a change that contributed to his isolation and the perpetuation of rumors regarding his fate. While religious considerations may have played a part in his identity transformation, it is more likely that he was, in fact, trying to make it harder for those he suspected were pursuing him. For all practical purposes, he was hiding out in plain sight. Occasionally, he would cross paths with someone from the earlier days on the streets of New York. The encounter was usually brief, with Gryce appearing nervous and fearful, as Ira Gitler recalled.

Now, I used to live at West End and 73rd and I ran into him in front of the subway station at 72nd street, and I can't tell you what year it was... It could have been late sixties... It could have been 1968 or whatever. We talked for a while and he was nervous. With all I knew plus his demeanor, I had a feeling he was a guy that was on the run... You know, not like ready to leave town but, fearful.

He was teaching, I know that. It was a short encounter and we were glad to see each other and that was it. That was the last time I saw him. (IG)

Gryce sent a remarkable letter to *Down Beat* magazine in 1968:

We get all kinds of letters, some from irate fans, and some from itinerant musicians. One of the latter turned up in August, although it was dated June 29. It read "(gigi gryce) (Trade Mark), who is legally named Basheer Qusim, will leave the United States to live in Switzerland. He will write, play and teach from there.

"His children, Bashir, Laila and Fdthia, will be educated completely there and live there in the family home. Mr. Qusim will use only his legal family name, consequently dropping the trade mark, but not relinquishing his rights to royalties and other benefits."

Qusim, as Gryce, was well-known in the 1950's as a composer-arranger, and for his alto saxophone work with Art Farmer, Donald Byrd, and his own groups, but has been off the jazz scene during most of the '60's, teaching in the Long Island, N.Y. school system. He has now joined the growing number of American jazzmen who have defected to Europe.[2]

Having the earmarks of an attempt to throw real or imagined pursuers off his trail, this communication contains plans that were never consummated and probably never could have been. There is no evidence that Gryce ever emigrated to another country, and at this point Eleanor and the children had been living apart from him for several years and were not under his influence. Fdthia, apparently a misspelling of Edthia, is a reference to Lynette under the name he had originally selected for her. The scenario Gryce described seems to be more of a dream than anything like a realistic sequence of events. Finally, reference to his teaching in the Long Island school system represents a widespread inaccuracy, still quoted, again probably publicized here to make himself more elusive. And in this regard he was quite successful. Gryce's isolation was so complete that when his mother, Rebecca, passed away in 1969, he could not be contacted because his whereabouts were unknown to his family. He did not attend her funeral.

In 1972, Gryce (now Qusim) met Ollie Warren, a school secretary in Community School District 9 in the Bronx, and the two married soon thereafter, living in Brooklyn. During their relationship, which lasted until his death, his earlier musical life was seldom mentioned, and the teaching of children became an obsession. She remembers him as a dedicated educator who often exceeded the call of duty in an attempt to elicit the highest level of achievement possible from his students, many of whom were at risk of failure. He used music to teach reading skills. In this regard, Gryce was on to something, as recent studies have demonstrated that music instruction increases reading and math skills among grade-school children.[3]

Around the time of his appointment as a permanent teacher, Gryce began working at Community Elementary School No. 53 located at 360 E. 168th Street in the Bronx. He would remain there until his death, creating a legacy that led to the school being renamed in his honor. This was also the time when his professional commitment to education was solidified. In the summer of 1975, he began graduate studies at Fordham University, which led to his being awarded an M.S. in Education Administration and Supervision from that institution on May 28, 1978. In contrast to the mediocre grades he received in high school and college, during his three years in graduate school he achieved nothing below a B in his courses. Aiming for a doctorate, he continued studies at Fordham into the spring of 1979, but at the time of his death had not completed the requirements for that degree. On July 12, 1979, he was initiated into the Fordham University chapter of Phi Delta Kappa, an organization whose mission is to promote quality public education. His ultimate goal was to have a school of his own, and he had even approached the city of Hartford, Connecticut about the possibility of starting a special school program, as Clifford Gunn recalled:

Community Elementary School No. 53
(Basheer Qusim/Gigi Gryce School), Bronx NY, Summer 2000

Some years later, in the sixties, he had an opportunity to come to Hartford… Well, he had a program about schools and he wanted Hartford to adopt this program in its schools. And, in fact, he had asked me to be one of the inspectors on the faculty there. And he had asked several others that I know here.

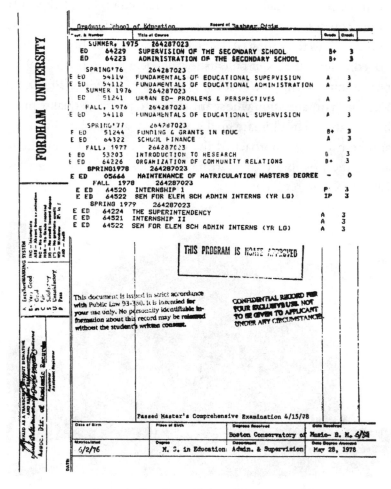

Gryce's Fordham University transcript

It was a music school. It was very similar… Today we have here in the school, the university where I was on the faculty, they have a new program, well, it's a black program, you know, with Jackie McLean. Well, the city didn't approve his [Gryce's] program. (CG)

Gryce's talents as teacher blossomed during his tenure at C.E.S. 53. Located in the South Bronx, the school's student population at that time was approximately half African-American and half Hispanic. Many of its students were at risk educationally. Reverend Jerome A. Greene and his wife, now New York State Assemblywoman Aurelia Greene, were on the board of School District 9 and active in community affairs in the Morrisania section. Reverend Greene remembered Mr. Qusim the teacher well.

He was a very strict disciplinarian and an excellent teacher! He had established a boys chorus here at P.S. 53 that was really heard all around the city, and highly respected. The children loved him. He brought to work with him, as a para-professional, someone who had played for Louis Armstrong, Edwin "Schubert" Swanston, who right now goes to Sweden and Russia giving concerts every year. Swanston had been a jazz pianist and so Mr. Swanston would play the piano [so that Qusim could conduct]. He [Qusim] was the music teacher but he had a para-professional who was a professional musician.

In the 1980s…because I had been an opera singer or was planning to be an opera singer and had studied music, and had, throughout my life, known the influence of music in my childhood, I sort of resurrected the arts after the Board of Ed had done away with most of it. But we had some powers at school boards to place emphasis on certain things. You didn't have a lot of money but you had some discretionary use. And so I proceeded to emphasize the arts and to spotlight them. That's why Mr. Qusim came to mind. I represented that school. My children went to that school. And so I saw what he was doing and appreciated it and wanted to spotlight it.

We used to give an annual Christmas program for the entire district and the boys chorus would be singled out to perform for us. And we'd usually have about a thousand parents there. And often we would feed everybody in the district because we'd get local businesses to donate and help us, and then the parents would come. We had such a community setting. And we could always count on him to bring his boys who were excellent. They were disciplined. When I tell you… I grew up in West Virginia. I went to college here. But I went through the southern music training in black schools growing up. And we didn't just arbitrarily get up. You had to practice how you stood and how you sat down after you finished performing, how you bowed in unison, all of those kinds of things. And all of a sudden in New York I saw it in Basheer Qusim.

He was very courteous. He respected parents. And he would talk business. He loved children, for you could get him involved in the aspirations of children. He'd talk about that. I never had a conversation with him about his musical background, what a genius he had been. I found that out from Mr. Swanston.

He was a brilliant man, highly articulate but he was a private man. Yes, he was a private man. I can just see his face now. He was well groomed. I guessed really that he carried a big hurt. So he was masked under his Muslim name. So no one even knew to ask about the good old days. (JG)

One of the few connections to the jazz world at this point on his life, Gryce's relationship with Swanston is intriguing. Swanston (1922–) worked and recorded with Louis Armstrong in the 1940s and even appeared in the motion picture *Pillow to Post* (1945) with Armstrong. A versatile musician who circulated widely, Swanston was also associated with such notables as trumpeter Oran "Hot Lips" Page, guitarist Tiny Grimes, and vocalists Joe Carroll, Dodo Greene, and King Pleasure during a long and illustrious career. He remains active in many contexts including the Harlem Blues & Jazz Band. Swanston had first met Gryce in the Lucky Thompson band in the early 1950s, and continued to interact occasionally in subsequent years in New York, sometimes dropping by the office of Totem Music to chat. After Gryce had left the scene, they encountered each other again at a school in Queens, and Swanston played organ at a junior high school graduation ceremony that Gryce was directing. Later Swanston was enlisted to assist Gryce with the music program at P.S. 53, beginning as a para-professional and then a substitute teacher.

And so I would see him [Gryce/Qusim] off and on and then sometime much later, in the eighties, I made a contact up in the Bronx where I went into the school first as a music professional or what they call as a para-professional but in the music department. And then later, I became a substitute teacher on a daily basis. And so while he was at the school, at 53, he would ask me to help him with the graduation program or different programs and I would come in and bring a trio to augment his school band and the chorus.

And so I was doing that and eventually I was working in the school with him. But like at first, he was doing it all by himself. I mean he was running the band and the chorus by himself. I mean he was very serious... So then I worked with him for, I guess, a couple of years in 53. (ESw)

Swanston reiterated Jerome Greene's assessment of Gryce's strengths as a teacher.

Listen, he was a disciplinarian. I mean, he could run that whole auditorium, full of students, by himself. Whatever he applied himself to, he actually mastered it. Now some of the teachers may have thought that he was a little bit too exacting. But there was no getting away from the fact that he was doing the job.

His whole manner of operations... I mean he was in charge of it from the time that he put his foot in the door. I remember at the other school where he was, he went into his pocket to buy uniforms for the girls in the chorus and for the boys. He got skirts for the girls and shirts for the boys. He went into his pocket. I mean he was willing to do anything that would build the morale for what he wanted to do. He wasn't afraid to spend his money. (ESw)

According to both Swanston and Ollie Qusim, Gryce seldom played his instruments either in the school setting or any other, except for demonstration purposes. The pianist noted how Gryce could reach some of the more difficult children and give them a sense of their own history.

See, I'm a pianist. So I was playing. He could conduct, et cetera, so forth like that. And he would set up rhythms for the kids who couldn't sing. I remember a couple of boys that were a little bit on the troublesome side and so he gave them this number that had a lot of rhythm in it and this kept them busy.

I know that he dealt a lot with relating music to where it came from, how the music came, through Africa and through the slave traditions and how, in New Orleans, on the weekends the slave owners would let the slaves have their dance routine that they'd be beating pots and pans and whatever, et cetera, until some of them later were able to get hold of old instruments and self-taught; and the beginnings of the Mardi Gras; and the learning of these instruments and the marches and participating in funerals and stuff like that; and then playing in the clubs; and then it branched off from there. (ESw)

Elements of this are apparent in the scores to works he wrote during his teaching career. His suite entitled "A.S.I.A." (for Africa, South America, India, and Asia) was designed to be performed in conjunction with narration discussing the spread of civilization. It proclaims, "Let us spotlight songs and chants, rhythms and dance," before proceeding into extended sections featuring drums and tambourines.

Gryce's dedication to helping children extended beyond his efforts at C.E.S. 53. He had also started a music program of his own in the South Bronx that emphasized discipline, as Aurelia Greene remembered:

I was the Executive Director of The Tremont Community Corporation and this was in the late 1970s. I do remember him as the executive director of a community agency that was teaching music to children or the youth. I remember he was in an old building. I don't remember the name of the agency. He was in an old building. I don't know how he was really even getting funded for it other than it was... Most of the money, I guess, was coming out of his pocket or maybe from playing he donated some of the proceeds towards the agency. But he was always struggling to keep it open.

Since we were the local corporation, we would recommend to them, to the community development agency, agencies that we felt were worthy of funding. And we would give them a recommended amount and they would approve them. Their moneys, however, would not flow through us but there was a separate entity that handled all of the accounting. And that was the entity that he was responsible to for the fiscal operations. What we did, primarily, was assist him with the pragmatic aspect.

I do recall that he had an outstanding program, one that we took a real keen [interest] in and we were trying to help him to get additional funding. At that time I was helping a number of the agencies, the community-based organizations to become incorporated as non-profits and training them in how to make their applications and what have you and he went through that process. But, as I said, the building that he was operating from was quite old and needed a lot of work.

It was somewhere in the Tremont/Southern Boulevard area. I'm not sure of the exact location. I don't even remember offhand the name of the agency. But I do remember he was running a music training program for young people and he was doing an outstanding job with them. In fact, it was a cadet corps as well. He organized it himself. He founded the agency. (AG)

Gryce received some funding for his program from the Community Development Division of the New York City Department of Youth and Community Development. This agency was established in 1966 to administer funds available from the federal Economic Opportunity Act of 1964, which had initiated the "War

On Poverty." But Gryce's personality was not suited to the politics involved in the acquisition of financial support, and the school ultimately closed in the early 1980s because the funding had been lost.

The only thing, he was a very quiet man, very reserved. I do remember that about him. And a lot of things that he had the potential to do I felt he just did not push it. And we tried to push him. I was really interested in his agency, very much so because he knew my uncle who was also a jazz musician, [bassist] Curley Russell. And so we talked and I was really trying to reach out to see what we could do to help him to keep that agency alive. Ultimately they did close it down. That was after I had left.

He was very, very quiet and there always appeared to be that he could accomplish so much more but he was not aggressive about looking for funding. (AG)

At the end of 1982, Gryce began to experience chest pains, fatigue, and difficulty sleeping, but initially did not seek medical care. He did sense that something was seriously wrong, however, because it was during this time that he would reach out to his siblings after years of isolation from them. He accepted an invitation to spend the Christmas holiday with Tommy and his family in Trenton, NJ.

He asked me one time, did I know any doctors in the Trenton area. And I told him I knew an excellent heart specialist. And he said, "Is he Muslim?" I don't know anything about the Muslim religion. I said, "Well, he's great friend of mine." And he just left it there. I said, "If you want me to contact him and set up an appointment, I would." But he never did get back to me.

He came over that Christmas. In fact I went over to New York to pick him up…and I brought him here and he spent the holidays with us and had a lovely time with my boys. In fact, I had to play several jobs in Philadelphia and I asked him to go with me and he said, "No,

I can't go." I mentioned the term jazz. He said, "Don't mention that word. Mention 'American Music.' That's what it is." And we talked and I went down in my playroom to practice and I purposely hit some wrong notes to make him critique me. And he just came down and smiled. And I took him back home. And right after that he went to Florida. (TG3)

So, even with his close family, there was a complete unwillingness to revisit, even for a moment, his other life as a jazz musician. Family was not the problem. It was playing music. That chapter of his life was closed, never to be reopened.

He looked kind of thin. But that Christmas, during the holidays, he was eating very well. In fact, my brother-in-law on my wife's side, was a retired general. And we went over to his house for the Christmas meal. And he and Gigi got along very well. Gigi was eating and eating and we were taking pictures. I don't know what's happened to the pictures. But when he left, he said he had a good time. And the next thing I knew my sister called and said, "He's coming home because I want him to come home and get some of this sunshine." (TG3)

Making his first visit in nearly thirty years, Gryce arrived in Pensacola in February of 1983 after taking medical leave from his teaching job at P.S. 53. Given his dedication to and enthusiasm for working with the children, he surely must have been feeling very poorly to abandon his responsibilities. Edwin Swanston had become very close to Gryce who would discuss with him at length his past experiences and setbacks. Despite the success he had found as a teacher, Gryce remained haunted by the loss of his family and musical career, even two decades after his earlier life had unraveled. Swanston remembered a very tired individual, worn down by years of bitterness and frustration and almost resigned to the end.

And so I remember one afternoon when he and I were walking up the hill on 168th Street and he was going to the subway. And he told me, "Swanston, if I stay it's all right and if I go it's all right." And I knew what he was telling me. It was like he was saying, "I don't care no more. I'm tired of fighting this thing, man." (ESw)

Gryce's siblings were most concerned about his health. Valerie had convinced him to return to Pensacola for rest, recuperation, and medical evaluation. After examination by physicians recommended by his sisters, he was given a portable heart monitor (Holter monitor[4]) to wear. He visited with his old friend and fellow clarinetist Aaron Long and the two had a joyful reunion, reminiscing about the old days in Pensacola. There was discussion of neither Gryce's accomplishments nor his misfortunes, but he seemed to be reaching back to make contact with his roots.

He kept very quiet. He didn't go [out] too much. I think he went to my church one Saturday to a meeting and I think he went to the old home church one time. But he didn't do too much going out.

Well, he just felt that he wanted to go to his old home church. And also, my sister, I remember we kept saying, "If you're not feeling well, it's time for you to read the 91st Psalm." I did observe him reading the 91st Psalm. He read the Koran, but he sure read the 91st Psalm! (VC1)

Psalm 91 is known as the Psalm of Protection, and is read when one faces danger and uncertainty: "I will say of the Lord, He is my refuge and my fortress: my God; in him will I trust… Thou shalt not be afraid for the terror by night; nor for the arrow that flieth by day; Nor for the pestilence that walketh in darkness; nor for the destruction that wasteth at noonday… There shall be no evil befall thee, neither shall any plague come nigh thy dwelling. For he shall give his angels charge over thee, to keep thee in all thy ways."[5]

The end came on March 14, 1983. Gryce had been staying at Valerie's home, but that day was visiting Kessel when he was found dead of a massive heart attack. At 57, he passed away at almost the same age as his father. He was buried in Holy Cross Cemetery in Pensacola, with very few people and none of his musical colleagues in attendance at the funeral. Twenty years after his withdrawal from the music scene, Gryce was a forgotten man at the time of his death.

On the other hand, the news of Gryce's passing came as a shock to the teachers, students, and parents of P.S. 53, all of whom had suffered a great loss. A memorial service was arranged by Rev. Greene.

He died unexpectedly. And there was not even a memorial service. And so I did a memorial service. And the community had high respect for him so we just improvised a memorial service at a church down the street…Morrisania Community Church. It wasn't his church.

I decided to ask a minister who was a teacher at the school at that time to lend me his church which was one block down the street, a block above me. And then we did a memorial service for him because he merited that. Everybody just… How do you bring this to closure? (JG)

The Greenes also set in motion a process by which P.S. 53 would be renamed in Gryce's honor.

But we did a public memorial service and then we determined to name the school. I went to my school board. I was the president. And usually, if there was going to be a change, the liaison to the school… Each school board member had two or three schools that he represented. I lived directly across the street from the school. My wife had been the PA president of the school years before. She's the Assemblywoman, Aurelia Greene. And she got into this whole thing by becoming a parent leader. So I've always had an interest in 53. And therefore I was close to Mr. Qusim because all the ethnic programs that we did, he was there. He would come to churches with the boys chorus to sing. And I noted he was respected as a disciplinarian in the school, a loving disciplinarian. (JG)

The resolution to rename the school was passed at a meeting of Community School Board 9 on June 22, 1983: "*Resolved*, That the District Nine Community School Board hereby authorize and approve the initial naming of C.E.S. 53 as: Basheer Qusim/GiGi Gryce Elementary School."[6] The school lobby contains a plaque with the following inscription:

COMMUNITY ELEMENTARY SCHOOL 53
"THE BASHEER QUSIM/G.G. GRYCE SCHOOL"

NOVEMBER 2, 1983

COMMUNITY SCHOOL BOARD NINE

JEROME A. GREENE, PRESIDENT
EDITH HICKS, 1st VICE PRESIDENT
JOSE M. GONZALES, 2nd VICE PRESIDENT
AURELIA A. GREENE, SECRETARY
CARMELO SAEZ, TREASURER
FRED BROWN
CURTIS JOHNSON
ISRAEL RUIZ
LOISE WASHINGTON

HAROLD M. CHAPNICK
COMMUNITY SUPERINTENDENT

This plaque is the only reminder of Gryce's presence there. Though

Gryce is one of the few jazz musicians to be honored with such a dedication, it was not his jazz career that prompted the renaming. Nearly two decades later, even his educational accomplishments have largely been forgotten, as new students and faculty take their places at the school.

Gryce's gravestone. Holy Cross Cemetary. Pensacola FL

Notes

1. Wright, Bruce, "Black Justice in a White World," Barricade Books, 1996, New York, pp. 145–146.
2. "Comings and Goings of Jazz Expatriates," *Down Beat*, October, 17, 1968, p. 13.
3. "Music Is Food for the Soul...And the Brain, Too," *International Musician*, September 2000, p. 10.
4. The Holter monitor, a small, portable electrocardiogram worn in a pouch around the neck or waist, is used to record the heart rhythm

over a period of, usually, 24 hours. It is used in patients who present symptoms such as chest pain, dizziness, or irregular heartbeat, and provides a correlation of the onset of such symptoms with daily activity.

5. Psalm 91, Authorized (King James) Bible.

6. Minutes of the New York City Board of Education, November 2, 1983, pp. 1412–1413; provided by David Ment, Head, Special Collections, The Milbank Memorial Library, Teachers College Columbia University.

epilogue

*D*ESPITE THE FACT that he was able to collaborate with the greatest artists of his era, Gigi Gryce seemed an outsider in his chosen field of jazz. His polite, formal manner was established early on, evident even as a child in Pensacola. Subsequent educational experiences strengthened this, enhancing his academic knowledge and the strong sense of aesthetics that made him demanding and unwilling to accept anything less than total involvement in and respect for his work. While he was able to find a few like-minded colleagues, Gryce refused to give in to the pressures of the commercial world to any meaningful extent or to reconcile his ideals with the harsh realities of the music business.

Gryce was something of a paradox even to his closest associates and family (and more so to those attempting to study him from an historical perspective). While he is usually remembered as outwardly courteous, friendly, calm and businesslike, the inner turmoil he experienced when dealing with adversity sometimes became apparent, manifesting itself in nervous mannerisms and, eventually, bizarre behavior. Further confounding an easy understanding of Gryce, the man, was his extreme suspicion of people and institutions leading to a reluctance to disclose many crucial details of personal and professional activities and relationships. He took bold and provocative stands on issues such as composers' rights, but instead of seeking assistance in dealing with the ramifications, he retreated into himself—with disastrous results.

Always a sensitive individual, Gryce encountered difficulties that not only caused him hardship and pain, but also led to drastically altered relationships with fellow musicians and family members. That he was able to start over and create a new life as a teacher is remarkable and a credit to his perseverance. He was doubly blessed in that he left two legacies: one from his educational career and another from his jazz years. Yet in retrospect, Gryce probably would have enjoyed a far less stressful and more fulfilling personal life had he chosen teaching as a profession initially as his siblings had done. His temperament seemed far better suited to instructing children than to dealing with record producers, club owners and chemically-dependent musicians.

As the new millennium begins, jazz is a relatively esoteric music, little appreciated by the general public, major record labels, or the media. Nonetheless, within this small artistic realm, the legacy of Gigi Gryce continues to be an influence on musicians, even those who came on the jazz scene after Gryce's departure from it in the early 1960s, even those who began performing in the mid-1980s and were not active during Gryce's lifetime. This lasting effect can be attributed in part to the introduction of the compact disc in the 1980s. Record companies found that there was a market, however limited, composed of collectors interested in replacing worn out LPs, and that there were also consumers eager to purchase material that had not been in print for decades. Only a few of Gryce's sessions have not seen a CD release in some form. Through these reissues the artistry of Gryce has been kept alive and contemporary players have been inspired by it.

There is no question that Gryce's influence as a writer exceeds his influence as an instrumentalist.

In my opinion, besides "Giant Steps," one of the most harmonically complex 16-bar tunes to improvise on is Gigi Gryce's "Minority." It's a challenging cyclical progression. My first introduction to the name Gigi Gryce was listening to Cannonball Adderley master these changes on his *Portrait of Cannonball* recording on the old Riverside label. That spurred me on to check out Gigi's recordings, and I was never disappointed. (MO)

In the era that was immediately post-Charlie Parker, along with Tadd Dameron, especially Tadd Dameron, Gigi Gryce's music codified a lot of the harmonic insights that Bird and the beboppers had. In other words, all they had was a normal, standard repertoire, harmonically, until people like Tadd and Gigi Gryce and a few other people, I guess you could include Horace Silver and Benny Golson, made "modern jazz compositions." And they're still as relevant today as they were the day they were written. That kind of harmonic insight doesn't come and go with time. It exists as a fact. And there's nothing old or especially new about it. It's just what it is. And it's important for people to learn it. (KG)

The world is waiting to discover Gigi in a way. His compositions have a quality just as Mingus's compositions have a quality. Just because Gigi leads you by the hand and Mingus grabs you by the throat doesn't make one superior to the other. And you have to remember that Monk thought so highly of Gigi as a composer. What Monk liked about it wasn't that Gigi's compositions sounded like Monk or anything, because they didn't, but Monk could recognize an individual quality, someone who could write songs with a quality. Horace Silver's tunes have a quality. That's why they last. All the great composers have a quality and Gigi had a quality in his playing and in his compositions. (BM)

Tadd Dameron was maybe the father of bebop composer-arrangers and he set the basic melodic and orchestral language. After World War II, a lot of people who were in the forefront of composing and arranging, like Eddie Sauter, Bill Finegan, John Carisi, George Russell, Mel Powell, Manny Albam, a bunch of others, they all started to study with classical teachers because they all wanted to learn more about their craft. Tadd never did, for whatever reasons. And he was somebody who really was gifted but who needed a good teacher. People like Gigi and Benny Golson and Quincy Jones kind of took the ball from Tadd and ran with it and, in some ways, I think, did Tadd one better. Gigi went after that kind of training with Alan Hovhaness at Boston Conservatory. And I think it really was evident because if you listen to the things he wrote for the Oscar Pettiford band or the nonet session for Signal or the big band session for Betty Carter, any of those things, the writing is crystal clear. I mean the voice leading is good. The voicings are good. Just craftwise, it's really first-rate writing. And there's a very definite harmonic and melodic language he just had down. (BK)

As a saxophonist, Gryce is remembered as an original voice but not one from which legends are made.

His tone was different, lighter, always very accurate, had great intonation, nice, smooth, cohesive style. The word that comes to mind to me is intelligent. He played an intelligent style. Some people play sort of haphazard, hit-and-miss style, but not Gigi. (HJ)

What Gigi did, along with Davey Schildkraut and, of course, a side of Bird was like that, and Konitz, was that he brought a vulnerability out in the alto. There was a gentle beauty that he had because beauty is timeless. And Gigi had a vulnerability to his playing and to his tone that was just a very... You get a certain loneliness in his sound that's kind of timeless. In other words, like a friend once said to me, which was a compliment, he said, "Man, sometimes you sound so fucking lonely." But basically, one is, sometimes. Music brings that out and there's that quality, that pristine vulnerability in Gigi's playing that, I think, is what makes him dear to me. The opposite of Gigi on the alto, in his period, who I like very much too, is Ernie Henry. And Ernie Henry had that street kind of toughness like Jackie McLean has. (BM)

It would not be right for me to say that Gigi Gryce was not a Sonny Stitt. He's not supposed to be a Sonny Stitt. He's not supposed to be a Charlie Parker. He's not supposed to be Jackie McLean. He's supposed to be Gigi Gryce. I mean he has something to say, you understand? (JC)

In the years since Gryce's death, his surviving colleagues have helped to keep his memory alive. Art Blakey, Eddie Bert, Charlie Rouse, Jimmy Gourley, even Lionel Hampton played his music through the 1980s and 1990s. Gryce's music has been revisited in tribute albums by Jacques Pelzer (1993) and Don Sickler (2000), and individual compositions have made their way into the repertoire of Kenny Barron and Bobby Watson. Artists as diverse as Anthony Braxton and Tito Puente have recorded Gryce tunes. There remains an appeal to his writing evident even in the wake of all the subsequent developments in music.

Regarding his musical goals, Gryce once said:

We're working in different forms; in attempts at fresher chord structures; in experiments with effects by way of more subtle dynamics and at other times with more specifically descriptive means.[1]

He was making a conscious effort to bring something new to the music and he was successful in this mission. He created a body of work that stands up to examination. This music is unquestionably jazz, but contains elements in the form and harmony that are fresh and different from the established tradition. Gryce found a new way of writing singable melodies that stemmed from bebop, extended the boundaries, but not so far as to be perceived as iconoclastic.

One time when we were at Birdland a lot of people came around and started telling us how much they liked his arrangements and his music. And it was hard to tell if they were, actually how sincere they were. But they were definitely very high! [Laughs] All of us said, "Thank you, thank you, thank you," and the people left. And Gigi said, "These people that try to be so hip are a bunch of phonies!" I remember I was so surprised to hear him use that word because he was such a gentleman and so scholarly and so sweet and kind to people. But again, he was upset because he thought that—probably rightly so—that the people were speaking to him so that they could get close to all the other musicians or the people who were friends of all the other musicians and seemed to want something besides sharing their love for the music. And this was the kind of thing that all of us got used to. But I could see that Gigi was so sensitive that a lot of the aspects of the nightlife and the fast lane were something that he couldn't stand.

And he used to talk to me privately and say, "You know people wouldn't act that way if they were going to hear the New York Philharmonic." He said, "They just don't take our music seriously enough." And Gigi really did have a sense of how serious the music was and also, he had a sense of how important *his* music was, not in an egotistical way, but because he objectively, could see how important all of this music was, how sophisticated it was, and what a high level it was on, harmonically, melodically, rhythmically, spiritually, and ultimately, musically which is something that you can't really put on a slide rule and prove. It's just something that you have to feel and understand, so that regardless of how much people appreciated him, he wanted them, I always felt, to really appreciate the whole history of jazz as being a tremendously important achievement in the 20th century.

Gigi, I think, felt about it in that spiritual way. He was almost like a minister sometimes when you were talking to him. He was very spiritual and on a very high level. And while he did have a good sense of humor, and was a very decent and kind, generous man, and a people person even though he was shy—he was very much of a people person—he had no snobbism in him at all. He understood how important this music was. And it hurt him deeply when there were any signs of disrespect to the music. So I could understand why, in the last years of his life, he withdrew from the whole scene. But I know he never withdrew from the music. (DA)

Gryce always had a respect for the history of the music and did nothing in his composing, arranging, or improvising to sever his ties with the rich lineage that preceded him. His work grew naturally from that tradition. Although innovative, it was conservative compared to the music of Cecil Taylor, Ornette Coleman, Albert Ayler, and late John Coltrane. Probably because of the rapid rate at which the jazz world was moving, Gryce's moment in the spotlight was brief. He was unable to succeed as a bandleader, almost certainly due to his aversion to travel. This prevented him from keeping up with Art Blakey or Horace Silver, both of whom played mainstream hard bop throughout their long careers and managed to ride out the low periods when jazz was in decline.

Had his disposition and priorities been different, Gryce might have been able to remain in music, perhaps working on film and television scores like his close friend Benny Golson, who was able to return to active playing in the late 1970s. He certainly had the talent and knowledge to do so. However, his uncompromising attitudes about his music being art that demands respect, together with his withdrawn and secretive personality, would not have helped in this regard.

Without a doubt an excellent musician and I think a misunderstood person. But, I mean, for every misunderstood person stands a person who was reluctant to expose themselves too. So that goes kind of both ways, hard to figure out. (CW)

We can only hope that Gryce's music continues to be made available for future generations so that they may be touched and inspired by his balance of intellect and emotion, his pursuit of compositional innovation without leaving the mainstream jazz idiom, and his commitment to beauty and art.

Notes

1. Gigi Gryce, quoted by Nat Hentoff, liner notes to *Modern Jazz Perspective*, 1957.

appendix a:
gigi gryce composition/
recording index

*T*HE FOLLOWING INDEX presents all of Gryce's recorded compositions, along with representative recordings on which the composition can be found. The year(s) of U. S. copyright registration is(are) given if known. Form, recorded key, and harmonic relationships to "standard" compositions are indicated where appropriate. It is an imposing task to comprehensively identify songs present on recordings issued worldwide, over a fifty-year period. Therefore, some examples may have been omitted and we apologize to any artists, or their heirs, whose versions of Gryce compositions have been overlooked. All issues of a given recording are not presented, but an effort has been made to list, primarily, CD reissues, known or presumed to be the most recently available. When no CD reissue exists, the original or a representative LP issue is given. Recording dates are given as year/month/day with 00 indicating that the month or day is unknown. Recording dates in italics can be found in the Discography.

Abbreviations: *(Dan.) Danish; (Eng.) English; (Eu.) European; (Fr.)*
French; (Ger.) German; (It.) Italian; (Jap.) Japanese; (Sp.) Spanish; (Swd.)
Swedish.

Anne Marie (I Need You So) 1955
32-bar form (ABAC), B-flat major
53/09/28: Lucky Thompson/Gigi Gryce, *Street Scenes*, Vogue (Fr.)
74321154672 (CD)
53/09/28: Lucky Thompson/Gigi Gryce, *In Paris*, Vogue RCA/BMG
09026-68216-2 (CD)

Au Tabou - *see* **Stupendous-Lee**

Autumn Serenade - *see* **In a Meditating Mood**

B.G.'s Holiday (Hannah's Holiday) 1957, 1958
64-bar form (AABA), C major
57/10/17: Benny Golson, *Benny Golson's New York Scene*, Contemporary
OJCCD-164-2 (CD)
Note: Liner notes incorrectly attribute this composition to Benny
Golson.

Baba's Blues 1958
12-bar form, blues in C
58/00/00: Gigi Gryce, *Gigi Gryce*, Metrojazz E1006 (LP)

Baby 1954
32-bar form (AABA), B-flat major
53/10/08: Clifford Brown, *The Complete Paris Sessions Vol. 2*, Vogue/BMG
45729 (CD)
61/02/15: Jacques Pelzer Quartet, *Featuring Dino Piana*, Cetra (It.) DLP 6
(LP)

Back Breaker, The 1960
32-bar form (AABA), B-flat major
60/03/11: Gigi Gryce, *Saying Somethin'!*, Prestige/New Jazz OJCCD-
1851-2 (CD)

Basheer's Dream 1955
32-bar form (AABA), G minor
55/03/29: Kenny Dorham, *Afro-Cuban*, Blue Note CDP 7 46815 2 (CD)

Batland (Bat Land) 1956
12-bar form, blues in F

57/02/25: Art Taylor, *Taylor's Wailers*, Prestige OJCCD-094-2 (CD); <u>Note</u>: Liner notes attribute this composition to "Lee Sears," which was a Gryce pseudonym.

57/07/05: Gigi Gryce–Donald Byrd, *Jazz Laboratory/Cecil Taylor Quartet at Newport*, Verve MGV 8238 (LP)

57/08/09: Gigi Gryce–Donald Byrd, *Jazz Lab*, Fresh Sound (Sp.) FSR-CD 82 (CD)

59/03/23: Nat Adderley, *Much Brass*, Riverside OJCCD-848-2 (CD); <u>Note</u>: Identified incorrectly as "Blue Concept" in liner notes.

Blue Concept (Blue Conception, Conception) 1956
12-bar form, blues in B-flat

53/09/29: Clifford Brown, *The Complete Paris Sessions Vol.1*, Vogue/BMG 45728 (CD)

54/05/19: Art Farmer, *When Farmer Met Gryce*, Prestige OJCCD-072-2 (CD)

57/01/13: Donald Byrd–Gigi Gryce, *Jazz Lab/Modern Jazz Perspective*, Collectables COL-CD-5674 (CD)

<u>Note</u>: This composition has no relation to George Shearing's "Conception."

Blue Getz Blues - *see* **Eleanor**

Blue Lights 1955
12-bar form, blues in F minor

54/05/19: Art Farmer, *When Farmer Met Gryce*, Prestige OJCCD-072-2 (CD)

57/03/12: Coleman Hawkins, *The Hawk Flies High*, Riverside OJCCD-027-2 (CD)

57/03/03: Clifford Jordan–John Gilmore, *Blowing in from Chicago*, Blue Note CDP 7243 8 28977 2 9 (CD)

57/08/09: Gigi Gryce–Donald Byrd, *Jazz Lab*, Fresh Sound (Sp.) FSR-CD 82 (CD)

59/01/29: Eddie Costa, *House of Blue Lights*, Dot DLP-3206 (LP); <u>Note</u>: Listed as "House of Blue Lights."

60/11/09: Gigi Gryce, *Reminiscin'*, Mercury MG 20628/SR 60628 (LP)

68/10/12: Art Farmer–Phil Woods, *What Happens…Art Farmer & Phil Woods Together*, Campi (It.) SJG12001 (LP)

93/05/10: Either/Orchestra, *Across the Omniverse*, Accurate AC-3372 (CD)

94/05/06: Junko Onishi, *Live at the Village Vanguard II*, Blue Note CDP

7243 8 33418 2 5 (CD); <u>Note</u>: Listed as "House of Blue Lights."

Blues for Tomorrow (Club Dues) 1958
12-bar form, blues in F major
57/06/25: Coleman Hawkins, *Blues Wail: Coleman Hawkins Plays the Blues*,
Prestige PRCD-11006-2 (CD)
57/06/25: Thelonious Monk, *The Complete Riverside Recordings*, Riverside
RCD-022-2 (CD)
57/06/25: Various Artists, *Blues for Tomorrow*, Riverside OJCCD-030-2
(CD)

Blues in the Jungle 1960
12-bar form (12/8), blues in G minor
60/03/11: Gigi Gryce, *Saying Somethin'!*, Prestige/New Jazz OJCCD-
1851-2 (CD)

Blues Shout 1961
12-bar form, blues in F
60/05/25: Hank Crawford/Leo Wright, *The Soul Clinic/Blues Shout*,
Collectables COL-CD-6281 (CD)

Boxer's Blues, The 1955
12-bar form, blues in F
Lyrics by Ira Gitler
60/06/07: Gigi Gryce, *The Rat Race Blues*, Prestige New Jazz OJCCD-
081-2 (CD)

Brown Skins 1956, 1958
Introductory section is 32-bar form (AABA), E-flat major; fast section
based on chord changes of "Cherokee", B-flat major
53/09/28: Clifford Brown, *The Complete Paris Sessions Vol.1*, Vogue/BMG
45728 (CD)

Capri 1956, 1958
36-bar form (ABAC, 8+8+8+12), B-flat major
53/06/22: J.J. Johnson, *The Eminent J.J. Johnson Vol. 1*, Blue Note CDP 7
81505 2 (CD)
53/06/22: Clifford Brown, *The Complete Blue Note and Pacific Jazz Recordings*, Blue Note CDP 7243 8 34195 2 4 (CD)
<u>Note</u>: Played in a different key (E-flat major), slightly different melody,
probably altered by Johnson on the recording of June 22, 1953, to fit
better on trombone.

53/11/02: Henri Renaud Quintet, *Bobby Jaspar/Henri Renaud*, Vogue (Fr.) 74321409372 (CD)

55/05/26: Art Farmer, *When Farmer Met Gryce*, Prestige OJCCD-072-2 (CD)

57/07/30: Donald Byrd/Gigi Gryce, *New Formulas from Jazz Lab*, RCA (Jap.) 6015M (LP)

57/10/17: Benny Golson, *Benny Golson's New York Scene*, Contemporary OJCCD-164-2 (CD)

Casbah, The 1957
32-bar form (AA´BA), second A up a fourth, E-flat minor/major

59/04/07: Buddy Rich and Max Roach, *Rich Versus Roach*, Mercury 826 987-2 (CD)

59/04/07: Max Roach, *The Complete Mercury Max Roach Plus Four Sessions,* Mosaic MD7-201 (CD)

Note: This composition is unrelated to "Casbah" by Tadd Dameron.

Casino 1955
32-bar form (AABA), G major
57/03/08: Art Blakey, *Midnight Session*, Savoy (Jap.) SV-0145 (CD)

Club Dues - *see* **Blues for Tomorrow**

Conception - *see* **Blue Concept**

Consultation 1954
32-bar form (AABA), D-flat major

53/11/02: Henri Renaud Quintet, *Bobby Jaspar/Henri Renaud*, Vogue (Fr.) 74321409372 (CD)

93/06/00: Jacques Pelzer Quartet, *Salute to the Band Box*, Igloo IGL 106 (CD)

Conversation Piece - *see* **Minority**

Deltitnu 1954
32-bar form (AABA), B-flat major, chord changes of "I Got Rhythm"

53/09/28: Clifford Brown, *The Complete Paris Sessions Vol. 1*, Vogue/BMG 45728 (CD)

54/05/19: Art Farmer, *When Farmer Met Gryce*, Prestige OJCCD-072-2 (CD)

93/06/00: Jacques Pelzer Quartet, *Salute to the Band Box*, Igloo IGL 106 (CD)

Early Morning Blues 1957, 1958

16-bar form (12/8) (AA´), F major
57/09/03: Donald Byrd–Gigi Gryce, *Jazz Lab/Modern Jazz Perspective*,
Collectables COL-CD-5674 (CD)

Eleanor 1954
12-bar form, blues in B-flat
51/10/28: Stan Getz, *The Complete Roost Recordings of Stan Getz*, Blue Note
CDP 7243 8 59622 2 6 (CD); Note: Listed as "Jumpin' with Symphony
Sid" which theme is also played on the same live track.
53/11/02: Henri Renaud Quintet, *Bobby Jaspar/Henri Renaud*, Vogue (Fr.)
74321409372 (CD)
54/05/20: Art Blakey, *Blakey*, Verve 314 538 634-2 (CD)
76/11/20: Woody Herman, *Early Autumn*, Bluebird 61062-2 (CD); Note:
Listed in liner notes as "Blue Getz Blues."
87/07/06: Stan Getz Quartet, *Anniversary*, EmArcy 838 769 (CD); Note:
Listed in liner notes as "Stan's Blues."
89/06/29: Stan Getz, *Soul Eyes*, Concord CCD-4783-2 (CD); Note:
Listed in liner notes as "Stan's Blues."
96/10/00: Andy LaVerne, *Stan Getz in Chappaqua*, SteepleChase SCCD
31418 (CD); Note: Listed in liner notes as "Stan's Blues."

Evening in Casablanca (An Evening in Casablanca, Gina) 1955
46-bar form (AA´BA´, 10+14+8+14), F minor
55/10/21: Art Farmer, *Art Farmer Quintet featuring Gigi Gryce*, Prestige
OJCCD-241-2 (CD)
57/08/30: Donald Byrd–Gigi Gryce, *Jazz Lab/Modern Jazz Perspective*,
Collectables COL-CD-5674 (CD)
85/05/04: Kjell–Ake Persson, *Samband*, MaNi (Swd.) 8505-041-02 (CD)

Exhibit A 1955
32-bar form (AABA), F major
57/02/11: Art Blakey, *Ritual*, Blue Note CDP 7 46858 2 (CD)
57/02/25: Art Taylor, *Taylor's Wailers*, Prestige OJCCD-094-2 (CD)
57/04/00: Art Blakey, *Percussion Discussion*, Chess CHC 2-92511 (CD)
57/07/30: Donald Byrd–Gigi Gryce, *New Formulas from Jazz Lab*, RCA
(Jap.) 6015M (LP)
Note: Liner notes attribute this composition to "Lee Sears," a Gryce
pseudonym.

Expansion 1954
32-bar form (AABA), F major

53/11/02: Henri Renaud Quintet, *Bobby Jaspar/Henri Renaud*, Vogue (Fr.)
74321409372 (CD)

Futurity 1954
32-bar form (ABAC), E-flat major, chord changes of "There Will Never
Be Another You"
53/05/20: Howard McGhee, *Howard McGhee Sextet Vol. 2/Tal Farlow
Quartet*, Blue Note 7243 4 95748 2 3 (CD)
54/05/20: Art Blakey, *Blakey*, Verve 314 538 634-2 (CD)

Gina - *see* **Evening in Casablanca**

Hannah's Holiday - *see* **B.G.'s Holiday**

Hello 1956, 1958
32-bar form (AABA), E-flat major
53/10/10: Lucky Thompson/Gigi Gryce, *Street Scenes*, Vogue (Fr.)
74321154672 (CD)
53/10/10: Lucky Thompson/Gigi Gryce, *In Paris*, Vogue RCA/BMG
09026-68216-2 (CD)
54/05/20: Art Blakey, *Blakey*, Verve 314 538 634-2 (CD)

House of Blue Lights - *see* **Blue Lights**

Hymn to the Orient (Hymn of the Orient) 1956
32-bar form (AABA), C minor
52/12/29: Stan Getz, *Stan Getz Plays*, Verve 833 535-2 (CD)
53/03/08: Stan Getz, *Live at the Hi-Hat 1953—Vol. 1*, Fresh Sound (Sp.)
FSCD 1014 (CD)
53/08/28: Clifford Brown, *Memorial Album*, Blue Note CDP
72435321412 (CD)
53/08/28: Clifford Brown, *Complete Blue Note and Pacific Jazz Recordings*,
Blue Note CDP 7243 8 34195 2 4 (CD)
57/12/19: Benny Golson, *The Modern Touch*, Riverside OJCCD-1797-2
(CD)

I Need You So - *see* **Anne Marie**

In a Meditating Mood (Autumn Serenade) 1957
56-bar form (AABA, 16+16+8+16), E-flat major
Lyrics by Jon Hendricks
55/10/30: Gigi Gryce, *Nica's Tempo*, Savoy 126 (CD)
55/11/00: Eddie Bert, *Let's Dig Bert (Eddie That Is)*, Trans World TWLP
208 (LP)

76/00/00: Eddie Bert, *Skeleton of the Band*, Backbone BRLP001 (LP)
Note: This composition is unrelated to "Autumn Serenade" by S. Gallop and P. DeRose, recorded by John Coltrane and Johnny Hartman.

In a Strange Mood 1959
32-bar form (AABA), C major
60/11/07: Gigi Gryce, *Reminiscin'*, Mercury MG 20628/SR 60628 (recorded but never issued on LP)

Infant's Song, The 1955
32-bar form (AABA), E-flat major
55/05/26: Art Farmer, *When Farmer Met Gryce*, Prestige OJCCD-072-2 (CD)

Kin Folks 1957, 1958
12-bar form, blues in C major
57/08/25: Lee Morgan, *City Lights*, Blue Note (Jap.) TOCJ-1575 (CD)
57/08/25: Lee Morgan, *The Complete Blue Note Fifties Sessions*, Mosaic MD4-162 (CD)

Leila's Blues (Laila's Blues, Kunteta's Blues, Movin') 1955, 1960
12-bar form, blues in B-flat major
60/03/11: Gigi Gryce, *Saying Somethin'!*, Prestige/New Jazz OJCCD-1851-2 (CD)

Li'l Daddee (Li'l Darlin')
Quincy Jones co-author.
53/08/02: Clifford Solomon, Okeh, 7010 (78)
Note: No copyright record of this composition could be found.

Melody Express 1956
32-bar form (AABA), F major
51/08/15: Stan Getz, *The Complete Roost Recordings*, Roost CDP 7243 8 59622 2 6 (CD)

Minority (Conversation Piece) 1956
16-bar form, F minor
53/10/08: Clifford Brown, *The Complete Paris Sessions Vol. 2*, Vogue/BMG 45729 (CD)
54/05/20: Art Blakey, *Blakey*, Verve 314 538 634-2 (CD)
57/02/27: Gigi Gryce, *Jazz Lab Quintet*, Riverside OJCCD-1774-2 (CD)
58/07/01: Julian Cannonball Adderley, *Portrait of Cannonball*, Riverside OJCCD-361-2 (CD)

58/09/29: Michael Naura Quintet, *Jazz in Deutschland*, Telefunken (Ger.) 6.22563 (LP)

58/12/15: Bill Evans, *Everybody Digs Bill Evans*, Riverside OJCCD-068-2 (CD)

60/05/03: Gigi Gryce, *The Hap'nin's*, Prestige New Jazz OJCCD-1868-2 (CD)

60/02/15: Slide Hampton, *Sister Salvation*, Collectables COL-CD-6173 (CD); <u>Note</u>: Listed in liner notes as "Conversation Piece."

61/02/15: Jacques Pelzer, *Quartet Featuring Dino Piana*, Fonit Cetra (It.) CDM5004 (CD)

64/10/28: Denny Zeitlin, *Cathexis/Carnival*, Collectables COL-CD-5891 (CD)

65/00/00: Sonny Simmons/Prince Lasha/Clifford Jordan/The Bossa Tres, *Jazz Tempo—Latin Accents*, Audio Fidelity AFL-2111 (LP)

65/02/26: Franco Ambrosetti, *A Jazz Portrait of Franco Ambrosetti*, Sound Hills SSCD 8071 (CD)

67/10/02: Pat Martino, *Strings!*, Prestige OJCCD-223-2 (CD)

73/11/13: Bobby Pierce, *New York*, Muse MR 5030 (LP)

76/12/17: Red Mitchell, *Blues For a Crushed Soul*, Sonet (Swd.) SNTF 762 (LP)

77/00/00: Ben Sidran, *The Cat and the Hat*, Horizon A&M LJ 741 (LP)

78/09/11: Billy Hart/Water Bishop, Jr., *The Trio*, Progressive 7044 (LP)

79/00/00: Romano Mussolini, *Soft & Swing*, Right Tempo 809 (CD)

80/04/17: Bill Hardman, *Focus*, Muse MR 5259 (LP)

80/09/07: Frank Sullivan, *First Impressions*, Revelation 34 (LP)

80/10/08: Tom McKinley/Miroslav Vitous, *Tom McKinley/Miroslav Vitous*, MMC 2013 (CD)

81/10/16: Frank Sullivan, *Incandescence*, Revelation 39 (LP)

83/04/11: Bobby Watson, *Beatitudes*, New Note KM 11867 (LP)

83/06/08: Frank Wess/Johnny Coles, *Two at the Top*, Uptown UP27.14 (LP)

83/11/13: Tommy Chase, *Tommy Chase Quartet*, Boplicity BOP 5 (LP)

84/04/29: Doug Raney, *Blue and White*, Steeplechase SCCD 31191 (CD)

84/08/23: Bill Barron, *Variations in Blue*, Muse MR 5306 (LP)

85/01/14: Jack DeJohnette, *Piano Album*, Landmark LCD-1504-2 (CD)

86/04/01: Alan Broadbent, *Everything I Love*, Discovery DSCD-929 (CD)

87/06/15: Arrigo Cappelletti, *Reflections*, Splasc(H) (It.) H134 (LP)

84/04/20: Mike Markaverich, *Two Sides*, Marktime MTR-102 (LP)

89/02/24: Ricky Ford, *Hard Groovin'*, Muse MCD 5373 (CD)

89/11/24: Frank Strazzeri, *Little Giant*, Fresh Sound (Sp.) FSR CD-184 (CD)
90/09/12: Manhattan Jazz Orchestra, *Moritat*, Sweet Basil (Jap.) ALCR-72 (CD)
91/08/22: Kenny Barron, *The Moment*, Reservoir RSR CD 121 (CD)
91/12/09: Bobby Watson, *Present Tense*, Columbia CK 52400 (CD)
92/00/00: Miles Osland, *Saxercize*, Sea Breeze (Night Life) CDNL-3009 (CD)
93/06/00: Jacques Pelzer Quartet, *Salute to the Band Boc*, Igloo IGL 106
93/06/11: Lanny Morgan, *Quartet*, V.S.O.P. 92 (CD)
93/06/22: Gary Bartz/Sonny Fortune, *Alto Memories*, Verve 523 268 (CD)
94/00/00: Sandra Booker, *Very Early*, Jersey Boy 1101 (CD)
94/06/15: Anthony Braxton, *Piano Quartet*, Music & Arts CD-849 (CD)
94/08/24: Robert Trowers Quartet, *Point of View*, Concord Jazz CCD-4656 (CD)
95/06/04: Phil Woods/Vincent Herring/Antonio Hart, *Alto Summit*, Milestone MCD-9265-2 (CD)
95/10/25: Robert Bootsie Barnes, *You Leave Me Breathless*, French Riviera 1022 (CD)
96/00/00: Henri Texier, *The Scene Is Clean*, Label Bleu (Fr.) 6540 (CD)
96/08/00: Harold Mabern Trio, *Mabern's Grooveyard*, DIW-621 (CD)
98/02/10: Boplicity, *Boplicity*, Imogena (Swd.) IGCD073 (CD)
99/12/27: Will Calhoun, *Live at the Blue Note*, Half Note 4912-2 (CD)

Mosquito Knees
32-bar form (AABA), F-major
51/10/28: Stan Getz, *The Complete Roost Recordings*, Roost CDP 7243 8 59622 2 6 (CD)
55/10/30: Max Bruel, *Live Odd Fellow Palaeet Copenhagen*, Olufsen (Dan.) unissued
Note: No copyright record of this composition could be found.

Movin' - *see* **Leila's Blues**

Music in the Air - *see* **Wildwood**

Nica's Tempo (Playhouse) 1955
44-bar form (AABA, 12+12+8+12), E-flat major
55/10/15: Gigi Gryce, *Nica's Tempo*, Savoy 126 (CD) Note: B-flat major
55/10/21: Art Farmer, *Art Farmer Quintet Featuring Gigi Gryce*, Prestige OJCCD-241-2 (CD)

Note: Only V7 chords are used in A section in this version (other recordings use ii–V7).

56/06/11: Oscar Pettiford, *Deep Passion*, Impulse GRD-143 (CD)

56/12/13: Art Blakey, *Drum Suite*, Columbia Legacy CK-65044 (CD)

57/01/13: Donald Byrd–Gigi Gryce, *Jazz Lab/Modern Jazz Perspective*, Collectables COL-CD-5674 (CD)

57/05/26: Oscar Pettiford, *Birdland Band—Jazz off the Air Vol. 6*, Spotlite (Eng.) SPJ 153 (LP)

60/05/03: Gigi Gryce, *The Hap'nin's*, Prestige New Jazz OJCCD-1868-2 (CD)

64/02/19: Denny Zeitlin, *Cathexis/Carnival*, Collectables COL-CD-5891 (CD)

81/10/00: Jazz Incorporated, *Walkin' On*, Dragon (Swd.) DRCD 348 (CD)

83/06/08: Frank Wess/Johnny Coles, *Two at the Top*, Uptown UP27.14 (LP)

90/02/17: Ned Otter, *The Right to Know*, Nelson Otter Productions NO-2 (CD)

90/04/10: Art Blakey, *One For All*, A&M 750215329 (CD)

93/06/26: Ravi Coltrane–Antoine Roney, *Grand Central—Tenor Titans*, Joshua Alfa Jazz (Jap.) ALCR-313 (CD)

94/00/00: Danny D'Imperio, *The Outlaw*, Sackville (Can.) SKCD2-3060 (CD)

95/00/00: Jon Mayer Trio, *Round Up the Usual Suspects*, Pullen Music PULL 2240 (CD)

95/00/00: Tito Puente, *Tito's Idea*, RMM RMD 81571 (CD)

95/06/15: Grant Stewart, *More Urban Tones*, Criss Cross (Du.) 1124 (CD)

96/05/28: Bill Perkins, *Swing Spring*, Candid CCD79752 (CD)

96/09/16: Jan Lundgren, *Cooking! At the Jazz Bakery*, Fresh Sound (Sp.) FSR 5019 (CD).

2000/05/28: Johnny Griffin/Steve Grossman, *Johnny Griffin & Steve Grossman Quintet*, Dreyfus Jazz FDM 36615-2

Night at Tony's, A 1956, 1958

32-bar form (AABA), E-flat major, chord changes of "Yardbird Suite."

54/05/19: Art Farmer, *When Farmer Met Gryce*, Prestige OJCCD-072-2 (CD)

57/04/02: Art Blakey, *Second Edition*, RCA Bluebird 07863-66661-2 (CD)

57/04/02: Art Blakey, *Theory of Art*, RCA/BMG 09026-68730-2 (CD)

57/12/17: Dizzy Gillespie, *The Greatest Trumpet of Them All*, Verve MGV-8352/MGVS-6117 (LP)

58/02/17: Michael Naura Quintet, *Jazz in Deutschland*, Telefunken 6.22563 (LP)

60/00/00: Modern Jazz Group Freiburg, Christopherus CV75020 (LP)

97/04/02: Paul Salomone Quartet, *Quickstep*, Paul Salomone Records PSQ97 (CD)

Now Don't You Know 1957

12-bar form, blues in F major

57/09/03: Donald Byrd–Gigi Gryce, *Jazz Lab/Modern Jazz Perspective*, Collectables COL-CD-5674 (CD)

Paris the Beautiful 1956

64-bar form (AA´BCA´´, 16+16+8+8+16), F major

53/09/26: Lucky Thompson/Gigi Gryce, *Street Scenes*, Vogue (Fr.) 74321154672 (CD)

53/09/26: Lucky Thompson/Gigi Gryce, *In Paris*, Vogue RCA/BMG 09026-68216-2 (CD)

Playhouse - *see* **Nica's Tempo**

Premonition of You, A (Premonitions of You) 1958

Lyrics by Jon Hendricks

60/11/07: Gigi Gryce, *Reminiscin'*, Mercury MG 20628/SR 60628 (recorded but never issued on LP)

Quick Step 1954

32-bar form (AABA), F major

53/10/09: Clifford Brown, *The Complete Paris Sessions Vol. 2*, Vogue/BMG 45729 (CD)

93/06/00: Jacques Pelzer Quartet, *Salute to the Band Box*, Igloo IGL 106 (CD)

97/04/02: Paul Salomone Quartet, *Quickstep*, Paul Salomone Records PSQ97 (CD)

Rat Race Blues, The

8-bar theme followed by improvisations on 12-bar blues form in several keys.

60/06/07: Gigi Gryce, *The Rat Race Blues*, Prestige/New Jazz OJCCD-081-2 (CD)

Reminiscing 1956

32-bar form (AABA), A-flat major

Lyrics by Jon Hendricks

56/06/08: Earl Coleman, *Earl Coleman Returns*, Prestige OJCCD-187-2 (CD)

56/11/23: Art Farmer, *Farmer's Market*, Prestige/New Jazz OJCCD-398-2 (CD)

57/12/17: Dizzy Gillespie, *The Greatest Trumpet of Them All*, Verve MGV-8352/MGVS-6117 (LP)

57/12/17: Dizzy Gillespie, *Jazz Round Midnight: Trumpet*, Verve 511057-2 IMS (CD)

59/02/00: Jimmy Cleveland, *Rhythm Crazy*, EmArcy MGE-26003/SRE-66003 (LP)

60/11/10: Gigi Gryce, *Reminiscin'*, Mercury MG 20628/SR 60628 (LP)

Reunion (Salute to the Band Box, Salute to Birdland) 1954, 1956

48-bar form (ABA), G major, chord changes of "I'll Remember April"

53/10/08: Clifford Brown, *The Complete Paris Sessions Vol. 2*, Vogue/BMG 45729 (CD); Note: Listed in liner notes as "Salute to the Band Box."

54/05/20: Art Blakey, *Blakey*, Verve 314 538 634-2 (CD); Note: Listed in liner notes as "Salute to Birdland."

56/03/08: Jacques Pelzer/Herman Sandy, *Jazz for Moderns*, Fiesta (Belg.) IS10043 (LP); Note: Listed in liner notes as "Salute to the Band Box."

57/12/19: Benny Golson, *The Modern Touch*, Riverside OJCCD-1797-2 (CD)

86/08/25: Jimmy Gourley, *The Left Bank of New York*, Uptown UPCD 27.32 (CD); Note: Listed in liner notes as "Salute to the Band Box."

93/06/00: Jacques Pelzer Quartet, *Salute to the Band Box*, Igloo IGL 106 (CD); Note: Listed in liner notes as "Salute to the Band Box."

Sans Souci 1955

32-bar form, (ABAC), G major, chord changes of "Out of Nowhere"

55/10/21: Art Farmer, *Art Farmer Quintet Featuring Gigi Gryce*, Prestige OJCCD-241-2 (CD)

57/02/05: Donald Byrd–Gigi Gryce, *Jazz Lab/Modern Jazz Perspective*, Collectables COL-CD-5674 (CD)

82/06/01: Lionel Hampton, *Made in Japan*, Timeless (Du.) CDSJP 175 (CD)

83/05/29: Lionel Hampton, *Air Mail Special*, West Wind WW 2401 (CD)

Satellite 1955

32-bar form (ABAC), D-flat major for head and piano solo; 56-bar form (AABA, 16+16 | 8+16) C major for horn solos

55/10/21: Art Farmer, *Art Farmer Quintet Featuring Gigi Gryce*, Prestige
OJCCD-241-2 (CD)

57/08/30: Donald Byrd–Gigi Gryce, *Jazz Lab/Modern Jazz Perspective*,
Collectables COL-CD-5674 (CD)

Shabozz 1956

32-bar form (AABA), E-flat minor

53/05/20: Howard McGhee, *Howard McGhee Sextet Vol. 2/Tal Farlow
Quartet*, Blue Note 7243 4 95748 2 3 (CD)

53/11/02: Henri Renaud Quintet, *Bobby Jaspar/Henri Renaud*, Vogue (Fr.)
74321409372 (CD)

55/10/21: Art Farmer, *Art Farmer Quintet Featuring Gigi Gryce*, Prestige
OJCCD-241-2 (CD)

57/12/17: Dizzy Gillespie, *The Greatest Trumpet of Them All*, Verve MGV-
8352/MGVS-6117 (LP)

Simplicity 1954

32-bar form (AABA), E-flat major

53/11/02: Henri Renaud Quintet, *Bobby Jaspar/Henri Renaud*, Vogue (Fr.)
74321409372 (CD)

54/05/20: Art Blakey, *Blakey*, Verve 314 538 634-2 (CD)

Smoke Signal 1955

64-bar form (AA´BA), E-flat major, chord changes of "Lover"

55/10/30: Gigi Gryce, *Nica's Tempo*, Savoy 126 (CD)

56/06/11: Oscar Pettiford, *Deep Passion*, Impulse GRD-143 (CD)

57/02/04: Various Artists (Donald Byrd–Gigi Gryce Jazz Lab), *Jazz
Omnibus*, Columbia CL 1020 (LP)

57/05/26: Oscar Pettiford, *Birdland Band—Jazz off the Air Vol. 6*, Spotlite
(Eng.) SPJ 153 (LP)

57/12/17: Dizzy Gillespie, *The Greatest Trumpet of Them All*, Verve MGV-
8352/MGVS-6117 (LP)

93/12/22: Gary Smulyan, *Saxophone Mosaic*, Criss Cross Jazz (Du.) 1092
(CD)

Social Call 1955

36-bar form (AABA´) last A adds 4-bar tag (not always used), D-flat
major (but key varies on recordings)

Lyrics by Jon Hendricks

55/05/26: Art Farmer, *When Farmer Met Gryce*, Prestige OJCCD-072-2
(CD)

55/10/22: Gigi Gryce, *Nica's Tempo*, Savoy 126 (CD)

56/04/25: Betty Carter, *Meet Betty Carter and Ray Bryant*, Columbia Legacy CK 64936 (CD)

56/06/08: Earl Coleman, *Earl Coleman Returns*, Prestige OJCCD-187-2 (CD)

57/04/02: Art Blakey, *Second Edition*, RCA Bluebird 07863-66661-2 (CD)

57/04/02: Art Blakey, *Theory of Art*, RCA/BMG 09026-68730-2 (CD)

57/08/30: Donald Byrd–Gigi Gryce, *Jazz Lab/Modern Jazz Perspective*, Collectables COL-CD-5674 (CD)

58/00/00: Ernestine Anderson, *Ernestine Anderson: The Toast of the Nation's Critics*, Mercury 514 076-2 (CD)

59/00/00: Jon Hendricks, *A Good Git-Together*, World Pacific WP-1283 (LP)

67/03/09: Einar Iversen, Nor Disc (Nor.) LPS17 (LP)

80/11/11: Stella Levitt, *With the Jacques Pelzer Quartet*, Adda 590066 (CD)

82/03/27: Betty Carter, *Whatever Happened to Love*, Verve 835 683-2 (CD)

82/00/00: Betty Carter, *Compact Jazz: Betty Carter*, Verve 843 274-2 (CD)

84/01/21: Charlie Rouse, *Social Call*, Uptown 27.18 (LP)

85/11/00: Mark Levine, *Smiley and Me*, Concord CCD-4352 (CD)

86/00/00: Eddie Bert, *One Bone—Four Strings*, Molshajala 1005 (LP)

87/06/14: Eddie Bert, *TNT: Eddie Bert and Impuls*, Key Bone KBLP 21987 (LP)

90/02/15: Harper Brothers, *Remembrance—Live at the Gavin Convention*, Verve HBGC-4 (promotional cassette)

90/07/31: Mary Stallings, *Fine and Mellow*, Clarity CCD-1001 (CD)

93/06/00: Jacques Pelzer Quartet, *Salute to the Band Box*, Igloo IGL 106 (CD)

93/06/09: Karrin Allyson, *Sweet Home Cookin'*, Concord Jazz CCD-4593 (CD)

94/00/00: Ann Dyer, *Ann Dyer & No Good Time Fairies*, Mr. Brown 896 (CD)

94/11/19: Dave Rasmussen, *Not So Tenderly*, Sea Breeze 2072 (CD)

96/06/30: Horace Tapscott, *Thoughts of Dar Es Salaam*, Arabesque AJO128 (CD)

97/07/24: Sherri Roberts, *Dreamsville*, Brownstone 9811 (CD)

97/12/30: Winard Harper, *Trap Dancer*, Savant 2013 (CD)

98/06/09: Rebecca Kilgore, *Moments Like This*, Moonburn MB0001 (CD)

99/00/00: Ray Vega, *Boperation*, Concord Jazz CCD-4867 (CD)

99/00/00: Doris Spears, *The Duchess*, Orchard 2072 (CD)

Square Dance Boogie 1953
16-bar form (AA´), C major, improvisations on 12-bar blues form
Quincy Jones co-author.
53/08/02: Various Artists (Clifford King Solomon & His Orchestra), *The OKeh Rhythm & Blues Story: 1949–1957*, Columbia Legacy E3K 48912 (CD)
Note: No copyright record of this composition could be found.

Stan's Blues - *see* **Eleanor**

Steppin' Out 1957, 1958
32-bar form (AABA), F major
57/08/30: Donald Byrd–Gigi Gryce, *Jazz Lab/Modern Jazz Perspective*, Collectables COL-CD-5674 (CD)

Straight Ahead 1957
12-bar form, blues in B-flat
57/02/27: Gigi Gryce, *Jazz Lab Quintet*, Riverside OJCCD-1774-2 (CD)
Note: Liner notes attribute this composition to "Lee Sears," a Gryce pseudonym.

Strange Feeling (Strange Feelin') 1961
16-bar form, E-flat major
Lyrics by Jon Hendricks
60/06/07: Gigi Gryce, *The Rat Race Blues*, Prestige New Jazz OJCCD-081-2 (CD)
Note: Liner notes attribute this composition to "Sam Finch," which may have been a Gryce pseudonym.

Strictly Romantic 1954
32-bar form (ABAC), A-flat major
53/10/08: Clifford Brown, *The Complete Paris Sessions Vol. 2*, Vogue/BMG 45729 (CD)
54/05/20: Art Blakey, *Blakey*, Verve 314 538 634-2 (CD)
61/02/15: Jacques Pelzer, *Quartet Featuring Dino Piana*, Fonit Cetra (It.) CDM5004 (CD)

Stupendous-Lee (Au Tabou) 1956
32-bar form (AABA), F major
53/11/02: Henri Renaud Quintet, *Bobby Jaspar/Henri Renaud*, Vogue (Fr.) 74321409372 (CD); Note: Listed in liner notes as "Au Tabou."

54/05/19: Art Farmer, *When Farmer Met Gryce*, Prestige OJCCD-072-2 (CD)

81/05/07: Pan Trio, *Pan Trio*, Sonet (Swd.) SLP2687 (LP)

86/08/25: Jimmy Gourley, *The Left Bank of New York*, Uptown UPCD 27.32 (CD); Note: Listed in liner notes as "Au Tabou."

Tiajuana 1956

32-bar form (AABA), C minor

54/06/07: Art Farmer, *Art Farmer Septet*, Prestige OJCCD-054-2 (CD)

Transfiguration 1956

32-bar form (ABAC), E-flat major, chord changes of "Gone With the Wind"

56/11/09: Mal Waldron, *Mal-1*, Prestige OJCCD-611-2 (CD)

57/04/00: Art Blakey, *Percussion Discussion*, Chess CHC 2-92511 (CD)

Note: Liner notes attribute this composition to "Lee Sears," a Gryce pseudonym.

Two French Fries 1956

32-bar form (AABA), E-flat major

56/06/11: Oscar Pettiford, *Deep Passion*, Impulse GRD-143 (CD)

57/05/26: Oscar Pettiford, *Birdland Band—Jazz off the Air Vol. 6*, Spotlite (Eng.) SPJ 153 (LP)

Up in Quincy's Room 1953

32-bar form (AABA), C minor

53/07/02: Art Farmer, *Art Farmer Septet*, Prestige OJCCD-054-2 (CD)

53/11/02: Henri Renaud Quintet, *Bobby Jaspar/Henri Renaud*, Vogue (Fr.) 74321409372 (CD)

56/05/14: Jimmy Raney, *Jimmy Raney in Three Attitudes*, ABC Paramount ABC-167 (LP)

83/04/29: Doug Raney Sextet, *Meeting the Tenors*, Criss Cross Jazz (Du.) 1006 (LP)

90/08/15: Hod O'Brien, *Ridin' High*, Reservoir 116 (CD)

Wake Up! 1956

32-bar form (AABA), B-flat major, chord changes of "I Got Rhythm."

57/02/11: Art Blakey, *Ritual*, Blue Note CDP 7 46858 2 (CD)

57/02/27: Gigi Gryce, *Jazz Lab Quintet*, Riverside OJCCD-1774-2 (CD)

Note: Liner notes attribute this composition to "Lee Sears," a Gryce pseudonym.

Wildwood (Music in the Air) 1952, 1956

32-bar form (AABA), G major
Lyrics by Jon Hendricks
51/08/15: Stan Getz, *The Complete Roost Recordings*, Roost CDP 7243 8
  59622 2 6 (CD)
54/06/07: Art Farmer, *Art Farmer Septet*, Prestige OJCCD-054-2 (CD)
57/00/00: Bob Brookmeyer, Hall Overton, Jimmy Raney, Jim Hall, Bill
  Crow, Dick Scott, *The Jazz Loft 1954-1965*, Jazz Magnet JAM-2002 (CD)
57/02/14: Conte Candoli/Lee Morgan, *Double or Nothin'*, Fresh Sound
  (Sp.) FSR-CD197 (CD)
59/00/00: Jon Hendricks, *A Good Git-Together*, World Pacific WP-1283
  (LP); <u>Note</u>: Listed in liner notes as "Music in the Air."
87/07/09: The Ritz, *The Ritz*, Denon CY-1839 (CD); <u>Note</u>: Listed in
  liner notes as "Music in the Air."
92/12/14: Ed Bennett, *Blues for Hamp*, Saphu SCD-0015 (CD)

Wolf Talk (Wolf's Talk) 1955
32-bar form (AABA), C major, chord changes of "I Got Rhythm"
56/06/25: Jimmy Cleveland (Various Artists), *Rhythm Plus One*, Epic LN
  3297 (LP)
<u>Note</u>: The composer credit is indicated as "Lee Sears" (a Gryce pseud-
  onym) on the LP label, but Gigi Gryce in the liner notes.

You'll Always Be the One I Love 1955
32-bar form (AABA), A major
Lyrics by Jon Hendricks
50/05/00: Margie Anderson, Columbia 30213 (78); <u>Note</u>: This is the
  earliest known recording of a Gigi Gryce composition. It has never
  been reissued on LP or CD.
55/10/22: Gigi Gryce, *Nica's Tempo*, Savoy 126 (CD)

You're Not the Kind 1955
32-bar form (ABA′C), C major, chord changes of "Pennies from
  Heaven"
58/11/17: Benny Golson, *Benny Golson and the Philadelphians*, Blue Note
  CDP 7243 4 94104 2 8 (CD)

Yvette 1952, 1956
32-bar form (ABAC), F major
51/08/15: Stan Getz, *The Complete Roost Recordings*, Roost CDP 7243 8
  59622 2 6 (CD)
53/12/01: Jack Noren Quartet, Lars Gullin, *Modern Sounds Vol. 2, 1953*,
  Dragon (Sw.) DRCD 234 (CD)

Unrecorded Compositions of Gigi Gryce

The following titles were never recorded, and could very well represent just a fraction of the Gryce compositions that have never seen the light of day. During the course of being interviewed on the subject of Gryce, several subjects recalled seeing a large body of works stored in Gryce's home. Unfortunately, that treasure-trove of material, if it remained intact, could never be located and it is quite possible that many of his manuscripts were either destroyed or given to parties unknown. This compilation was drawn from Library of Congress, BMI, and ASCAP records. It was possible to examine some, but not all, of Gryce's copyright depositions, and the approximate year of registration is given, followed by occasional comments on form and structure. It is interesting to note that several of these pieces were apparently composed during his later years, after Gryce had left the music business.

5-3 X March 1975
A.S.I.A. Suite 1975 (A.S.I.A. stands for: "Africa, South America, India, Asia")
Al-Gashiya (Al Ghashiya, Gashiya) 1953, 1956; <u>Note</u>: The title refers to a Chapter or Surah in the Quran describing "The Overwhelming Event." The 1956 copyright deposition outlines a suite based on three themes:
Theme I ("bounce," 18 bars)
Theme II ("slow," 8 bars)
Theme III ("fast," 12 bars)

Bananas 1968
Bassology 1956
Blues - Part 1 (Manhattan Blues) 1955
Blues - Part 2 (Pensacola Blues) 1955
Blues You Choose (Blues U Choose) 1956
But Most of All 1957
Can This Be Love 1956 (32-bar form (AABA), E-flat major)
Chase Me with a Melody 1956 (32-bar waltz (AABA), C major)
Clock Work (Clockwork) 1954

Concerto (Unaccompanied alto saxophone) 1964
Concerto for Cookie 1968
Count Ali Carte (Scalpin') 1958
Dance of the Green Witches 1964; <u>Note</u>: This piece was composed in the early 1950s.
Dancing the Gigi 1961
Denise 1955
Do Not Sleep My Children 1975
Down Home Boy 1956
Duck Strut Blues 1956 (12-bar blues in C major)
Easter's Coming 1955 (19-bar form (AABA, 5+5+4+5), E-flat major)
Echo, The 1957
Edthia 1968
Es Tut Mir Leid 1967
Evening in Pakistan 1957
Fool in Love, A 1956 (32-bar form (AABA), E-flat major)
For Beauty's Sake 1955 (32-bar form (AABA), F major)
Fugue (Brass quartet) 1964
God's Gift to Man 1964
Gryce Suite 1, The (Pepsi Cola Trailers) 1960
   Kids
   Drive In
   Tickets
   Magician
Gryce Suite 2, The (On the Sound - Background Music for the Film, "Jazz Dance USA") 1960
   Blues in the Morning
   Despair
   Rat Race Blues (<u>note</u>: this theme was recorded on Prestige/New Jazz OJCCD-081-2.)
   Lighthouse
   Search
   Sequence
   Ratology
Holiday Drums (Holiday for Drums) 1976
Holiday on Broadway 1955
Home Boy 1957 (56-bar form (AABA, 16+16+8+16), Gospel-style, C major)
I'll Wait for You 1956 (32-bar form (ABAC), E-flat major)

I'm Going to Skin Your Natural Hide 1957

If It Don't Get Better Then It's Gonna Get Worse 1958

In Memory of Gene 1962; <u>Note</u>: Composed in memory of Hartford
pianist Gene Nelson

Junior's Bounce 1968

Just Groovin' 1955

Lady Luck 1955 (32-bar form (AABA), F major); <u>Note</u>: This composition is very similar to "So That's How It's Gonna Be."

Lailatul-Qadr. 1967; <u>Note</u>: The title, taken from the Koran, means "The
Night of Power."

Latin, The 1968

Let's Face It 1962

Little Folks 1955 (32-bar form (AABA), B-flat major)

Loneliness 1955

Lost Love 1955 (32-bar form (AABA), F major)

Lover's Mood 1954 (32-bar form (AABA), E-flat major)

Mambo in Eb 1955

Mambo Velasco 1956

March on America (Wake Up Young America) 1956, 1958; Lyrics by
Jon Hendricks; standard march with two 16-bar themes

Mood in Blue 1954 (32-bar form (AABA), E-flat major); <u>Note</u>: Although the sheet music published in 1955 indicates that this composition was recorded by Earl Bostic on King Records, no such recording
could be found.

Moon Beams 1955 (32-bar form (ABAC), A-flat major)

Night That We Met, The 1955, 1956 (32-bar form (AABA), E-flat
major); Lyrics by Leo Corday

Now How Do You Know 1957

Now That I Found You (She's (He's) My Baby) 1956, 1959; Lyrics by
Leo Corday

Oh Baby Please 1957

Pee Wee 1956

Please Come Back to Me Dear 1955

Prelude 1967

Premonitions of Basheer (Baby G) 1958 (28-bar form (AABA,
8+8+4+8), C major)

Quartet for Brass Instruments 1977

Rosie (Josie) 1957

Seven Senses 1968

Since You've Come to Me 1954 (32-bar form (ABAC), E-flat major)
So That's How It's Gonna Be 1955 (32-bar form (AABA), F major);
  Note: This composition is very similar to "Lady Luck."
Sol'in 1955 (altered 12-bar blues in A major)
Sonata (Violin Sonata) 1964
Soul 1959
Spring Is Coming 1977
Starvation 1964
Take a Little Tip from Me 1957 (12-bar blues in C major)
Trolly Tracks 1954 (32-bar form (AABA), F major)
Waltz of the Willow Tree 1956
Where Do We Go from Here 1956
Wishing 1954 (32-bar form (AABA), G major)
Wishing Song, The 1956

The following may comprise a suite. All of the titles date from 1968 and
  have Islamic references:
  Al-Hikmat (Wisdom)
  Hajj (The annual pilgrimage to Mecca, a major Islamic celebration)
  Jihad (The striving or struggle carried out by Muslims in their effort to
  follow and defend the teachings of Allah)
  Safa (A small mountain involved in an Islamic ritual called the sa'i,
  performed as part of the pilgrimage to Mecca (Hajj))
  Shaitan (Satan, the source of evil in the world)
  Yarun (The title may refer to a village in what is now Lebanon.)
  Zemzem (A sacred well in the city of Mecca known as "The Well of
  Ishmael" thought to have healing powers)

The following may comprise a suite. All of the titles date from 1977:
  Break! Break!
  Brown! Brown! Brown!
  Down! Up!
  Scuffle! Scuffle!

appendix b: publishing company holdings

In the following tables, Reg. Date indicates the year of registration with the U.S. Copyright Office. Gigi Gryce's compositions (see Appendix A) are not listed but most of them were published by these companies during the time periods indicated.

Melotone Music, Inc. Holdings 1955–1963

Composer(s)	Title	Reg. Date
Bailey, Joe	Fleetwind	1961
Bailey, Joe	Lament	1961
Bailey, Joe	Meditation	1961
Bailey, Joe	Movin'	1961
Bailey, Joe	Perfume Blue	1961
Bailey, Joe	Psycho	1961
Bailey, Joe	Say Something	1961
Bailey, Joe	Third Rail	1961
Belgrave, Marcus	Cellar Groove	1961
Best, Denzil	Forty Five (45) Degree Angle	1957
Bethea, Jimmie	Passion Eyes	1960
Bolden, Walter	Ittapnna	1958

Composer(s)	Title	Reg. Date
Brown, Clifford	All Weird	1957
Brown, Clifford	Blue and Brown	1957
Brown, Clifford	Brownie Speaks	1956
Brown, Clifford	Larue [rec. as Tribute to Brownie as by D. Pearson]	1957
Brown, Clifford	Minor Mood	1956
Bryant, Ray	Little Susie	1961
Carter, Betty	I Can't Help It	1958
Coles, Johnny	Room Three	1961
Copeland, Ray	Somewhere	1957
Davis, Charles	Turbo Village (Turbo)	1960
Donaldson, Lou	Cookin'	1956
Donaldson, Lou	Down Home	1956
Donaldson, Lou	Lou's Blues	1956
Farmer, Art	Stretch in F	1958
Gardner, Billy	Billy's Blues	1961
Gardner, Billy	One for Elena	1961
Golson, Benny	And You Call My Name [rec. as ...Called...]	1955
Golson, Benny	Are You Real	1956
Golson, Benny	Beauty and the Blues	1957
Golson, Benny	Big Ben (I'm Cool Not Hot)	1955
Golson, Benny Blue	Sophisticate	1956
Golson, Benny	Blue Walk	1955
Golson, Benny	Blues It	1957
Golson, Benny	Celedia	1957
Golson, Benny	Day Dreams All Come True	1956
Golson, Benny	Finger Poppin' and Hip Shakin'	1956
Golson, Benny	Four Eleven West	1956
Golson, Benny	Four Strings	1957
Golson, Benny	Hasaan's Dream	1956
Golson, Benny	I Found My Love in Mexico	1956
Golson, Benny	I Want to Mambo Too	1956
Golson, Benny	Just by Myself (All by Myself)	1957
Golson, Benny	Latin Hangover	1957
Golson, Benny	Long Way Home	1955
Golson, Benny	Mesabi Chant	1955
Golson, Benny	Minor Run-Down	1957
Golson, Benny	My Heart Just Told Me So	1956
Golson, Benny	Night in Philly, A	1956

Composer(s)	Title	Reg. Date
Golson, Benny	Park Avenue Petite	1956
Golson, Benny	Reggie of Chester	1956
Golson, Benny	Sahara	1956
Golson, Benny	Shades of Dameron	1956
Golson, Benny	Slightly Hep [rec. as Slightly Hip]	1957
Golson, Benny	Step Lightly	1955
Golson, Benny	Strut, The	1955
Golson, Benny	Theme for Jeri	1956
Golson, Benny	Tip Toeing	1957
Golson, Benny	Voice from the West	1956
Golson, Benny	When You Find the One You Love	1956
Golson, Benny & Jon Hendricks	I Remember Clifford	1957
Gryce, Tommy	New Tune	1956
Hall, Nancy	Nancy	1957
Haynes, Frank	Frankly Speaking	1961
Jones, Hank	Bangoon	1957
Jones, Hank	Ergo the Blues (Jones Bones)	1957, 1958
Jones, Hank	Hank's Blues	1957
Jones, Hank	Passade (Under the Stars)	1957, 1958
Jones, Hank	So It's Spring	1957
Jones, Sam	Blues Funk [rec. as Blue Funk]	1958
Jordan, Duke	Flight to Jordan (East of Cairo)	1955, 1958
Jordan, Duke	Forecast	1955
Jordan, Duke	Oh Yeah	1955
Jordan, Duke	Scotch Blues	1955
Jordan, Duke	Sheila (Pannonica)	1955, 1958
Jordan, Duke	Sultry Eve	1955
Jordan, Duke	Tracey	1955
Jordan, Duke	Vacker Flicka	1956
Keyes, Donald	Just Last Spring	1956
Keyes, Donald	Night That We Fell in Love, The	1956
Keyes, Donald	There's Love	1956
Keyes, Donald & Eric Springer	Lady's Sad Now, The	1956
Keyes, Donald & Eric Springer	Woman Has to Be Told, A	1956
Knittel, Wolf	First at Lancaster	1961
Legge, Wade	Cold Breeze	1958
Little, Booker	Booker's Blues	1961
Little, Booker	Cliff Walk	1961
Little, Booker	Looking Ahead	1961

Composer(s)	Title	Reg. Date
Little, Booker	Victory and Sorrow	1961
Mance, Junior	Jubilation	1958
Mapp, Norman	Blues in Bloom	1960
Mapp, Norman	Foul Play	1958
Mapp, Norman	Monday through Sunday	1960
McGhee, Howard	Belle from Bunnyock [rec. as ...Bunnycock]	1956
McGhee, Howard	Down Home	1956
McGhee, Howard	Flip Lip [rec. as Flip Lid]	1956
McGhee, Howard	Short Life	1956
McIntyre, Ken	Contsy [rec. as Curtsy]	1960
McIntyre, Ken	George's Tune [rec. as Geo's Tune]	1960
McIntyre, Ken	Twinkle Toes	1961
Mitchell, Hal	Confidentially	1956
Mitchell, Hal	Hong Pong Blues	1958
Mitchell, Hal	I Got Money Too	1956
Mitchell, Hal	Is This Real	1956
Mitchell, Hal	Mitch's Blues	1956
Mitchell, Hal	Rockin' and Rollin'	1956
Mitchell, Hal	Rough Sailin'	1956
Mitchell, Leon	Late Spring	1958
Mitchell, Leon	To Lady	1961
Mitchell, Richard "Blue"	Bluzie	1958
Mitchell, Richard "Blue"	Brother Ball	1958
Monk, Thelonious	Brake's Sake	1955
Monk, Thelonious	Gallop's Gallop	1955
Monk, Thelonious	Shuffle Boil	1955
Morgan, Lee	Juba	1957
Ousley, Harold	Alpha	1958
Ousley, Harold	Baby You're the Only One	1958
Ousley, Harold	'Cause It's So Groovy	1958
Ousley, Harold	Celestria	1958
Ousley, Harold	Del-A-Vonn	1958
Ousley, Harold	Minor Revelation, A	1958
Ousley, Harold	Stratus Sphere	1958
Ousley, Harold	That Happy Feeling	1958
Payne, Cecil	Arnetta	1956
Payne, Cecil	Blues for O.P. (Bringing Up Father)	1956, 1958
Payne, Cecil	Man of Moods	1956

Composer(s)	Title	Reg. Date
Phelps, Tony	Get Yourself Together	1961
Phelps, Tony & Cyril Mumford	Ain't That a Shame	1961
Priester, Julian	In the Know	1961
Priester, Julian	Juliano (Julian's Tune)	1961
Priester, Julian	Looking Up	1961
Priester, Julian	On Your Toes	1961
Priester, Julian	Push Come to Shove	1961
Priester, Julian	Since When	1961
Priester, Julian	Why Not	1961
Priester, Julian & Abbey Lincoln	Retribution	1961
Roach, Max & Oscar Brown, Jr.	All Africa	1961
Roach, Max & Oscar Brown, Jr.	Driva Man	1961
Roach, Max & Oscar Brown, Jr.	Freedom Day	1961
Roach, Max & Oscar Brown, Jr.	Tears for Johannesburg	1961
Silver, Horace	Speculation	1955
Simmons, Norman	Ain't That News	1961
Simmons, Norman	Message, The	1959
Simmons, Norman	Venus and the Moon	1959
Smalls, Danny (Singh, Darshon)	Don't Weep for the Lady	1959
Smith, Hale	Feathers	1961
Stevenson, Rudy	B.M.T. Express, The	1961
Stevenson, Rudy	Break Through	1961
Stevenson, Rudy	Carefree	1961
Stevenson, Rudy	Lady Iris B	1961
Stevenson, Rudy	Not a Tear Will I Shed [rec. as Not a Tear]	1961
Stevenson, Rudy	Off Color	1961
Stevenson, Rudy	Reaching Out	1961
Stevenson, Rudy	Smoothie	1961
Stevenson, Rudy	Two Feet in the Gutter	1961
Tucker, Ben	Begin	1961
Tucker, Ben	Flick of a Trick	1961
Tucker, Ben & Bob Dorough	Comin' Home Baby	1961
Watkins, Julius	Eileen	1958
Watkins, Julius	Glad That I Found You	1958
Watkins, Julius	Moods in Motion	1958
Weston, Randy	Chessman's Delight	1956
Weston, Randy	Earth Birth	1957
Weston, Randy	Fe-Double-U-Blues	1957
Weston, Randy	Ginger Bread	1957

Composer(s)	Title	Reg. Date
Weston, Randy	Little Niles	1957
Weston, Randy	Pam's Waltz	1957
Weston, Randy	Saucer Eyes	1956
Weston, Randy	Softness	1957
Williams, Richard	Blues in a Quandary	1960
Williams, Richard	Raucous Notes	1960
Williams, Richard	Renita's Bounce	1960
Wyands, Richard	Candied Sweets	1960
Wyands, Richard	Ferris Wheel	1960
Wyands, Richard	Half 'n' Half	1961

Totem Music, Inc. Holdings 1958–1963

Items marked with an asterisk were registered in both companies.

Composer(s)	Title	Reg. Date
Alexander, Roland	Libra	1958
Alexander, Roland	Pleasure Bent	1958
Best, Denzil	Forty Five (45) Degree Angle*	1958
Blakey, Art	Art's Mambo	1958
Bryant, Ray	Calgary	1958
Bryant, Ray	Little Susie*	1960
Bryant, Ray	Reflection	1958
Bryant, Ray	Stacatto Swing	1959
Cassey, Sara	Very Near Blue	1958
Dorough, Bob & Bobby Timmons	This Here	1962
Fuller, Curtis	Bit of Heaven	1959
Fuller, Curtis	Down Home	1959
Golson, Benny	Along Came Betty	1958
Golson, Benny	Are You Real*	1958
Golson, Benny	Blue Thoughts	1958
Golson, Benny	Blues on Down	1958
Golson, Benny	Blues on My Mind	1958
Golson, Benny	City Lights	1958
Golson, Benny	Cry a Blue Tear	1958
Golson, Benny	Drum Thunder	1958
Golson, Benny	Fair Weather	1958
Golson, Benny	Golson Suite	1959
Golson, Benny	Harlem's Disciples	1958
Golson, Benny	Out of the Past	1958
Golson, Benny	Paris Suite	1958

Composer(s)	Title	Reg. Date
Golson, Benny	Strut Time	1958
Golson, Benny	Tempo De Waltz	1958
Golson, Benny	Theme for Jeri*	1958
Golson, Benny	Thursday's Theme	1959
Golson, Benny	Venetian Breeze	1958
Hardman, Bill	Politely	1958
Hardman, Bill	Theme for Tomorrow	1958
Hendricks, Jon	Minor Catastrophe	1958
Hendricks, Jon & Bobby Timmons	Moanin'	1961
Hendricks, Jon & Randy Weston	Little Niles*	1958
Hendricks, Jon & Randy Weston	Where?	1958
Hughes, Langston	Introduction to Uhuru Kwanza	1961
Jones, Hank	Get Set	1958
Jones, Hank	Jones' Bones* [rec. as Ergo the Blues]	1960
Jones, Hank	Levitation (In and Out of the Waldorf)	1958
Jones, Hank	Low Bridge	1958
Jones, Hank	Vignette	1958
Jones, Hank & Jon Hendricks	Let Me Know	1958
Lee, Bill	Brownie's Mood	1961
Lee, Bill	Deeds, Not Words	1961
Lee, Bill	Jodie's Chacha	1961
Lee, Bill	Sporty	1961
Lee, Bill & Bill Campbell	Mirage	1961
Lee, Bill & Bill Campbell	No More	1961
Lee, Bill & Bill Campbell	Quiet As It's Kept	1961
Lincoln, Abbey & Mal Waldron	Straight Ahead	1961
Liston, Melba	Blues Melba	1959
Liston, Melba	The Way I Feel about My Lord	1962
Liston, Melba	Tone Poem	1961
Liston, Melba	We Never Kissed, What a Shame	1958
Liston, Melba	You Don't Say	1959
Little, Booker	Dungeon's Waltz	1959
Little, Booker	Jewel's Tempo	1959
Little, Booker	Rounders Mood	1959
Mitchell, Leon & Charles Gaston	I'm Always a Brother	1960
Moorehead, Consuela Lee	Connie's Bounce	1961
Moorehead, Consuela Lee	Prelude	1961
Morgan, Lee	Lee's Blues Lines (Blues Pour Doudou)	1962
Richardson, Jerome	According to J.R.	1958

Composer(s)	Title	Reg. Date
Richardson, Jerome	Freelance	1958
Richardson, Jerome	Funk Box	1958
Shihab, Sahib	Hum-Bug	1959
Shihab, Sahib	My Pretty Little French Girl	1958
Shihab, Sahib	Please Don't Leave	1958
Timmons, Bobby	Bobby's Theme (Pasquier)	1962
Timmons, Bobby	Moanin'	1958
Timmons, Bobby	Quick Trick	1959
Timmons, Bobby	This Here (Dis Hyunh)	1959, 1961
Timmons, Bobby; Blakey, Art; Morgan, Lee	Bobby's Blues Lines (Blues Pour Marcel; Pasquier)	1962
Weston, Randy	204	1961
Weston, Randy	Babe's Blues	1958
Weston, Randy	Bantu Suite	1958
Weston, Randy	Bass Jones	1961
Weston, Randy	Beef Blues Stew	1958
Weston, Randy	Blues for Cannonball	1961
Weston, Randy	Blues for Kim	1961
Weston, Randy	Bobby 3/4	1961
Weston, Randy	Cornet New Blues	1961
Weston, Randy	Cry Me Not	1961
Weston, Randy	Deep Affection	1961
Weston, Randy	Gee Blues Gee (Kucheza)	1961
Weston, Randy	Hi-Fly	1958
Weston, Randy	Honk Honk [rec. as Honky Tonk]	1961
Weston, Randy	Let's Climb a Hill	1958
Weston, Randy	Lifetime	1958
Weston, Randy	Lisa Lovely	1959
Weston, Randy	Little Dru	1961
Weston, Randy	Little Niles*	1958
Weston, Randy	Machine Blues	1958
Weston, Randy	Nice Ice	1958
Weston, Randy	Portrait of Patsy J.	1961
Weston, Randy	Portrait of Vivian	1961
Weston, Randy	Pretty Strange	1958
Weston, Randy	Sketch of Melba, A	1959
Weston, Randy	Spot 5 Blues	1961
Weston, Randy	Tweetle Drum Dum	1961
Weston, Randy	Uhuru Kwanza	1961

Composer(s)	Title	Reg. Date
Weston, Randy	Uncle Neemo [rec. as …Nemo]	1961
Weston, Randy	Where?	1958
Weston, Randy & Jon Hendricks	Babe's Blues	1958
Weston, Randy & Langston Hughes	African Lady	1961
Wilkins, Ernie	Posterity	1958
Williams, Pinkey A. K.	Stop Cheating on Me	1959

discography

In an attempt to present an intelligible guide to Gryce's recording activities, for the most part only original long-playing and most recent U.S. CD (re-)issues are included. Exceptions are made for items which were never issued in long-playing or CD format or when foreign issues are first or only sources. (Please contact the authors regarding corrections and additional issue details.)

The following format is used:

<u>Session number</u> (Derived from year-month-day; these numbers are referenced in Appendix A.)
Artist - Album Title (When later issues are given different titles, this is noted. Titles in [brackets] were not commercially issued as such.)
Date, Location
Personnel (see below for instrument abbreviations); arrangers are indicated when known, using their initials.

| Matrix number | Song title | Timing | Composer | Issue numbers (a " - " indicates that the issue number is the same as indicated above it; for country abbreviations see below.) |

Notes:

<u>Abbreviations</u>: (acc) accordion; (alt) alternative take; (arr) arranger; (as) alto saxophone; (b) string bass; (bar) baritone saxophone; (bcl) bass clarinet; (bgo) (bongo); (bnj) banjo; (btb) bass trombone; (cel) cello; (cga) conga; (cl) clarinet; (con) conductor; (d) drums; (eb) electric bass; (fh) French horn; (fl) flute; (flg) flugelhorn; (g) guitar; (hp) harp; (mc) master of ceremonies; (ob) oboe; (p) piano; (perc) percussion; (pic) piccolo; (sx) saxophone; (tamb) tambourine; (tb) trombone; (tp) trumpet; (ts) tenor saxophone; (tu) tuba; (vb) vibraphone; (vln) violin; (voc) vocal; (v tb) valve trombone; (ww) woodwinds. (Eng.) English; (Fr.) French; (Jap.) Japanese; (Sp.) Spanish; (Swd.) Swedish.

500600
Margie Anderson
Early June 1950, New York

Margie Anderson (voc), Milton Hayes (voc), unknown (g), possibly Duke Anderson (p), unknown (b), possibly Milton Hayes (d)

CO43859	Hurry, Hurry, Margie (ensemble voc)	2:07	Duke Anderson, Margie Anderson, Lester Harris	Columbia 30213 [78]
CO43860	You'll Always Be the One I Love	2:33	Gigi Gryce	-
CO43861	It's Time You Cried	2:41	Berman & Baron	Columbia 30226 [78]
CO43862	Always Love Him (Never Leave Him Blues)	2:00	Jerry Bressler & Alan Norman Jackson	-

Note 1: Margie Anderson confirms that Gryce was present in the studio for this session.
Note 2: Hayes is featured singing on CO43862 only. A Milton Hayes did perform on drums in the Newark NJ area and may be the drummer on this session.

510000
[Jam Session]
Winter 1950–Spring 1951, Christy's Restaurant, Framingham MA

Howard McGhee, unknown (tp), Bob Wilber (cl), Gigi Gryce (as, p), Joe Roland (vb), Duke Jordan, Nat Pierce (p), Oscar Pettiford (cel, b), Tommy Potter (b), unknown (d), Eddie Curran (mc):

			Unissued
Rockin' in Rhythm/Jumpin' with Symphony Sid	15:30	Duke Ellington/Lester Young	-
Don't Blame Me	5:47	Jimmy McHugh, Dorothy Fields	-
Perdido	8:53	Juan Tizol	-
Swingin' 'Till the Girls Come Home	10:11	Oscar Pettiford	-
Star Dust	2:50	Hoagy Carmichael & Mitchell Parish	-
Ad lib			-
These Foolish Things	2:51	Jack Strachey, Harry Link, Holt Marvell	-
Imagination	5:37	Jimmy Van Heusen	-
Perdido		Juan Tizol	-
Move (breakdown)	0:36	Denzil Best	-
Move	8:00	Denzil Best	-
Embraceable You	9:50	George Gershwin	-
Jumpin' with Symphony Sid	9:42	Lester Young	-
Body and Soul	5:33	John Green, Edward Heyman, Robert Sour, Frank Eyton	-

			Unissued
Donna Lee	2:51	Miles Davis	-
Untitled piano solo			-
Untitled piano solo			-
Anthropology	6:43	Charlie Parker & Dizzy Gillespie	-
I Got Rhythm	6:22	George Gershwin & Ira Gershwin	-
I'll Remember April	11:30	Don Raye, Gene DePaul, Bat Johnson	-
Unknown title			-
Unknown title			-

Titles with timings were to be issued on the Zim label. Art Zimmerman is in possession of the tapes.

Note 1: This collective personnel is somewhat speculative and incomplete.
Note 2: The first selection is not a medley but a merging of the two melodies.
Note 3: Many titles are fragmentary and the sound quality varies.
Note 4: Gryce plays piano on the two piano solos.

530410
Max Roach - Featuring Hank Mobley

April 10, 1953, New York
Idrees Sulieman (tp), Leon Comegys (tb), Gigi Gryce (as, fl, arr), Hank Mobley (ts, arr), Walter Davis Jr. (p), Franklin Skeete (b), Max Roach (d, arr):

A105	Mobleyzation	2:42	Hank Mobley	Debut DEP-451, OJCCD-202-2
	Orientation (alt)	3:04	Hank Mobley	Debut DEB-198, OJC-115
B105	Orientation	2:50	Hank Mobley	Debut DEP-451, OJCCD-202-2, 4DEBCD-4420-2
A106	Glow Worm	2:27	Paul Lincke, Johnny Mercer, Lilla C. Robinson	Debut DEP-451, OJCCD-202-2
B106	Sfax	2:17	Max Roach	Debut DEP-451, OJCCD-202-2, 4DEBCD-4420-2

Note 1: All compositions arranged by their composers except Glow Worm by Gigi Gryce.
Note 2: Debut 198 and OJC-115 are titled Autobiography in Jazz. Debut 4420 is titled The Debut Records Story.

530520
Howard McGhee Sextet - Volume 2

May 20, 1953, WOR Studios, New York
Howard McGhee (tp, arr), Gigi Gryce (as, fl, arr), Tal Farlow (g), Horace Silver (p), Percy Heath (b), Walter Bolden (d):

BN483-2	Shabozz	3:56	Gigi Gryce	*Blue Note BLP 5024*
BN484-2	Tranquility	4:07	Howard McGhee	-
BN485-1	Futurity	4:01	Gigi Gryce	-
BN486-0	Jarm (fast version)	3:54	Howard McGhee	
BN486-1	Jarm	4:32	Howard McGhee	*Blue Note BLP 5024*
BN487-1	Ittapnna	3:46	Walter Bolden	

Gryce out:

| BN488-2 | Goodbye | 4:06 | Gordon Jenkins | *Blue Note BLP 5024* |

All takes on Blue Note 7243 4 95748 2 3, titled *Howard McGhee Volume 2/Tal Farlow Quartet*.

Note: Gryce arranged his own compositions.

530611
Tadd Dameron Orchestra - A Study in Dameronia

June 11, 1953, WOR Studios, New York

Clifford Brown, Idrees Sulieman (tp), Herb Mullins (tb), Gigi Gryce (as), Benny Golson (ts), Oscar Estelle (bar), Tadd Dameron (p, arr), Percy Heath (b), Philly Joe Jones (d):

490	Philly JJ	5:05	Tadd Dameron	*Prestige PRLP 159*
491-1	Choose Now	4:50	Tadd Dameron	
491-2	Choose Now	3:20	Tadd Dameron	*Prestige PRLP 159*
492	Dial "B" for Beauty	4:30	Tadd Dameron	*Prestige PRLP 159*
493	Theme of No Repeat	5:15	Tadd Dameron	*Prestige PRLP 159*

All takes on Prestige PRLP 7055, OJCD-017-2, titled *Clifford Brown: Memorial Album*.

Note: Some sources incorrectly list the studio as Van Gelder. The issue names the engineer as Doug Hawkins who is known to have worked at WOR.

530620
Tadd Dameron

c. late June 1953, Paradise Club, Atlantic City, NJ

Clifford Brown, Johnny Coles (tp), Steve Pulliam (tb), Gigi Gryce (as), Benny Golson (ts), Kellice Swaggerty (bar), Tadd Dameron (p, arr), Jymie Merritt (b), Philly Joe Jones (d); Bob Bailey (mc):

| | Introduction | | Tadd Dameron | *Unissued* |

| | [Theme Music] | Tadd Dameron | - |
| | All Aboard for the Caribbean | Tadd Dameron | - |

Note 1: This six-minute excerpt from a longer tape was broadcast on WKCR-FM. Gryce solos briefly.
Note 2: Composer uncertain for these pieces.

530702
Art Farmer Septet
July 2, 1953, WOR Studios, New York

Art Farmer (tp), Jimmy Cleveland (tb), Clifford Solomon (ts), Oscar Estelle (bar), Quincy Jones (p), Monk Montgomery (eb), Sonny Johnson (d), Gigi Gryce (arr, con):

| 506 | Up in Quincy's Room | 4:00 | Gigi Gryce | *Prestige PRLP 162, PRLP 7031, OJCCID 054-2* |

Note: In subsequent liner notes, Ira Gitler confirms Gryce was in the studio for this session.

530802
Clifford "King" Solomon and His Orchestra
August 2, 1953, New York

Jimmy Cleveland (tb), Clifford Solomon (ts), Oscar Estelle (bar), Wade Legge (p), Monk Montgomery (eb), Max Roach (d), Ernestine Anderson, Gigi Gryce (voc), Quincy Jones (arr):

CO49881	Lil' Daddee (EA, GG voc)	2:24	Gigi Gryce & Quincy Jones	*Okeh 7010 [78]*
CO49882	Square Dance Boogie (EA voc)	2:24	Gigi Gryce & Quincy Jones	*Okeh 7022, Epic/Okeh/Legacy CD E3K 48912*
CO49883	Street Walking			*Okeh 7022 [78]*
CO49884	But Officer (GG voc)	2:49	Incencio & Wainright	*Okeh 7010, Epic/Okeh/Legacy CD E3K 48912*

Note: Epic 48912 is titled *The Okeh Rhythm & Blues Story: 1949–1957.*

530828
Clifford Brown Sextet - New Star on the Horizon
August 28, 1953, Audio-Video Studios, New York

Clifford Brown (tp), Gigi Gryce (as, fl*, arr), Charlie Rouse (ts), John Lewis (p, arr), Percy Heath (b), Art Blakey (d); Quincy Jones (arr):

BN524-0	Wail Bait (alt)	4:01	Quincy Jones	*Blue Note BST 84428*
BN524-2	Wail Bait	3:56	Quincy Jones	*Blue Note BLP 5032, BLP 1526*
BN525-1	Hymn to the Orient	4:01	Gigi Gryce	*Blue Note BLP 5032, BLP 1526*

379

BN525-3	Hymn to the Orient (alt)	4:00	Gigi Gryce	Blue Note BST 84428
BN526-1	Brownie Eyes *	3:52	Quincy Jones	Blue Note BLP 5032, BST 84428
BN527-0	Cherokee (alt)	3:40	Ray Noble	Blue Note BST 84428
BN527-1	Cherokee	3:23	Ray Noble	Blue Note BLP 5032, BLP 1526
BN528-0	Easy Living (arr. JL) *	3:40	Leo Robin & Ralph Rainger	Blue Note BLP 5032, BLP 1526
BN529-0	Minor Mood	4:31	Clifford Brown	Blue Note BLP 5032, BLP 1526

All takes on Blue Note CDP 7243 5 32141 2, titled *Memorial Album*, CDP 7243 8 34195 2 4, titled *The Complete Blue Note and Pacific Jazz Recordings*.

Note 1: Gryce and Jones each arranged their own compositions.
Note 2: Blue Note 1526 is titled *Memorial Album*. Blue Note 84428 is titled *Alternate Takes*.

530900
Lionel Hampton and His Orchestra
September 1953, Concert, Sweden

Clifford Brown, Art Farmer, Quincy Jones, Walter Williams (tp), Al Hayse, Jimmy Cleveland, George "Buster" Cooper (tb), Anthony Ortega, Gigi Gryce (as), Clifford Scott, Clifford Solomon (ts), Oscar Estelle (bar), Lionel Hampton (vb, voc), Billy Mackel (g), George Wallington (p), Monk Montgomery (eb), Alan Dawson, Curley Hamner (d):

The Opener	4:13	Lionel Hampton	IAJRC 31, Natasha CD NI 4010
Summertime	3:57	George Gershwin & DuBose Heyward	-
On the Sunny Side of the Street	4:04	Dorothy Fields & Jimmy McHugh	-
Oh, Rock!	7:05	Lionel Hampton	-
How High the Moon	4:34	Morgan Lewis & Nancy Hamilton	-
Star Dust	3:53	Hoagy Carmichael & Mitchell Parish	-
I Only Have Eyes for You	4:28	Al Dubin & Harry Warren	-
Blue Boy	9:19	Lionel Hampton	-

Note 1: Some issues list Sonny Parker and/or Annie Ross (voc) who are not heard on these tracks.
Note 2: Hampton appears as vocalist on On the Sunny Side of the Street only.
Note 3: IAJRC 31 is titled *Live In Sweden 1953*. Natasha 4010 is titled *Ob, Rock! Live in Sweden 1953*.

530914
Annie Ross
September 14, 1953, Sweden

Annie Ross (voc), Jimmy Cleveland (tb), Anthony Ortega (as), Clifford Solomon (ts), Lars Gullin (bar), Quincy Jones (p), Simon Brehm (b), Alan Dawson (d), Gigi Gryce (arr, con):

| 516 | The Song is You | 3:07 | Jerome Kern | Metronome (Sud.) B647 [78], Prestige SP 879 [78], P-7828 |
| 517 | Jackie | 2:44 | Hampton Hawes (& Annie Ross) | Metronome (Sud.) B647, Prestige SP 879, P-7828, CD 24216-2 |

Note 1: Studio could well be Europa Film Studios, Sundbyerg, Stockholm, where Clifford Brown discographer Bob Weir places the Clifford Brown/Art Farmer recording of the following day.

Note 2: Prestige 7828 and 24216 are titled *The Bebop Singers*.

530926
Gigi Gryce Ensembles
September 26, 1953, Paris

Art Farmer (tp), Jimmy Cleveland (tb), Gigi Gryce (as, arr), Anthony Ortega (as, fl), Clifford Solomon (ts), William Boucaya (bar), Henri Renaud (p), Pierre Michelot (b), Alan Dawson (d), Quincy Jones (arr):

| 53V4650-1 | Paris The Beautiful | 4:16 | Gigi Gryce | Vogue (Fr.) LD 724, CD 7 4321 15467 2, BMG CD 0026-68216-2 |
| 53V4651-1 | Purple Shades | 2:51 | Quincy Jones | |

same session but Ortega (fl) only, Quincy Jones (p, arr) replaces Renaud:

53V4652-1	La Rose Noire (inc.)	1:32	Quincy Jones	Vogue (Jap.) DY5903-3
53V4652-2	La Rose Noire (inc.)	2:04	Quincy Jones	-
53V4652-3	La Rose Noire	3:36	Quincy Jones	Vogue (Fr.) LD 724, CD 7 4321 15467 2, BMG CD 0026-68216-2

Note 1: Gryce and Jones each arranged their own compositions.

Note 2: Farmer does not appear on 53V4650.

Note 3: Vogue 15467 is titled *Lucky Thompson/Gigi Gryce: Street Scenes*. BMG 68216 is titled *Lucky Thompson/Gigi Gryce: in Paris*.

Note 4: Although labeled as rehearsals on Vogue DY5903-3, the incomplete takes of La Rose Noire are obviously fragments that were spliced together to form the issued take.

Note 5: Vogue DY5903-3 titled Gigi Gryce: *The Complete Paris Collection Vol. 5* is a bonus LP never sold individually but given to purchasers of volumes 1–4.

530926
Gigi Gryce Ensembles
September 26, 1953, Paris

Gigi Gryce (as, fl*), Jimmy Gourley (g), Henri Renaud (p), Pierre Michelot (b), Jean-Louis Viale (d):

| 53V4653 | I Can't Get Started * | 0:46 | Vernon Duke & Ira Gershwin | *Vogue (Jap.) DY5903-3* |

Alan Dawson (d) replaces Viale:

53V4654-1	Anne Marie (I Need You So)	1:03	Gigi Gryce	*Vogue (Jap.) DY5903-3*
53V4654-2	Anne Marie (I Need You So)	1:00	Gigi Gryce	-
53V4654-3	Anne Marie (I Need You So)	3:55	Gigi Gryce	-

<u>Note</u>: Vogue DY5903-3 titled Gigi Gryce: *The Complete Paris Collection Vol. 5* is a bonus LP never sold individually but given to purchasers of volumes 1-4.

530928
Gigi Gryce Orchestra

September 28, 1953, Vogue Studio, Schola Cantorum, Paris

Gigi Gryce (as, arr), Henri Renaud (p), Pierre Michelot (b), Alan Dawson (d):

| 53V4654-? | Anne Marie (I Need You So) | 3:34 | Gigi Gryce | *Vogue (Fr.) CD 7 4321 15467 2, BMG CD 09026-68216-2* |

add Clifford Brown, Art Farmer, Walter Williams, Fernand Verstraete, Fred Gerard (tp), Quincy Jones (tp, arr), Jimmy Cleveland, Bill Tamper, Al Hayse (tb), Anthony Ortega (as), Clifford Solomon, Henri Bernard (ts), Henri Jouot (bar):

| 53V4655-1 | Brown Skins | 6:04 | Gigi Gryce | *Vogue (Fr.) LD 607-30, Prestige OJCCD-359-2* |
| 53V4655-2 | Brown Skins | 6:07 | Gigi Gryce | *Vogue (Fr.) LD 173, Prestige OJCCD-359-2* |

Gerard out:

53V4656	Deltitnu	3:53	Gigi Gryce	*Vogue (Fr.) LD 173*
53V4658-1	Keepin' Up with Jonesy	7:05	Quincy Jones	*Vogue (Fr.) LD 173, Prestige OJCCD-359-2*
53V4658-2	Keepin' Up with Jonesy	6:27	Quincy Jones	*Vogue (Fr.) LD 723, Prestige OJCCD-359-2*

All takes on Vogue (Fr.) CD 45728 titled *Clifford Brown: The Complete Paris Sessions, Vol. 1.*

<u>Note 1</u>: Gryce and Jones each arranged their own compositions.

<u>Note 2</u>: Take numbers may indicate choice, not order.

<u>Note 3</u>: Prestige OJC 359 is titled *Clifford Brown Big Band in Paris.*

<u>Note 4</u>: The version of Anne Marie listed here is the commonly known take. It has been reported as from this date however doubt remains on the accuracy of recording details. Although Jimmy Gourley is sometimes listed as playing on this, no guitar can be heard.

530929
Clifford Brown Sextet

September 29, 1953, Vogue Studio, Schola Cantorum, Paris

Clifford Brown (tp), Gigi Gryce (as), Jimmy Gourley (g), Henri Renaud (p), Pierre Michelot (b), Jean-Louis Viale (d):

53V4659-1	Blue Concept (Conception)	3:18	Gigi Gryce	Vogue (Fr.) CLD 802
53V4659-2	Blue Concept (Conception)	3:18	Gigi Gryce	Vogue (Fr.) LD 723
53V4660-1	All the Things You Are	3:52	Jerome Kern	Vogue (Fr.) CLD 802
53V4660-2	All the Things You Are	4:20	Jerome Kern	Vogue (Fr.) LD 723
53V4661-11	Cover the Waterfront	3:55	Johnny Green & Edward Heyman	Vogue (Fr.) LD 607-30
53V4662-1	Goofin' with Me	4:48	Clifford Brown	Vogue (Fr.) LD 607-30

All takes on Prestige OJCCD-358-2 titled *Clifford Brown Sextet in Paris* and Vogue (Fr.) CD 45728.
Note 1: Gourley does not play on 53V4661 but is not absent on 53V4662 as sometimes reported.
Note 2: Take numbers may indicate choice, not order.

531004
Lionel Hampton and His Orchestra
October 4, 1953, Sportpalast, Berlin, Germany
Clifford Brown, Art Farmer, Walter Williams (tp), Quincy Jones (tp, p), Al Hayse, Jimmy Cleveland, George "Buster" Cooper (tb), Anthony Ortega, Gigi Gryce (as),
Clifford Scott, Clifford Solomon (ts), Oscar Estelle (bar), Lionel Hampton (vb, voc), Billy Mackel (g), Monk Montgomery (eb), Alan Dawson, Curley Hamner (d),
Sonny Parker (voc):

Air Mail Special	Lionel Hampton	*Unissued*
I Only Have Eyes for You	Al Dubin & Harry Warren	-
Stompin' at the Savoy/Oh, Rock!	Edgar Sampson & Benny Goodman	-
Star Dust	Hoagy Carmichael & Mitchell Parish	-
How High the Moon	Morgan Lewis & Nancy Hamilton	-
The Mess Is Here	Lionel Hampton	-
Always	Irving Berlin & Israel Balin	-
Drinking Wine Spo-Dee-O-Dee	Sticks McGhee & Williams	-
Jelly Roll Blues		-
I'm Beginning to See the Light	Duke Ellington, Johnny Hodges, Harry James, D. George	-
Summertime	George Gershwin & DuBose Heyward	-
Hey Ba-ba-re-bop	Lionel Hampton & Curley Hamner	-
Piney Brown Blues	Joe Turner & Johnson	-

Note: Concert was broadcast on German radio.

531008

Gigi Gryce - Clifford Brown Sextet

October 8, 1953, Rue Jouvenet Studio, Paris

Clifford Brown (tp), Gigi Gryce (as), Jimmy Gourley (g), Henri Renaud (p), Pierre Michelot (b), Jean-Louis Viale (d):

(tk.1)	Minority	5:30	Gigi Gryce	Vogue (Fr.) LD 175, Prestige OJCCD-358-2
(tk.2)	Minority	5:27	Gigi Gryce	Vogue (Fr.) LD 723, Prestige OJCCD-358-2
(tk.3)	Minority	5:33	Gigi Gryce	Vogue Jazz Legacy (Fr.) JL 86
(tk.1)	Salute to the Bandbox	5:39	Gigi Gryce	Vogue (Fr.) LD 175, Prestige OJCCD-358-2
(tk.2)	Salute to the Bandbox	5:43	Gigi Gryce	Vogue (Fr.) LD 724, Prestige OJCCD-358-2
	Strictly Romantic	4:14	Gigi Gryce	Vogue (Fr.) LD 175, Prestige OJCCD-358-2
(tk.2)	Baby (inc.)	4:48	Gigi Gryce	Inner City IC 7019
(tk.1)	Baby	5:45	Gigi Gryce	Vogue (Fr.) LD 175, Prestige OJCCD-358-2

All takes on Vogue (Fr.) CD 45729 titled *Clifford Brown: The Complete Paris Sessions, Vol. 2.*

Note 1: Salute to the Bandbox is also known both as Salute to Birdland and as Reunion.

Note 2: Gourley does not play on Strictly Romantic but is not absent on Baby as sometimes reported.

Note 3: Take numbers may indicate choice, not order.

531009

Gigi Gryce Orchestra

October 9, 1953, Paris

Clifford Brown, Art Farmer, Walter Williams (tp), Quincy Jones (tp, arr), Jimmy Cleveland, Benny Vasseur, Al Hayse (tb), Gigi Gryce (as, arr), Anthony Ortega (as), Clifford Solomon, Andre Dabonneville (ts), William Boucaya (bar), Henri Renaud (p), Pierre Michelot (b), Jean-Louis Viale (d):

Quick Step (tk. 1)	2:41	Gigi Gryce	Vogue (Fr.) LD 173
Quick Step (tk. 2)	2:42	Gigi Gryce	Vogue (Fr.) 500.102
Quick Step (tk. 3)	2:43	Gigi Gryce	-
Bum's Rush (tk. 1)	3:11	Quincy Jones	Vogue (Fr.) LD 173, Prestige OJCCD-359-2
Bum's Rush (tk. 2)	3:07	Quincy Jones	Vogue (Fr.) 500.102
Bum's Rush (tk. 3)	3:11	Quincy Jones	-

All takes on Vogue (Fr.) CD 45729.

Note 1: Gryce and Jones each arranged their own compositions.

Note 2: Take numbers may indicate choice, not order.
Note 3: Vogue 500.102 is titled *Clifford Brown: The Complete Paris Collection, Vol. 3*.

531009

Gigi Gryce Quartet

October 9, 1953, Paris

Gigi Gryce (as), Henri Renaud (p), Pierre Michelot (b), Jean-Louis Viale (d):

Anne Marie (I Need You So)	4:58	Gigi Gryce	*Vogue (Jap.) DY5903-3*

Note: Vogue DY5903-3 titled *Gigi Gryce: The Complete Paris Collection Vol. 5* is a bonus LP never sold individually but given to purchasers of volumes 1–4.

531010

Gigi Gryce - Clifford Brown Ensembles

October 10, 1953, Paris

Clifford Brown (tp), Jimmy Cleveland (tb), Gigi Gryce (as), Clifford Solomon (ts), William Boucaya (bar), Jimmy Gourley (g), Henri Renaud (p), Marcel Dutrieux (b), Jean-Louis Viale (d):

No Start No End	11:47	Jean Feline, **Paul** Moise Misrachi, R. Bruce Sievier	*Vogue (Fr.) LD 175, CD 45729, Prestige OJCCD-359-2*
(Venez Donc) Chez Moi	7:49	Jean Feline, **Paul** Moise Misrachi, R. Bruce Sievier	*Vogue (Fr.) LD 724, CD 45730, Prestige OJCCD-359-2*

Gourley out:

Hello	4:17	Gigi Gryce	*Vogue (Fr.) LD 724, CD 7 4321 15467 2, BMG CD 09026-68216-2*

Note 1: No Start No End is a rehearsal for (Venez Donc) Chez Moi.
Note 2: Most issues use a 2:15 excerpt of No Start, No End. Complete version on Vogue (Fr.) CD 45729.
Note 3: Vogue 45730 is titled *Clifford Brown: The Complete Paris Sessions, Vol. 3*.

531011

Gigi Gryce - Clifford Brown Ensembles

October 11, 1953, Paris

Gigi Gryce (as, arr), Jimmy Gourley (g), Quincy Jones (p, arr), Marcel Dutrieux (b), Jean-Louis Viale (d):

Evening in Paris (tk. 1)	3:52	Quincy Jones	*Vogue (Jap.) DY5903-3*
Evening in Paris (tk. 2)	3:56	Quincy Jones	*Vogue (Fr.) LD 724, CD 7 4321 15467 2, BMG CD 09026-68216-2*
Evening in Paris (tk. 3)	3:53	Quincy Jones	*Vogue (Jap.) DY5903-3*

Note 1: Gryce and Jones each arranged their own compositions.

Note 2: Take numbers may indicate choice, not order.

Note 3: Vogue DY5903-3 titled Gigi Gryce: *The Complete Paris Collection Vol. 5* is a bonus LP never sold individually but given to purchasers of volumes 1–4.

531011

Gigi Gryce - Clifford Brown Ensembles

October 11, 1953, Paris

Clifford Brown (tp), Jimmy Cleveland (tb), Gigi Gryce, Anthony Ortega (as), Clifford Solomon (ts), William Boucaya (bar), Quincy Jones (p), Marcel Dutrieux (b), Jean-Louis Viale (d):

(tk.1)	All Weird	5:17	Clifford Brown	*Vogue (Fr.) LD 706-30, CD 45730, Prestige OJCCD-359-2*
(tk.2)	All Weird (excerpt)	1:55	Clifford Brown	*Vogue (Fr.) LD 723, CD 45730, Prestige OJCCD-359-2*
(tk.3)	All Weird	4:59	Clifford Brown	*Vogue (Fr.) CD 45730*

Note: Take numbers may indicate choice, not order.

531102

Henri Renaud Quintet - Joue Gigi Gryce

November 2, 1953, Paris

Bobby Jaspar (ts), Jimmy Gourley (g), Henri Renaud (p), Jean-Marie Ingrand (b), Jean-Louis Viale (d), Gigi Gryce (arr, con):

Eleanor	3:25	Gigi Gryce	*Vogue (Fr.) LD 174, CD 7 4321 40937 2*
Capri	3:24	Gigi Gryce	-
Shabozz	2:50	Gigi Gryce	-
Simplicity	2:50	Gigi Gryce	-
Up in Quincy's Room	4:12	Gigi Gryce	-
Consultation	3:28	Gigi Gryce	-
Stupendous-Lee	2:48	Gigi Gryce	-
Expansion	3:48	Gigi Gryce	-

Note 1: Henri Renaud confirms that Gryce was present in the studio for this session.

Note 2: Eleanor was issued as "Eleanore" and Shabozz was issued as "Schabozz."

Note 3: Stupendous-Lee was issued as "Au Tabou."

Note 4: Vogue 40937 is titled *Bobby Jaspar/Henri Renaud.*

531112
International Jam Session

November 12, 1953, Forsvarsbrodrenes Hus, Copenhagen

Clifford Brown, Jørgen Ryg, possibly Quincy Jones, Art Farmer (tp), Jimmy Cleveland (tb), Anthony Ortega, Gigi Gryce (as), Clifford Solomon (ts), Max Brüel (bar), Jørgen Bengston or Jørgen Lausen (p), Erik Moseholm (b), possibly Ole Jørgensen (d):

CA113	Perdido	15:23	Juan Tizol	*Unissued*
CA114	All the Things You Are	18:07	Jerome Kern	*Unissued*
CA115	Back Home Again in Indiana	10:51	Ballard MacDonald & James Hanley	*Xanadu 122*

<u>Note</u>: Gryce cannot be heard on the issued track, which is an excerpt from an amateur tape recorded by Chris Albertson.

531115
[Jam Session]

c. November 15, 1953, Hotel Aletti, Algiers

Clifford Brown, Quincy Jones, Art Farmer (tp), Jimmy Cleveland (tb), Anthony Ortega (as), Gigi Gryce, Guy Combres, Lucky Starway (p), Joe Ford (b):

Back Home Again in Indiana	Ballard MacDonald & James Hanley	*Unissued*
Midnight Sun	Sonny Burke & Lionel Hampton	-
Keepin' Up with Jonesy	Quincy Jones	-
Come Rain or Come Shine	Harold Arlen & Johnny Mercer	-
Minority	Gigi Gryce	-

<u>Note</u>: Date is positively earlier than 11/24, 25, or 26 which is as listed in Bob Weir's Clifford Brown discography. Hampton band departed from Paris on 11/24/53 for New York (via London and Glasgow). Unknown French musicians from Algiers also participated in this session. This tape is lost and report is based on an eyewitness.

540228
Henri Renaud Band

February 28, 1954, New York

Jerry Hurwitz (Lloyd) (tp), J.J. Johnson (tb), Al Cohn (ts, arr), Gigi Gryce (bar), Henri Renaud (p, arr), Curley Russell (b), Walter Bolden (d):

Wallington Special (arr. HR)	6:05	Henri Renaud	*Swing (Fr.) M 33327, Fresh Sound (Sp.) FSR-CD 170*
Lisa (arr. AC)	6:02	Al Cohn	-
Something for Lili (arr. AC)	2:50	Al Cohn	-
Boo Wah (arr. AC)	4:56	Al Cohn	-

387

Note 1: Sometimes incorrectly listed as from March 7, 1954.
Note 2: Fresh Sound 170 is titled *The Birdlanders*.

540519
Art Farmer Quintet
May 19, 1954, Van Gelder Studio, Hackensack NJ
Art Farmer (tp), Gigi Gryce (as, arr), Horace Silver (p), Percy Heath (b), Kenny Clarke (d):

Prestige PRLP 181, PRLP 7085, OJCD-072-2

574	A Night at Tony's	5:06	Gigi Gryce	
575	Blue Concept	4:56	Gigi Gryce	-
576	Deltitnu	4:18	Gigi Gryce	-
577	Stupendous-Lee	5:47	Gigi Gryce	-

Note: Prestige 7085 and OJC 072 are titled *When Farmer Met Gryce*.

540520
Art Blakey - Blakey
May 20, 1954, Fine Sound Studio, New York
Joe Gordon (tp), Gigi Gryce (as), Walter Bishop, Jr. (p), Bernie Griggs (b), Art Blakey (d), unknown (perc):

EmArcy MG 26030, Verve CD 314 538 634-2

10542	Minority	3:06	Gigi Gryce	
10543	Salute to Birdland	2:58	Gigi Gryce	-
10544	Eleanor	2:52	Gigi Gryce	-
10545	Futurity	2:54	Gigi Gryce	-
10546	Simplicity	2:49	Gigi Gryce	-
10547	Strictly Romantic	2:45	Gigi Gryce	-
10548	Hello	2:39	Gigi Gryce	-
10549	Mayrah (Mayreh)	3:12	Horace Silver	-

Note 1: Salute to Birdland is also known both as Salute to the Bandbox and as Reunion.
Note 2: Additional percussionist (possibly Sabu Martinez) appears on 10545 only.

540607
Art Farmer Septet
June 7, 1954, Van Gelder Studio, Hackensack, NJ

Art Farmer (tp), Jimmy Cleveland (tb), Charlie Rouse (ts), Danny Bank (bar), Horace Silver (p), Percy Heath (b), Art Taylor (d), Gigi Gryce (arr):

583	Wildwood	2:55	Gigi Gryce	
585	Tiajuana	2:49	Gigi Gryce	Prestige PRLP 7031, OJCCD 054-2
				-

Note: Although unconfirmed, it is likely that Gryce and Quincy Jones were present to direct their arrangements.

550307
Gigi Gryce & Duke Jordan Quartet - Jazz Laboratory Series, Vol. 1
March 7, 1955, Van Gelder Studio, Hackensack NJ
Gigi Gryce (as), Duke Jordan (p), Oscar Pettiford (b), Kenny Clarke (d):

105	Sometimes I'm Happy	5:54	Vincent Youmans & Irving Caesar	Signal S 101, Savoy MG 12145, MG 12146, CD SV 0130
106	Embraceable You	7:30	George Gershwin	-
107	Jordu	5:00	Duke Jordan	-
108	Oh Yeah!	4:30	Duke Jordan	

Note 1: These four tracks were also issued without the overdubbed alto saxophone as a play-along on Signal S 101 and on Savoy MG 12145 subtitled *Do It Yourself Jazz, Vol. 1*.
Note 2: Savoy 12146 is titled *Jordu*.

550329
Kenny Dorham Octet - Afro-Cuban
March 29, 1955, Van Gelder Studio, Hackensack NJ
Kenny Dorham (tp), J.J. Johnson (tb), Hank Mobley (ts), Cecil Payne (bar), Horace Silver (p), Oscar Pettiford (b), Art Blakey (d), Carlos 'Patato' Valdez (cga), probably Richie Goldberg (perc), Gigi Gryce (arr):

| tk. 5 | Basheer's Dream | 5:00 | Gigi Gryce | Blue Note BLP 5065, BLP 1535, CDP 7 46815-2 |

Note: Although unconfirmed, it is likely that Gryce was present to direct his arrangement.

550526
Art Farmer Quintet
May 26, 1955, Van Gelder Studio, Hackensack NJ
Art Farmer (tp), Gigi Gryce (as, arr), Freddie Redd (p), Addison Farmer (b), Art Taylor (d):

| 741 | Blue Lights | 5:19 | Gigi Gryce | Prestige PRLP 209, PRLP 7085, OJCCD-072-2 |
| 742 | Capri | 5:01 | Gigi Gryce | - |

743	The Infant's Song	5:15	Gigi Gryce	-
744	Social Call	6:04	Gigi Gryce	-

Note: Prestige 7085 and OJC 072 are titled *When Farmer Met Gryce*.

550812
Oscar Pettiford Octet - Oscar Pettiford

August 12, 1955, New York

Ernie Royal, Donald Byrd (tp), Bob Brookmeyer (v tb), Gigi Gryce (as, cl, arr), Jerome Richardson (ts, cl, fl), Don Abney (p), Oscar Pettiford (b, cel*, arr), Osie Johnson (d); Tom Talbert, Tom Whaley, Quincy Jones, Ernie Wilkins (arr):

6470	Titoro (arr. TT)	4:14	Billy Taylor	*Bethlehem BCP 33, CD R2 75910-2*
6471	Scorpio (arr. TW)	7:36	Mary Lou Williams	-
6472	Oscalypso (arr. GG)	2:22	Oscar Pettiford	-
6473	Another One (arr. QJ)	4:09	Quincy Jones	-
	Bohemia After Dark (arr. OP)	5:33	Oscar Pettiford	-
	Don't Squawk (arr. EW)	4:15	Oscar Pettiford	-
	Minor Seventh Heaven *	4:09	Osie Johnson	-
	Kamman's A'Comin' (arr. EW)	5:08	Oscar Pettiford	-
	Star Dust (p, b only)	3:29	Hoagy Carmichael & Mitchell Parish	-

Note 1: Kamman's A'Comin' and Another One are reversed on sleeve of CD 75910-2.

Note 2: Master numbers were assigned when the four selections were reissued as singles.

Note 3: Gryce and Richardson play clarinet on Scorpio. Richardson plays flute on Oscalypso, Bohemia After Dark, and Don't Squawk.

550912
Dizzy Gillespie - Big Band Sound of Dizzy Gillespie

September 12, 1955, New York

Dizzy Gillespie (tp, arr), Taft Jordan, Ermet Perry, Ernie Royal (tp), Jimmy Cleveland, Matthew Gee, Jimmy Wilkins (tb), Gigi Gryce, Hilton Jefferson (as), Budd Johnson, Ernie Wilkins (ts), Sahib Shihab (bar), Wade Legge (p), Nelson Boyd (b), Charli Persip (d), Herb Lance (voc), Buster Harding (arr):

2514-1	Seems Like You Just Don't Care (HL voc)	3:27	R. McCoy & K. Nobel	*Norgran MGN-1083*
2514-4	Evening Sound (arr. BH)	4:44	Dizzy Gillespie	*Verve (Eng.) 2317080, CD 314 513 875-2*
2516-3	Bout to Wail (arr. BH)	6:46	Dizzy Gillespie	*Verve (Eng.) 2317080, American Recording Society G-405, Verve CD 314 513 875-2*

| 2517-7 | Begin the Beguine (arr. DG) | 4:52 | Cole Porter | Verve (Eng.) 2317080, CD 314 513 875-2 |
| 2518-2 | The Shout by Rail (arr. BH) | 7:29 | Dizzy Gillespie | Verve (Eng.) 2317080, American Recording Society G-405 |

Note: Norgran 1083 is titled *Dizzy Gillespie and His Orchestra*. American Recording Society 405 is titled *Jazz Creations of Dizzy Gillespie*. Verve 314 513 875 is titled *Dizzy's Diamonds*.

550917
Oscar Pettiford
September 17, 1955, Birdland New York

Joe Wilder, Art Farmer (tp), Eddie Bert (tb), Gigi Gryce (as, cl, arr), Jerome Richardson (ts, cl, fl), Danny Bank (bar), Hank Jones (p), Oscar Pettiford (b, cel*, arr), Osie Johnson (d), Ernie Wilkins (arr):

Bohemia After Dark (arr. OP)	0:26	Oscar Pettiford	Unissued
Kamman's A'Comin' (arr. EW)	2:34	Oscar Pettiford	-
You'd Be So Nice to Come Home To	3:16	Cole Porter	-
Jack the Bear	2:56	Duke Ellington	-
Bohemia After Dark (arr. OP)	1:30	Oscar Pettiford	-

Note 1: Reported in Oscar Pettiford discography by Coover Gazdar, timings supplied by Dr. William Miner.
Note 2: Personnel based on published review.

551015
Gigi Gryce Quartet - Nica's Tempo
October 15, 1955, Van Gelder Studio, Hackensack, NJ

Gigi Gryce (as), Thelonious Monk (p), Percy Heath (b), Art Blakey (d):

114	Brake's Sake	4:45	Thelonious Monk	Signal S 1201, Savoy MG 12137, CD SV 0126
115	Gallop's Gallop	5:31	Thelonious Monk	-
116	Shuffle Boil	5:02	Thelonious Monk	-
117	Nica's Tempo	6:06	Gigi Gryce	-

551021
Art Farmer Quintet Featuring Gigi Gryce
October 21, 1955, Van Gelder Studio, Hackensack, NJ

Art Farmer (tp), Gigi Gryce (as), Duke Jordan (p), Addison Farmer (b), Philly Joe Jones (d):

804	Forecast	4:48	Duke Jordan	Prestige PRLP 7017, OJCD 241-2
805	Sans Souci	6:39	Gigi Gryce	-
806	Evening in Casablanca	5:20	Gigi Gryce	-
807	Satellite	4:21	Gigi Gryce	-
808	Nica's Tempo	7:50	Gigi Gryce	-
809	Shabozz	5:32	Gigi Gryce	-

Note: Gryce and Jordan each arranged their own compositions.

551022
Gigi Gryce Orchestra - Nica's Tempo
October 22, 1955, Van Gelder Studio, Hackensack, NJ
Art Farmer (tp), Julius Watkins (fh), Eddie Bert (tb), Bill Barber (tu), Gigi Gryce (as, arr), Cecil Payne (bar), Horace Silver (p), Oscar Pettiford (b), Art Blakey (d), Ernestine Anderson (voc):

| 118 | Social Call (EA voc) | 2:43 | Gigi Gryce (& Jon Hendricks) | Signal S 1201, Savoy MG 12137, CD SV 0126 |
| 119 | You'll Always Be the One I Love (EA voc) | 3:28 | Gigi Gryce | - |

551022
Gigi Gryce Orchestra - Nica's Tempo
October 30, 1955, Van Gelder Studio, Hackensack, NJ
Art Farmer (tp), Gunther Schuller (fh), Jimmy Cleveland (tb), Bill Barber (tu), Gigi Gryce (as, arr), Danny Bank (bar), Horace Silver (p, arr), Oscar Pettiford (b), Kenny Clarke (d):

120	Smoke Signal	3:42	Gigi Gryce	Signal S 1201, Savoy MG 12137, CD SV 0126
121	In a Meditating Mood	4:29	Gigi Gryce	-
122	Speculation (arr. HS)	4:21	Horace Silver	-
123	Kerry Dance	3:02	James Molloy	-

Note: All arrangements except Speculation by Gigi Gryce.

560106
Teddy Charles - The Teddy Charles Tentet
January 6, 1956, Coastal Studios, New York
Art Farmer (tp), Don Butterfield (tu), Gigi Gryce (as), J. R. Monterose (ts), George Barrow (bar), Teddy Charles (vb, arr), Jimmy Raney (g), Mal Waldron (p),

Teddy Kotick (b), Joe Harris (d), Jimmy Giuffre (arr):

1806	Green Blues		Teddy Charles	Unissued
1807	Nature Boy	6:22	Eden Ahbez	Atlantic LP 1229, Collectables CD COL 6161
1808	The Quiet Time	5:48	Jimmy Giuffre	-

Note: All arrangements by their composers except Nature Boy arranged by Teddy Charles.

560111
Teddy Charles - The Teddy Charles Tentet
January 11, 1956, Coastal Studios, New York, same as January 6, 1956 but Gil Evans and Bob Brookmeyer (arr) replace Jimmy Giuffre:

1813	Green Blues	4:07	Teddy Charles	Atlantic LP 1229, Collectables CD COL 6161
1814	You Go to My Head	4:27	Haven Gillespie & J. Fred Coots	-
1815	Show Time		Bob Brookmeyer	Unissued

Note: All arrangements by their composers except You Go to My Head arranged by Gil Evans.

560117
Teddy Charles - The Teddy Charles Tentet
January 17, 1956, Coastal Studios, New York
Art Farmer (tp), Don Butterfield (tu), Gigi Gryce (as), J. R. Monterose (ts), Sol Schlinger (bar), Teddy Charles (vb, arr), Jimmy Raney (g), Mal Waldron (p, arr), Teddy Kotick (b), Joe Harris (d), George Russell (arr):

1831	Vibrations	6:14	Mal Waldron	Atlantic LP 1229, Collectables CD COL 6161
1832	The Emperor	8:08	Teddy Charles	-
1833	Lydian M-1	4:26	George Russell	-
1834	Majors			Unissued

Note 1: Art Farmer was listed on Atlantic LP 1229 as "Peter Urban".
Note 2: All arrangements by their composers.

560301
Various Artists - Know Your Jazz
March 1, 1956, New York
Gigi Gryce (as), Billy Taylor (p), Oscar Pettiford (b), Kenny Clarke (d):

| 5136 | Come Rain or Come Shine | 3:51 | Harold Arlen & Johnny Mercer | ABC Paramount ABC LP 115 |

add Tony Scott (cl), Mundell Lowe (g)

5137	In a Mellotone	2:43	Duke Ellington	*ABC Paramount ABC LP 115*

560302
Earl Coleman - Earl Coleman Returns
March 2, 1956, New York

Earl Coleman (voc), Art Farmer (tp), Gigi Gryce (as), Hank Jones (p), Oscar Pettiford (b), Shadow Wilson (d):

856	No Love No Nothing	5:21	Leo Robin & Harry Warren	*Prestige PRLP 7045, OJCCD-187-2*
857	It's You or No One	5:19	Sammy Cahn & Jule Styne	-
858	Come Rain or Come Shine	4:15	Harold Arlen & Johnny Mercer	-

560300
Mat Mathews - The Modern Art of Jazz by Mat Mathews
March 1956, Carl Fischer Concert Hall, New York

Art Farmer (tp), Gigi Gryce (as), Mat Mathews (acc, arr), Dick Katz (p, arr), Oscar Pettiford (cel, b), Kenny Clarke (d):

Not So Sleepy (arr. MM)	6:30	Mat Mathews	*Dawn DLP-1104, (Jap.) CD 32WD-7015*
Summertime	2:20	George Gershwin & DuBose Heyward	-
Knights at the Castle (arr. DK)	5:30	Dick Katz	*Dawn DLP-1104, (Jap.) CD 32WD-7015, Biograph BCD 120*

Clarke out:

Now See How You Are	2:03	Oscar Pettiford & Harris	*Dawn DLP-1104, (Jap.) CD 32WD-7015*

<u>Note 1</u>: Farmer, Gryce, and Katz appear on Not So Sleepy and Knights at the Castle only.
<u>Note 2</u>: Biograph 120 is a compilation titled *The Modern Art of Jazz*.

560425
Betty Carter - Social Call
April 25, 1956, New York

Betty Carter (voc), Gigi Gryce (arr, leader), Bernie Glow, Nick Travis, Conte Candoli, Joe Ferrante (tp), Urbie Green, Jimmy Cleveland (tb), Sam Marowitz (as), Al Cohn, Seldon Powell (ts), Danny Bank (bar), Hank Jones (p), Milt Hinton (b), Osie Johnson (d):

CO55871	Social Call	2:38	Gigi Gryce (& Jon Hendricks)	*Columbia JC 36425, Columbia Legacy CD CK 64936*
CO55872	Run Away	2:29	Coleman & Lee	-
CO55873	Frenesi	2:31	Charles, Dominguez, Russell	-

CO55874   Let's Fall in Love   1:57   Ted Koehler & Harold Arlen

Note: Columbia 64936 is titled *Meet Betty Carter and Ray Bryant*.

560608

Earl Coleman - Earl Coleman Returns

June 8, 1956, Van Gelder Studio, Hackensack, NJ

Earl Coleman (voc), Art Farmer (tp), Hank Jones (p), Wendell Marshall (b), Wilbert Hogan (d):

| 911 | Social Call | 6:29 | Gigi Gryce (& Jon Hendricks) | *Prestige PRLP 7045, OJCCD-187-2* |
| 912 | Reminiscing | 5:50 | Gigi Gryce (& Jon Hendricks) | - |

Note: While unconfirmed, it is likely that Gryce was present in the studio to direct his compositions.

560611

Oscar Pettiford - Orchestra in Hi-Fi

June 11, 1956, New York

Ernie Royal, Art Farmer (tp), Julius Watkins, David Amram (fh), Jimmy Cleveland (tb), Gigi Gryce (as, arr), Jerome Richardson (ts, fl), Lucky Thompson (ts, arr), Danny Bank (bar), Tommy Flanagan (p), Oscar Pettiford (b, cel), Osie Johnson (d):

| 5246 | Nica's Tempo (arr. GG) | 3:45 | Gigi Gryce | *ABC Paramount ABC LP 135, Impulse CD GRD-143* |
| 5247 | Deep Passion (arr. LT) | 3:40 | Lucky Thompson | - |

Note: Impulse 143 is titled *Deep Passion*.

560612

Oscar Pettiford - Orchestra in Hi-Fi

June 12, 1956, New York

same as June 11, 1956 but add Gordon "Whitey" Mitchell (b), Janet Putnam (hp):

5248	Smoke Signal (arr. GG)	4:11	Gigi Gryce	*ABC Paramount ABC LP 135, Impulse CD GRD-143*
5249	Sunrise-Sunset (arr. GG)	3:58	Oscar Pettiford	*ABC Paramount ABC LP 135, Impulse CD GRD-143*
5250	Speculation (arr. GG)		Horace Silver	*Unissued*
5251	Not So Sleepy (arr. GG)	4:50	Mat Mathews	*ABC Paramount ABC LP 135, Impulse CD GRD-143*
5252	Perdido (arr. LT)	4:00	Juan Tizol	-

Note 1: Mitchell plays bass on 5248 only. Pettiford plays only cello.

Note 2: Pettiford overdubbed cello on 5251 and 5252.

560619
Oscar Pettiford - Orchestra in Hi-Fi
June 19, 1956, New York
same as June 11, 1956 but David Kurtzer (bar) replaces Danny Bank:

5250(A)	Speculation (arr. GG)	4:03	Horace Silver	ABC Paramount ABC LP 135, Impulse CD GRD-143	
5253	Two French Fries (arr. GG)	2:48	Gigi Gryce		

add Janet Putnam (hp)

5254	The Pendulum at Falcon's Lair (arr. GG)	2:58	Oscar Pettiford	ABC Paramount ABC LP 135, Impulse CD GRD-143	
5255	The Gentle Art of Love (arr. LT)	3:33	Oscar Pettiford	-	

Note: Pettiford overdubbed cello on 5250(A).

560702
Tony Scott Orchestra - The Touch of Tony Scott
July 2, 1956, Webster Hall, New York
Jimmy Maxwell, Jimmy Nottingham, Idrees Sulieman (tp), Jimmy Cleveland, Urbie Green, Rex Peer (tb), Bart Varsalona (btb), Tony Scott (cl, arr), Gigi Gryce, Sam Marowitz (as), Seldon Powell, Zoot Sims (ts), Danny Bank (bar), Mundell Lowe (g), Bill Evans (p), Milt Hinton (b), Osie Johnson (d), Eddie Sauter (arr), unknown (hp), unknown (fh):

G2JB5901	You're Driving Me Crazy	3:07	Walter Donaldson	RCA Victor LPM 1353	
G2JB5902	Poinciana	3:12	Buddy Bernier & Nat Simon	-	
G2JB5903	Rock Me But Don't Roll Me	2:26	Tony Scott	-	
G2JB5904	The Moon Walks	3:39	Eddie Sauter	-	

560703
Tony Scott Orchestra - The Touch of Tony Scott
July 3, 1956, New York, same as preceding:

G2JB5943	Yesterdays	2:49	Jerome Kern	RCA Victor LPM 1353	

560707
Teddy Charles Tentet
July 7, 1956, Newport Jazz Festival, Newport, RI

Jon Eardley (tp), Don Butterfield (tu), Gigi Gryce (as), Hal Stein (ts), George Barrow (bar), Teddy Charles (vb, arr), Barry Galbraith (g), Hall Overton (p), Addison Farmer (b), Ed Shaughnessy (d), Bob Brookmeyer, Jimmy Giuffre, Gil Evans (arr):

Show Time	4:33	Bob Brookmeyer	*Unissued*
The Quiet Time	5:35	Jimmy Giuffre	-
You Go to My Head	4:01	Haven Gillespie & J. Fred Coots	-
Green Blues	4:28	Teddy Charles	-
The Emperor	12:15	Teddy Charles	-

add David Broekman (con):

Word from Bird	9:23	Teddy Charles	*Unissued*

Voice Of America tapes held in the Library of Congress.
Note: All compositions arranged by their composers except You Go to My Head (arr. Gil Evans).

561109
Mal Waldron - Mal 1
November 9, 1956, Van Gelder Studio, Hackensack NJ
Idrees Sulieman (tp), Gigi Gryce (as), Mal Waldron (p), Julian Euell (b), Arthur Edgehill (d):

1013	Shome	5:07	Idrees Sulieman	*Prestige PRLP 7090, OJCCD-611-2*
1014	Transfiguration	7:17	Gigi Gryce	-
1015	Dee's Dilemma	6:58	Mal Waldron	-
1016	Stablemates	4:51	Benny Golson	-
1017	Bud Study	5:48	Mal Waldron	-
1018	Yesterdays	7:47	Jerome Kern	-

561120
Johnnie Ray - The Big Beat
November 20, 1956, Columbia 30th Street Recording Studio, New York
Johnnie Ray (voc), Ray Conniff (ldr, arr), Tony Fasso, Stan Fishelson, Jimmy Nottingham, Clark Terry (tp), J.J. Johnson, Jack Satterfield, Tom Mitchell, Chauncey Welsh (tb), Al Epstein, Henry Freeman, Gigi Gryce, Nick Peters, Joe Palmer (sax), Al Casamente, Ed O'Connor, Hy White (g), Andrew Ackers (p), Frank Carroll (b), Herman Grove Kapp, Ed Shaughnessy (d):

CO56757	I'm Gonna Move to the Outskirts of Town	2:46	William Weldon	*Columbia CL 961, Bear Family BCD 16285-4/15*

CO56758 Sent for You Yesterday 2:26 Jimmy Rushing, Count Basie, Eddie Durham   *Columbia CL 961, Sony 65157, Bear Family BCD 16285-4/15*

CO56759 Pretty-Eyed Baby 2:20 Mary Lou Williams & William Johnson   *Columbia CL 961, Bear Family BCD 16285-4/15*

<u>Note</u>: Bear Family 16285 is titled *Cry*. Sony 65157 is titled *High Drama: The Real Johnnie Ray*.

561211

Tony Scott Orchestra - The Complete Tony Scott

December 11, 1956, Webster Hall, New York

John Garisi (tp, arr), Thad Jones, Jimmy Nottingham, Clark Terry (tp), Henry Coker, Quentin Jackson, Benny Powell (tb), Sonny Truitt (tb, arr), Tony Scott (cl), Gigi Gryce (as), Zoot Sims, Frank Wess (ts), Danny Bank, Sahib Shihab (bar), Freddie Green (g), Bill Evans (p), Milt Hinton (b), Osie Johnson (d), Nat Pierce (arr):

G2JB9813	Moonlight Cocktail (arr. ST)	2:52	Kim Cannon & Lucky Roberts	*RCA Victor LPM 1452, CD 7 4321 42132 2*
G2JB9814	I Surrender Dear (arr. NP)	2:23	Harry Barris & Gordon Clifford	-
G2JB9815	Under a Blanket of Blue (arr. NP)	2:25	Livingston, Symes, Neiburg	-
G2JB9816	I'll Remember April (arr. JC)		Don Raye, Gene DePaul, Bat Johnson	*Unissued*

561213

Tony Scott Orchestra - The Complete Tony Scott

December 13, 1956, Webster Hall, New York

same as December 11, 1956 but Bernie Glow (tp), Les Grinage (b), and Paul Motian (d) replace Jimmy Nottingham, Milt Hinton, and Osie Johnson, respectively:

G2JB9817	I Found a Million Dollar Baby (arr. ST)	2:18	Rose, Dixon, Morton	*RCA Victor LPM 1452, CD 7 4321 42132 2*
G2JB9818	Skylark (arr. JC)	2:50	Hoagy Carmichael	-
G2JB9819	Finger Poppin' Blues (arr. TS)	6:35	Tony Scott	-

561214

Tony Scott Orchestra - The Complete Tony Scott

December 14, 1956, Webster Hall, New York

same as December 13, 1956 but Jimmy Nottingham (tp), Frank Foster (ts), Milt Hinton (b), and Osie Johnson (d) replace Bernie Glow, Zoot Sims, Les Grinage, and Paul Motian, respectively:

G2JB9821	A Blues Serenade (arr. ST)	2:26	Frank Signorelli, V. Grande, Mitchell Parish	*RCA Victor LPM 1452, CD 7 4321 42132 2*
G2JB9822	Just One of Those Things (arr. NP)	2:37	Cole Porter	-
G2JB9823	Walkin' (arr. Bill Evans)	2:56	Richard Carpenter	-

570112
Big Maybelle Sings

January 12, 1957, Van Gelder Studio, Hackensack NJ

Big Maybelle (voc), Gigi Gryce (as), Ernie Wilkins (ts, arr), George Barrow (bar), Don Abney (p), Leonard Gaskin (b), Bobby Donaldson (d):

			Savoy MG 14005, CD 93018
SBM6930	If I Could Be with You	J. Johnson & H. Creamer	2:26	-
SBM6931	Jim	Caesar Petrillo, Milton Samuels, Nelson A. Shawn	3:21	-
SBM6932	It's a Sin to Tell a Lie	William P. Mayhew	2:47	-
SBM6933	I Could Make You Care	Sammy Cahn & Saul Chaplin	2:39	-

Note 1: Recording date (not January 7, 1957) and bassist (not Wendell Marshall) revised based on contract information from the Savoy files.
Note 2: Savoy 93018 is titled *Big Maybelle: Candy – On Savoy 1956–59.*

570113
Donald Byrd & Gigi Gryce - Jazz Lab

January 13, 1957, New York

Donald Byrd (tp), Julius Watkins (fh), Jimmy Cleveland (tb), Don Butterfield (tu), Gigi Gryce (as, arr), Sahib Shihab (bar), Wade Legge (p), Wendell Marshall (b), Art Taylor (d):

			Columbia CL 998, Collectables CD COL 5674
CO56457	I Remember Clifford	Benny Golson	4:57	-
CO56458	Little Niles	Randy Weston	7:04	-

570128
Big Maybelle - Big Maybelle Sings

January 28, 1957, Van Gelder Studio, Hackensack NJ

Big Maybelle (voc), Frank Rehak (tb), Gigi Gryce (as), Jerome Richardson (ts), George Barrow (bar), Hank Jones (p), Wendell Marshall (b), Bobby Donaldson (d), Ernie Wilkins (arr):

			Savoy MG 14005, CD 93018
SBM6936	All of Me	Gerald Marks & Seymour Simons	2:38	-
SBM6937	Stay as Sweet as You Are	Mack Gordon & Harry Revel	3:28	-
SBM6938-1	Baby Won't You Please Come Home	Charles Warfield & Clarence Williams	3:26	-
SBM6939-1	Say It Isn't So	Irving Berlin	2:28	-

Note: Savoy 93018 is titled *Big Maybelle: Candy – On Savoy 1956–59.*

399

Thad Jones - The Magnificent Thad Jones Vol. 3

February 2, 1957, Van Gelder Studio, Hackensack, NJ

Thad Jones (tp, arr), Benny Powell (tb), Gigi Gryce (as), Tommy Flanagan (p), George Duvivier (b), Elvin Jones (d) :

tk. 05	Slipped Again	6:15	Thad Jones	*Blue Note BLP 1546*
tk. 06	Going Off Stage	8:28	Thad Jones	
tk. 09	Let's	8:43	Thad Jones	*Blue Note BLP 1546*
tk. 10	Ill Wind	7:00	Harold Arlen & Ted Koehler	-
tk. 14	Thadrack	5:40	Thad Jones	-

Note: Slipped Again is also known as Thad's Blues.
All takes on Mosaic MQ5-172, CD MD 3-172, titled *The Complete Blue Note/UA./Roulette Recordings of Thad Jones.*

Donald Byrd & Gigi Gryce - Jazz Lab

February 4, 1957, New York

as January 13, 1957 but Benny Powell (tb), Tommy Flanagan (p) replace Cleveland and Legge, respectively:

CO57304	Nica's Tempo	5:33	Gigi Gryce	*Columbia CL 998, Collectables CD COL 5674*
CO57305	Smoke Signal	3:26	Gigi Gryce	*Columbia CL 1020*
CO57306	Speculation	3:43	Horace Silver	*Columbia CL 998, Collectables CD COL 5674*

Note: Columbia 1020 is titled *Jazz Omnibus.*

Donald Byrd & Gigi Gryce - Jazz Lab

February 5, 1957, New York

same as preceding but Julius Watkins, Benny Powell, Don Butterfield, Sahib Shihab out:

| CO57307 | Over the Rainbow | 8:21 | E. Y. Harburg | *Columbia CL 998, Collectables CD COL 5674* |
| CO57308 | Sans Souci | 7:17 | Gigi Gryce | - |

Tony Scott Orchestra - The Complete Tony Scott

February 6, 1957, Webster Hall, New York

Wendell Culley, Thad Jones, Jimmy Maxwell, Joe Newman (tp), Henry Coker, Bill Hughes, Quentin Jackson, Benny Powell (tb), Tony Scott (cl, arr), Gigi Gryce (as), Frank Foster, Frank Wess (ts, fl), Charlie Fowlkes, Sahib Shihab (bar), Freddie Green (g), Bill Evans (p), Les Grinage (b), Osie Johnson (d); Bill Finegan, John Carisi (arr):

H2JB1449	The Lady Is a Tramp (arr. BF)	2:16	Richard Rodgers & Lorenz Hart	RCA Victor LPM 1452, CD 7 4321 42132 2
H2JB1450	Time to Go (arr. TS)	11:35	Tony Scott	-
H2JB1451	I'll Remember April (arr. JC)	2:25	Don Raye, Gene DePaul, Bat Johnson	-

570227
Gigi Gryce and The Jazz Lab Quintet
February 27, 1957, Reeves Sound Studios, New York
Donald Byrd (tp, arr), Gigi Gryce (as, arr), Wade Legge (p), Wendell Marshall (b), Art Taylor (d):

Love for Sale (arr. DB)	7:59	Cole Porter	Riverside RLP 12-229, RSLP 1110, OJCD-1774-2
Geraldine	5:34	Wade Legge	-
Minority (arr. GG)	6:26	Gigi Gryce	-

570307
Gigi Gryce and The Jazz Lab Quintet
March 7, 1957, Reeves Sound Studios, New York, same as preceding:

Zing! Went the Strings of My Heart (arr. DB)	5:59	James F. Hanley	Riverside RLP 12-229, RSLP 1110, OJCD-1774-2
Straight Ahead (arr. DB)	9:29	Gigi Gryce	-
Wake Up! (arr. GG)	4:37	Gigi Gryce	-

570308
Art Blakey - Midnight Session
March 8–9, 1957, Carl Fischer Concert Hall, New York
Bill Hardman (tp), Jackie McLean (as), Sam Dockery (p), Spanky DeBrest (b), Art Blakey (d)

Casino	5:00	Gigi Gryce	Elektra EKL 120, Savoy MG 12171, CD SV 0145

Note: While unconfirmed, it is likely that Gryce was present in the studio to direct his composition.

570313
Donald Byrd & Gigi Gryce - Jazz Lab
March 13, 1957, New York.

same as February 5, 1957 but Wade Legge (p) replaces Flanagan:

| CO57309 | Blue Concept | 5:03 | Gigi Gryce | Columbia CL 998, Collectables CD COL 5674 |

570324
Lee Morgan - Volume 3
March 24, 1957; Van Gelder Studio, Hackensack, NJ
Lee Morgan (tp), Gigi Gryce (as, fl*), Benny Golson (ts, arr), Wynton Kelly (p), Paul Chambers (b), Charli Persip (d):

tk. 03	Hasaan's Dream *	8:40	Benny Golson	Blue Note BLP 1557, Blue Note CDP 7 46817 2, Mosaic CD MD4-162
tk. 05	I Remember Clifford	7:00	Benny Golson	
tk. 07	Mesabi Chant	6:05	Benny Golson	-
tk. 10	Tip-Toeing (alt)	6:30	Benny Golson	Blue Note CDP 7 46817 2, Mosaic CD MD4-162
tk. 11	Tip-Toeing	6:30	Benny Golson	Blue Note BLP 1557, Blue Note CDP 7 46817 2, Mosaic CD MD4-162
tk. 13	Domingo	9:15	Benny Golson	-

Note: Mosaic 162 is titled *The Complete Blue Note Fifties Sessions*.

570402
Art Blakey - Jazz Messengers Plus Four
April 2, 1957, RCA Studio 3, New York
Lee Morgan, Bill Hardman (tp), Melba Liston (tb), Sahib Shihab (as), Johnny Griffin (ts), Cecil Payne (bar), Wynton Kelly (p), Spanky DeBrest (b), Art Blakey (d), Gigi Gryce (arr):

H4JB2892-3	A Night at Tony's	4:37	Gigi Gryce	BMG 07863 66661-2
H4JB2892-4	A Night at Tony's	4:20	Gigi Gryce	RCA 6286-2, BMG 07863 66661-2, BMG 09026-68730-2
H4JB2893-4	Social Call	5:36	Gigi Gryce	BMG 07863 66661-2
H4JB2893-5?	Social Call	5:16	Gigi Gryce	RCA 6286-2, BMG 09026-68730-2

Note 1: While unconfirmed, it is likely that Gryce was present in the studio to direct his arrangements.
Note 2: The arrangement of Social Call is the same as the one used for session 551022.
Note 3: BMG 66661 is titled *Second Edition*. RCA 6286 and BMG 68730 are titled *Theory of Art*.

570418
Herbie Mann - Salute to the Flute
April 18, 1957, New York

Herbie Mann (alto fl), Anthony Ortega (as, cl), Dick Hafer (ts, cl), Dave Kurtzer (bar, bcl), Joe Puma (g), Hank Jones (p, celeste), Oscar Pettiford (b), Philly Joe Jones (d), Gigi Gryce (arr):

| CO57718 | Little Niles | 6:10 | Randy Weston | Epic LN 3395, Portrait CD RK44095 |
| CO57720 | Song for Ruth | 4:22 | Herbie Mann | - |

<u>Note</u>: While unconfirmed, it is likely that Gryce was present in the studio to direct his arrangements.

570526
Oscar Pettiford and His Birdland Band - Jazz off the Air Vol. 6
May 26, 1957, Birdland, New York

Ray Copeland, Donald Byrd (tp), David Amram, Ed London (fh), Al Grey (tb), Gigi Gryce (as, arr), Benny Golson or J.R. Monterose (ts), Jerome Richardson (ts, fl), Sahib Shihab (bar), Dick Katz (p), Oscar Pettiford (b, cel), Shadow Wilson (d), Betty Glamman (hp):

The Gentle Art of Love (Theme)	1:47	Oscar Pettiford	Spotlite (Eng.) SPJ 153
Nica's Tempo	3:32	Gigi Gryce	-
Seventh Heaven	3:00		-
Perdido	2:47	Juan Tizol	-
Two French Fries	2:36	Gigi Gryce	-
He's My Guy	2:33	Don Raye & Gene DePaul	-
Smoke Signal	3:53	Gigi Gryce	-
The Gentle Art of Love (Theme)	0:38	Oscar Pettiford	-

<u>Note 1</u>: Gryce arranged his own compositions; Lucky Thompson arranged The Gentle Art of Love and Perdido.
<u>Note 2</u>: The track listed as Seventh Heaven has no connection to Minor Seventh Heaven.
<u>Note 3</u>: The Oscar Pettiford discography by Coover Gazdar divides this material between two dates, but neither he nor we have been able to locate the tapes to confirm the existence of additional material.

570527
Kenny Dorham - Jazz Contrasts
May 27, 1957, Reeves Sound Studios, New York

Kenny Dorham (tp), Sonny Rollins (ts *), Betty Glamman (hp), Hank Jones (p), Oscar Pettiford (b), Max Roach (d), Gigi Gryce (arr):

| LaRue | 7:54 | Clifford Brown | Riverside RLP-239, OJCCD-028-2 |
| My Old Flame * | 8:24 | Sam Coslow & Arthur Johnston | - |

Note 1: While unconfirmed, it is likely that Gryce was present in the studio to direct his arrangements.

Note 2: LaRue is also known as Tribute to Brownie.

570624

Gigi Gryce - [Signal Records Party]

June 24, 1957, Golden Thread Café at The Hotel New Yorker, New York

Gigi Gryce (as), Cecil Payne (bar), Duke Jordan (p), Wendell Marshall (b), Art Taylor (d), Hugh Downs (mc):

All the Things You Are	Jerome Kern	*Unissued*
Arnetta	Cecil Payne	-
How Deep is the Ocean	Irving Berlin	-
Saucer Eyes	Randy Weston	-
Scotch Blues	Duke Jordan	-
Star Eyes	Don Raye & Gene DePaul	-
There Will Never Be Another You	Mack Gordon & Harry Warren	-

NBC-TV broadcast of Tonight! America After Dark, hosted by Al "Jazzbo" Collins.

Note: Recording may not have survived. Information based on NBC program scripts held in the Library of Congress.

570625

Thelonious Monk - Monk's Music

June 25, 1957, Reeves Sound Studios, New York

Ray Copeland (tp), Gigi Gryce (as), Coleman Hawkins (ts), John Coltrane (ts), Thelonious Monk (p), Wilbur Ware (b), Art Blakey (d):

Crepuscule with Nellie (tk. 1)	4:34	Thelonious Monk	*Riverside RCD-022-2*
Crepuscule with Nellie (breakdown)	1:01	Thelonious Monk	*Riverside RCD-022-2*

Monk out.

Blues for Tomorrow	13:32	Gigi Gryce	*Riverside RLP 12-243, OJCCD-030-2, RCD-022-2*

Note 1: Blues for Tomorrow originally issued as by the East Coast All-Stars.

Note 2: Riverside 243 and OJC 030 are titled *Blues for Tomorrow*. Riverside 022 is titled *The Complete Riverside Recordings*.

570626

Thelonious Monk - Monk's Music

June 26, 1957, Reeves Sound Studios, New York

same as June 25, 1957 but add Thelonious Monk (p)

Off Minor (tk. 4)	5:14	Thelonious Monk	*Jazzland J (9) 46, OJCCD-039-2*
Off Minor (tk. 5)	5:08	Thelonious Monk	*Riverside RLP 12-242, 1102, OJCCD-084-2*
Abide with Me	0:53	William H. Monk	*Riverside RLP 12-242, 1102, OJCCD-084-2*
Crepuscule with Nellie (tks. 4/5)	4:46	Thelonious Monk	*Riverside OJCCD-084-2*
Crepuscule with Nellie (tk. 6)	4:39	Thelonious Monk	*Riverside RLP 12-242, OJCCD-084-2*
Epistrophy (fragment)	1:46	Thelonious Monk	*Jazzland J (9) 46, OJCCD-039-2*
Epistrophy	10:45	Thelonious Monk	*Riverside RLP 12-242, 1102, OJCCD-084-2*
Well You Needn't (fragment)	1:25	Thelonious Monk	
Well You Needn't	11:23	Thelonious Monk	*Riverside RLP 12-242, 1102, OJCCD-084-2*

Copeland, Gryce, and Coltrane out:

Ruby My Dear	5:25	Thelonious Monk	*Riverside RLP 12-242, 1102, OJCCD-084-2*

All takes on Riverside RCD-022-2.

Note 1: Monk, Ware, and Blakey do not appear on Abide with Me.
Note 2: Jazzland 46 and OJC 039 are titled *Thelonious Monk with John Coltrane*.

570705
Gigi Gryce & Donald Byrd Jazz Laboratory at Newport
July 5, 1957, Newport Jazz Festival, Newport RI
Donald Byrd (tp), Gigi Gryce (as), Hank Jones (p), Wendell Marshall (b), Osie Johnson (d):

Batland (Bat Land)	7:02	Gigi Gryce	*Verve MG V-8238*
Splittin' (Ray's Way)	6:57	Ray Bryant	-
Love for Sale	7:26	Cole Porter	-

Note: Voice of America tapes held in the Library of Congress indicate that there is no unissued material from this performance. George Wein apparently allotted 20–25 minutes for each non-headliner set.

570730
Donald Byrd & Gigi Gryce - New Formulas from Jazz Lab
July 30, 1957, New York
Donald Byrd (tp), Gigi Gryce (as), Hank Jones (p), Paul Chambers (b), Art Taylor (d):

H4JB5811-3	Exhibit A		8:30	Gigi Gryce	RCA (Jap.) 6015M
H4JB5812-2	Ergo the Blues (Jones Bones)		7:42	Hank Jones	
H4JB5812-3	Ergo the Blues		6:20	Hank Jones	RCA (Jap.) 6015M

570731
Donald Byrd & Gigi Gryce - New Formulas from Jazz Lab
July 31, 1957, New York, same as preceding:

| H4JB5813-3 | Capri | 4:53 | Gigi Gryce | RCA (Jap.) 6015M |
| H4JB5814-4 | Splittin' (Ray's Way) | 5:15 | Ray Bryant | RCA (Jap.) 6015M |

570801
Donald Byrd & Gigi Gryce - New Formulas from Jazz Lab
August 1, 1957, New York, same as preceding:

| H4JB5815-8 | Passade (Under the Stars) | 6:25 | Hank Jones | RCA (Jap.) 6015M |
| H4JB5816-3 | Byrd in Hand (High Step) | 9:35 | Barry Harris | RCA (Jap.) 6015M |

All takes from the above three sessions on RCA (Fr.) PL 43698; These sessions were intended for Vik LX 1138, which was never issued.

570809
Gigi Gryce & Donald Byrd Jazz Lab
August 9, 1957, New York

Donald Byrd (tp), Gigi Gryce (as), Hank Jones (p), Paul Chambers (b), Art Taylor (d):

JB931	Blue Lights	4:00	Gigi Gryce	Jubilee JLP 1059, Fresh Sound (Sp.) FSR-CD 82
JB932	Isn't It Romantic	4:51	Richard Rodgers & Lorenz Hart	-
JB933	Onion Head	4:44	Donald Byrd	-
JB934	Bangoon	4:57	Hank Jones	-
JB935	Imagination	5:40	Johnny Burke & Jimmy Van Heusen	-
JB936	X-tacy	8:32	Donald Byrd	-
JB937	Bat Land (Batland)	7:05	Gigi Gryce	-

570823
Oscar Pettiford - Orchestra in Hi-Fi, Volume 2
August 23, 1957, New York

Ray Copeland, Art Farmer (tp), Julius Watkins, David Amram (fh), Al Grey (tb), Gigi Gryce (as, arr), Benny Golson (ts, arr), Jerome Richardson (ts, fl), Sahib Shihab (bar), Dick Katz (p), Oscar Pettiford (b, cel), Gordon "Whitey" Mitchell (b), Gus Johnson (d):

add Betty Glamman (hp):

5607	Now See How You Are	5:10	Oscar Pettiford & Harris	ABC Paramount ABC 227, Impulse CD GRD-143
5608	I Remember Clifford (arr. BG)	4:42	Benny Golson	ABC Paramount ABC 227, Impulse CD GRD-143
5609	Aw! Come On	3:55	Oscar Pettiford	-

570830
Oscar Pettiford - Orchestra in Hi-Fi, Volume 2
August 30, 1957, New York
same as August 23, 1957 but Betty Glamman out:

5613	Somewhere	4:00	Ray Copeland	ABC Paramount ABC 227, Impulse CD GRD-143

add Betty Glamman (hp):

5614	Laura	3:40	David Raksin	ABC Paramount ABC 227, Impulse CD GRD-143
5615	Two Basses		Oscar Pettiford	Unissued

Note: Pettiford plays cello on 5613. It is not known if overdubbed.

570830
Donald Byrd & Gigi Gryce - Modern Jazz Perspective/Jazz Lab. Volume 2
August 30, 1957, New York
Donald Byrd (tp), Gigi Gryce (as, arr), Wynton Kelly (p), Wendell Marshall (b), Art Taylor (d):

CO59677	Satellite	4:26	Gigi Gryce	Columbia CL 1058, Collectables CD COL 5674
CO59678	Evening in Casablanca	5:05	Gigi Gryce	-
CO59679	Social Call	4:44	Gigi Gryce	-

570903
Donald Byrd & Gigi Gryce - Modern Jazz Perspective/Jazz Lab. Volume 2
September 3, 1957, New York, Jackie Paris (voc, bnj) added:

CO59684	Early Morning Blues/Now Don't You Know (JP voc)	3:46	Gigi Gryce	Columbia CL 1058, Collectables CD COL 5674
CO59685	Early Bird (JP voc)	6:23	Donald Byrd	Columbia CL 1058
CO59686	Elgy (JP voc)	6:28	Donald Byrd	Columbia CL 1058, Collectables CD COL 5674

570905
Donald Byrd & Gigi Gryce - Modern Jazz Perspective/Jazz Lab. Volume 2
September 5, 1957, New York
Donald Byrd (tp), Julius Watkins (fh), Jimmy Cleveland (tb), Don Butterfield (tu), Gigi Gryce (as, arr), Sahib Shihab (bar), Wynton Kelly (p), Wendell Marshall (b), Art Taylor (d), Benny Golson (arr):

| CO59690 | Stablemates (arr. GG) | 5:00 | Benny Golson | Columbia CL 1058, Collectables CD COL 5674 |
| CO59691 | Steppin' Out (arr. BG) | 5:30 | Gigi Gryce | - |

570906
Oscar Pettiford - Orchestra in Hi-Fi, Volume 2
September 6, 1957, New York,
same as August 30, 1957 but Kenny Dorham (tp) replaces Art Farmer:

5616	Little Niles (arr. GG)	4:40	Randy Weston	ABC Paramount ABC 227, Impulse CD GRD-143
5617	Seabreeze	2:54	Larry Douglas	-
5618	Bohemia After Dark		Oscar Pettiford	Unissued

Note: Pettiford plays cello on 5616. It is not known if overdubbed.

571014
Benny Golson - Benny Golson's New York Scene
October 14, 1957, New York
Art Farmer (tp), Benny Golson (ts, arr), Wynton Kelly (p), Paul Chambers (b), Charli Persip (d), Gigi Gryce (arr):

| Something in B Flat (arr. GG) | 6:01 | Ray Bryant | Contemporary C-3552, OJCCD-164-2 |
| B.G.'s Holiday (arr. GG) | 5:34 | Gigi Gryce | - |

Note: While unconfirmed, it is likely that Gryce was present in the studio to direct his arrangements.

571017
Benny Golson - Benny Golson's New York Scene
October 17, 1957, New York
Art Farmer (tp), Julius Watkins (fh), Jimmy Cleveland (tb), Gigi Gryce (as, arr), Benny Golson (ts, arr), Sahib Shihab (bar), Wynton Kelly (p), Paul Chambers (b), Charli Persip (d), Ernie Wilkins (arr):

| Whisper Not (arr. BG) | 5:57 | Benny Golson | Contemporary C-3552, OJCCD-164-2 |

| Just by Myself (arr. EW) | 4:57 | Benny Golson | - |
| Capri (arr. GG) | 3:56 | Gigi Gryce | - |

571217

Dizzy Gillespie Octet - The Greatest Trumpet of Them All

December 17, 1957, New York

Dizzy Gillespie (tp), Henry Coker (tb), Gigi Gryce (as, arr), Benny Golson (ts, arr), Pee Wee Moore (bar), Ray Bryant (p, celeste), Tommy Bryant (b), Charli Persip (d):

21849	Blues After Dark	6:27	Benny Golson	*Verve MG V-8352, MG VS-6117, 2304-382, CD 314 513 875-2*
21850	Sea Breeze	3:15	Larry Douglas	*Verve MG V-8352, MG VS-6117, 2304-382, CD 510088-2*
21851	Out of the Past	5:30	Benny Golson	*Verve MG V-8352, MG VS-6117, 2304-382*
21852	Shabozz	6:00	Gigi Gryce	-
21853	Reminiscing	4:50	Gigi Gryce	*Verve MG V-8352, MG VS-6117, 2304-382, CD 511057-2 IMS*
21854	A Night at Tony's	5:10	Gigi Gryce	*Verve MG V-8352, MG VS-6117, 2304-382*
21855	Smoke Signals	5:10	Gigi Gryce	-
21856	Just by Myself	4:45	Benny Golson	

Note 1: Benny Golson arranged his own compositions, all others arranged by Gryce.

Note 2: Verve 511057 is titled *Jazz Round Midnight: Trumpet*.

571219

Benny Golson - The Modern Touch

December 19, 1957, Reeves Sound Studios, New York

Kenny Dorham (tp), J.J. Johnson (tb), Benny Golson (ts), Wynton Kelly (p), Paul Chambers (b), Max Roach (d), Gigi Gryce (arr):

| Hymn to the Orient | 4:07 | Gigi Gryce | *Riverside RLP 12-256, OJCCD 1797-2* |

Note: It is implied in the original liner notes that Gryce was present to direct his arrangements.

571223

Benny Golson - The Modern Touch

December 23, 1957, Reeves Sound Studios, New York

Kenny Dorham (tp), J.J. Johnson (tb), Benny Golson (ts), Wynton Kelly (p), Paul Chambers (b), Max Roach (d), Gigi Gryce (arr):

| Reunion | 7:14 | Gigi Gryce | *Riverside RLP 12-256, OJCCD 1797-2* |

Note 1: It is implied in the original liner notes that Gryce was present to direct his arrangements.
Note 2: Reunion is also known both as Salute to the Bandbox and Salute to Birdland.

580200
Betty Carter - Out There with Betty Carter - Progressive Jazz
February 1958, New York

Betty Carter (voc), Kenny Dorham, Ray Copeland (tp, arr), Melba Liston (tb, arr), Gigi Gryce (as, arr), Jimmy Powell (as), Benny Golson (ts, arr), Tommy Gryce (ts, arr), Sahib Shihab (bar), unknown (fl, bcl), Wynton Kelly (p), Sam Jones, Peck Morrison (b), Specs Wright (d):

Peacock PLP 90, Impulse ASD 9321, CD GRD 114

	You're Driving Me Crazy	1:45	Walter Donaldson	-
	Foul Play	2:21	Norman Mapp	-
FR 6002	On the Isle of May	2:02	Mack David & Andre Kostelanetz	-
	Make It Last (arr. ML)	4:30	Paxton & Haynes	
	Blue Bird of Happiness (arr. TG)	1:30	Edward Heyman & Sandor Harmati	
	Something Wonderful (arr. ML)	3:37	Richard Rodgers & Oscar Hammerstein	

Note 1: Tommy Gryce listed as "Tommy Bryce."
Note 2: Impulse 9321 is titled *What a Little Moonlight Can Do*. Impulse 114 is titled *I Can't Help It*.

580200
Betty Carter - Out There with Betty Carter - Progressive Jazz
February 1958, New York

Betty Carter (voc), Ray Copeland (tp, arr), Melba Liston (tb), Jerome Richardson (ts, fl *), Wynton Kelly (p), Peck Morrison (b), Specs Wright (d):

Peacock PLP 90, Impulse ASD 9321, CD GRD 114

	I Can't Help It (tp, tb out)	2:44	Betty Carter	-
	By the Bend of the River	2:07	Clara Edwards	-
	Babe's Blues *	2:49	Randy Weston (& Jon Hendricks)	
	You're Getting to Be a Habit with Me	2:30	Harry Warren & Al Dubin	
FR 6003	But Beautiful *	3:58	Jimmy Van Heusen & Johnny Burke	
	All I've Got	2:15	D. Cole	

Note: Gryce's participation in this session is uncertain but he may have arranged and/or conducted the material.

580600
Gigi Gryce Quartet - Gigi Gryce

Probably early June 1958, New York
Gigi Gryce (as, ts, cl, bar, fl, pic, arr), Hank Jones (p, celeste), Milt Hinton (b), Osie Johnson (d):

58-XY-629	Little Susan	2:20	Randy Weston	*Metrojazz E 1006*
58-XY-630	Lullaby for Milkman	2:30	Jack Lazare	-
58-XY-631	My Ideal (bar)	2:48	Newell Chase, Leo Robin, Richard Whiting	-
58-XY-632	Bangoon	2:43	Hank Jones	-
58-XY-633	Blues March	3:03	Benny Golson	-
58-XY-634	Sea Breeze	2:30	Larry Douglas	-

580600
Gigi Gryce Quartet - Gigi Gryce
Probably early June 1958, New York, same as preceding:

58-XY-641	Somewhere	2:36	Ray Copeland	*Metrojazz E 1006*
58-XY-642	Cold Breeze	2:36	Wade Legge	-
58-XY-643	Rich and Creamy (cl)	3:29	Jack Lazare	-
58-XY-644	Baba's Blues (ts)	2:59	Gigi Gryce	-
58-XY-645	In a Sentimental Mood (ts)	3:35	Duke Ellington	
58-XY-646	It Don't Mean a Thing	3:00	Duke Ellington	

580910
Art Farmer - Modern Art
September 10, 11, or 14, 1958, Nola's Penthouse Studios, New York
Art Farmer (tp), Benny Golson (ts), Bill Evans (p), Addison Farmer (b), Dave Bailey (d), Gigi Gryce (arr):

Cold Breeze	3:52	Wade Legge	*United Artists UAL-4007, UAS-5007, Blue Note CDP 7 84459-2*

Note: While unconfirmed, it is likely that Gryce was present in the studio to direct his arrangement.

581113
Gerry Mulligan
November 13, 1958, TV Studio, New York
Art Farmer (tp), Jimmy Cleveland (tb), Gigi Gryce (as), Gerry Mulligan (bar), Kenny Burrell (g), Hank Jones (p), Bill Crow (b), Donald Bailey (d), Candido Camero (cga), Art Ford (mc):

Selections from *I Want to Live*   Gerry Mulligan   *Unissued*

TV broadcast of Art Ford's Jazz Party.

Note: Recording may not have survived.

581117

Benny Golson - And the Philadelphians

November 17, 1958, New York

Lee Morgan (tp), Benny Golson (ts), Ray Bryant (p), Percy Heath (b), Philly Joe Jones (d), Gigi Gryce (arr):

You're Not the Kind	4:20	Gigi Gryce	*United Artists UAL 4020, UAS 5020, Blue Note CD 7243 4 94104 2 8*
Calgary	3:39	Ray Bryant	-

Note: While unconfirmed, it is likely that Gryce was present in the studio to direct his arrangements.

581120

Gerry Mulligan

November 20, 1958, TV Studio, New York

Art Farmer (tp), Jimmy Cleveland (tb), Gigi Gryce (as), Gerry Mulligan (bar), Kenny Burrell (g), Jimmy Jones (p), possibly Vinnie Burke (b), possibly Barry Miles (d), Candido Camero (bgo), Art Ford (mc):

What Is This Thing Called Love	12:02	Cole Porter	*Jazz Band EB 418, EBCD 2101-2*

TV broadcast of Art Ford's Jazz Party.

Note 1: Recording may not have survived.

Note 2: Jazz Band 418 and 2101 are titled Miles Davis All-Stars Live in 1958–1959. The above listing corrects personnel errors.

590200

Jimmy Cleveland - Rhythm Crazy

February 1959, New York

Art Farmer (tp), Jimmy Cleveland (tb), Jerome Richardson (fl), Benny Golson (ts), Hank Jones (p), Milt Hinton (b), Osie Johnson (d), Gigi Gryce (arr):

Crazy Rhythm	3:55	Joseph Mayer, Roger Kahn, Irving Caesar	*EmArcy MGE-26003, SRE-66003*
We Never Kissed	3:46	Melba Liston	-
Reminiscing	3:02	Gigi Gryce	-

Note 1: While unconfirmed, it is likely that Gryce was present in the studio to direct his arrangements.

Note 2: Jimmy Cleveland credits Melba Liston with the arrangement of We Never Kissed, contrary to liner notes.

Curtis Fuller - Sliding Easy

March 9, 1959, Nola's Penthouse Studios, New York

Lee Morgan (tp), Curtis Fuller (tb), Hank Mobley (ts), Tommy Flanagan (p), Paul Chambers (b), Elvin Jones (d), Gigi Gryce (tamb*, arr):

tk. 5	Down Home *	4:02	Curtis Fuller	United Artists UAL-4041, UAS-5041
tk. 6	Down Home *	4:29	Curtis Fuller	Unissued
tk. 7	C.T.A.	5:06	Jimmy Heath	United Artists UAL-4041, UAS-5041

All takes on Mosaic MD3-166, titled *The Complete Blue Note/UA Sessions.*

Buddy Rich & Max Roach - Rich Versus Roach

April 7,8, 1959, Fine Sound Studio, New York

Tommy Turrentine (tp), Willie Dennis, Julian Priester (tb), Phil Woods (as), Stanley Turrentine (ts), John Bunch (p), Phil Leshin, Bobby Boswell (b), Buddy Rich, Max Roach (d), Gigi Gryce (arr, con):

JB487-6	Yesterdays	5:41	Jerome Kern	Mercury MG 20448, SR 60133, CD 826 987-2
JB488-3	Limehouse Blues (alt)	3:43	Douglas Furber & Philip Braham	Mercury CD 826 987-2
JB488-7	Limehouse Blues	3:56	Douglas Furber & Philip Braham	Mercury MG 20448, SR 60133, CD 826 987-2
JB489-6	The Casbah (alt)	4:28	Gigi Gryce	Mercury CD 826 987-2
JB489-8	The Casbah	4:58	Gigi Gryce	Mercury MG 20448, SR 60133, CD 826 987-2
JB490-2	Big Foot (first alt)	5:01	Charlie Parker	
JB490-3	Big Foot	5:02	Charlie Parker	Mercury MG 20448, SR 60133, CD 826 987-2
JB490-7	Big Foot (second alt)	5:14	Charlie Parker	Mercury CD 826 987-2
JB491-10	Sleep	3:18	Earl Lebieg	Mercury MG 20448, SR 60133, CD 826 987-2
JB492-2	Toot, Toot, Tootsie Goodbye	3:57	Gus Kahn, Ernie Erdman, Dan Russo, Ted Riorito	Mercury MG 20448, SR 60133, CD 826 987-2
JB493-4	Sing, Sing, Sing (alt)	4:08	Louis Prima	Mercury CD 826 987-2
JB493-8	Sing, Sing, Sing	4:22	Louis Prima	Mercury MG 20448, SR 60133, CD 826 987-2
JB503-1	Figure Eights (drums only)	4:29	Buddy Rich & Max Roach	Mercury MG 20448, SR 60133, CD 826 987-2

All takes on Mosaic MD7-201, titled *The Complete Mercury Max Roach Plus Four Sessions.*

Note 1: Photos confirm Gryce was present in the studio for these sessions.
Note 2: The Rich and Roach quintets were recorded on separate channels.

413

Note 3: First track of session was Liza (All the Clouds'll Roll Away) but no tape survives.
Note 4: The original LP issue edits out the bass introduction to Big Foot.
Note 5: Mercury CD 826 987-2 mislabels master and alternative takes for Limehouse Blues and The Casbah. These are labeled correctly in the Mosaic boxed set.

600311
Gigi Gryce - Saying Somethin'!
March 11, 1960, Van Gelder Studio, Englewood Cliffs, NJ
Richard Williams (tp), Gigi Gryce (as), Richard Wyands (p), Reggie Workman (b), Granville "Mickey" Roker (d):
New Jazz NJLP 8230, Prestige/New Jazz OJCD-1851-2

2077	Leila's Blues	6:47	Gigi Gryce	
2078	Blues in the Jungle	6:16	Gigi Gryce	-
2079	Down Home	8:19	Curtis Fuller	-
2080	Back Breaker	6:08	Gigi Gryce	-
2081	Let Me Know	4:43	Hank Jones	-
2082	Jones Bones (Ergo the Blues)	7:10	Hank Jones	-

600503
Gigi Gryce - The Hap'nin's
May 3, 1960, Van Gelder Studio, Englewood Cliffs, NJ
Richard Williams (tp), Gigi Gryce (as), Richard Wyands (p), Julian Euell (b), Granville "Mickey" Roker (d):
New Jazz NJLP 8246, Prestige/New Jazz OJCD-1868-2

2212	Summertime	8:04	George Gershwin & DuBose Heyward	
2213	Lover Man	5:37	James E. Davis, Ram Ramirez, James Sherman	
2214	Minority	6:33	Gigi Gryce	-
2215	Don't Worry 'Bout Me	7:42	Rube Bloom & Ted Koehler	-
2216	Frankie and Johnny	7:33	Traditional	-
2217	Nica's Tempo	4:05	Gigi Gryce	-

600525
Leo Wright - Blues Shout
May 25, 1960, Atlantic Recording Studio, New York
Richard Williams (tp), Leo Wright (as), Junior Mance (p), Art Davis (b), Charli Persip (d), Gigi Gryce (arr, con):
Atlantic SD-1538, Collectables CD COL-6281

| 4569 | A Night in Tunisia | 5:21 | Dizzy Gillespie |

4570 The Wind 4:37 Russ Freeman -
4572 Blues Shout 4:58 Gigi Gryce -

Note 1: Art Davis confirms that Gryce was in the studio for this session.
Note 2: Collectables 6281 is titled *Hank Crawford/Leo Wright: Soul Clinic/Blues Shout.*

600607

Gigi Gryce - The Rat Race Blues

June 7, 1960, Van Gelder Studio, Englewood Cliffs, NJ

Richard Williams (tp), Gigi Gryce (as), Richard Wyands (p), Julian Euell (b), Granville "Mickey" Roker (d):

2293	Blues in Bloom	7:44	Norman Mapp	New Jazz NJLP 8262, Prestige/New Jazz OJCCD-081-2
2294	Boxer's Blues	6:58	Gigi Gryce	-
2295	Strange Feelin'	7:45	Gigi Gryce	-
2296	The Rat Race Blues	6:35	Gigi Gryce	-
2297	Monday Through Sunday	11:09	Norman Mapp	-

600329

Leo Wright - Blues Shout

August 29, 1960, Atlantic Recording Studio, New York

Leo Wright (f), Harry Lookofsky (vln), Junior Mance (p), Art Davis (b), Charli Persip (d), Gigi Gryce (arr, con):

4869	Indian Summer	7:00	Victor Herbert & Al Dubin	Atlantic 1358, Collectables COL-6281
4870	Angel Eyes	4:09	Matt Dennis & Earl Brent	-

Note: Art Davis confirms that Gryce was in the studio for this session.

600000-A

Gigi Gryce Quintet - [Demo Disc]

Probably 1960, Nola's Penthouse Studios, New York

Richard Williams (tp), Gigi Gryce (as, arr), probably Richard Wyands (p), unknown (b), unknown (d):

Sonor	3:32	Gerald Wiggins & Kenny Clarke	Unissued
Down Home	4:15	Curtis Fuller	-
Take the 'A' Train	4:00	Billy Strayhorn	-
Stompin' at the Savoy	2:36	Edgar Sampson & Benny Goodman	-

| I'll Walk Alone | 4:33 | Sammy Cahn & Jule Styne | - |
| Caravan | 5:00 | Juan Tizol & Duke Ellington | - |

Disc in the collection of the Rutgers Institute of Jazz Studies.

<u>Note</u>: The arrangements of Take the 'A' Train and Caravan are the same as those issued on *Reminiscin'* (below), suggesting a similar time period, probably before.

<u>600000-B</u>

Gigi Gryce Orchtette - [Soundtrack for the Fred Baker film *On the Sound*]

Second half of 1960, Bell Sound Studios, New York [date unknown]

Richard Williams (tp), Gigi Gryce (as, cl, fl, arr), Eddie Costa (vb), Richard Wyands (p), Reggie Workman (b), Mickey Roker (d)

The Rat Race Blues	Gigi Gryce	*Unissued*
Despair	Gigi Gryce	-
Blues in the Mornin'	Gigi Gryce	-
Search	Gigi Gryce	-
Sequence	Gigi Gryce	-
Lighthouse	Gigi Gryce	-
Ratology	Gigi Gryce	-

<u>Note</u>: Titles taken from copyright deposit held in the Library of Congress.

<u>601107</u>

Gigi Gryce Orchtette - Reminiscin'

November 7, 1960, New York

Richard Williams (tp), Gigi Gryce (as, arr), Eddie Costa (vb), Richard Wyands (p), Reggie Workman (b), Walter Perkins (d):

20627	A Night in Tunisia	5:12	Dizzy Gillespie	*Mercury MG 20628, SR 60628*
20628	In a Strange Mood		Gigi Gryce	*Unissued*
20629	A Premonition of You		Gigi Gryce	*Unissued*

<u>601109</u>

Gigi Gryce Orchtette - Reminiscin'

November 9, 1960, New York

Richard Williams (tp), Gigi Gryce (as, arr), Richard Wyands (p), Julian Euell (b), Walter Perkins (d):

| 20630 | Dearly Beloved | 4:20 | Jerome Kern & Johnny Mercer | *Mercury MG 20628, SR 60628* |

| 20631 | Blue Lights | 3:25 | Gigi Gryce |
| 20632 | Gee Blues Gee | 3:22 | Randy Weston |

Note: Gee Blues Gee is also known as Kucheza Blues.

601110

Gigi Gryce Orchtette - Reminiscin'

November 10, 1960, New York

Richard Williams (tp), Gigi Gryce (as, arr), Eddie Costa (vb), Richard Wyands (p), George Duvivier (b), Robert Thomas, Jr. (d):

20633	Caravan	4:26	Juan Tizol & Duke Ellington	*Mercury MG 20628, SR 60628*
20634	Yesterdays	4:46	Jerome Kern	-
20635	Take the 'A' Train	3:36	Billy Strayhorn	-
20636	Reminiscing	4:01	Gigi Gryce	-

601116

Randy Weston Orchestra - Uhuru Afrika

November 16-18, 1960, Bell Sound Studios, New York

Clark Terry (tp, flg), Benny Bailey, Richard Williams, Freddie Hubbard (tp), Slide Hampton, Jimmy Cleveland, Quentin Jackson (tb), Julius Watkins (fh), Gigi Gryce (as, fl), Yusef Lateef (ts, fl, ob), Cecil Payne, Sahib Shihab (as, bar), Budd Johnson (ts, cl), Jerome Richardson (bar, pic), Les Spann (g, fl), Kenny Burrell (g), Randy Weston (p, arr), George Duvivier, Ron Carter (b), Max Roach, Charli Persip, G.T. Hogan, Babatunde Olatunji, Armando Peraza (dm, perc), Martha Flowers, Brock Peters (voc), Tuntemeke Sanga (narrator):

Intro - Uhuru Kwanza	2:44	Randy Weston	*Roulette R 65001, CD CDP 7 94510 2*
Movement 1 - Uhuru Kwanza	5:53	Randy Weston	-
Movement 2 - African Lady	8:44	Randy Weston & Langston Hughes	-
Movement 3 - Bantu	8:22	Randy Weston	-
Movement 4 - Kucheza Blues	8:05	Randy Weston	-

Note: Kucheza Blues is also known as Gee Blues Gee.

610819

Gigi Gryce

August 19, 1961, Birdland, New York

Richard Williams (tp), Gigi Gryce (as, arr), Eddie Costa (vb), possibly Richard Wyands (p), unknown (b), possibly Mickey Roker (d):

417

Blues in Bloom	11:00	Norman Mapp	*Unissued*
A Premonition of You	4:30	Gigi Gryce	-
A Night in Tunisia	7:15	Dizzy Gillespie	-
Down Home	5:30	Curtis Fuller	-

Broadcast recorded by Boris Rose.

610930
Gigi Gryce
September 30, 1961, Birdland, New York
Richard Williams (tp), Gigi Gryce (as, arr), Eddie Costa (vb), possibly Richard Wyands (p), unknown (b), possibly Mickey Roker (d):

Round about the Blues	7:15		*Unissued*
Take the 'A' Train	4:30	Billy Strayhorn	-
Down Home	5:00	Curtis Fuller	-

Broadcast recorded by Boris Rose.

<u>Note</u>: Round about the Blues may be the Don Sebesky composition recorded by Maynard Ferguson on June 20, 1961; this is unconfirmed.

418

bibliography

Amram, David, *Vibrations*, New York, The Macmillan Company, 1968.

Arnold, Denis (ed.), "Hovhaness, Alan," *The New Oxford Companion to Music*, New York, Oxford University Press, 1984, pp. 431–33.

Blume, August, "An Interview with John Coltrane," *The Jazz Review*, January 1959, p. 25.

Cardell, Victor T. with Nina Davis-Mills, "Hartford," *The New Oxford Companion to Music*, New York, Oxford University Press, 1984, pp. 342–43.

Catalano, Nick, *Clifford Brown: The Life and Art of the Legendary Jazz Trumpeter*, New York, Oxford University Press, 2000.

Cohen, Noal and Michael Fitzgerald, "Emotional Eloquence: An Historical Overview of Gigi Gryce," *Coda*, #283, January–February 1999, pp. 26–30.

Dance, Stanley, *The World of Earl Hines*, New York, Da Capo Press, 1977.

Gitler, Ira, *The Masters of Bebop: A Listener's Guide* (formerly *Jazz Masters of the '40's*), New York, Da Capo Press, 2001.

Goldblatt, Burt, *Newport Jazz Festival*, New York, The Dial Press, 1977.

Griffiths, Paul, "Boulanger, Nadia," *The New Oxford Companion to Music*, New York, Oxford University Press, 1984, pp. 245–46.

———, "Honegger, Arthur," *The New Oxford Companion to Music*, New York, Oxford University Press, 1984, p. 872.

419

Hampton, Lionel with James Haskins, *Hamp: An Autobiography*, New York, Warner Books, 1989.

Harrison, Max, "Teddy Charles," *A Jazz Retrospect*, Boston, Crescendo Publishing Company, 1976.

Hentoff, Nat, "A New Jazz Corporation—Gryce, Farmer," *Down Beat*, October 19, 1955, pp. 10–11.

————, *Jazz Is*, New York, Ridge Press/Random House, 1976.

————, "Memories of Thelonious Monk," *Listen to the Stories*, HarperCollins Publishers, 1995.

Horricks, Raymond, *Quincy Jones*, New York, Hippocrene Books, 1985.

Horricks, Raymond, "The Search for Orchestral Progression," *Jazzbook 1955*, McCarthy, Albert J. (ed.), London, Cassell and Company, 1955.

Horricks, Raymond, "Gigi Gryce: Smoke Signals," *These Jazzmen of Our Time*, London, Gollancz, 1959.

Keepnews, Orrin, "Charlie Parker," *The Jazz Makers*, New York, Da Capo Press, 79.

Lyons, Len and Don Perlo, "Donald Byrd," "Sam Rivers," *Jazz Portraits*, New York, William Morrow & Co., 1989.

Meeker, David, *Jazz in the Movies*, New York, Da Capo Press, 1981.

Morgan, Alun and Raymond Horricks, *Modern Jazz: A Survey of Developments Since 1939*, London, Victor Gollancz, 1956.

Nevard, Mike and Max Jones, "A Guy Named Gigi," *Melody Maker*, 29/1054 (November 28, 1953), p. 7.

Owens, Thomas, *Bebop: The Music and Its Players*, New York, Oxford University Press, 1995.

————, "Gryce, Gigi," *The New Grove Dictionary of Jazz*, Kernfeld, Barry (ed.), New York, St. Martins's Press, 1996, p. 456.

Porter, Lewis, *John Coltrane*, Ann Arbor, University of Michigan Press, 1998.

Reisner, Robert G., "Gigi Gryce," *The Jazz Titans*, New York, Doubleday, 1960.

Reisner, Robert G. (ed.), *Bird: The Legend of Charlie Parker*, New York, Da Capo Press, 1979.

Rosenthal, David H., *Hard Bop: Jazz and Black Music 1955–1965*, New York, Oxford University Press, 1992.

Schuller, Gunther, "The Future of Form in Jazz," *Musings*, New York, Oxford University Press, 1986.

————, "Thelonious Monk," *Jazz Panorama*, New York, Collier Books, 1962, pp. 216–38.

Sidran, Ben, *Talking Jazz: An Oral History*, New York, Da Capo Press, 1995.

Spellman, A. B., "Cecil Taylor," "Herbie Nichols," *Four Lives in the Bebop Business*, Pantheon Books, 1966.

Steinberg, Michael, "Pinkham, Daniel," *The New Grove Dictionary of Music and Musicians*, Sadie, Stanley (ed.), London, Macmillan Publishers, 1980, p. 756.

Taylor, Arthur, "Randy Weston," *Notes and Tones*, New York, Coward, McGann & Geohegan, 1982, pp. 22–25.

Ward, Tyrone, *When Art Farmer Remembered Gigi Gryce: An Oral History of a Life in Jazz*, Chicago, 1992.

Williams, Martin, "New Ears for Jazz," *Metronome*, 78/6 (June 1961), pp. 12–13.

Woideck, Carl (ed.), *The John Coltrane Companion*, New York, Schirmer Books, 1998.

Wright, Bruce, *Black Justice in a White World: A Memoir*, New York, Barricade Books, Inc., 1996, pp. 13, 145–46.

Wynn, Ron (ed.), "Gigi Gryce," *All Music Guide to Jazz*, San Francisco, Miller Freeman Books, 1994, p. 299.

Discographies and Reference Materials

Bruyninckx, Walter, *70 Years of Recorded Jazz 1917–1987*, Mechelen, Belgium, Walter Bruyninckx.

Carlu, Pierre, "Clifford Brown–Gigi Gryce & Co.," *Micrography*, no. 58, pp. 16–17.

Cuscuna, Michael & Michel Ruppli, *The Blue Note Label*, Westport, CT, Greenwood Press, 1988.

Feather, Leonard, *New Edition of The Encyclopedia of Jazz*, New York, Horizon Press, 1960.

Feather, Leonard & Ira Gitler, *The Biographical Encyclopedia of Jazz*, New York, Oxford University Press, 1999.

Gazdar, Coover, *First Bass: Oscar Pettiford*, International Association Of Jazz Record Collectors, 1993.

Lord, Tom, *The Jazz Discography*, Redwood, NY, Cadence Jazz Books, 1992–2001.

Neely, Tim, *Goldmine Jazz Album Price Guide*, Iola, WI, Krause Publications, 2000.

The Prestige Book: Discography of All Series, Jazz Critique Magazine, Special Edition (Japanese), 1996, vol. 3.

Ruppli, Michel, "Art Farmer: His Complete Discography," International Records News, 1/5, 1/6 (October, November 1982), The Fini Editions, Imola, Italy.

———, "Discographie: Clifford Brown," *Jazz Hot*, March 1978, pp. 24–27.

———, *Atlantic Records: A Discography*, Westport, CT, Greenwood Press, 1979.

———, *Discographies Vol. 2: The Vogue Label*, Paris, AFAS, 1992.

Ruppli, Michel and Novitsky, Ed, *The Mercury Labels: A Discography*, Westport, CT, Greenwood Press, 1993.

———, *The MGM Labels: A Discography*, Westport, CT, Greenwood Press, 1998.

Ruppli, Michel and Porter, Bob, *The Prestige Label: A Discography*, Westport, CT, Greenwood Press, 1980.

———, *The Savoy Label: A Discography*, Westport, CT, Greenwood Press, 1980.

———, *The Clef/Verve Labels: A Discography*, Westport, CT, Greenwood Press, 1986.

Umphred, Neal, *Goldmine's Price Guide to Collectible Jazz Albums, 1949–1969*, Iola, WI, Krause Publications, 1994.

Weiler, Uwe, *The Debut Label: A Discography*, Norderstedt, Germany, Uwe Weiler, 1994.

Weir, Bob, *Clifford Brown Discography*, Cardiff, Wales, Bob Weir, 1984.

index

ABC Paramount Records 194, 201, 236–237, 244n

Adams, Park "Pepper" 232, 248, 283

Adderley, Julian "Cannonball" 2, 10, 34n, 233, 255, 257, 259

"African Lady" 293–94

"Al Gashiya" ("Al Ghashiya," "Gashiya") 52–53, 191

Alexander, Willard 193, 272

"All God's Chillun Got Rhythm" 153, 232

"All the Things You Are" 125

"All Weird" 133–134

Allen Chapel A.M.E., Pensacola, FL 15

Ammons, Gene "Jug" 48, 195

Amram, David 54–55, 166–167, 198–199, 200, 202, 204–205, 210n, 340–341

Anderson, Duke 184n

Anderson, Ernestine 93, 95, 96, 99, 172

Anderson, Margie 68–70, 179

Andrews, Harold 21–23, 34n

"Angel Eyes" 281

"Anne Marie" ("I Need You So") 130

"Another One" 164

"Anthropology" 40, 48

Apollo Theatre, New York 69, 97

Armstrong, Louis 218, 279, 323–324

Art Ford's Jazz Party (television show) 254

ASCAP (American Society of Composers, Authors and Publishers) 170, 247

A.S.I.A. Suite 326

Atlantic Records 188, 191, 193, 194, 209

"B.G.'s Holiday" 240, 241

"Baba's Blues" 251

"Babe's Blues" 248, 251

"Baby" 28, 128, 129, 154

Bach, Johann Sebastian 43, 136, 214

"Back Breaker" 275

Baker, Fred 298–304

Band Box Club, The, New York 96, 98–99, 105–106

"Bangoon" ("Allison's Uncle") 233, 250

Bank, Danny 164, 176, 203, 228

"Bantu" 293–94

Barber, John William "Bill" 176, 180

Barrow, George 187, 192

Bartok, Bela 54

"Basheer's Dream" 160–161

Basie, William "Count" 57, 58, 60, 63, 125, 130, 216, 234

"Batland" 148, 229, 234

Bauer, Billy 187
Bee Hive Club, Chicago, IL 151, 197
Benny Golson's New York Scene 239–241, 264
Berendt, Joachim 127, 145n
Berklee College of Music, Boston, MA 42, 57
Berkshire Music Barn, Lenox, MA 163
Bert, Eddie 164, 176, 187, 339
Bethlehem Records 163
Big Beat, The (Johnnie Ray LP) 209
"Big Foot" 263
Big Maybelle 212, 216
Birdland, New York 96, 98, 150, 164, 174, 181, 197, 200, 204, 224, 297, 340
Birth of the Cool 176, 177, 250
Bishop, Jr., Walter xiii, 153
Blakey, Art viii, 2, 49, 100–102, 128, 129, 143, 153, 154, 161, 166, 171, 173, 213, 216, 218, 219–220, 223, 226–227, 231, 234, 242–243, 250, 254, 266, 314, 339, 341
Blanchard, Elvis Grice (sister of Gigi Gryce) xiii, 11–14
"Blue Concept" 125, 152, 153, 219, 254
"Blue Lights" ("House of the Blue Lights") 162, 220, 285, 291–92
Blue Note Records 80–81, 85, 99, 107n, 135, 152, 168, 217, 219, 221, 231, 237, 262, 278
Blues for Tomorrow 227
"Blues in Bloom" 282–83
"Blues in the Jungle" 275
"Blues March" 250, 264
"Blues Shout" 230, 238, 264, 280
"Blues Walk" 277
BMI (Broadcast Music, Inc.) 149, 165, 247
Board, Clyde 38–41, 43–45, 49–51, 66
Boccherini, Luigi 136, 138
"Bohemia after Dark" 164
Bolden, Walter 45, 47, 48, 49, 63, 64, 80, 82

Booker T. Washington High School, Pensacola, FL 16–17, 21, 22, 24, 25, 26, 27
Bostic, Earl 183n
Boston Conservatory viii, 32, 38, 39, 47, 49, 51, 53, 54, 55, 56, 59, 61, 70–71, 73, 75, 77n, 268, 338
Boulanger, Nadia 71–73, 77n, 213
"Boxer's Blues, The" 281
Bradshaw, "Tiny" 33, 184n
Braxton, Anthony 61, 339
Broekman, David 186, 190, 192–193
Brookmeyer, Bob 164, 186, 188, 192
"Brown Skins" 123–124, 175
Brown, Clifford ix, xi, 2, 5, 65, 84–87, 94–96, 98, 99–102, 104, 106n, 107n, 110, 111, 113, 114, 115, 118, 122–129, 133–136, 138–140, 143, 148, 206, 216, 224, 231, 235, 239, 244, 263, 269, 277, 291
"Brownie Eyes" 102
Brubeck, Dave 159, 195, 216, 218, 234, 239, 283
Bryant, Ray 214, 229, 240, 242, 254, 272, 285
Buckley, Richard "Lord" 295–296
"Bud Study" 208
"Budo" 250
"Bum's Rush" 130
Burns, Ralph 165
"But Officer" 91–92
Butterfield, Don 187, 188, 191, 192
Byard, Jaki xiii, 59, 60, 61, 63
Byas, Don 85, 110, 198
"Bye Bye Blackbird" 231, 283
"Byrd in Hand" ("High Step") 232
Byrd, Donald 6, 53, 71, 164, 194, 203, 209, 211–216, 220–221, 224, 228–234, 237–239, 248, 274, 282, 298, 319

"C.T.A." 262
Café Bohemia, New York 156, 197, 248, 300

"Calgary" 254

Calloway, Cab 29, 32

Calloway, Joe 47–49, 63–64

"Capri" 140, 141, 162, 231, 240, 241, 243, 264

"Caravan" 220, 272–273, 276, 291–292

Carter, Benny 305

Carter, Betty (Lillie Mae Jones) xiii, 88, 205, 247–248, 251, 259, 268, 338

"Casbah" (Dameron) 174

"Casbah, The" (Gryce) 174, 263

"Casino" 220

Chaloff, Margaret 55

Chambers, Paul 198, 215, 221, 231, 232, 243–244

Charles, Teddy 7, 52, 185–194, 207, 209, 284

"Cherokee" 7, 101, 123–124, 175

"Chez Moi" 133

Chicago Conservatory of Music 31

"Choose Now" 86

Claiborne, Valerie Grice (sister of Gigi Gryce) 11–16, 24, 34n, 330

Clarke, Kenny 79, 83, 151, 152, 158, 180, 194, 218, 272

Cleveland, Jimmy ix, 45–47, 90–92, 94, 95, 97, 103–105, 107n, 113–116, 118, 119, 121, 125, 131–134, 140–142, 145n, 156–157, 176–178, 194, 199–202, 210n, 216, 254, 260–261, 290, 293, 339

Club Ruby, Queens, NY 267

Cohn, Al 149, 194, 244

"Cold Breeze" 250, 252

Cole, Don 87

Coleman, Earl 195, 295

Coleman, Ornette 187, 259, 272, 284, 296, 307, 341

Coles, Johnny ix, xiii, 87

Colomby, Jules 158, 160, 172–173

Coltrane, John 3, 30, 41, 42, 75n, 120, 171, 189, 213, 226–227, 232, 266, 276, 297, 298, 307, 341

Columbia Records 69–70, 179, 216, 218, 220, 230, 233, 237, 239, 240

Combs, Charles 37, 315–316

Combs, Harriet Grice (sister of Gigi Gryce) xiii, 11–15, 37, 38, 315–316

"Come Rain or Come Shine" 195, 196

"Comin' Home Baby" 314

"Consultation" 140, 154

Contemporary Records 239

Cooper Union, New York 52, 186, 190

Cooper, George "Buster" 94, 143

Copa City, Jamaica, NY 265

Copeland, Ray 203, 226–227, 237, 248, 250, 267

Coss, Bill 186, 192

Costa, Eddie 28, 248–249, 284–88, 290, 292, 295, 297, 304, 309

Counce, Curtis 186, 272

Couperin, Francois 136

Cranshaw, Bob 258, 279, 286–288, 295

"Crazy Rhythm" 261

Crosson, Tasker 62

Curtis, Harry 32–33

Dameron, Tadd ix, 7, 44, 83–89, 94, 100, 104, 174, 179, 227, 337–338

"Dance of the Green Witches, The" 52

Davis, Dr. Art 280–281, 296–298

Davis, Miles 57, 60, 79, 100, 135, 151, 152, 174, 176, 177, 208, 216, 221, 234, 243, 250, 262, 276, 278, 284

Dawson, Alan ix, 61–63, 95, 96, 104, 106n, 123, 130, 141, 143, 144

de Koenigswarter, Baroness Pannonica ("Nica") 173

"Dear Old Stockholm" 82, 135, 243

"Dearly Beloved" 291

Debut Records 79

"Dee's Dilemma" 208

"Deep Passion" 203

Delaunay, Charles 117, 118, 135

"Deltitnu" 124–125, 152, 153, 154

Dennard, Oscar 94–96

Desmond, Paul 54, 159, 195, 256–257
"Dial B for Beauty" 86
Distel, Sacha 118
Dolphy, Eric 67, 282, 307
"Domingo" 222, 276
Don Byrd–Gigi Gryce Jazz Lab 218–219
"Don't Blame Me" 48
"Don't Worry about Me" 279
Donaldson, Lou 30, 85, 148, 244, 255–257
Dorham, McKinley "Kenny" 3, 160–161, 166, 203, 224, 233, 243–244, 267, 284
Douglas, Larry 242, 250
Down Beat 32, 65, 83, 93, 106, 160, 163, 165, 177, 193, 203, 228, 230, 237, 244, 259, 282, 285, 291, 295, 308, 319
"Down Home" 262, 272–273, 275, 284
Downs, Hugh 225
Dreares, Al 265, 286
DuBose, Evelyn "Baby" 15, 17, 27–28, 128, 290
Dunlop, Frankie 296–297
Duvivier, George 289

Eager, Allen 83, 284
Eardley, Jon 188, 192
"Early Bird" 238
"Early Morning Blues" 238
"Easy Living" 102
Eckstine, Billy 33, 83, 100
Edelhagen, Kurt 127
Edgehill, Arthur 207, 297
Edison, Harry "Sweets" 196, 295
Edthia 317, 319–320
Edwards, Esmond 277
"Eleanor" 64–65, 140, 141, 153, 154
"Elgy" 238
Ellington, Edward Kennedy "Duke" 7, 29, 33, 54, 57–58, 60, 123, 156, 189, 193, 216, 251, 278, 285, 290, 298
EmArcy Records 34n, 153, 261
"Embraceable You" 158
Emerson, Harold "Bunky" 62

"Emperor, The" 188, 189, 192, 193
Engel, Owen 295
Epic Records 205, 224, 244n, 284
"Epistrophy" 227
"Ergo the Blues" ("Jones Bones") 231, 275–276
Estelle, Oscar 87, 90, 94, 143
Euell, Julian 53, 172–173, 207, 208, 259, 271, 286, 289
Evans, Bill 209, 252, 255
Evans, Gil 176, 177, 187, 188, 192, 244
"Evening in Casablanca" ("Gina") 166, 175
"Evening in Paris" 132
Everybody Digs Bill Evans 4, 255
"Exhibit A" 148, 220, 231
"Expansion" 140, 154

Farlow, Tal 80–81
Farmer, Addison 98, 160, 161, 163, 192, 197, 252, 297, 305n
Farmer, Art ix, xiii, 89–90, 94, 96, 98, 104, 106n, 114, 118, 119, 124, 126–127, 135, 138, 140, 141, 143, 144n, 145n, 148, 150–153, 156, 157, 160, 162–164, 166, 174–177, 179, 180, 183n, 184n, 185, 186, 188, 191, 194, 196, 197, 199–202, 205, 206, 209, 213, 238, 240, 241, 252, 256, 264, 270, 272, 274, 282, 298, 319
"Farmer's Market" 98, 150
Feather, Leonard 142, 165, 167, 183n, 217, 244n
Federal Music Project (FMP) 18, 22
Fega, Mort 296
"Figure Eights" 264
"Filthy McNasty" 281
Finch Records 295
Finch, Sam 284, 295
"Fine and Dandy" 82
Fitzgerald, Ella 57, 270, 279
Five Spot Club, The, New York 171, 172, 265–266, 272, 286, 295–297, 300
Flanagan, Tommy 196, 199, 201, 202,

214–215, 217, 218, 219, 295
Floyd, Samuel, Jr. 30, 35n
"Flying Home" 96, 97, 105
Fordham University, New York 321–322
"Forecast" 174
"Foul Play" 248
"Frankie and Johnny" 80, 278
Fulbright Scholarship 70–74, 76n, 77n, 155–156
Fuller, Curtis 262, 274–275, 284
"Futurity" 81, 153, 156

Galbraith, Barry 192
"Gallop's Gallop" 172, 184n
Gardner, Andrew "Goon" 32
Garner, Erroll 57, 218, 275, 288
"Gee Blues Gee" ("Kucheza Blues") 290–291, 293–294
"Geraldine" 221
"Get Happy" 7
Getz, Stan 48, 49, 58, 60, 63–66, 100, 111, 140, 154, 229
"Giant Steps" 42, 337
GI Bill of Rights 14, 18, 33, 38
Gigi Records 295
Gillespie, John Birks "Dizzy" 32, 33, 45, 47, 48, 54, 58, 66, 80, 83, 85, 96, 124, 125, 163, 165, 171, 178, 183n, 184n, 221, 223, 229, 234, 238, 241–243, 261, 280, 296–297
Gilmore, John 220
"Gina" ("Evening in Casablanca") 166
Gitler, Ira 90, 160, 184n, 281, 291, 319
Giuffre, Jimmy 185, 187, 188, 191, 192, 209, 296
Glamman, Betty 199
"Glow Worm" 80
Goldberg, Richie 161, 207
Golson, Benny 3, 83, 85–87, 89, 94, 95, 106n, 112, 144n, 166, 170, 179, 198, 203, 208, 214, 216, 221–223, 235, 237, 239–244, 245n, 247, 250, 252, 254–

55, 260, 262, 270, 272, 298, 304, 311–312, 337–338, 341
Gonsalves, Paul 61
Goodman, Benny 42, 144, 274
"Goofin' with Me" 126
Gordon, Joe 61, 63, 153
Gourley, Jimmy 119, 125, 130, 339
Graham, Martha 299
Grant, Bill "Baggy" 63
Gray, Wardell 83, 98, 150
Great Day in Harlem, A 251
Greatest Trumpet of Them All, The 241–243
"Green Blues" 188, 192
Green, Bennie 32
Greene, Aurelia 323, 326–328, 331–332
Greene, Reverend Jerome A. 323–325, 331–332
Greenwich, Lorenzo 268
Grey, Al iii, 203
Grice, George General, Sr. (father of Gigi Gryce) 10, 11, 14
Grice, Harriet 10
Grice, Rebecca Rials (mother of Gigi Gryce) 11–16, 17, 20, 24, 34n, 37, 38, 103, 320
Grice, Thomas, Jr. "Baby" 11–12
Griggs, Bernie 153
Gryce Lynette (daughter of Gigi Gryce) 308, 316
Gryce, Bashir (son of Gigi Gryce) 234, 236, 251, 253, 308, 316–317, 319
Gryce, Bilil (son of Gigi Gryce) 253
Gryce, Eleanor Sears (Lee Sears; wife of Gigi Gryce) 1, 97, 140, 148–149, 157, 181, 196, 211–212, 228, 234–236, 253, 308, 311, 313–314, 316–318, 320
Gryce, Gigi
  aversion to travel 181, 206, 309, 341
  classical compositions viii, 51–55
  college education 38, 39, 47, 49, 51, 53, 54, 55, 56, 59, 61, 70–71, 73, 75, 77n

health problems 328, 330
marital problems 316–17
military service 28–34
nervous breakdown viii, 72–74, 76n–
    77n, 156, 309
publishing efforts 2, 4–5, 50, 154–
    155, 165–170, 213, 236, 247, 258,
    271–272, 290, 304–305, 309–16, 319
religion 51, 53, 74, 235–236, 316, 328
rumors concerning xii, 307, 309–311,
    318–19
school renamed for 320, 331–32
teaching career 5, 317–18
Gryce, "Tommy" (Thomas Grice,
    brother of Gigi Gryce) 2, 11–16, 17–
    18, 20, 24, 32, 33, 34n, 35n, 38, 53, 74,
    103, 107n, 206, 247–248, 265, 315,
    328–329
Gryce-Smith, Laila (daughter of Gigi
    Gryce) 238, 277, 308, 316–317, 319
Gullin, Lars 111, 141
Gunn, Clifford 38, 47, 50, 63, 70, 321–
    323

Haig, Al 140
Hamner, Curley 95, 99, 104, 143
"Hamp's Boogie Woogie" 98, 105
Hampton, Gladys 95, 114–115, 127, 142
    144
Hampton, Lionel ix, 7, 28, 45–47, 73,
    89–91, 93–99, 103–106, 109–144, 147,
    150, 224, 229, 249, 257, 268, 339
Hampton, Locksley "Slide" 279–280,
    283, 296
Hap'nin's, The 277, 279
Hardy, Hagood 297
Hart, George 114, 139
Hartman, Johnny 195
Hartt School of Music 38, 45, 75n
"Hasaan's Dream" 222–223
Hawk Flies High, The 220
Hawkins, Coleman viii, 85, 214, 220,
    226–227, 229, 284

Haynes, Roy 61, 76n, 298
Hayse, Al 94, 104, 127, 143
"He's Just My Bill" 159
Heath, Jimmy 83, 262
Heath, Percy 80, 87, 100, 148, 151, 152,
    171
"Hello" 132, 153
Henderson, Luther 30
Hendricks, Jon 4, 65, 170, 178, 179, 196,
    248, 251, 306n
Hentoff, Nat 8n, 53, 65, 75n, 76n, 147,
    183n, 197–198, 210n, 235, 237–238,
    239
Herbert L. Clarke Trumpet Studies 40
Herman, Woody 60, 63, 130
"High Step" ("Byrd in Hand") 232
Hi-Hat Club, Boston, MA 57–58, 64,
    171
Hines, Earl 10, 32, 34n, 35n
Hinkson, Mary "Bunny" 299
Hinton, Milt 229, 249–250
Honegger, Arthur 71–73, 76n, 77n, 283
"Honeysuckle Rose" 65, 86, 238
Horricks, Raymond xi, 74, 76n, 77n,
    123, 141, 144n, 145n
"Hot House" 33, 83
House of the Blue Lights 285
Hovhaness, Alan xiii, 51–53, 75n, 338
Howard McGhee Volume Two 81–83
"Hymn to the Orient" ix, 65, 100–101,
    155, 159, 161, 244
"Hymn, The" 219, 277

"I Can't Help It" 248
"I Cover the Waterfront" 126
"I Got Rhythm" 86, 125, 180, 202, 221,
    231, 233, 262
"I Remember Clifford" 216
"I'll Remember April" 128, 208, 244
"I'll Walk Alone" 273–274
"If You Could See Me Now" 83, 227
"Ill Wind" 217
"Imagination" 234

"In a Meditating Mood" ("Autumn Serenade") 178

"In a Mellotone" 194

"In a Sentimental Mood" 249

"In a Strange Mood" 289, 305n

"In Memory of Gene" 50

"Indian Summer" 281

"Indiana" ("Back Home Again in Indiana") 7, 126

"Infant's Song, The" 162, 180, 197

"Isn't It Romantic" 234

"It Ain't Necessarily So" 222, 279

"It Don't Mean a Thing (If It Ain't Got That Swing)" 251

"It's You or No One" 196

"Ittapnna" 82

Jackson, "Bull Moose" 83, 87

Jacogg Publications, Inc. 315–316

Jaffe, Hy 114, 115

James, Leon 163, 238

James, Thomas, Dr. 14, 16, 17, 23, 24, 26, 27

Jamieson, Kessel Grice (sister of Gigi Gryce) xiii, 11–16, 330

"Jarm" 82

Jaspar, Bobby 140

Jazz Ain't Nothin' But Soul 284

Jazz Composers Workshop 186

Jazz Gallery, New York 284, 296, 298

Jazz Hot magazine 116, 117, 134

Jazz Lab (Donald Byrd–Gigi Gryce Jazz Lab) 2, 6, 130, 207, 212–219, 224, 229–234, 236, 237–240, 248, 250

Jazz Laboratory (Signal Records Play-Along) 158–160, 225

Jazz Messengers, The 2, 100, 216, 219, 229, 233, 254, 266, 314

Jazz Omnibus 218

Jazztet 272, 296

Jessie, Joseph 18–23

Johnson, Buddy 44–45

Johnson, Gus 196, 204, 295

Johnson, J.J. 135, 140, 149, 161, 209, 218, 243–244, 304

Johnson, Lennie 63

Johnson, Osie 30, 164, 199, 201, 215, 229, 230, 232–233, 249–250, 261

"Jones Bones" ("Ergo the Blues") 232, 275–276

Jones, "Philly" Joe ix, 85–86, 174, 224, 255, 298

Jones, Hank viii, 132, 164, 196, 204, 214–215, 224, 229, 231, 233, 234, 249–251, 254, 275, 278, 305n, 310

Jones, Quincy ix, 7, 8n, 45, 60, 71, 90, 91, 93, 94, 96, 99, 102–105, 106n, 112, 114, 118, 119, 121, 122, 125, 130–132, 136, 138, 139, 141, 143, 144, 145n, 148, 163–165, 219, 241, 242, 245n, 278, 289, 304, 310, 338

Jones, Sam 255

Jones, Thad 3, 216–217, 310

Jordan, Clifford 220

Jordan, Irving "Duke" 3, 158, 159, 174, 197, 200, 225, 249

"Jordu" 158–159

Jubilee Records 230, 233

Juilliard School of Music, New York 185, 187

"Jumpin' with Symphony Sid" 65

"Just by Myself" 240, 241

"Just One of Those Things" 209

Kaba, Léon 118

Kaleidophone (Schillinger) 42

"Kamman's A'Comin" 164

Kane, Art 251

Karpe, Kenneth 199, 200

Katz, Dick 196–197, 203

"Keeping up with Jonesy" 125

Keepnews, Orrin 226–227, 245n

Kelly, Wynton 157, 214–215, 221, 223, 243, 255

Kenton, Stan 60, 111, 280

"Kerry Dance" 180

"Kin Folks" 237
King Saxophones 308
King, Morgana 200, 254
"King's Chimney, The" 54
Kirk, Andy 10, 22
"Knights at the Castle" 197
Know Your Jazz 194
Koenig, Lester 239
"Koko" 101
"Kokomo" 22
Konitz, Lee 111, 119, 138, 338
Korall, Burt 200–201, 210n
(Koran) 53, 235–236, 330
"Kucheza Blues" ("Gee Blues Gee")
    290–291, 293–294
Kunstler, William 165
Kurtzer, Dave 203

La Porta, John 187
"La Rose Noire" 119–120, 126
Lacy, Steve 282, 298
"Lady Bird" 83
Lambert, Hendricks and Ross 248
"LaRue" ("Tribute To Brownie") 224
Lateef, Yusef 282, 293
"Laura" 237
Lazare, Jack 249, 251
"Lazy Bones" 81
Legge, Wade 215, 219–221, 250, 252
"Leila's Blues" ("Movin'") 238, 277
"Let Me Know" 275
"Let's" 217
"Let's Fall in Love" 205
Lewis, John 61, 100–102, 123, 176, 188,
    191, 255
Lewis, Shari 225
Lewis, William Sebastian "Sabby" 57,
    61–62, 69, 143
Liberty Records 222
"Li'l Daddee" 93
"Limehouse Blues" 264
Liston, Melba xiii, 223, 248, 261, 293–
    294
"Little Bandmaster, The" 245n

"Little Niles" 216, 224, 237
"Little Rootie Tootie" 172
"Little Susan" 250
Little, Booker 4, 297–298
Lloyd, Jerry (Hurwitz) 149
Lomax, Alan 11
London, Ed 203
Long, Aaron 20, 24–26, 29, 31–32, 330
Lookofsky, Harry 280–281
"Love for Sale" 220, 230
Lovelle, Herbie 160
"Lover" x, 180
"Lover Man" 279
"Lover's Mood" 154
Lowe, Mundell 194
"Lullaby for Milkman" 249, 251
Lydian Chromatic Concept of Tonal Organization 277
"Lydian M-1" 188, 191, 192

Macero, Teo 52, 186, 187, 190, 191
Mackel, Billy 104, 143
Macklin, Norman 38, 39
Magnificent Thad Jones, The, Volume 3 217
Mal-1 207
Malachi, John 33
Mandel, Johnny 7
Manhattan School of Music, New York
    213, 269
Mann, Herbie 160, 163, 224, 314
Manne, Shelly 186
Mapp, Norman 248, 271, 281, 284–285
Mariano, Charlie 60, 68
Marshall, Wendell 215, 218, 219, 225,
    229, 231–233
Martin, Jimmy 62–63
Mathews, Mat 196, 202, 203, 228
"Mau Mau" 90
"Mayreh" 153
McGhee, Howard viii, 57, 59, 80–83,
    140, 154, 175
McIntyre, Dr. Makanda Ken xiii, 67–
    68, 76n, 282
McKayle, Donald 299

McLean, Jackie 135, 138, 213, 222, 255–259, 267, 323, 339
McKusick, Hal 163
McMillan, Herman 23–24
McShann, Jay 21, 245n
"Melody Express" 64–65
Melody Maker magazine 94, 141, 142, 148
Melotone Music, Inc. 149, 165, 225, 247, 250, 271, 281, 310–315
Mercury Records 260, 272, 288–290, 293
Merritt, Jymie ix, 87
"Mesabi Chant" 223
MetroJazz Records 249, 259, 264
Metronome magazine 52, 99, 186, 191, 193, 200, 209, 210n, 295
Metronome Records 111, 113, 119
Mialy, Louis-Victor 72, 111, 134–140
Michelot, Pierre 119
Milhaud, Darius 54–55
Millinder, "Lucky" 21, 22, 69
Mills Music 167–169
Mingus, Charles 4, 151, 186–187, 191, 192, 239, 256, 268–269, 284, 289, 299–301, 337
Minns, Al 163, 238
"Minor Mood" 102
"Minor Seventh Heaven" 164
"Minority" ix, 4, 128, 153, 154, 221, 255, 276, 279, 337
Mitchell, Gordon 'Whitey' 198
"Moanin'" 314
Mobley, Hank 4, 79–80, 161, 175
"Mobleyzation" 80
Modern Art 252
Modern Jazz Perspective 236, 238–239
Modern Jazz Quartet, The (MJQ) 2, 61, 100, 152, 197, 213
Modern Sounds Vol. 1 and 2 154–156
Modern Touch, The 243
"Monday Through Sunday" 282–284
Monk, Thelonious 4, 45–46, 54, 57–59, 66, 82, 96, 100, 151, 157, 171–174, 200, 205–206, 217, 226–228, 252, 284, 286, 297–298, 337
Monk's Music 226–228, 259
Monterose, J.R. 185, 188, 199
Montgomery, William "Monk" ix, 94–95, 104
"Mood in Blue" 154, 183n
Moore, Brew 158
Morgan, Lee 175, 221–223, 237, 254
Morton, Jelly Roll 11, 34n, 169
"Mosquito Knees" 64–65, 140
Mosse, Sandy 119
Most, Sam 163
"Movin'" ("Leila's Blues") 238
Mulligan, Gerry xiii, 176, 177, 229, 234, 254
Mullins, Herb 87
"Music in the Air" ("Wildwood") 65
"My Ideal" 249
"My Man" 164, 221, 279
"My Old Flame" 224

Nance, Ray 33
"Nature Boy" 188, 192
Navarro, Theodore "Fats" 83, 84, 292
Nelson, Gene 50
Nevard, Mike 145n, 148, 183n
New Directions 185
New Jazz Records 99, 232, 270, 272, 274, 277, 281–282, 290
Newborn, Phineas Jr. 173, 192
Newport Jazz Festival, Newport, RI 186, 192–193, 228, 268, 284
"Nica's Dream" 233, 291
"Nica's Tempo" ("Playhouse") 166, 173–175, 197, 201, 218, 224, 279
"Night at Tony's, A" 151, 223, 241, 242
"Night in Tunisia, A" 192, 280, 291–292
"No Love, No Nothing" 196
No Room for Squares 175
"No Start, No End" 133
Nola's Studio, New York 45, 261, 273

Norén, Jack 111, 141
Norgran Records 65
Norvo, Red (Kenneth Norville) 186
"Not So Sleepy" 197, 202
Nottingham, Jimmy 30, 209, 267
"Now Don't You Know" 238
"Now See How You Are" 236–237
"Now's the Time" 40

"Oh Yeah" 158
Okeh Records 91–93
"Ol' Man River" 153
Oliver, Joe "King" 18, 169
On the Sound 298–304
"Onion Head" 233
Open Door Club, New York 157–158
Orch-tette (Gigi Gryce Orch-tette) 6,
    285–286, 288, 291–292, 295–298, 309
Ore, John 298
Ortega, Anthony 94, 95, 104, 109–110,
    119–122, 125, 133, 143, 224, 249, 257,
    305n
"Our Delight" 83, 89
"Oscalypso" 164
Ousley, Harold 170
"Out of Nowhere" 174
"Over the Rainbow" 218
Overton, Hall 185–187, 189, 191, 192
"Ow" 48

Pad Club, The, New York 207
Paich, Marty 244
Palais de Chaillot, Paris, France 116, 117
Panassié, Hugues 115, 117
Paradise Club, Atlantic City, NJ 86–89
"Paris the Beautiful" 120
Paris, Jackie 215, 228, 237–238
"Parisian Thoroughfare" 231
Parker, Charlie 32, 33, 48, 54, 55, 57,
    59–60, 66–68, 76n, 79, 93, 101, 120,
    125, 151, 157–160, 162, 171, 173, 180,
    195, 198, 214, 217, 219, 232, 257–259,
    263, 274, 276, 337–339
Parker, Leo 33

Parker, Sonny 95, 99, 104, 141
Payne, Cecil ix, 87, 172, 176, 223, 225
Peacock Records 247
Pearson, Columbus "Duke" 224
"Pennies from Heaven" 82, 166, 254
Pepsi-Cola Co. 304
"Perdido" 127, 128, 203
Perkins, Walter 286–289, 295
Perry, Bay 59
Perry, Joe 59
Perry, Ray 59, 61
Persip, Charli 221, 240, 242, 243, 255,
    280
Peterson, Oscar 58
Pettiford, Oscar 59, 135, 158, 163–165,
    185, 191, 194, 196–205, 209, 218, 224,
    228, 236–237, 338
"Philly J.J." 85
Pinkham, Daniel 55, 71, 77n
Plater, Bobby 95, 103
"Playhouse" ("Nica's Tempo") 166,
    173–175, 197, 201, 218, 224, 279
Pomeroy, Herb 57–58, 76n, 143
Porcelli, Bob 255–257
Porgy and Bess 278–279
Portrait of Cannonball 337
Potter, Tommy 33, 59
Powell, Benny 217
Powell, Earl "Bud" 58, 96, 125, 208
"Premonition of You, A" 289
Prestige Records 84, 90, 98, 99, 119,
    150–152, 156, 161, 169–170, 180, 185,
    195, 197, 207, 219, 245n, 267, 271–
    272, 274, 281–282, 289
Priester, Julian 263
Prysock, Arthur 44–45
Pulliam, Steve 87
"Purple Shades" 119

"Quick Step" 130, 154, 239
"Quiet Time, The" 188, 191, 192
Quill, Gene 203
Qusim, Basheer (Gigi Gryce) 74, 77n,
    160

Qusim, Basheer/Gigi Gryce School, (Community Elementary School No. 53, Bronx, NY (P.S. 53)) 318, 320–321, 323, 325–326, 329, 331–332
Qusim, Ollie Warren (wife of Basheer Qusim) 320, 326

Randall's Island Jazz Festival, New York, NY 234
Raney, Jimmy 157, 186–188, 190, 191, 194
Rat Race Blues, The 281–284
"Rat Race Blues" (song) 282–283, 298
Ray, Johnnie 208–209
RCA Victor Records 176, 233
Redd, Freddie 161, 163
Reese, Hampton 63
Reinhardt, Django 133
Reminiscin' 289, 291
"Reminiscing" 196, 242, 261, 290
Renaud, Henri 72, 118, 119, 121, 125, 128, 140, 141, 145n, 149, 152
"Reunion" ("Salute to Birdland," "Salute to the Band Box") 119–120, 126, 128–129, 132, 153–155, 244, 250
"Rich and Creamy" 249
Rich, Bernard "Buddy" 262–264
Richardson, Jerome xiii, 30, 163, 164, 199, 202, 228, 267, 298
Rivers, Sam 30, 51, 53, 58–63, 70, 74–75
Riverside Records 4, 220–221, 224, 226, 230, 243, 252, 255, 289
Roach, Max 79–80, 84, 92–93, 129, 151, 166, 179, 243–244, 262–264, 277, 284, 291, 298–300
Rogers, Shorty (Milton Rajonsky) 176, 186
Roker, Granville "Mickey" 266, 269–270, 275, 277, 283, 286, 302, 304
Roland, Joe 59, 194
Rollins, Theodore Walter "Sonny" 157, 214, 298

Roost Records 64–65
Ross, Annie (Annabelle Lynch) 96, 105–106, 112, 115
"Round Midnight" 206
Rouse, Charlie 100–102, 194, 195, 339
Royal, Ernie 30, 164, 199, 201
Russell, Dillon "Curley" 328
Russell, George 187, 188, 191, 192, 277, 306n, 338
Russo, Bill (William Russo) 123, 191

"Salt Peanuts" 33, 238
"Salute to Birdland" ("Reunion," "Salute to the Band Box") 119–120, 126, 128–129, 132, 153–155, 244, 250
"Salute to the Band Box" ("Reunion," "Salute to Birdland") 119–120, 126, 128–129, 132, 153–155, 244, 250
"Sans Souci" 44, 166, 174, 218
"Satellite" 175–176, 197
Savoy Records 212, 231, 272
Saying Somethin'! 266, 271, 274–275
Schillinger System of Musical Composition, The 42, 83, 162, 276–277
Schlitten, Don 157–158, 160, 171, 225, 282
Schuller, Gunther 176, 188, 191
"Scorpio" 164
Scott, Clifford 94
Scott, Tony 194, 209, 228
"Sea Breeze" 236, 237, 242, 249
Sears, Lee (Eleanor Sears Gryce; Gigi Gryce pseudonym) 148, 207, 221, 238
"Señor Blues" 275
"Shabozz" 81–82, 140, 161, 175, 242
Shaughnessy, Ed 186, 192, 193, 209
Shearing, George 57, 125
Sheppard, Raymond 10, 20, 22–24, 26–29, 32
Shihab, Sahib (Edmund Gregory) 47, 199, 223, 231
Shirley, Donald 10, 12–19, 21–24, 180–181

"Shome" 208
"Show Time" 188, 192, 193
Signal Records 70, 158–160, 170–174, 176, 217, 218, 225–226, 243, 249, 338
Silhouette Music Corp. 219
Silver, Horace 2, 4, 47–50, 63–64, 75n, 80, 82, 100, 111, 143, 148, 151–153, 157, 167–169, 176, 180, 202, 203, 206, 210n, 213, 219, 228, 232, 233, 235, 271, 274–275, 277, 281, 291, 310, 337, 341
"Simplicity" 140, 153, 154
Sims, John Haley 'Zoot' 60, 111, 119, 228
"Since You've Come To Me" 154
"Sing, Sing, Sing" 263
"Sleep" 264
Slonimsky, Nicolas 41, 276
Smalls, Cliff 10
Smith, Emery 39–45, 47–51, 58, 61, 66, 172
Smith, Willie 30, 244
"Smoke Signal" x, 105, 165, 180, 201, 218, 224, 243
"Social Call" x, 4, 40, 162, 178–179, 182, 196, 197, 205, 223
Solomon, Clifford 72, 73, 90–93, 94, 97, 98, 103, 110–111, 114, 117, 121, 122, 124, 125, 133
"Something in B-flat" 240
"Sometimes I'm Happy" 158–159
"Somewhere" 237, 250
"Song for Ruth" 224
"Song Is You, The" 112
"Sonor" 272–273
Spann, Les 293
"Speculation" 176, 202, 217
"Splittin'" ("Ray's Way") 232
Springfield Gardens, Queens, New York 236, 265, 267, 270, 308
"Square Dance Boogie" 93
"Stablemates" 208, 239, 255
"Stan's Blues" ("Eleanor") 65–66
"Star Dust" 127

Stearns, Marshall 157, 163, 225, 238
Stein, Hal 191, 192
"Steppin' Out" 130, 239
Stewart, Rex 279
Stitt, Edward "Sonny" 339
"Stompin' at the Savoy" 273–274
Storyville Club, Boston, MA 57–58, 66
"Straight Ahead" 221
"Strange Feelin'" 282, 284, 295
"Strictly Romantic" 129, 153, 154
Study in Dameronia, A 86
"Stupendous-Lee" ("Au Tabou") 140, 152
Subject Is Jazz, The 254
Sulieman, Idrees (Leonard Graham) 51, 79, 84, 86, 148, 178–179, 207–208
"Summertime" 119, 279
Sundown Club, Hartford, CT 47, 48
"Sunrise-Sunset" 202
Swaggerty, Kellice 87–89
Swanston, Edwin "Schubert" 79, 323–326, 329
"Sweet Georgia Brown" 189, 192
"Swinging Till the Girls Come Home" 228

"Take the 'A' Train" 263, 272–273, 291
Taylor, Art xiii, 161, 163, 197, 215, 218, 220, 221, 225, 230, 231, 232, 234
Taylor, Billy 194, 195, 210n
Taylor, Cecil 58, 67, 68, 76n, 230, 341
Taylor, Creed 194, 201, 210n
"Tenderly" 40–41, 127
Terry, Clark 30, 31, 209
"Theme of No Repeat" 86
Thesaurus of Scales and Melodic Patterns (Slonimsky) 41, 276
"These Foolish Things" 48
Thomas, Bobby 281, 289
Thompson, Eli "Lucky" 4, 48, 79, 167, 169, 198, 201–203, 205, 228, 324
"Tijuana" 156
Tijuana Club, Baltimore, MD 150

Timmons, Bobby 4, 314
"Tip-toeing" 223
Tonight! America after Dark 225–226
"Toot, Toot, Tootsie Goodbye" 263
Torme, Mel 314
Totem Music, Inc. 149, 166, 247, 251, 262, 271, 310–315, 325
Town Hall, New York 157, 200
Tracy, Jack 210n, 262
"Tranquility" 82
"Transfiguration" 148, 207
"Trolly Tracks" 154
Tucker, Ben 314
Turbo Village, Brooklyn, NY 266, 267
Turney, Matt 299
Tuskegee Institute 21, 22, 29
"Two Basses" 237
"Two French Fries" 202, 224

U.S. Navy 28–33
U.S. State Department 70, 241
Uhuru Afrika 292–294
"Up in Quincy's Room" 90–91, 140, 161

Van Gelder, Rudy 2, 152, 158, 161, 277
Vaughan, Sarah 41, 57, 83, 112
Verve Records 165, 229, 241
Viale, Jean-Louis 119, 130
"Vibrations" 188, 190, 191
Vik Records (RCA) 230–231, 233
Vogue Records 118, 122, 129, 135, 149

"Wail Bait" 102
"Wake Up" 148, 197, 220, 221
Waldron, Mal 4, 186–191, 194, 206–209, 282
Wallington, George 7, 96, 105–106, 112, 113, 115, 119, 213, 278
Ware, Wilbur 206, 226
Washington, Dinah 204–205
Watkins, Julius 176, 199, 202
"We Never Kissed" 261
Webster, Ben 33, 85
Weinstock, Bob 98–99, 150–153, 161–

163, 169–170, 195, 207, 258, 274, 277
"Well, You Needn't" 228
Weston, Randy 4, 216, 224, 238, 250, 251, 284, 290, 292–294
"What Is This Thing Called Love" 254
When Farmer Met Gryce 150
"When the Saints Go Marching In" 97
"Whisper Not" 240
White, Chris 177–178, 182–183, 341
Wilder, Joe 164
"Wildwood" ("Music in the Air") 64–65, 156, 222
Wilkins, Ernie xiii, 30, 164, 212, 239
"William Tell Overture" 21, 231
Williams, Charles "Cootie" 6
Williams, Floyd "Floogie" 143
Williams, Martin 8n, 285
Williams, Mary Lou 69, 164, 252
Williams, Richard "Notes" 265–270, 275, 277–282, 286, 292–293, 295–296, 304
Williams, Walter 94, 143
Wilson, Rossiere "Shadow" 32, 204, 224
"Wind, The" 280
"Wishing" 154
"Wolf Talk" 148
Woode, Jimmy 68
Woods, Phil 159–160
"Woody'n You" 85, 174
"Word from Bird" 192–193
Workman, Reggie 3, 196, 259, 265–267, 269, 281, 286–287, 289, 295, 304, 311
Works Progress Administration (WPA) 14, 18, 20, 23
Wright, Bruce 166, 310, 312–313, 315
Wright, Leo 280–281, 291
Wright, Phil 265–268
Wyands, Richard 267–270, 272, 275, 277, 279, 281, 286–288, 292, 304, 308–309

"Xtacy" 233

"Yardbird Suite" 151

"Yesterdays" 208, 263, 291–292
"You Go to My Head" 188, 192
"You'll Always Be the One I Love" 70, 179–180
"You're Not the Kind" 166, 254

Young, James "Trummy" 32–33, 35n
"Yvette" 64–65, 141

"Zing! Went the Strings of My Heart" 220–221

IF YOU ENJOYED THIS BOOK, you may be interested in our other jazz titles. Please use this order form—or call our toll-free number—to order one or more for yourself or a friend. Each paperback title features many photographs and an extensive discography. Shipping is free. Thank you for your order.

Thelonious Monk: His life and music. Thomas Fitterling. 240 pages, $15.95.
The life, the style, and the recorded legacy of the bebop great. "Lays the groundwork for anyone interested in addressing Monk the musician, Monk the composer, and Monk the arranger." — John Ephland, *Down Beat*

Ornette Coleman: His life and music. Peter Wilson. 256 pages, $15.95.
The only comprehensive book available on a living legend. Foreword by Pat Metheny. "It is not easy to explain the music of Ornette Coleman with both accuracy and clarity, but Peter Wilson has done so with *Ornette Coleman: His life and music.*" — Bill Shoemaker, *JazzTimes*

Chet Baker: His life and music. Jeroen de Valk. 308 pages, $15.95.
The first book devoted to the legendary singer and trumpeter—famous as much for his tragic life as his beautiful music.
"A classic of modern Jazz biography." — Larry Nai, *Cadence*

Sonny Rollins: The definitive musical guide. Peter Wilson. 252 pages, $15.95.
"The definitive musical guide, this will reward anyone who wants to understand who Rollins is, what he accomplished musically, and the culture in which he flourished." — *Library Journal*

Ben Webster: His life and music. Jeroen de Valk. 292 pages, $15.95.

The first biography of the one of the most beloved of all jazz saxophonists, and a central figure of jazz in its heyday.
"Finally a book about my friend Ben Webster which is both accurate and honest." — Joe Zawinul
"A valuable contribution." — Whitney Balliett

Rat Race Blues: The musical life of Gigi Gryce. Noal Cohen & Michael Fitzgerald. 456 pages, $18.95.

A fascinating account of the enigmatic composer and alto saxophonist. Best known for his work with Clifford Brown, Gryce was also one of the first jazz musicians to found his own publishing company and work for jazz composers' rights.

To order, mail or fax this form, or you may call us toll-free at (888) 848-7303 to use your Visa or MasterCard. Shipping is free.

— —

Berkeley Hills Books • P.O. Box 9877 • Berkeley, CA 94709
1-888-848-7303 (phone) • (510) 525-2948 (fax) • rob@berkeleyhills.com

Please send me ____ copies of *Thelonious Monk: His life and music* at $15.95 each
Please send me ____ copies of *Ornette Coleman: His life and music* at $15.95
Please send me ____ copies of *Chet Baker: His life and music* at $15.95
Please send me ____ copies of *Sonny Rollins: The definitive musical guide* at $15.95
Please send me ____ copies of *Ben Webster: His life and music* at $15.95
Please send me ____ copies of *Rat Race Blues: The musical life of Gigi Gryce* at $18.95

Enclosed: check payable to Berkeley Hills Books for $_____

Charge my Visa or MasterCard # _____

Expiration date _____

Name _____

Address _____

City/State/Zip _____

Phone _____